THE
CON

THE INFORMAL CONSTITUTION

UNWRITTEN CRITERIA IN SELECTING JUDGES FOR THE SUPREME COURT OF INDIA

ABHINAV CHANDRACHUD

OXFORD
UNIVERSITY PRESS

OXFORD
UNIVERSITY PRESS

Oxford University Press is a department of the University of Oxford.
It furthers the University's objective of excellence in research, scholarship,
and education by publishing worldwide. Oxford is a registered trademark of
Oxford University Press in the UK and in certain other countries

Published in India by
Oxford University Press
22 Workspace, 2nd Floor, 1/22 Asaf Ali Road, New Delhi 110 002, India

ISBN-13: 978-0-19-012766-4
ISBN-10: 0-19-012766-X

Typeset in Bell MT Std 10.5/13
by Alphæta Solutions, Puducherry, India 605 009
Printed in India by Rakmo Press, New Delhi 110 020

To Radha
for reminding me that only love is real

CONTENTS

TABLES AND FIGURES

TABLES

FIGURES

ACKNOWLEDGEMENTS

MY INTEREST IN THIS TOPIC first arose while I was working at a law firm in Mumbai in 2005. Having to read numerous Supreme Court judgments to answer client queries, I realized that I knew almost nothing about the actual judges who had written the Court's opinions, except for some famous ones like Justices Vivian Bose, P.N. Bhagwati, or Krishna Iyer. For a long time, the website of the Supreme Court did not contain any biographical information on many of the Court's former puisne judges, especially those who had served on the Court in the early decades of its existence. I pointed this out in a post on the blog, *Law and Other Things*, in 2009.[1] Then, while working at an international law firm in Singapore in 2010, I spent my free time writing an empirical paper in which I examined the background characteristics of the judges who had served on the Court since 1985. I owe a lot to Nick Robinson, who forwarded me a couple of papers written by Professor George H. Gadbois, Jr, and who helped shape the course of my research. Once my paper was published in the *Economic and Political Weekly* in 2011, Professor Gadbois wrote

---

[1] Abhinav Chandrachud. 2009. 'Puisne Matters', *Law and Other Things*, 1 October, available online at http://lawandotherthings.blogspot.com/2009/10/puisne-matters.html (last accessed on 18 July 2013).

to me himself, and since then, he has been an enormous resource, a mentor, supervisor, and guide. My original plan as a SPILS (Stanford Program in International Legal Studies) student at Stanford was to replicate Professor Gadbois's research, to carry out a semi-biographical study of the Court's judges since 1989. I soon realized, however, that this was going to be a very difficult task. Some of the Supreme Court's former judges were not interested in talking to me when I contacted them for information. Interviewing judges was not easy either—one judge hung up on me when I asked him a question. However, most of the judges I contacted for my thesis at Stanford were enormously kind to me, and I am deeply grateful and indebted to them for speaking with me, writing to me, or meeting me in person. This book is the product of the most interesting story I was able to put together using these interviews. Some information in this volume has been updated and presented in chapter endnotes.

I owe a debt of gratitude to many. My supervisor at Stanford, Professor David Engstrom, encouraged me to look beyond the specific, and to engage with broader questions. Professor Gadbois tirelessly went through several drafts of this book, and I benefited a great deal from his very frank advice. The teaching fellow of the SPILS programme, Sergio Puig, treated us all like members of his own family, and his guidance during the programme was invaluable. I am also very grateful to Professor Deborah Hensler, Professor Lawrence Friedman, and Professor Rogelio Perez-Perdomo for their guidance these past few years. The staff at the Robert Crown Law Library at Stanford has been a tremendous help. I must especially thank Sonia Moss, who tirelessly got books for me from various libraries scattered across the United States. This book could not have been written without her help. I would also like to thank others with whom I have come into contact at the library, including George D. Wilson, Naheed Zaheer, Sergio Stone, George Vizvary, and Kelly S. Kuehl. My SPILS classmates at Stanford were all a source of support and encouragement. I am especially grateful to my good friend, Fernan Restrepo, who patiently helped me through the quantitative components of this book, and gave up time he could have spent working on his own thesis to help me work on mine.

I would like to thank the following people for corresponding with me, at various times, about different issues I was dealing with in my research: Kate Malleson, Rohit De, Graham Gee, Kyela Leakey, Nicholas Georgakopoulos, Dong Won Kim, Carl Baar, Sari Aziz, Shiri Krebs, Anirudh Wadhwa, and K.K. Wadhwa. A portion of Chapter 4 of this book was first published in the *Connecticut Journal of International Law* (vol. 28, no. 2) in 2013, and I am grateful to Randall S. Blowers and his team. The literature review section in Chapter 5 of this book was first published in the *Brooklyn Journal of International Law* (vol. 38, no. 2) in 2013, and I am grateful to Nicholas Cade and his team. I would like to thank Sumeet Malik and Abhinandan Malik for the kindness they have always shown me. I am especially grateful to the editorial team at Oxford University Press.

Last, but not the least, I would like to thank my family, which has always been a source of strength and support. Thank you Dad, Chintan, and Kalpana for being so wonderfully supportive and encouraging. Thank you Aai and Baba (my wife's parents), for treating me like your own son. Thank you Nani, for always cheering me up and encouraging me to follow my dreams. Thank you Shridhar Mama, Shalini Mami, Pranay, and Vinayak. Thank you Sharda and Gaurav, Saloni and Raj. Thank you Neema Atya and Dilda, Charu Didi and Mohit, Priya Didi and Greg. Thanks are also due to those who have treated me like a member of their family: Dr P.B. Desai and Meena Aunty, Dr Satyavan Sharma and Meeta Aunty, and Alpana Ghone. Though they are not here with us, I would like to thank my grandfather (Aaju), my mother (Aai), and my grandmother (Prabha): none of this would have been possible without your love, vision, encouragement, and sacrifice. Since disclaimers are a lawyer's trade, the usual ones must apply here. The views expressed here are mine alone.

INTRODUCTION

BACKGROUND

BETWEEN 1950 AND 2009, 189 judges (including 37 chief justices) served on the Supreme Court of India, which is considered to be one of the world's most powerful courts.[1] Not enough is known about who these judges were, especially those who served on the Court in relatively recent times, and the criteria that were used to select them for the Court. Broadly speaking, the Indian Constitution formally provides that three types of individuals can be appointed to the Supreme Court: (*a*) high court judges of five years' standing, (*b*) high court lawyers of 10 years' standing, or (*c*) 'distinguished jurists', that is, law professors or others.[2] However, this says very little, perhaps nothing, about the kind of candidates that are appointed to the Court. Informal norms have evolved over a period of 60 years, which coexist alongside formal constitutional rules—norms that govern who will be considered fit and eligible for appointment to the Supreme Court. In this book, which has originated from my thesis in the JSM program at Stanford Law School, I quantitatively and qualitatively

---

[1] S.P. Sathe. 2002. *Judicial Activism in India: Transgressing Borders and Enforcing Limits.* New Delhi: Oxford University Press.
[2] Article 124(3), Constitution of India.

demonstrate that three informal eligibility criteria, in particular, are used to select judges for the Supreme Court, criteria that have not been formally specified in any constitutional document: (a) a judge should be at least 55 years of age in order to be considered eligible to be appointed to the Supreme Court, (b) he should be a senior high court judge, or, especially over the last 20 years, the chief justice of a high court, and (c) judges should reflect the geographic (and demographic) diversity of India, that is, judges are selected for the Supreme Court by taking into account the state or region they belong to, and whether they belong to non-traditional backgrounds, in terms of religion, caste, or gender.

When six judges took their seats at the inaugural session of the Supreme Court of India on 28 January 1950,[3] they were manifestly aware of the 'historical significance'[4] of the occasion. In an All India Radio (AIR) broadcast only five days earlier, a former high court judge, Bakshi Tek Chand, had said that this would be an 'epoch-making event in the annals of our ancient land'.[5] Standing up that day in a hall packed with ministers, ambassadors, chief justices, advocates-general, and diplomatic representatives from several countries, the first Attorney General of India, M.C. Setalvad, reminded the Court's judges that the powers of the Supreme Court would be 'wider than [the powers] exercised by the highest court of any country in the Commonwealth or by the Supreme Court of the United States'.[6] In response, the Chief Justice of India, Harilal J. Kania, said that '[p]olitical considerations should not influence appointments to the Bench'.[7] Enacted for historical reasons on 26 January 1950,[8] the Constitution of India provided that the Supreme Court of India, situated in New Delhi, was to have one Chief Justice of India, and not

---

[3]   *Times of India*. 1950. 'Supreme Court Takes Seat: Simple Ceremony at Delhi', *Times of India*, 29 January, p. 3.

[4]   *Times of India*, 'Supreme Court Takes Seat'.

[5]   *Times of India*. 1950. 'Supreme Court of India: Epoch-Making Event', *Times of India*, 24 January, p. 9.

[6]   Motilal C. Setalvad. 1970. *My Life: Law and Other Things*. London: Sweet and Maxwell, p. 148.

[7]   *Times of India*, 'Supreme Court Takes Seat'.

[8]   See Ramachandra Guha. 2007. *India after Gandhi: The History of the World's Largest Democracy*. New York: HarperCollins, p. 20.

more than seven judges.[9] Today, the Court has 30 judges* in addition to the Chief Justice of India. But who are these judges, and where did they come from?

In the past 20 years of constitutional governance in India, the process of appointing judges to the Supreme Court of India has spurred widespread debate.[10] If the jurisprudence of the first three decades of the Court was defined by a struggle for custody of India's Constitution, the politics of the next three decades were delineated by a tussle for custody of the Court's composition.[11] When the Constitution came into being, it said that appointments to the Supreme Court were to be made by the President of India, and that the Chief Justice of India only had to be 'consulted' in the process. In 1981, in perhaps one of the longest set of judicial opinions ever written by the Court,[12] the Court held that the power to appoint judges lay with the executive—that recommendations made by the Chief Justice of India would not be binding on the executive. As political power at the centre weakened in the late 1980s, the judiciary sought to wrest control of its composition from the executive. In the 1990s,[13] the Court held that the advice of a 'collegium' of judges consisting of the Chief Justice of India and the four most senior judges of the Court was binding on the executive. Today, Supreme Court judges are selected by this body—the collegium. Substantially weakened by the pressures of coalitional politics, and with only fractured majorities at

---

[9] Article 124(1), Constitution of India.

[10] See for example, S.P. Sathe. 1998. 'Appointment of Judges: The Issues', *Economic and Political Weekly*, 33(32): 2155–7; Lord Cooke of Thorndon. 2000. 'Where Angels Fear to Tread', in B.N. Kirpal, Ashok H. Desai, Gopal Subramanium, Rajeev Dhavan, and Raju Ramachandran (eds) in *Supreme but Not Infallible: Essays in Honour of the Supreme Court of India*. New Delhi: Oxford University Press, pp. 97–106; K.G. Kannabiran. 2004. 'Selection and Impeachment of Judges: Issues for Debate', *Economic and Political Weekly*, 39(49): 5221–5; T.R. Andhyarujina. 2009. 'Appointment of Judges by Collegium of Judges', *Hindu*, 18 December, available online at http://www.thehindu.com/opinion/op-ed/article66672.ece (last accessed on 21 April 2012).

[11] See Abhinav Chandrachud. 2011. 'An Empirical Study of the Supreme Court's Composition', *Economic and Political Weekly*, 46(1): 71–7.

[12] *S.P. Gupta* v. *President of India*, AIR 1982 SC 149; (1982) 2 SCR 365.

[13] *Supreme Court Advocates on Record Association* v. *Union of India*, AIR 1994 SC 268; *In re Presidential Reference*, AIR 1999 SC 1.

the centre, the executive now did not have the political power to be able to undo this holding. So it came to be that Supreme Court judges get to decide who gets appointed to the Supreme Court of India.[14]

The phenomenon of increased judicial independence occurred against the backdrop of serious (though often wildly speculative) allegations of corruption levelled against the judiciary, and the wider movement against corruption in India.[15] The judiciary is

---

[14] On the basis of interviews conducted with judges, Gadbois argues that judges appointed judges even before—prior to 1970, although he acknowledges that a judge would seldom admit that he had been appointed by the executive as he would then be considered 'less deserving'. George H. Gadbois, Jr. 2011. *Judges of the Supreme Court of India: 1950–1989*. New Delhi: Oxford University Press, pp. 4–6. However, even if the Chief Justice of India exercised wide powers of appointment prior to 1970, now it is not merely the Chief Justice of India who exercises this power, but a group of five judges, the collegium. Further, where the executive could potentially or at least theoretically reject appointments suggested by the Chief Justice of India previously, now this power no longer exists if the collegium unanimously insists on the appointment despite the president's reservations.

[15] In the not-so-distant past, a senior lawyer and former law minister, Shanti Bhushan, cast serious, though perhaps speculative, allegations of corruption against eight former chief justices of India. *Indian Express*. 2010. '8 CJIs Corrupt: Ex-Law Minister to SC', *Indian Express*, 17 September, available online at http://www.indianexpress.com/news/8-cjis-corrupt-exlaw-minister-to-sc/682677/ (last accessed on 23 March 2012); *Hindustan Times*. 2010. '8 out of 16 former CJIs Corrupt', *Hindustan Times*, 17 September, available online at http://www.hindustantimes.com/India-news/NewDelhi/8-out-of-16-former-CJIs-corrupt/Article1-601069.aspx (last accessed on 23 March 2012). Further, the problem of corruption in the judiciary came into the limelight again when a judge, against whom serious allegations of corruption had been levelled, almost became a Supreme Court judge. On 27 August 2009, a report appeared in a newspaper that five names had been cleared by the collegium for appointment to the Supreme Court of India. V. Venkatesan. 2009. 'Controversial Choice', *Frontline*, 26(22), available online at http://www.frontlineonnet.com/fl2622/stories/20091106262212200.htm (last accessed on 2 December 2011). One of these names was Justice P.D. Dinakaran, Chief Justice of the Karnataka High Court. Senior and respected lawyers in the Supreme Court petitioned the Chief Justice not to go ahead with his appointment, reportedly submitting evidence of irregularities in his assets and judicial orders. Eventually, only four of the five judges previously reported were appointed to the Court on 17 November 2009—these were Justices A.K. Patnaik, T.S. Thakur, K.S. Panicker Radhakrishnan, and S.S. Nijjar—and an inquiry was initiated against Dinakaran,

still perhaps widely perceived to be the last bastion of integrity in public service in India, but the fear of corruption among a few members of India's judiciary has generated a debate as to the criteria to be employed in selecting judges. In a recent impeachment motion against a judge of the Calcutta High Court (Soumitra Sen[16]), the leader of the opposition in the Rajya Sabha, Arun Jaitley, spoke in favour of adopting 'objective criteria' in the selection of judges:

> What is your academic qualification? How bright were you during your academic days? What is your experience as a lawyer? If you are a judge, how many judgments have you written? How many have been set aside? How many have been upheld? How many juniors have you trained? How many cases have you argued? How many cases have been reported which you have argued? Have you got laws laid down? Have you written papers on legal subjects?[17]

Recently, a former Supreme Court judge publicly declared that the secrecy shrouding the process of selecting judges to the Supreme Court and the high courts was a 'sin'.[18] It was, in her words, 'one of the best kept secrets' in India. She opined that although the process of selecting judges has changed, and judges now select judges in a self-perpetuating cycle, things have substantively remained the same: the process has only 'changed the actors without any change either

---

who consequently resigned. J. Venkatesan. 2011. 'Justice Dinakaran Resigns', *Hindu*, 29 July 2011, available online at http://www.thehindu.com/news/national/article2305932.ece (last accessed on 23 March 2012).

[16] The Rajya Sabha, the upper house of India's Parliament, voted to impeach the judge. Before the lower house, the Lok Sabha, could vote on the question of his impeachment, he chose to resign. *Times of India*. 2011. 'Justice Soumitra Sen, Facing Impeachment, Resigns', *Times of India*, 1 September, available online at http://articles.timesofindia.indiatimes.com/2011-09-01/india/29953339_1_impeachment-motion-justice-soumitra-sen-common-citizen (last accessed on 23 March 2012).

[17] 'Uncorrected Verbatim Rajya Sabha Debates, 18 August 2011', available online at http://164.100.47.5/newdebate/223/18082011/Fullday.pdf (last accessed on 2 December 2011), p. 161.

[18] Justice Ruma Pal. 2011. 'An Independent Judiciary', V.M. Tarkunde Memorial Lecture, New Delhi, 10 November, available online at http://www.theradical humanist.com/index.php&option=com_radical&controller=article&cid=431& Itemid=56.

in the roles or the method of acting'. The former judge highlighted key drawbacks in the selection mechanism prevalent today:

> The very secrecy of the process leads to an inadequate input of information as to the abilities and suitability of a possible candidate for appointment as a judge. A chance remark, a rumour or even third-hand information may be sufficient to damn a judge's prospects. Contrariwise a personal friendship or unspoken obligation may colour a recommendation. Consensus within the collegium is sometimes resolved through a trade-off resulting in dubious appointments with disastrous consequences for the litigants and the credibility of the judicial system. Besides, institutional independence has also been compromised by growing sycophancy and 'lobbying' within the system.[19]

A great deal of speculation has gone into the question of what criteria are used to appoint judges to the Supreme Court of India. When the author of the famous Naz Foundation decision,[20] Chief Justice A.P. Shah, retired from the Delhi High Court in 2010, many wondered why he had not been elevated to the Supreme Court.[21] More recently, the Chief Justice of the Gujarat High Court, Bhaskar Bhattacharya, accused a retiring Chief Justice of India, Altamas Kabir, of blackballing his elevation to the Supreme Court as a way of retaliating against him for refusing to appoint Kabir's sister to the Calcutta High Court.[22] Though we may not know what the truth is anytime soon, all this has brought judicial appointments to the heart of controversy in recent times.

The Constitution of India provides that a person may be eligible for appointment to the Supreme Court of India if he or she has either five years' experience serving as a high court judge, 10 years'

---

[19] Pal, 'Independent Judiciary'.
[20] *Naz Foundation* v. *Delhi*, (2009) 160 DLT 277.
[21] See Abhinav Chandrachud. 2010. 'Supreme, but Not Superior', *Indian Express*, 23 February, available online at http://www.indianexpress.com/news/supreme-but-not-superior/583098/ (last accessed on 18 July 2013).
[22] *Indian Express*. 2013. 'Gujarat CJ Says He Lost SC Berth because He Opposed HC Judgeship for CJI Kabir's Sister', *Indian Express*, 12 July, available online at http://www.indianexpress.com/news/gujarat-cj-says-he-lost-sc-berth-because-he-opposed-hc-judgeship-for-cji-kabir-s-sister/1140908/0 (last accessed on 18 July 2013). Interestingly, allegations like these were around even before the collegium system. One of the judges I interviewed for this book informed me that his own appointment to the Supreme Court in the 1970s might

standing as a high court advocate, or is otherwise a 'distinguished jurist' in the opinion of the President of India.[23] But this hardly gives us any idea of who Indian Supreme Court judges are at all. In 60 years, not once has the president ever appointed a 'distinguished jurist', that is, a legal scholar or law professor who has not practised as a lawyer or worked as a judge, to the Supreme Court.[24] Further, only a handful of lawyers in India's history were ever appointed as Supreme Court judges directly, without having first served as high court judges, though several other lawyers may have been invited to be appointed to the Court and declined. The overwhelming majority of judges have twice, or in some cases, three times, the basic requirement of five years' experience as high court judges.

There appears to be a distinction, then, between Indian constitutional law on the books and Indian constitutional law in action, between the formal eligibility criteria prescribed by the Indian Constitution for the appointment of judges to the Supreme Court of India, and informal criteria employed in finally selecting and making appointments to the Supreme Court. Said another way, the Indian Constitution prescribes some basic threshold qualifications for appointment to the Supreme Court, but those by no means give us any indication of who an Indian Supreme Court judge will be. There are additional threshold criteria, which the Indian Constitution does not spell out, but which informally prevail nonetheless. There is an unwritten convention or understanding about what type of person will be appointed an Indian Supreme Court judge—this book seeks to shed light upon that convention, and to measure any changes in that constitutional convention. It is the central thesis of this book that informal norms have seeped into the cracks of India's written Constitution and live in its shadows. At a broader level of abstraction, this book adds to the literature that even written constitutions can

---

have been blackballed by a senior Supreme Court judge, because a proposed marriage between their two families had not worked out (Interview 23).

[23] Article 124(3), Constitution of India.

[24] In the 1970s, Nagendra Singh came close to being appointed to the Supreme Court of India. Had he been appointed to the Court, he would have been appointed under the 'distinguished jurist' category. Gadbois, *Judges of the Supreme Court*, p. 156. However, this did not happen.

have unwritten, 'invisible'[25] features or 'silences'[26] characteristic of unwritten constitutions.

PREVIOUS RESEARCH

Although the informal norms being analysed in this book are widely known within India's legal community, they have seldom been studied. Legal research in India has been dominated by doctrinal studies. Serious quantitative studies that analyse the court's structural and behavioural processes can be counted on one's fingertips.[27] In order to carry out quantitative studies that attempt to understand whether the demographic characteristics of judges pressure or bias the manner in which they decide cases, an accurate and comprehensive map of the judges first needs to be prepared. Very few studies have accomplished or even attempted this, and very little is particularly known about judges who served on the Supreme Court of India in the last 20 years.

In a study published in 1977, Rajeev Dhavan prepared a portrait of 55 judges who had served on the Supreme Court of India between 1950 and 1975.[28] Dhavan analysed the composition of the Court

---

[25] Laurence H. Tribe. 2008. *The Invisible Constitution*. New York: Oxford University Press.

[26] Fali S. Nariman. 2006. 'The Silences in Our Constitutional Law', *Supreme Court Cases*, 2:15.

[27] See Vijay Gupta. 1995. *Decision Making in the Supreme Court of India*. Delhi: Kaveri; George H. Gadbois, Jr. 1969. 'Selection, Background Characteristics, and Voting Behavior of Indian Supreme Court Judges, 1950–1959', in Glendon Schubert and David J. Danelski (eds), *Comparative Judicial Behavior: Cross-cultural Studies of Political Decision-making in the East and West*. New York: Oxford University Press, pp. 221–51; Rajeev Dhavan. 1977. *The Supreme Court of India: A Socio-legal Critique of Its Juristic Techniques*. Bombay: Tripathi; Nick Robinson, Anjana Agarwal, Vrinda Bhandari, Ankit Goel, Karishma Kakkar, Reeba Muthalaly, *et al.* 2011. 'Interpreting the Constitution: Supreme Court Constitution Benches since Independence', *Economic and Political Weekly*, 46(9): 27–31; Shyam Krishnan Sriram. 2006. 'Caste and the Court: Examining Judicial Selection Bias on Bench Assignments on the Indian Supreme Court', *Political Science Theses*, Paper 6, available online at http://digitalarchive.gsu.edu/political_science_theses/6 (last accessed 26 December 2013).

[28] Dhavan, *Supreme Court of India*. See further, Rajeev Dhavan and Alice Jacob. 1978. *Selection and Appointment of Supreme Court Judges: A Case Study*. Bombay: Tara.

until 1975, measuring the variables that I propose to investigate in this book. Further, in a seminal study published recently, George H. Gadbois,[29] Jr, prepared a 'collective portrait' of 93 judges who served on the Supreme Court between 1950 and 1989, including the ones studied by Dhavan. Gadbois too measured the variables I propose to investigate. However, these lucid studies of Supreme Court judges do not shed light on judicial appointments made to the Supreme Court in the last two decades of its existence, and consequently there is a gap in the literature.

First, the process of selecting judges for the Supreme Court of India is fundamentally and significantly different today from what it used to be during the time that Dhavan and Gadbois studied the composition of the Court. At that time, the power to select judges for the Supreme Court theoretically rested with the executive, and during the Indira Gandhi years in particular, the executive influenced judicial appointments. However, starting 6 October 1993, the Supreme Court seized the power to select judges in India, consequent to a decision which is popularly referred to as the second Judges case.[30] As a result, for close to 20 years, judges have been selected for appointment to the Supreme Court in a manner fundamentally different from the manner in which they were selected previously. The studies of Dhavan and Gadbois do not extend to this period, and there is consequently a large gap in the literature for this period.

Second, between 1989 and 2009, more judges have served on the Supreme Court of India than even those that served on the Court between 1950 and 1989. Gadbois studied 93 judges who served on the Court between 1950 and 1989. However, between 1989 and 2009, there have been 96 more judges who have served on the Court. The task of investigating the demographic features of these 96 judges who served during the shorter time span of 1989–2009 is therefore no less challenging than the task Gadbois had embarked upon. The fact that almost no studies have been conducted concerning these

---

[29] Gadbois, *Judges of the Supreme Court*. See further, George H. Gadbois, Jr. 1970. 'Indian Judicial Behavior', *Economic and Political Weekly*, 5(3/5): 149, 151, 153–5, 157, 159, 161, 163, 165–6.

[30] *Supreme Court Advocates on Record Association* v. *Union of India*, AIR 1994 SC 268.

96 judges speaks to the large gap in the literature that this book hopes to address.

This book builds upon the studies conducted by Dhavan and Gadbois, while specifically exploring the prevalence of informal, unwritten norms in selecting judges for the Supreme Court of India. This book will shed light on any impact the second and third Judges cases have had on judicial appointments in action—one of the questions that I will ask in each empirical chapter will be: have the second and third Judges cases had an impact or made any difference to the type of candidate selected for appointment to the Supreme Court? My approach will partly be comparative—I will draw upon the international and comparative literature on the norms investigated in this book to situate the discussion within a broader framework.

It must be clarified at the outset that this book is not a catalogue of semi-biographical vignettes, but a monograph which makes an analytical argument about the nature of judicial appointments to the Supreme Court of India. This book does not directly address the normative question of whether the present collegium system of appointing judges to the Supreme Court is legitimate, particularly because that question has long occupied other authors.[31] This book does, however, address the questions of whether the criteria adopted by the collegium in appointing judges are any different from those adopted previously, whether those criteria are legitimate, and whether the collegium has produced a more legitimate, efficient, or diverse judiciary than that which existed between 1950 and 1989.

RESEARCH QUESTIONS

Age

The age at which a judge is appointed to the Supreme Court of India is inextricably intertwined with the length of the term the judge will serve in office. Since Supreme Court judges retire at the age of 65,[32] younger judges serve longer terms in office. Intuitively, this naturally creates incentives for political authorities that seek to control the Court to appoint judges younger—so that they will

[31] See for example, Andhyarujina, 'Appointment of Judges'; Fali S. Nariman. 2010. *Before Memory Fades: An Autobiography.* New Delhi: Hay House, pp. 399–405.
[32] Article 124(2), Constitution of India.

last longer on the Court. These incentives are very similar to those that exist for appointment to the US Supreme Court,[33] where judges serve life terms in office, as distinguished from constitutional courts where judges serve in office for a fixed, typically non-renewable term, usually in civil law countries that follow Hans Kelsen's 'continental model' of constitutional design, where powers of constitutional adjudication are centralized and concentrated in one constitutional court, and not dispersed amongst various courts (for example, France, Italy, Spain, and Portugal).[34]

Interestingly, although Supreme Court judges retire at age 65, high court judges retire at age 62 (earlier, it was 60).[35] By way of background, this book will seek to understand why legislators in India thought it appropriate that the judges of the high courts and the Supreme Court should retire at different ages. It will be demonstrated that this was done in order to provide an incentive for high court judges to serve on India's new Supreme Court. I will seek to empirically demonstrate that the fact that India's Supreme Court now consists of (and has increasingly consisted of) a majority of high court chief justices offers reason to suggest that this 'retirement age gap' is no longer necessary.

In this book, I will measure the age at which judges have been appointed to the Supreme Court of India, and examine whether this variable has changed over the years, or whether it has changed consequent to a change in political regime. The questions that I will ask are: how old were the judges when they were appointed to the Supreme Court of India? In particular, is there an unwritten convention that a Supreme Court judge cannot be appointed younger than the age of 55?

Seniority

Seniority is arguably the single most important unwritten norm prevalent in the Indian judiciary. When the Chief Justice of India

[33] Steven G. Calabresi and James Lindgren. 2006. 'Term Limits for the Supreme Court: Life Tenure Reconsidered', *Harvard Journal of Law and Public Policy*, 29(3): 769–877.
[34] Judges of the Constitutional Court of these countries serve nine-year terms (typically non-renewable) in office. See Vicki C. Jackson and Mark Tushnet. 2006. *Comparative Constitutional Law*. Foundation Press, pp. 498–9.
[35] Article 124(2) and Article 217(1), Constitution of India.

retires, the most senior puisne judge on the Court at the time is almost[36] always picked as the next chief justice. This practice is also followed in the high courts. Seniority is also important for other reasons. How senior you are could determine whether you get to write the judicial opinion in a case, whether you can decide who gets appointed to the judiciary, and even what kind of apartment you get to stay in, or what kind of car you get to drive—both being benefits Indian higher court judges are entitled to. Judges in India also sit on the bench in their order of seniority, much in the same way as constitutional courts the world over. Thus, the Chief Justice of India or most senior judge sits in the centre, the next most senior judge sits to his right, the next to his left, and so on, with the result that the most senior judges are concentrated towards the centre of the bench, while the junior judges sit in the flanks.

This book will seek to answer the following questions: what was a judge's seniority on a high court when he was appointed to the Supreme Court of India? In other words, if a judge was a high court judge before he was appointed to the Supreme Court (as was always the case, barring only a few exceptions),[37] (a) how many years did he serve on a high court before being elevated to the Supreme Court and (b) what was his position of seniority in his own court before he was appointed to the Supreme Court? Additionally, was he always a chief justice of a high court? Was he the chief justice of more than one high court? Most importantly, is there any correlation between the greater number of high court chief justices and older judges being appointed to the Court?

Diversity

This book will demonstrate that an attempt is made to ensure regional diversity in the Supreme Court of India. A judge is considered to represent the state or region in which the high court on which he served is located, irrespective of where he was born, where he lived for most of his life, or what language that he speaks. I will seek

---

[36] This practice has been followed, barring five exceptions. See Abhinav Chandrachud. 2012. 'Supreme Court's Seniority Norm: Historical Origins', *Economic and Political Weekly*, 47(8): 26–30, 29n1.

[37] See Chandrachud, 'Age Factor'.

answers to the following questions: how have the states of India been represented on the Supreme Court? In particular, (*a*) what share or percentage of seats on the Supreme Court belong or have typically belonged to the puisne judges of each high court of India and (*b*) what share or percentage of seats on the Supreme Court belong or have typically belonged to the chief justices of each high court of India?[38] How does the size of the population of a state, its representation in Parliament, or the sanctioned strength and size of its high court determine the likelihood that judges from that state's high court will get to serve on the Supreme Court?

It will be demonstrated that an attempt is made to appoint religious minorities, and occasionally, 'backward' castes, and women, to the Court, and that this too serves as an informal criterion for appointment to the Supreme Court of India. This is despite the fact that the Indian Constitution does not specify any formal policy of affirmative action on the basis of religion, caste, or gender on the Supreme Court. In fact, in October 2011, I filed a right to information application with the Ministry of Law and Justice, Government of India, seeking to know the religion and caste of each judge who served on the Court between 1950 and 2011. The response that I received a month later was that since judges are appointed to the Supreme Court under Article 124 of the Constitution, which 'does not provide for reservation for any caste or class of persons', 'no such information is maintained' officially by the government.[39]

Answers will be sought to the following questions: how have minorities been represented on the Court? What is the religious, caste, and gender composition of the Court? How do these statistics stand in comparison with the characteristics of the total population of India?

METHODOLOGY

My research approach is both quantitative and qualitative. In each chapter, I begin by setting out the results of my qualitative study, and then determine whether those results prove to be quantitatively true.

---

[38] Consequent to the policy on transfer of judges, chief justices typically do not belong to the same high court in which they were puisne judges.

[39] Letter dated 23 November 2011, 162/DS(J)/2011-RTI, from the Department of Justice, Ministry of Law and Justice, Government of India; on file with me.

Data for the quantitative investigation were first obtained from publicly available sources of information (for example, the website of the Supreme Court of India,[40] websites of high courts, law journals). Next, I obtained non-public quantitative data by personally speaking with 49 former or sitting Supreme Court judges, and 11 close personal relatives of former or sitting Supreme Court judges. For the qualitative component of my study, amongst the 49 judges I personally spoke with, I conducted semi-structured interviews with 29 former judges of the Supreme Court, including former chief justices of the Court and members of the collegium who were instrumental in selecting judges for the Supreme Court.

I adopted a decision rule of convenience in attributing judicial appointments to chief justices. In other words, since it is beyond the scope of this book to investigate who was responsible for the appointment of each individual justice to the Court, I uniformly attributed the appointment of a judge to the chief justice during the term of whom the judge was appointed to the Court.[41]

The decision rule that I have adopted in Chapter 6 for geographic representation also needs to be stated here. Assume that a judge is born in State 1, practises law and lives for most of his life in State 2, his mother tongue is the language spoken in State 3, he is first appointed to the High Court of State 4 as a judge, he is then transferred to the High Court of State 5 as a puisne judge, and finally, he is transferred

---

[40] See http://supremecourtofindia.nic.in.

[41] For example, Justice T.L. Venkatarama Ayyar was appointed on 4 January 1954, the day on which Justice M.C. Mahajan became Chief Justice of India. Even so, in order to be consistent, I attributed his appointment to M.C. Mahajan, and all other judges were similarly considered as having been appointed by the chief justice during whose term they were appointed to the Court, even though their appointment may have been recommended by a predecessor chief justice. Since the study in this book does not investigate who was responsible for each individual judicial appointment, but only examines quantitative and qualitative data to observe trends in appointments, this decision rule does not take away from the study. Although George H. Gadbois, Jr has attributed judicial appointments to individual chief justices, based on his interviews with judges (Gadbois, *Judges of the Supreme Court*), since I do not have the same insider accounts of judicial appointments after 1989, I preferred to apply my decision rule consistently, even for judicial appointments made before 1989.

to the High Court of State 6 as chief justice—the question which arises is: which state should the judge be attributed to? The decision rule I adopted, which, I believe, closely approximates the official decision rule, is that a judge is considered to belong to the state to which he was first appointed as a high court judge, irrespective of other considerations. Thus, in this hypothetical, the judge will be considered as belonging to State 4.

A stylistic note is also necessary here: in this book, a judge will often be termed as having been 'appointed' to the Supreme Court of India by the collegium of judges, or by the Chief Justice of India. Wherever this occurs, it should be understood that the collegium or Chief Justice only selected the judge for appointment, and it was the President of India under whose warrant the judge was finally appointed to the Supreme Court of India. Under the Constitution of India, judges are appointed to the Supreme Court by the president,[42] though the distinction between selection and appointment becomes a little tenuous especially in the last 20 years, as the process of judicial appointments has virtually been seized by the judiciary, by virtue of decisions which will be closely examined in Chapter 2.

This book does not employ a methodology substantially different from the one adopted by Dhavan or Gadbois. Like these authors, the approach here is both quantitative and qualitative, though in the quantitative analysis, tests of statistical significance will be employed to measure the variables of interest. However, the research questions pursued in this book differ from those pursued by these authors—particularly, this book strongly focuses on the prevalence of informal, unwritten norms in appointing judges to the Supreme Court of India, while also addressing the gap in the literature for the period 1989–2011.

Quantitative Data

The Supreme Court's website provides brief résumés of each judge who has been appointed to the Court between 1950 and 2009. However, this information suffers from three shortcomings.

[42] Article 124(2), Constitution of India.

First, it is not always complete.[43] For this reason, wherever possible, the judges' résumés obtained from the Court's website were corroborated against other sources of information, in particular the websites of certain high courts which provide biographical information concerning their former judges (including those who later served on the Supreme Court). Other sources of data include: law reports (for example, the journal section of the All India Reporter) and a periodical published by the Ministry of Law and Justice, entitled *Judges of the Supreme Court of India and the High Courts*. Sources of data for historical information include: *Indian Yearbook* and *Who's Who (Times of India)*, the *Proquest Times of India* electronic database (1838–2002), and the *Oxford Dictionary of National Biography*.

Second, the information on the Supreme Court's website is not systematically organized, and had to be extensively organized in order to measure variables. The courts of 37 chief justices of India were reconstructed in order to figure out which judges served on the Court at what time, which of them retired (or in rare cases, died or resigned), and which judges were appointed to the Court. This enabled me to study not merely differences in the regional composition of the Court, but also differences in judges appointed to the Supreme Court by different chief justices.

Third, from the publicly available sources of information I was able to get certain kinds of reasonably accurate and comprehensive data, for example, a judge's date of birth, whether he worked as a government lawyer, the high court or high courts he served on as a judge, the dates of his appointment as high court judge, high court chief justice, Supreme Court judge, and Chief Justice of India (if applicable), and the date of his retirement from the Supreme Court. However, certain kinds of data, especially required for the purposes of ascertaining demographic diversity in Chapter 5, were not publicly available (for example, whether the judge was the first lawyer in his family, or what his religion and caste were), or public sources of certain data were unreliable and patchy (for example, the judge's educational background). Upon filing requests for information under

---

[43] For example, the résumés of some judges do not tell us that they were formerly high court chief justices. On one occasion, a judge who died in harness was shown as having retired on the date of his death.

the Right to Information Act, 2005, I found that the Supreme Court of India does not maintain information concerning the religion and caste of judges,[44] and neither does the Ministry of Law and Justice.[45] Demographic data for the purposes of Chapter 5 were obtained in the following manner.

For the 93 judges who were appointed to the Supreme Court of India between 1950 and 1989, these data have been provided in Gadbois's study.[46] However, 96 more judges were appointed to the Supreme Court between 1989 and 2009. I have obtained data concerning these judges from the following sources: (*a*) I personally spoke with or corresponded with 47 judges, retired or active, of the Supreme Court, who were appointed to the Court between 1989 and 2009; (*b*) data for 11 judges of the Supreme Court, who were appointed to the Court between 1989 and 2009, were obtained by personally speaking with the judge's spouse or close relative (son, daughter, granddaughter, grandson); (*c*) data concerning the caste of 27[47] judges were obtained from a list prepared by the Lawyer's Forum for Social Justice (New Delhi, 2002); and (*d*) I was able to ascertain data for nine other judges with reasonable accuracy.[48] I was unable to ascertain the caste of two judges who were appointed to the Supreme Court in the 1990s, who have since passed away. Accordingly, the

[44] On 3 June 2011, I filed a right to information application under the Right to Information Act, 2005, with the Central Public Information Officer (CPIO) of the Supreme Court of India. I requested details concerning the religion and caste of every one of 193 judges who had served on the Court between 1950 and that date. On 7 July 2011, I received a response from the Additional Registrar and CPIO informing me that the data I requested were 'neither maintained nor available'. Letter on file with me.

[45] Letter dated 23 November 2011, 162/DS(J)/2011-RTI, from the Department of Justice, Ministry of Law and Justice, Government of India.

[46] Gadbois, *Judges of the Supreme Court.*

[47] One of these judges was identified in this source as belonging to a Scheduled Tribe. However, the judge's personal secretary informed me that he was not a Hindu, and information about that judge's religion has been categorized accordingly.

[48] These data were obtained either from reliable media articles, other judges, close relatives of other judges, or from a scholar who corresponded with the judges. Where information concerning the father of a judge was accessible, the judge was attributed the same demographic characteristics as his father.

demographic diversity section of Chapter 5 relies on data for 98.9 per cent of the judges who served on the Court between 1950 and 2009.

Qualitative Data

Barring two judges, the 29 judges I interviewed all served on the Supreme Court of India sometime between October 1989 (when Gadbois's study ends) and December 2009. During that time, 96 judges were appointed to the Supreme Court. How did I select 29 of these judges for the interviews? Carving out a random sample of the 96 judges would have been the best method of deciding whom to interview, but my difficulty was that not every judge was accessible, interested, or willing to go through the relatively lengthy interview. Amongst the 49 judges I personally spoke with or corresponded with (some preferred to answer my questions over email), I managed to ask some for nothing more than basic background information about themselves which was not publicly available—whether they were the first lawyers in their family, what their mother tongue, religion, and caste were, and where they had studied. From amongst the judges I spoke or corresponded with, I was able to conduct lengthier, semi-structured interviews with 29 judges. The interviews were all conducted between July 2011 and February 2012, in person, over the telephone, or via an email questionnaire. The interviews typically ranged roughly 10–25 minutes. Every effort was made to ensure that the judges I interviewed were as diverse a group as possible. The judges were promised confidentiality before each interview, even though most did not request it, and in this book I will not identify the judges I interviewed. Instead, each judge has been assigned a number, according to the order in which he or she was interviewed, and interviews will be cited accordingly. I agree that the anonymity of the interviewees makes the research less convincing, but the use of anonymous interviews is not unknown in the social science literature,[49] and I felt that

---

[49] See for example, David C. Potter. 1986. *India's Political Administrators 1919–1983*. Oxford: Clarendon Press, p. 17.

by promising confidentiality, I could get information which would otherwise not be accessible to me.

CONTRIBUTIONS

A researcher ought always to be interested in why anybody else would be interested in his research question, and so I too must ask: why are the variables of interest I am investigating, namely, age, seniority, and diversity, important? I would argue that they are important for at least three reasons. First, my book examines the use of informal, unwritten criteria in the appointment of judges to the Supreme Court of India. My variables of interest are not catalogued in any legislative document, although they may be known to members of India's legal profession. To that extent, my book adds to the vast law and society literature on the prevalence of informal norms in legal systems.[50] Second, my book also serves as a foundation for quantitative studies that may be carried out in the future. The results of the study contained in this book might facilitate future studies that build regression models to determine whether the background of judges has an impact on the way in which they decide cases—for example, to answer questions such as whether the tenure of a judge in office has an impact on the manner in which cases are decided. Third, my book situates judicial appointments in India within a broader normative and comparative framework. I seek answers to questions such as: are

[50] See for example, Richard D. Schwartz. 1954. 'Social Factors in the Development of Legal Control: A Case Study of Two Israeli Settlements', *Yale Law Journal*, 63(4): 471–91; Masaki Abe. 1995. 'The Internal Control of a Bureaucratic Judiciary: The Case of Japan', *International Journal of the Sociology of Law*, 23(1): 303–20; Daniel H. Foote. 1992. 'The Benevolent Paternalism of Japanese Criminal Justice', *California Law Review*, 80(2): 317–90; Robert C. Ellickson. 1986. 'Of Coase and Cattle: Dispute Resolution among Neighbors in Shasta County', *Stanford Law Review*, 38(1): 623–87; Jane Kaufman Winn. 1994. 'Relational Practices and the Marginalization of Law: Informal Financial Practices of Small Businesses in Taiwan', *Law and Society Review*, 28(2): 193–232; Stewart Macaulay. 1963. 'Non-contractual Relations in Business: A Preliminary Study', *American Sociological Review*, 28(1): 55–67; Yang Su and Xin He. 2010. 'Street As Courtroom: State Accommodation of Labor Protest in South China', *Law and Society Review*, 44(1): 157–84.

terms on the Supreme Court of India too short, are life terms as in the United States, or fixed, non-renewable terms as in South Africa and Colombia, preferable? Should constitutional court judges be appointed from amongst scholars, lawyers, or judges? In appointing judges to constitutional courts, how should the appointing authority account for the 'merit/diversity' paradox,[51] that is, should diversity trump merit or supplement merit, and if so, to what extent, and what kind of diversity?

NOTE

* In 2019, the strength of the Supreme Court was increased to 33 judges (excluding the Chief Justice).

[51] See Leny E. De Groot-Van Leeuwen. 2006. 'Merit Selection and Diversity in the Dutch Judiciary', in Kate Malleson and Peter H. Russell (eds), *Appointing Judges in an Age of Judicial Power: Critical Perspectives from around the World*, pp. 145–58. Toronto: University of Toronto Press.

HISTORICAL BACKGROUND

THIS CHAPTER BEGINS BY ANALYSING historical debates surrounding the establishment of the Federal Court during British rule in India, a court which would be the predecessor to the Supreme Court of India. An attempt will be made to answer the following questions: what were the qualifications for appointment to the Federal Court of India? For what length of time were Federal Court judges meant to serve on the court? (This question is answered by analysing debates surrounding the age at which its judges were meant to retire.) Did any debate spell out specific guidelines concerning the criteria that were to be employed in appointing judges; for example, were religious 'quotas' to be prevalent in the court? Next, this chapter will provide a biographical glimpse into the judges who served on the Federal Court of India. It will be seen that informal criteria were adopted in appointing judges to the Federal Court—criteria not specifically discussed or set out in a constitutional document. Foremost among these was that out of the three judges on the Federal Court, one would be British, one Hindu, and one Muslim. This was an informal 'quota' in the court, which was not set out in the Government of India Act, 1935, but which prevailed nonetheless, and perhaps set the tone for future informal 'quotas' based on region, caste, gender, and religion in the Supreme Court. The judges who served on the Federal Court of India prior to independence will then be contrasted against those who served on the Federal Court after independence (but before the creation of the Supreme Court), in order to determine whether there were any discernible differences amongst the judges who served on the court in these two periods of India's history. This discussion will serve as a reference point against which the composition of the Supreme Court will be compared in subsequent chapters. Finally, this chapter will analyse historical debates, primarily debates of the Constituent Assembly of India and its sub-committees, specific to the establishment of the Supreme Court—the qualifications of its judges, and the criteria that were to be employed in appointing judges.

While analyzing historical debates, we will particularly focus on debates concerning the retirement age at the Federal Court and Supreme Court of India. This is because the retirement age of judges in India is important for at least three reasons:

1. Judges in India do not serve fixed terms in office, and on account of the retirement age, the age at which a judge is appointed to the court works to determine the length of the judge's tenure in the Supreme Court of India. Chapter 3 analyses this phenomenon in greater detail.
2. Supreme Court judges in India retire at age 65, which is perhaps one of the earliest retirements in the world (judges in many countries typically retire at age 70, or in rare cases, at 75). Historical debates surrounding the creation of the Court will be analysed in order to determine when and why the age of 65 was picked for Federal Court and Supreme Court judges to retire, and whether an argument is capable of being made today to increase the age of retirement, from a policy standpoint.
3. Although Supreme Court judges in India retire at age 65, high court judges in India retire at age 62 (until 1963,[1] it was 60). At first, this 'retirement age gap' seems odd—was this purely supported by hierarchical considerations, that is, were Supreme Court judges meant to retire later than high court judges only because they were hierarchically 'superior' to high court judges? Or was there another reason why legislators in India decided to fix different

---

[1] Constitution (Fifteenth Amendment) Act, 1963.

mandatory retirement age limits for the Supreme Court and the high courts? This chapter demonstrates that there was a specific reason why Supreme Court judges were to serve terms of five years more than high court judges, and in Chapter 4, a policy recommendation will be made that this reason has no empirical basis today.

The data set out in this chapter have typically been obtained from the following sources: the Federal Court Reports, the *Indian Yearbook and Who's Who* (*Times of India*), the *Oxford Dictionary of National Biography*, autobiographies (where available) and biographical studies, speeches delivered at high courts in memory of judges, and biographical pages available on the websites of high courts or on the website of the United Nations.

BACKGROUND

The first serious courts in British India were established in the three presidency towns[2] of Madras, Bombay, and Calcutta—the 'Mayor's Courts' set up by the charter of King George I in 1726. The Mayor's Courts were staffed by three non-professional judges, drawn from amongst the Mayor and aldermen of the corporation in each presidency town.[3] The Regulating Act in 1773 authorized the Crown to establish a supreme court, and in 1774, the Crown established a supreme court in Calcutta.[4] The supreme court consisted of a Chief Justice and three puisne judges.[5] Only a barrister of five years' standing could be appointed a judge on the court.[6] The court's first Chief Justice was Sir Elijah Impey,[7] and its other judges were Robert Chambers,[8]

---

[2] Gradually, as more territories were added to the presidency towns, these became provinces. See M.P. Jain. 1981. *Outlines of Indian Legal History*, 4th ed. Bombay: Tripathi, p. 221.

[3] Jain, *Outlines of Indian Legal History*, pp. 37–8.

[4] Jain, *Outlines of Indian Legal History*, pp. 67–109. Although the court was called a 'supreme court', it was not a federal court.

[5] Section 13, The East India Company Act, 1773, 13 Geo. 3, c. 63.

[6] Section 13, East India Company Act, 1773.

[7] *Oxford Dictionary of National Biography*, under 'Sir Elijah Impey'.

[8] *Oxford Dictionary of National Biography*, under 'Sir Robert Chambers'.

Stephen Caesar LeMaistre, and John Hyde.[9] A supreme court was similarly established later in Madras (1800) and Bombay (1823).[10]

Before 1861, a dual system of courts prevailed in British India. On the one hand there was a supreme court in each of the three presidency towns,[11] which was distinctly British in flavour. On the other hand, in the rural districts of British India called the 'mofussils', there were civil courts (Diwani Adalats) and criminal courts (Nizamat or Fozdari Adalats), from which appeals lay to civil appellate courts (Sadar Diwani Adalats) and criminal appellate courts (Sadar Nizamat Adalats).[12] The supreme courts of the presidency towns were bound by English law, whereas the Sadar Adalats applied local personal laws.[13] The supreme courts derived their legitimacy from the Crown, the Sadar Adalats from the East India Company.[14] In 1861, Britain's Parliament enacted the Indian High Courts Act, authorizing the Crown 'by Letters Patent under the Great Seal of the United Kingdom' to 'erect and establish' High Courts of Judicature at Fort William in Bengal (that is, Calcutta), Madras, and Bombay.[15] Each high court was to have one chief justice and not more than 15 puisne judges.[16] Judges were to be selected from amongst the following:

1. Barristers of not less than five years' standing; or
2. Members of the Covenanted Civil Service of not less than ten years' standing, and who shall have served as Zillah judges, or shall have exercised the like Powers as those of a Zillah judge for at least three years of that period; or

---

[9] Jain, *Outlines of Indian Legal History*, p. 71.

[10] Jain, *Outlines of Indian Legal History*, p. 112.

[11] The supreme court also exercised personal jurisdiction beyond the presidency towns over certain classes of individuals, namely, British subjects and servants of the East India Company. See Jain, *Outlines of Indian Legal History*, p. 262.

[12] Jain, *Outlines of Indian Legal History*, pp. 262–8.

[13] Jain, *Outlines of Indian Legal History*, pp. 262–8.

[14] Jain, *Outlines of Indian Legal History*, p. 273.

[15] Section 1, Indian High Courts Act, 1861, 24 & 25 Vict. c. 104.

[16] Section 2, Indian High Courts Act, 1861. Later, under the Indian High Courts Act, 1911, 1 & 2 Geo. 5, c. 18, the number was increased to 20 (including the chief justice).

3. Persons who have held judicial office not inferior to that of Principal Sudder Ameen or Judge of a Small Causes Court for a period of not less than five years; or

4. Persons who have been Pleaders of a Sudder Court or High Court for a Period of not less than ten years, if such Pleaders of a Sudder Court shall have been admitted as Pleaders of a High Court[17]

The law discriminated between British-trained barristers and Indian-trained pleaders—the former could become judges only five years into their practices, while the latter had to wait 10 years. However, for the first time, Indian lawyers could become judges on superior appellate courts in British India. A third of the seats on the high courts were reserved for barristers, and a third were reserved for members of the civil service.[18] All judges were to hold office 'during Her Majesty's Pleasure',[19] meaning that there was formally no security of tenure for judges. The chief justice of a high court had to be a barrister[20]—in other words a member of the civil service or an Indian pleader could not rise to the position of chief justice of a high court. Significantly, the chief justice of each high court was given the power to determine the composition of benches.[21] In 1862, Queen Victoria issued charters which established a high court in each of the three presidency towns, formally bringing an end to the dual system of courts prevalent in the presidency towns.[22] The ordinary original jurisdiction of the high courts mirrored the jurisdiction of the erstwhile supreme courts, while the appellate jurisdiction of the high courts mirrored the jurisdiction of the Sadar Adalats.[23]

The Indian High Courts Act, 1861, also contained an interesting provision, which established a hierarchy amongst judges appointed to the high courts in India. It provided that 'all the Judges of each High Court shall have Rank and Precedence according to the Seniority

[17] Section 2, Indian High Courts Act, 1861.
[18] Proviso to Section 2, Indian High Courts Act, 1861.
[19] Section 4, Indian High Courts Act, 1861.
[20] Proviso to Section 2, Indian High Courts Act, 1861.
[21] Section 14, Indian High Courts Act, 1861.
[22] Section 8, Indian High Courts Act, 1861.
[23] Jain, *Outlines of Indian Legal History*, p. 274.

of their Appointments'.[24] Once appointed to a high court, a judge was not formally considered to be of equal status as the rest of his brethren—he had 'rank and precedence' to those appointed after him, and he was subject to the 'rank and precedence' of those appointed before him. It is tempting to hypothesize that the seniority system prevalent in Indian courts today, especially the seniority norm in the matter of appointing the Chief Justice of India discussed in Chapter 2, and the seniority criterion for appointments to the Supreme Court of India discussed in Chapter 4, had its historical origins in this provision. However, this type of provision was not unique to British India,[25] and consequently, the 'seniority' system prevalent in Indian courts today cannot simply be explained away by this formal legal provision, although it may have contributed to the entrenchment of the present seniority system, which will be discussed in the coming chapters.

Not much of the constitution of the courts changed as a result of the Government of India Act, 1915.[26] The law continued to discriminate between British-trained barristers and Indian-trained pleaders: as before, a barrister of five years' standing could become a high court judge, whereas a pleader had to wait 10 years in order to be considered eligible.[27] As before, an Indian pleader or member of the civil service could not become the chief justice of a high court[28]—a

---

[24] Section 5, Indian High Courts Act, 1861.

[25] For example, in Britain at the time, Section III of the Court of Chancery Act, 1851, c. 83, provided that Lords Justices of the Court of Appeal in Chancery had 'Rank and Precedence' after the Lord Chief Baron of the Court of Exchequer, and as between themselves, 'according to the Order and Time of their Appointment'. Even in the United States, § 1 of the Judiciary Act, 1789 provided that the associate justices of the Supreme Court had 'precedence according to the date of their commissions', or if their commissions bore the same date, 'according to their respective ages'.

[26] Under Section 101(3), Government of India Act, 1915, 5 & 6 Geo. 5, c. 61, in order to be considered eligible for appointment to a high court, a person had to be:

> (a) a barrister of England or Ireland, or a member of the Faculty of Advocates in Scotland, of not less than five years' standing; or (b) a member of the Indian Civil Service of not less than ten years' standing, and having for at least three years served as, or exercised the powers of, a district judge; or (c) a person having held judicial office, not inferior to that of a subordinate judge or a judge of a small cause court, for a period of not less than five years; or (d) a person having been a pleader of a high court for a period of not less than ten years.

[27] Section 101(3), Government of India Act, 1915.

[28] Section 101(4), Government of India Act, 1915.

position formally reserved for British-trained barristers or advocates. Formally speaking, there was no security of tenure for high court judges, who continued to hold office during 'His Majesty's pleasure'.[29] As before, the chief justice of a high court had 'rank and precedence before the other judges of the same court', and puisne judges had 'rank and precedence according to the seniority of their appointments, unless otherwise provided in their patents'.[30]

However, although federal executive and legislative authorities were established in British India fairly early on, a federal judicial authority was conspicuously absent.

THE GOVERNMENT OF INDIA ACT, 1935

A resolution to establish a 'Court of Ultimate Appeal in India' was first introduced in the Central Legislative Assembly of British India on 26 March 1921,[31] by Dr Hari Singh Gour,[32] who hoped that British India would follow the example of 'the great Colonies of England, such as, Canada, Australia, and South Africa',[33] by setting up a supreme court in India. Gour urged three grounds in support of his proposed resolution: first, it was too expensive to file an appeal before the Privy Council, second, there was invariably a delay of around two–five years as a consequence of filing an appeal before the Privy Council, and third, the method of disposing cases there was unsatisfactory, particularly because the Privy Council did not have advisers on 'Hindu and Muhammadan Law and ... law which is not founded on English Law'.[34] Who would the judges on this proposed Ultimate Court of Appeal be? Gour did not want to overload his

---

[29] Section 102(1), Government of India Act, 1915.

[30] Section 103, Government of India Act, 1915.

[31] *Legislative Assembly Debates*, dated 26 March 1921, vol. 1, no. 15, p. 1606. See George H. Gadbois, Jr. 1963. 'Evolution of the Federal Court of India: An Historical Footnote', *Journal of the Indian Law Institute*, 5: 19–45.

[32] Dr Hari Singh Gour was a lawyer, later the first Vice Chancellor of the University of Delhi, the leader of the National Party in the Assembly, and leader of the opposition. *Times of India*. 1922. *The Indian Yearbook*, vol. 9. Bombay: Bennett Coleman, p. 825; *Times of India*. 1933–4. *The Indian Yearbook*, vol. 20. Bennett Coleman, p. 1028–9.

[33] *Legislative Assembly Debates*, 26 March 1921, p. 1606.

[34] *Legislative Assembly Debates*, 26 March 1921, p. 1608.

resolution with such 'details', but he only proposed that a majority of the judges on the court should 'come from this country', while two or three judges could be imported from England to 'strengthen the Bench for the determination of Indian cases'.[35] Indian judges were to be in the majority.

A strong debate took place as to whether Indian judges should serve on the proposed court, if such a court were to be set up. One member of the assembly, T.V. Seshagiri Ayyar,[36] disagreed with the proposal that a majority of the judges on the proposed court should be Indians. English judges, he argued, did not have any 'legal prejudice' and were therefore very impartial, even more so that retired high court judges who left India to serve on the Privy Council.[37] Eardley Norton[38] argued that the Privy Council had in the past 'openly complimented' Indian judges 'from the time of the late Mr. Justice Mahmood of Allahabad down to recent days', although he expressed doubts as to whether Indian judges could completely attain self-detachment, impartiality, and 'inamenability to collateral and outside influences which almost invariably exist at Home'.[39]

The Law Member of the Viceroy's Executive Council, Tej Bahadur Sapru, moved an amendment to the proposed resolution, seeking, instead of establishing a Court of Ultimate Appeal, to 'collect the opinions of the Local Governments, the High Courts and other legal authorities and to ascertain public opinion generally as to the desirability of establishing a supreme court of appeal in India',[40] and the motion and resolution were adopted.[41]

Dr Gour introduced another such resolution 18 months later, but now the resolution met with considerable opposition. One objection was that a federal court in India would 'impair the independence of the High Courts' since judges would seek appointment

---

[35] *Legislative Assembly Debates*, 26 March 1921, p. 1610.

[36] T.V. Seshagiri Ayyar was a retired high court judge and law professor. *Times of India, Indian Yearbook*, vol. 9, p. 806.

[37] *Legislative Assembly Debates*, 26 March 1921, p. 1612.

[38] Eardley Norton was a barrister and an advocate in the High Courts of Bengal and Madras. *Times of India, Indian Yearbook*, vol. 9, p. 845.

[39] *Legislative Assembly Debates*, 26 March 1921, pp. 1612–13.

[40] *Legislative Assembly Debates*, 26 March 1921, pp. 1610–11.

[41] *Legislative Assembly Debates*, 26 March 1921, p. 1615.

to this 'court of Ultimate Appeals' and be incentivized to favour the executive.[42]

On 17 February 1925, Dr Gour once again moved a resolution in the Legislative Assembly for the establishment of a supreme court, arguing that there was a very large body of official opinion in favour of the establishment of such a court.

Colonel Sir Henry Stanyon[43] stood up to oppose the motion, arguing that it was premature. In particular, he added that the 'selection and appointment of the Judges [of the supreme court] would be an extremely delicate and difficult business'.[44] In his speech, he highlighted the difficulty with appointing judges to the proposed supreme court from the different regions of India:

[M]en would have to be found who, not only in fact but also in the opinion of the public, were competent to sit in judgment over the decisions of the provincial High Courts. If wholly recruited in India, would their *dicta* be better or command higher respect, than those of any of the existing chartered High Courts? We have no all-India lawyers available. On the Indian Benches and at the Indian Bars we have men of provincial experience only. Would the decision of, say, a Bengal *ex*-Judge or a Madras lawyer of eminence, presiding in our Supreme Court, be any better or be accepted as any better … than the decision of a Bombay High Court on a case demanding the interpretation of the Mayukha, or a judgment of the Punjab High Court on a case of pre-emption in accordance with Punjab custom?[45]

Stanyon said that the most 'eminent and successful' members of the provincial bars would not be attracted to the supreme court by any emoluments which 'the tax-payer in India could afford to pay'. He also added that the proposed supreme court would 'inevitably and materially' lower the prestige of the high courts, which would 'seriously affect the recruitment of Judges in those Courts with catastrophic results'.[46] However, M.A. Jinnah strongly contested the idea that establishing a supreme court would lower the prestige of the

[42] Gadbois, 'Evolution of the Federal Court', p. 24.
[43] Henry Stanyon served as Additional Judicial Commissioner for approximately 20 years in Nagpur, and then retired to practise law. *Times of India*, 24 October 1917, p. 10.
[44] *Legislative Assembly Debates*, dated 17 February 1925, p. 1167.
[45] *Legislative Assembly Debates*, 17 February 1925, p. 1167.
[46] *Legislative Assembly Debates*, 17 February 1925, pp. 1167.

high courts—he argued that the Privy Council had not diminished the high courts' prestige, despite the fact that a few of its judges had been appointed from Indian courts.[47]

Maulvi Muhammad Yakub[48] opposed the motion, amongst other reasons, because he feared that if a supreme court were to be established, almost all high court judges would aspire to acquire a seat on the bench of the supreme court, and that this would compromise their independence, as they would be 'inclined to work in such a way as they may be able to win the favour of the authorities in whose power lies the bestowing of that post of honour'.[49] Pandit Motilal Nehru also opposed the resolution. He argued that it would be difficult to find 'competent men' to appoint to the proposed supreme court of India 'outside the ranks of superannuated judges or Chief Justices or perhaps also equally superannuated members of the Bar'.[50]

The resolution was defeated by a vote of 15–56.[51]

Soon thereafter, the demand for an all-India federal court caught on. Gadbois[52] and Pylee[53] have separately documented the history of the formation of the Federal Court of India. On 31 August 1927, a resolution was introduced in the Council of State by a former high court judge, Sir Sankaran Nair, for the establishment of a supreme court. A member of the council, Sir Maneckji Dadabhoy, an industrialist lawyer-politician,[54] argued against the resolution by highlighting problems associated with how the proposed court's judges were to be staffed. He also suggested that a supreme court in India would undermine the prestige of the high courts, although

---

[47] *Legislative Assembly Debates*, 17 February 1925, p. 1175.

[48] The *Times of India* described Maulvi Muhammad Yakub as 'perpetually a lugubrious member of the Swarajist Party'. *Times of India*. 1924. 'A Session's Work: Principal Achievement the Wrecking of Prestige', *Times of India*, 27 March, p. 10.

[49] *Legislative Assembly Debates*, 17 February 1925, p. 1170.

[50] *Legislative Assembly Debates*, 17 February 1925, p. 1172.

[51] *Legislative Assembly Debates*, 17 February 1925, p. 1180.

[52] Gadbois, 'Evolution of the Federal Court'.

[53] M.V. Pylee. 1966. *The Federal Court of India*. Bombay: Manaktalas, pp. 64–82.

[54] *Oxford Dictionary of National Biography*, under 'Maneckji Dadabhoy'.

other members[55] disagreed that it would take away from the position of the high courts:

> Now, sir, as regards the constitution of the Supreme Court, one fundamental and vital gap in the speech of my Honourable friend has been his failure to refer to the constitution of the Supreme Court. *He has not enlightened us as to how the Judges are to be appointed, from what cadre the Judges are to be taken, whether they are to be barrister Judges or whether they are to be wholly Indian Judges, or whether they are to be selected from mixed ranks....* Further, my Honourable friend ought to know that the constitution of a Supreme Court will *absolutely undermine the authority and the prestige of our various High Courts....* We know in India how much reverence is attached to the opinions of the various High Courts. If you establish in the same country in some isolated place another court having ... jurisdiction to supervise, superintend and revise the authority and the judgments of these courts, you can under-stand what respect it would carry in the minds of the general public and how it will affect the dignity of the several High Courts.[56]
>
> (emphasis supplied)

Another member, Saiyid Alay Nabi,[57] supported this argument and added that he could not 'by any stretch of imagination' believe that if a supreme court were to be established in India, that it would have judges of 'greater calibre, of higher standing and greater status' than High Court judges, unless 'angels from the Indian heavens' were brought to serve on the court.[58] The Law Member of the Viceroy's Executive Council, S.R. Das, elaborated this argument, and said that if such a court were to be established, it needed to have judges of 'greater eminence', as it would not be worthwhile staffing the pro-posed supreme court with judges of the 'same calibre' as high court judges. He argued that top-notch high court lawyers were the right men for the job, but they were unlikely to accept positions on the proposed supreme court. Viewed today in retrospect, these words are especially prescient:

> Now, Sir, what is going to be the constitution of this court? Is it going to be a glorified High Court or a court consisting of judges far superior to

---

[55] V. Ramadas Pantulu, *Council of State Debates,* vol. 2, no. 26, p. 904; G.S. Khaparde, p. 909.
[56] *Council of State Debates,* pp. 896–8.
[57] Saiyid Alay Nabi was a *vakil* of the Agra High Court. *Times of India.* 1913. 'Personal News', *Times of India,* 18 April, p. 7.
[58] *Council of State Debates,* p. 900.

the High Court Judges whom we have now?.... *[I]f you are going to have a Supreme Court, it is no use having the same calibre of Judges as you have in the High Courts. There is no satisfaction to the litigant to go in appeal from one judge to another judge of the same calibre; you want men of greater eminence.* Where are you going to get them? I do not suggest you have not got men in India who would be suitable for the Supreme Court, but what happens now? Do you get in your High Courts as Judges men who are at the top of the profession? Do they accept High Court Judgeships? *Do we not know cases of men who have got very good practice, who are great lawyers, who refuse to be appointed High Court Judges? These are the men you have to get if you want men of higher calibre;* and if you get these men you will not get them for Rs. 4,000 or Rs. 5,000; you will have to pay them very handsomely if you want to attract them to the Supreme Court; and even then I doubt if you will be able to induce many of them to give up there [*sic*] very lucrative practice for the purpose of sitting on the Supreme Court.[59]

(emphasis supplied)

The Law Member also insightfully pointed out that there would be practical difficulties in determining how to staff the courts. He feared that communal considerations would end up determining how the court's judges would be appointed. His words are especially prescient because the Federal Court of India that would be established later would have an informal communal 'quota'.

If you have a Supreme Court, communal questions will arise. Are you going to appoint so many Hindus, so many Muhammadans, etc., or are you going to appoint Judges simply from the point of view of the merits of the persons concerned? Will you be able to do so? *I am quite certain that communal questions will arise in the matter of appointments. Would you be satisfied with such a court?*[60]

(emphasis supplied)

G.S. Khaparde[61] agreed that communal considerations might prevail in judicial appointments in the beginning, but argued that this would not last long. He hoped that the proposed supreme court of India would be staffed by retired high court judges and 'able lawyers'.[62]

[59] *Council of State Debates*, pp. 906–7.
[60] *Council of State Debates*, p. 907.
[61] G.S. Khaparde was an advocate and politician. *Times of India*. 1928. *The Indian Yearbook*, vol. 15. Bombay: Bennett Coleman, p. 857.
[62] *Council of State Debates*, p. 910.

In the end, the resolution was defeated 15–25.[63]

In 1928, the Nehru Report[64] called for the establishment of a supreme court of India. In 1929 the Viceroy, Lord Irwin, announced that a 'Round Table Conference' would be held to discuss changes in India's Constitution.[65] The first Round Table Conference was held in 1930, but it lacked serious significance, given that the Congress party did not participate in its deliberations.

At the second Round Table Conference held in 1931, one of the sub-committees presented a report to the conference in which it opined that the Federal Court should consist of a chief justice and a fixed number of puisne judges, appointed by the Crown, holding office during good behaviour, retiring at age 65, removable before that age only on an address passed by both houses of the legislature, and 'moved with the Fiat of the Federal Advocate General'.[66] With regard to the qualifications of the judges, it was suggested that the following should be eligible for appointment—any barrister or advocate of 15 years' standing, and any person who has been, for not less than five years, a judge of a high court or of a state court.[67] Law professors were not included in this list.

Between the second and third Round Table Conferences, and nearly 11 years after the first resolution calling for the establishment of a Federal Court in India was introduced in the Central Legislative Assembly, on 10 February 1932, a resolution calling for the establishment of such a court was passed in the Central Legislative Assembly.

[63] *Council of State Debates*, pp. 916–17.
[64] The Nehru Report was submitted by Motilal Nehru, chairman of the committee appointed by the All Parties Conference in Bombay (19 May 1928), to Dr M.A. Ansari, President of the All Parties Conference, on 10 August 1928. Articles 46–51 of the 'draft bill' dealt with the federal judiciary. In particular, Article 46 called for the establishment of a supreme court, consisting of a Lord President and other Justices, as 'Parliament may fix', to 'exercise such jurisdiction as Parliament shall determine'. See All Parties Conference. 1975. *The Nehru Report: An Anti-Separatist Manifesto.* New Delhi: Michiko and Panjathan.
[65] See Marquess of Reading. 1933. 'The Progress of Constitutional Reform in India', *Foreign Affairs*, 11(4): 609–20.
[66] Proceedings of the Indian Round Table Conference (Second Session), 7 September 1931–1 December 1931, 1931–2, Cmd. 3997, p. 30.
[67] Proceedings of the Indian Round Table Conference (Second Session), 1931–2, Cmd. 3997, p. 30.

The resolution was moved by B.R. Puri,[68] and called for the assembly to recommend to the Governor General in Council to take

> early steps to secure that a Supreme Court is established in India with power—(a) to interpret and uphold the constitution; (b) to act as a court of final criminal appeal against all sentences of death; (c) to act as a revising court in specified serious cases; (d) to hear civil appeals now heard by His Majesty's Privy Council; and (e) generally to carry out the work at present entrusted to His Majesty's Privy Council; provided that such court shall not affect His Majesty's prerogative safeguarded in the constitutions of Canada, Australia, and South Africa.[69]

The resolution was identical to the one introduced in the Council of State by Sir Sankaran Nair on 31 August 1927.[70] During the debate, terminologically speaking, the terms 'Federal Court' and 'Supreme Court' were used to convey different meanings.[71] In the words of one member,[72] a 'Federal Court' was a court that would interpret the Constitution and adjudicate any disputes between one state and another, or between one member of the federation and another, but a 'Supreme Court' was a court that would either take the place of the Privy Council or act as an intermediary between the high court and the Privy Council. B.R. Puri, the member who introduced the resolution in the Assembly in 1932, used the term 'Supreme Court' in his resolution, although his resolution left room for a person to choose either to appeal to the 'Supreme Court' or to the Privy Council.[73] Perhaps this distinction between the terms 'Federal Court' and 'Supreme Court' is important from the point of view of understanding why the term 'Federal Court' was dropped under independent India's Constitution, and the framers of India's Constitution preferred the term 'Supreme Court'. The Supreme Court envisioned by India's legislators had always had broader powers.

---

[68] It seems that B.R. Puri was a barrister who practised in the Lahore High Court. Cf. *Times of India*. 1928. 'Finance Department Fraud Case: Petition for Transfer', *Times of India*, 16 October, p. 5; *Times of India*. 1929. 'Evidence Act: Conflicting Rulings by Judges', *Times of India*, 9 February, p. 8.

[69] *Legislative Assembly Debates*, dated 10 February 1932, vol. 1, no. 10, p. 571.

[70] *Council of State Debates*, p. 885.

[71] See speech by Hari Singh Gour, *Legislative Assembly Debates*, 10 February 1932, p. 586.

[72] R.K. Shanmukham Chetty, *Legislative Assembly Debates*, 10 February 1932, pp. 592–3.

[73] *Legislative Assembly Debates*, 10 February 1932, p. 603.

B.R. Puri supported his proposed resolution strongly on the grounds that a second appeal was necessary in criminal cases. At the time, in civil cases there were two appeals from the trial court: the first before the district judge, and the second before the high court (in some cases where the value of the suit exceeded a certain pecuniary threshold, the first appeal lay before the high court, and the second appeal before the Privy Council). However, in criminal cases, there was only one appeal—either before the sessions court, or in some cases involving large sentences, before the high court. The Privy Council had declared that it was not a court of appeal in criminal cases. For this reason amongst others, Puri argued, it was necessary to establish a supreme court in India.[74]

Addressing the proposed resolution, R.K. Shanmukham Chetty[75] recalled Pandit Motilal Nehru's objection to a similar resolution brought by Hari Singh Gour in 1925. Nehru had said that it would be 'difficult to find competent men to occupy seats on the bench of the Supreme Court of India outside the ranks of the superannuated Judges or Chief Justices or perhaps also equally superannuated members of the Bar'. Now, Chetty argued that although circumstances might have changed, and although eminent men like 'our friend Sir Hari Singh Gour' might be willing to make the 'sacrifice' of accepting a judgeship on a supreme court, the question of who the judges would be on this court was one which deserved to be 'seriously considered'.[76] C.C. Biswas[77] argued that judges in India were susceptible to executive influence, whereas judges of the Privy Council were not, and for this reason, it did not make sense to supplant the Privy Council.[78] The Law Member of the Viceroy's Executive Council, Sir Brojendra Mitter, vehemently opposed the establishment of a supreme court, calling it a 'mock Privy Council',[79] and he supported

---

[74] *Legislative Assembly Debates*, 10 February 1932, pp. 574–5.
[75] R.K. Shanmukham Chetty was a lawyer, and had a distinguished political career. He was elected Deputy President of the Legislative Assembly in January 1931. *Times of India, Indian Yearbook*, vol. 20, p. 1012.
[76] *Legislative Assembly Debates*, 10 February 1932, p. 593.
[77] C.C. Biswas was an advocate in the Calcutta High Court, and a law professor. *Times of India, Indian Yearbook*, vol. 20, p. 1005.
[78] *Legislative Assembly Debates*, 10 February 1932, pp. 594–5.
[79] *Legislative Assembly Debates*, 10 February 1932, p. 598.

the objections raised by Chetty concerning the competence of judges who would serve on the proposed court. One member immediately asked him not to call the court a 'mock' council, because he might be called upon to preside over it. Mitter replied by saying that he did not want to preside over such a court, although he may want to practise there. As things turned out, Mitter became the first advocate general before the Federal Court of India several years later.

B.R. Puri rose to address the objections to his proposed resolution. He took umbrage to Brojendra Mitter's speech, which called the proposed supreme court a 'mock' tribunal. Puri argued that if the proposed supreme court were called a 'mock tribunal', then one would logically have to extend this statement to the high courts, and call them 'mock' courts too, since supreme court vacancies would be staffed from amongst high court judges. This remarkable statement made by B.R. Puri in 1932 gives us an indication that it had always been envisioned that supreme court judges would be picked from amongst high court judges. Nearly 70 years later, this statement still rings true:

> Now, Sir, if that is a good argument, then I think the sooner you abolish the High Courts the better it will be; *because after all for some time to come at least, perhaps for all time to come, we shall have to draw upon the existing personnel of the High Courts in order to find our Judges for the Supreme Court.* And if the Supreme Court composed of these Judges is to be looked upon as a mockery, then I submit your High Courts will be occupying no better place.[80]

(emphasis supplied)

The resolution was passed by a vote of 34–17.[81]

At the third session of the Round Table Conference in November–December 1932, Sir Tej Sapru, former Law Member in the Governor General's Council and an Indian representative at the conference, suggested that the Federal Court of India should have between nine and twelve judges, as this size would be impressive enough to 'command confidence and attract talent'.[82] It was suggested that 'paramount importance' be given to 'keeping the judiciary absolutely

[80] *Legislative Assembly Debates*, 10 February 1932, p. 603.
[81] *Legislative Assembly Debates*, 10 February 1932, p. 606.
[82] Proceedings of the Indian Round Table Conference (Third Session), 17 November 1932–24 December 1932, Cmd. 4238, p. 71.

independent of all political taint', and that judges' salaries should be fixed.[83] Interestingly, it was suggested that no 'religious or racial considerations should influence the appointment of judges who should be taken from any community, European or Indian, provided that they could command confidence by reason of their independence, of their competence and their impartiality'.[84]

Very soon after the conclusion of the third Round Table Conference, in 1933, a white paper entitled 'Proposals for Indian Constitutional Reform' was published, containing the blueprint for a law that would propose a federal structure of government in India for perhaps the first time—a prelude to the Government of India Act, 1935. It was proposed that a federal court, with appellate and original jurisdiction, be established.[85] The court would consist of a chief justice and a specified number of judges, appointed by the Crown, and holding office during good behaviour.[86] On the question of whether a supreme court should additionally be set up, it was noted that there was strong support for the view that it would be difficult to find, in addition to the judges required for the federal court and the provincial courts, 'a body of judicial talent of the calibre essential ... to justify its existence'.[87]

Soon, a Joint Committee on Indian Constitutional Reform was established to discuss the white paper's proposals. It had 32 members—16 from each House of Britain's Parliament, with the second marquess of Linlithgow, Victor Alexander John Hope, as its Chairman. Hope would go on to serve as Governor General of India for a record seven-and-a-half-year term following this assignment.[88] The Joint Committee consulted 'representatives of Indian states and of British India', who included B.R. Ambedkar, Hari Singh Gour, M.R. Jayakar, and Zafrulla Khan. Two of these (Jayakar and Khan) would go on to serve as judges of the Federal Court of India. Ambedkar would later

---

[83] Proceedings of the Indian Round Table Conference (Third Session), 1932–3, Cmd. 4238, p. 71.

[84] Proceedings of the Indian Round Table Conference (Third Session), 1932–3, Cmd. 4238, p. 71.

[85] Proposals for Indian Constitutional Reform, 1933, Cmd. 4268, pp. 32–3.

[86] Proposals for Indian Constitutional Reform, 1933, Cmd. 4268, pp. 32–3.

[87] Proposals for Indian Constitutional Reform, 1933, Cmd. 4268, pp. 32–3.

[88] *Oxford Dictionary of National Biography*, under 'Victor Alexander John Hope'.

serve as the chief architect of independent India's Constitution. Gour had been the most persistent advocate in the Central Legislative Assembly for the establishment of a supreme court in India. The report[89] of the Joint Committee was a key document which shaped the subsequent Government of India Act, 1935. In its report, the Joint Committee recommended that the proposed Federal Court of India should 'consist of a Chief Justice and not more than six or eight judges', although it did not think that 'for some time to come it will be necessary to appoint more than three or four'.[90] The Joint Committee opined that the Federal Court of India could sit in two divisions or benches, one to decide federal disputes, and the other to hear appeals from the high courts. Importantly, the Joint Committee felt that judges of the Federal Court should retire at age 65, although it had been debated whether they should retire at age 62 instead. At the time, although there was no statutory retirement age for high court judges, the Secretary of State had instituted a practice that judges would be required to retire at age 60.[91] On the age of retirement, the Joint Committee had this to say:

> It has been represented to us that the retiring age of [High Court] Judges should not be raised to sixty-two, but should continue to be sixty; and we concur. We have suggested that in the case of the Federal Court the age should be sixty-five, *because it might otherwise be difficult to secure the services of High Court Judges who have shown themselves qualified for promotion to the*

[89] Joint Select Committee. 1934. *Report of the Joint Select Committee on Indian Constitutional Reform* (Session 1933–1934). London: His Majesty's Stationery Office.
[90] Joint Select Committee, *Report of the Joint Select Committee*, para. 323.
[91] Sir John Beaumont. 1946. 'The Indian Judicial System: Some Suggested Reforms', *Bombay Law Reporter*, 48: 12–184. The reason that there was no statutory rule for retirement was that there was 'room for modification'. Beaumont, 'Indian Judicial System'. Beaumont himself was offered the post of Chief Justice of Bombay at the age of 52, and he refused to accept it if he was made to retire at the age of 60. His undertaking required him to retire at the age of 65, and his retirement was postponed by an additional year at the request of the Secretary of State. See further, Jain, *Outlines of Indian Legal History*, p. 356. Accordingly, the retirement age was not specified in any successive constitution of British India until 1935. For example, under Section 102(1) of the Government of India Act, 1915, every judge of a high court was to hold office during 'His Majesty's pleasure', but there was no formal constitutional provision that a high court judge would retire at the age of 60. The Letters Patent establishing high courts

Federal Court; but the evidence satisfies us that in India a Judge has in general done his best work by the time he has reached the age of sixty.[92]

(emphasis supplied)

Accordingly, the Joint Committee recommended that Federal Court judges retire at age 65. Naturally, this would mean that the term of each Federal Court judge would be limited according to the age at which the judge was appointed to the court—the older a judge was appointed to the court, the shorter would be the term of office served by the judge. However, at the same time the Joint Committee opined that high court judges should continue to retire at age 60. What was the reason for this difference, namely, why were Federal Court judges and high court judges meant to retire at ages 65 and 60 respectively, instead of each retiring at a common, uniform age?

---

in India did not prescribe the retirement age either. See for example, Letters Patent for Constituting the High Court of Judicature of the Bengal Division of the Presidency of Fort William, 14 May 1862. Section 6 of the Indian High Courts Act, 1861 provided that the Secretary of State in Council of India was entitled to fix, amongst other things, the 'Retiring Pensions' of the chief justices and judges of the high courts, which suggests that judges did indeed retire. Further, during the time that the Government of India Act, 1935 was being debated, the Joint Committee on Indian Constitutional Reform opined that the age of retirement of high court judges in India should 'continue to be sixty', which implies that high court judges did, in fact, retire at the age of 60 at that time. The retirement age for high court judges was built into their contracts of appointment. It was customary for the Secretary of State in Council to conclude a contract with officers appointed to government service in India—a contract which also typically specified the term of service. See Sir Courtenay Ilbert. 1915. *The Government of India: Being a Digest of the Statute Law Relating Thereto*, 3rd ed. Oxford: Clarendon Press, p. 184. This also appeared to be so for high court judges. Section 220(2) of the Government of India Act, 1935, 25 & 26 Geo. 5, c. 42 formally prescribed the retirement age of 60 for high court judges.

Taking a step back, it is interesting that judges in colonial India had to retire at all, given that mandatory retirement came to courts in Britain only in the 20th century. Why did judges in India have to retire at a time when judges in Britain did not? Perhaps a retirement age for judges was considered sound policy, but one that was difficult to impose at home. Perhaps the retirement age was a form of colonial distrust of the judiciary in India—a way to control judges and ensure that they did not become too powerful. Perhaps it was a mechanism whereby judges, who served during the 'pleasure' of the Crown, got some form of security of tenure.

[92] Joint Select Committee, *Report of the Joint Select Committee*, para. 331.

Was this merely because Federal Court judges were hierarchically 'superior' to high court judges? The paragraph quoted above reveals the rationale for what has been termed in this book as the 'retirement age gap'. The Joint Committee felt that it would be difficult to staff the new Federal Court of India with reputed judges from the high courts if the retirement age at the Federal Court was 60—in other words, that a high court judge or chief justice would not be willing to give up his position of seniority and the remaining years of his service on an established court, and take up a junior position on a new Federal Court with an uncertain future and tiny caseload. Perhaps the five extra years of judicial service were meant to serve as an incentive for retiring high court judges to agree to serve on the Federal Court of India. A retirement age of 65 in the Federal Court would mean that a retiring high court judge would be able to serve five more years in high constitutional office, and would perhaps not have to give up too many years of service on his prestigious high court. Why else would it have been 'difficult to secure the services of High Court judges who have shown themselves qualified for promotion' to the Federal Court without a 'retirement age gap'? After all, if a judge has 'done his best work' in India by age 60, why should he be promoted to the Federal Court after he has crossed his prime?

This argument, namely, that the five-year 'retirement age gap' was necessitated by the fact that high court judges and chief justices would otherwise not have easily given up their positions on the high courts in favour of a position on the Federal Court, is borne out by what happened subsequently. Between 1937 and 1947, only four out of eight judges on the Federal Court were actually high court judges before appointment to the Federal Court, of whom only two were high court chief justices. There is no historical evidence to suggest that other high court chief justices were offered appointments which they turned down, but this is not entirely implausible given that there were numerous reputable high court chief justices at the time who were not appointed to the Federal Court. Further, as Gadbois[93]

[93]   George H. Gadbois, Jr. 1969. 'Selection, Background Characteristics, and Voting Behavior of Indian Supreme Court Judges, 1950-1959', in Glendon Schubert and David J. Danelski (eds), *Comparative Judicial Behavior: Cross-cultural Studies of Political Decision-making in the East and West.* New York: Oxford University Press, p. 223.

points out, after independence, the practice was to offer Supreme
Court judgeships to the chief justice of a high court, but the fact that
no Bombay High Court chief justice or Madras High Court chief
justice was eventually appointed to the Supreme Court in 1950–9,
and the fact that only one chief justice, of the Calcutta High Court,
Das Gupta, was appointed to the Court during that time, points to
the fact that 'the Chief Justices of these High Courts considered their
position to be one of greater prestige and importance than an associate judgeship on the Supreme Court'.[94]

This five-year difference in retirement ages would also mean that
a Federal Court judge in India would serve a term of at least five
years in office—hypothetically speaking, if a high court judge were
appointed to the Federal Court a day before he retired from the high
court, that is, a day before his 60th birthday, he would serve five
years in office, that is, until he reached the age of 65.[95]

Another factor for pegging the retirement age in the Federal
Court at 65 instead of 60 could have been that the Joint Committee
wanted mature judges to sit on the court—judges who had more
high court experience,[96] or generally more experience and wisdom
than the average high court judge. Picking high court judges for

[94] Gadbois, 'Selection, Background Characteristics, and Voting Behavior'. Gadbois
points out that the following high court chief justices (or judges at the threshold of
being appointed chief justices) declined offers to be elevated to the Supreme Court:
M.C. Chagla, P.B. Chakravartti, P.V. Rajamannar, P.N. Mookerjee, S.P. Mitra, V.S. Malimath, M.M. Ismail, Satish Chandra, Bhimiah, and Sarwar Ali. George H. Gadbois, Jr.
2011. *Judges of the Supreme Court of India: 1950–1989*. New Delhi: Oxford University
Press, pp. 17, 59, 61n16, 137, 157, 264, 314. Also see, Abhinav Chandrachud. 2014.
'My dear Chagla', *Frontline*, 31(2), available online at http://www.frontline.in/the-
nation/my-dear-chagla/article5589838.ece (last accessed on January 26, 2014). To
be sure, not all of these judges declined Supreme Court judgeship offers because
they considered their high court positions to be superior to the Supreme Court.
Many declined for personal reasons. However, many, especially in earlier times,
declined because they considered their positions in their respective high courts to be
preferable to junior positions on the Supreme Court. Further, high court chief justices had little or no financial incentives to accept Supreme Court judgeships, as will
be discussed in Chapter 4, since the salary and pension structures of Supreme Court
judges and high court chief justices were (and continue to be) the same.
[95] Theoretically, nothing would preclude the appointment of a judge after he
retired from a high court, but this turned out to be very rare.
[96] Pylee, for example, indicates that the Joint Committee was concerned not
merely with life expectancy in India, but also with 'mature judicial experience'

appointment to the Federal Court could also have been that much easier, since the judges could be 'judged' for appointment to the court based on a longer service record. Judges who were 59 or even 60 would presumably have a longer service record on a high court, and it would have been that much easier to judge whether they were 'worthy' of promotion to the Federal Court of India.

The Joint Committee report was published in 1934. Today, the retirement age in the Supreme Court of India is still 65 years. Is there a policy argument for now enhancing the retirement age? Pylee points to the fact that the life expectancy in India at the time was very low, only 26 years according to the census conducted in 1931, and later, according to the 1951 census, it was 32 years.[97] Accordingly, a retirement age of 65 may not have been unjustified at the time. However, life expectancy at birth in India rose consistently thereafter to 41.3 (1951–61), 45.6 (1961–71), 52.3 (1976–80), 57.7 (1986–90), 61.9 (1996–2000), and 63.4 (2002–6).[98] The projected life expectancy at birth in India now goes past the retirement age for Supreme Court judges—it is 67.3 (2011–15).[99] It is surprising that the retirement age of independent India's Supreme Court judges has remained 65 years, nearly 80 years after the Joint Committee's report was written—a person born at around the time the report was written could grow up, become Chief Justice of India, retire, and even more than a decade after his retirement, the retirement age in the Supreme Court of India would remain the same.[100]

The Joint Committee also hoped that judges on the high courts would bring a diversity of perspectives to the cases they decided. In particular, they hoped that judges from the Indian Civil Service (ICS) would rise to serve on the courts, because the committee was 'satisfied that [ICS judges] bring to the Bench a knowledge of Indian

---

and being able to serve on the court, while fixing the retirement age at 65. Pylee, *Federal Court of India*, p. 91.

[97] Pylee, *Federal Court of India*, p. 91.

[98] All figures have been obtained from the website www.indiastat.com, where they have been sourced either from the Ministry of Statistics and Programme Implementation, Government of India, or from the Ministry of Health and Family Welfare, Government of India.

[99] www.indiastat.com

[100] For example, Chief Justice J.S. Verma was born in 1933.

country life and conditions which barristers and pleaders from the towns may not always possess'.[101] In fact, an early draft of the report of the Joint Committee also contained the following paragraph, which was eventually deleted from the text of the final report. In this paragraph, the Joint Committee was discussing whether ICS judges ought not to be appointed to the Federal Court.

> A suggestion was made that a High Court Judge who is a member of the Civil Service ought not to be regarded as qualified. *We do not agree to so invidious a distinction being drawn between one High Court Judge and another,* though it may well be that His Majesty may in practice see fit to appoint only such qualified persons as have had a legal training before their appointment to the High Court bench.[102]

(emphasis supplied)

It will be recalled that the Indian High Courts Act, 1861 had provided that one-third of the seats on the high courts established in India were to be reserved for members of the ICS, and one-third would be reserved for barristers. However, the Government of India Act, 1935 abolished these quotas.

The Government of India Act, 1935 was enacted on 2 August 1935. With 478 sections and 16 schedules, it was longer than any previously drafted law in the Commonwealth. Section 200 of the Act established a Federal Court in India consisting of a 'Chief Justice of India' and not more than six puisne judges. The strength of the court could be increased if an address were presented to that effect by the federal legislature to the Governor General. Security of tenure for judges was now formally a part of the Constitution. Earlier, high court judges could be removed by the Crown at any time, although M.P. Jain finds that a convention had evolved that they would not be removed except under the rarest of circumstances.[103] The Government of India Act, 1935 now crystallized that convention, and judges could only be removed for 'misbehaviour' or 'infirmity of mind or body' if the Privy Council made a recommendation that the judge be so removed.[104] The doctrine of 'pleasure', under which judges held office only during the pleasure of the Crown, was accordingly done

---

[101] Joint Select Committee, *Report of the Joint Select Committee*, para. 331.
[102] Removed from para. 310 of an initial draft of the report.
[103] Jain, *Outlines of Indian Legal History*.
[104] Sections 200(2)(b) and 220(2)(b), Government of India Act, 1935.

away with. Section 200 provided that Federal Court judges would retire at age 65.[105] High court judges were now to formally retire at age 60.[106] However, prior to reaching the age of retirement, either could resign. The salaries and rights in respect of leave of absence or pension could not be varied to a judge's disadvantage after appointment, in order to ensure judicial independence and freedom from executive pressure.[107] However, there was no elaborate impeachment process for the removal of a judge by the federal legislature.

Most importantly, however, Section 200(3) set out the qualifications for judges of the Federal Court of India:

> A person shall not be qualified for appointment as a judge of the Federal Court unless he: (a) has been for at least *five years a judge of a High Court* in British India or in a Federated State; or (b) is a barrister of England or Northern Ireland of at least *ten years standing*, or a member of the Faculty of Advocates in Scotland of at least ten years standing; or (c) has been for at least *ten years a pleader of a High Court in British India* or in a Federated State or of two or more such Courts in succession.

(emphasis supplied)

In other words, the Government of India Act, 1935 removed the distinction between British-trained barristers and Indian-trained pleaders—either could be appointed to the Federal Court or to the high court after 10 years of practice,[108] and either could become the Chief Justice of India[109] or the chief justice of a high court.[110] However, as before, there was no provision for the Crown to appoint 'distinguished jurists' to the court, that is, law professors or legal scholars who had not practised law or served as judges. Only a high

---

[105] Section 200(2), Government of India Act, 1935.
[106] Section 220(2), Government of India Act, 1935.
[107] Proviso to Section 201, Government of India Act, 1935. This was also a safeguard for high court judges. Proviso to Section 221, Government of India Act, 1935. Today, constitutional court judges in India do not enjoy the same rights with respect to their salaries under India's Constitution. See proviso to Article 125, Constitution of India; proviso to Article 221, Constitution of India.
[108] Section 220(3), Government of India Act, 1935.
[109] Proviso (i) to Section 200(3), Government of India Act, 1935. In order to become the Chief Justice of India, a duly qualified lawyer had to have 15 years' standing. Proviso (ii) to Section 200(3), Government of India Act, 1935.
[110] Proviso to Section 220(3), Government of India Act, 1935.

court judge of five years' standing, or a suitably qualified lawyer of 10 years' standing, could be a judge of the Federal Court of India.

A proviso to Section 200(3) set out certain additional qualifications necessary for appointment to the post of Chief Justice of India:

> (i) a person shall not be qualified for appointment as Chief Justice of India unless he is, or when first appointed to judicial office was, *a barrister, a member of the Faculty of Advocates or a pleader*; and (ii) in relation to the Chief Justice of India, for the references in paragraphs (b) and (c) of this subsection to ten years there shall be substituted references to *fifteen years*.

(emphasis supplied)

The Chief Justice of India was required to be a suitably qualified lawyer before he was first appointed a judge.[111] This was designed to ensure that members of the ICS could not hold the post of Chief Justice of India.[112] Interestingly, although the Government of India Act, 1935 prohibited a member of the civil service from becoming Chief Justice of India, it did not persist with the restriction that had existed earlier against a civil service member becoming chief justice of a high court.[113] All that the Government of India Act, 1935 required was that a civil service member serve as a judge of a high court for at least three years before he could be appointed chief justice of a high court.[114] At the time, there was a strong public sentiment in India against civil service judges, who were perceived to entertain a natural bias towards the government.[115] Significantly, provisions contained in the Indian High Courts Act, 1861, and in the Government of India Act, 1915, which specified the 'rank and precedence' of high court judges according to the 'seniority of their appointments' were absent in the Government of India Act, 1935.[116]

---

[111] In other words, one could become the Chief Justice of India only if one were a barrister, advocate, or pleader prior to one's first appointment to judicial office, or if one were a barrister, advocate, or pleader of 15 years' standing immediately prior to the appointment as Chief Justice of India.

[112] George H. Gadbois, Jr. 1964. 'The Federal Court of India: 1937-1950', *Journal of the Indian Law Institute*, 6: 253–315.

[113] Jain, *Outlines of Indian Legal History*, pp. 357–8.

[114] Proviso to Section 220(3), Government of India Act, 1935.

[115] Jain, *Outlines of Indian Legal History*, p. 357.

[116] See Section 5, Indian High Courts Act, 1861; Section 103, Government of India Act, 1915; and the text in notes 24 and 30 above. It is not entirely clear

The Federal Court had original, appellate, and advisory juris-dictions. Its original jurisdiction extended to federal disputes.[117] In British India, its appellate jurisdiction extended to decisions of the high courts, only if the high court issued a certificate that the case involved a substantial question of law as to the interpretation of the Constitution.[118] The Federal Court's appellate jurisdiction was therefore purely exercisable in constitutional cases, and not in civil or criminal cases. The federal legislature was empowered to extend this jurisdiction to civil cases, subject to certain conditions, in which event the legislature could also preclude direct appeals to the Privy Council from the high courts in such cases.[119] In cases where a certificate was granted by a high court, no direct appeal would lie to the Privy Council.[120] A decision of the Federal Court could be appealed before the Privy Council, without leave, if the decision was issued under the court's original jurisdiction and involved a certain type of dispute, but with leave of either the Federal Court or Privy Council in other cases.[121] The Governor General could invoke the

---

why the Government of India Act, 1935 did not specify the order of precedence amongst judges of the Federal Court and the high courts, as between them-selves. Statutes in Britain did not cease to specify the order of precedence amongst judges. For example, Section 16 of the Supreme Court of Judicature (Consolidation) Act, 1925, c. 49, provided that Lords Justices of Appeal ranked 'according to the priority of the dates at which they respectively became judges of the Court of Appeal', and the same principle applied to High Court judges. To this date, Section 13 of the Senior Courts Act, 1981, c. 54, provides that judges of the Supreme Court of the United Kingdom rank next after the Master of the Rolls, and as between themselves, 'according to the priority of the dates on which they respectively became judges of the Supreme Court', and the same principle applies to judges of the Court of Appeal and to judges of the High Court. Similarly, to this date, associate justices of the Supreme Court of the United States have 'precedence according to the seniority of their commissions', and if their commissions bear the same date, 'according to seniority in age'. 28 U.S.C.A. § 4. The same principle applies to federal circuit court judges in the United States. 28 U.S.C.A. § 45.

[117] Section 204, Government of India Act, 1935.

[118] The specific words were 'this Act or any Order in Council made thereunder'. Section 205, Government of India Act, 1935.

[119] Section 206, Government of India Act, 1935.

[120] Section 205(2), Government of India Act, 1935.

[121] Section 208, Government of India Act, 1935.

court's advisory jurisdiction, in his discretion, on questions of public importance.[122]

In short, the Federal Court under the Government of India Act, 1935 was a weak court, with limited jurisdiction—importantly, it had no appellate jurisdiction in criminal or civil cases, it did not swallow all direct appeals from a high court to the Privy Council, and its decisions could be appealed before the Privy Council. This was clearly not the supreme court that B.R. Puri and the Central Legislative Assembly had asked for in 1932.

FEDERAL COURT JUDGES (1937–47)

The Federal Court of India was established on 1 October 1937, when its first three judges were sworn in by the Governor General at the Viceregal Lodge in Simla,[123] six months after the inauguration of provincial autonomy.[124] However, it was formally inaugurated only on 6 December 1937,[125] when the first session[126] was held at the Chamber of Princes in a circular three-sectored building known as the Council House,[127] the judges dressed in 'black and gold gowns', an event at which 'messages of good wishes' were read from Lord Chancellor Hailsham, and the Chief Justices of Canada

---

[122] Section 213, Government of India Act, 1935.
[123] *Times of India.* 1937. 'Federal Court Judges Sworn In: Oath Administered by Lord Linlithgow', *Times of India*, 2 October, p. 14.
[124] Pylee, *Federal Court of India*, p. xi.
[125] Harihar Prasad Dubey. 1968. *A Short History of the Judicial Systems of India and Some Foreign Countries.* Bombay: Tripathi, p. 350.
[126] *Times of India.* 1954. 'Most Striking Changes', *Times of India*, 28 March, p. 6; *Times of India.* 1937. 'Federal Court Holds First Session', *Times of India*, 7 December, p. 11; *Times of India.* 1938. 'First Case Before Federal Court', *Times of India*, 1 June, p. 10. In fact, the inaugural session of the Supreme Court of India was held in this chamber, where the new court continued to convene until the increase in the number of judges created the necessity for a separate building, which was formally declared open in August 1958. *Times of India.* 1958. 'Supreme Court Building', *Times of India*, 15 July, p. 8; *Times of India.* 1958. 'New Supreme Court Building Opened', *Times of India*, 6 August, p. 8. See also *Times of India.* 1953. 'Supreme Court Construction Plans Finalised', *Times of India*, 23 January, p. 5.
[127] The Council House itself, later India's Parliament building, was inaugurated on 17 January 1927. *Times of India.* 1927. 'Magnificent Home for India's Parliament', *Times of India*, 18 January, p. 10.

and Australia, in a chamber packed with barristers from all parts of India, Lady Linlithgow, and prominent members of the Viceroy's staff.[128] The Federal Court of India never had its own building[129]—in fact, until 1958, even the Supreme Court of India would convene at the Chamber of Princes.

Before Indian independence on 15 August 1947, the court always had three judges—one British Chief Justice of India,[130] and two puisne judges, one Hindu and the other Muslim.[131] This was despite the fact that the Government of India Act, 1935 did not establish any such religious or racial quotas for the Federal Court. The first judges of the Federal Court of India were Chief Justice Sir Maurice Linford Gwyer,[132] and Justices Sir Shah Muhammad Sulaiman and Mukund Ramrao Jayakar, the last of whom would later serve on the Judicial Committee of the Privy Council. In the coming years, prior to independence, Sir William Patrick Spens would replace Gwyer as Chief Justice, Justices Sir Muhammad Zafrulla Khan and Syed Fazl Ali would occupy the Muslim seat on the court, while Justices S. Varadachariar and Harilal Kania would occupy the Hindu seat on the court.

Between its establishment in 1937, and Indian independence in 1947, the court had eight judges,[133] never more than three at a time. There was no convention that the most senior judge on the court

[128] *New York Times*. 1937. 'New Federal Court Inaugurated in India', *New York Times*, 7 December.

[129] In fact, a month before the inaugural session, the Public Works Department was worried about what would happen a few months later, in February, when a session of the Chamber of Princes was due to be held. *Times of India*. 1937. 'Housing Federal Court', *Times of India*, 2 November, p. 6.

[130] Even otherwise, there seemed to be a convention that the chief justice of a court would typically be British. See Chapter 2.

[131] See *Times of India*. 1936. 'Federal Court of India: Advocate General Sir B.L. Mitter Accepts Post', *Times of India*, 24 November, p. 11.

[132] Interestingly, although Harilal J. Kania is said in most accounts to be the first Chief Justice of India, this is not so, strictly speaking. Under the Government of India Act, 1935, the Chief Justice of the Federal Court was termed the 'Chief Justice of India'. For this reason, Maurice Gwyer could rightly be termed the first Chief Justice of India, and Harilal J. Kania the first Chief Justice of independent India, the first Chief Justice of the Supreme Court of India, or the first Indian Chief Justice of India.

[133] On occasion, acting judges may have been appointed to make up for a judge's absence. For example, when Shah Muhammad Sulaiman passed away, Sir John Beaumont, the Chief Justice of the Bombay High Court, served on the court

should become Chief Justice of India on the eve of the retirement of the outgoing Chief Justice. Accordingly, William Patrick Spens replaced Maurice Gwyer on the court as its Chief Justice when Gwyer retired, although at the time, S. Varadachariar, who had served as acting Chief Justice in the interim, was the most senior judge on the court. Apparently, the outgoing Chief Justice, Maurice Gwyer, was not pleased that he had not been consulted before the appointment of Spens to the court. In fact, Gwyer 'bitterly opposed' Spens' appointment, on three grounds: (*a*) an Indian ought to have been considered for the post, (*b*) Spens' political background would affect the perception of his being impartial, and (*c*) Spens' professional qualifications were inadequate.[134] Even otherwise, the announcement of Spens had 'provoked a certain amount of criticism'.[135] The appointment of Spens over Varadachariar must be considered the first 'supersession' of a senior judge for the post of the Chief Justice of India, and even at that point in time it was not taken too well.

Before Spens was offered the post of Chief Justice of India, it seems that three other British lawyers were considered for the job—Sir Walter Monckton,[136] Sir Cyril Radcliffe,[137] and Sir William Jowitt,[138]

---

as an acting judge between 15 April and 31 May 1941. *Federal Court Reports*, 1941, vol. 3. Similarly, in 1942, when Zafrulla Khan briefly served as Agent-General to the Indian government in China, Beaumont served once again as an acting judge during 21 April–31 May 1942. *Federal Court Reports*, 1942, vol. 4. See *Times of India*. 1942. 'New Federal Court Judge', *Times of India*, 17 April, p. 1. Similarly, Sir Torrick Ameer Ali and Francis George Rowland also seemed to have served on the court. Gadbois, 'Federal Court of India'.

[134] *Oxford Dictionary of National Biography*, under 'William Patrick Spens'.

[135] *Times of India*. 1942. 'The Federal Court', *Times of India*, 4 December, p. 6.

[136] Walter Turner Monckton was a barrister who studied at Oxford University, was called to the bar at the Inner Temple, legal adviser to the Simon Commission for Constitutional Reform in India, and constitutional adviser to the Nizam of Hyderabad. *Oxford Dictionary of National Biography*, under 'Walter Turner Monckton'.

[137] Cyril John Radcliffe was a barrister who studied at Oxford University, was called to the bar at the Inner Temple, and later the first man (apart from former law officers) to be appointed to the House of Lords directly from the bar in over 60 years, and appointed chairman of the Boundary Commissions for India. *Oxford Dictionary of National Biography*, under 'Cyril Radcliffe'.

[138] William Allen Jowitt was a lawyer-politician who studied at Oxford University, was called to the bar at the Middle Temple, attorney general in the Labour

but none accepted.[139] Before Varadachariar was appointed to the court, Sir Nripendra Sircar was offered the position on the Federal Court, which he declined.[140] Varadachariar was Gwyer's nominee. Gwyer's list, in the order of merit, consisted of Varadachariar, Venkata Subba Rao, and Madhavan Nair, all from Madras.[141] Gwyer was apparently also anxious to make B.N. Rau a Federal Court judge.[142]

The mean age of the judges appointed to the court was 56.9 years. Appointed at age 48, Zafrulla Khan was the youngest, and no judge would be appointed to either the Federal Court of India or to the Supreme Court of India younger than him. In fact, had he not resigned a month prior to independence, he would have been Chief Justice of India until 1958, depriving four judges of the post of Chief Justice of India—Kania, Sastri, Mahajan, and Mukherjea—everything else remaining the same. After Spens resigned in 1947, Khan would have served as Chief Justice of India for close to 11 years—no Chief Justice of India has served for as long a term. Sir Shah Muhammad Sulaiman was also young when appointed to the Federal Court, only 51, and he would have been Chief Justice of India before Zafrulla Khan, had he not died in office only less than four years after his appointment to the Federal Court. Jayakar was the oldest, appointed at age 63[143]—there has not been an older judge appointed to either the Federal Court or the Supreme Court since.

---

government, a Labour Party member of Parliament (MP), solicitor-general in Churchill's wartime coalition government, a minister without portfolio, and later lord chancellor. *Oxford Dictionary of National Biography*, under 'William Allen Jowitt'.

[139] *Oxford Dictionary of National Biography*, under 'William Patrick Spens'.

[140] IOR/L/PO/8/89(Ii) L/PO/203(Ii) (Gwyer to Varadachariar), item 282-285, as conveyed to me by Mr Rohit De. Also see, National Archives of India, M.R. Jayakar Papers, Reel 112, Murthy to Jayakar, letter dated 30 January 1939.

[141] Ibid.

[142] Sir Benegal Rau. 1963. *India's Constitution in the Making*, 2nd ed., Bombay: Orient Longmans, p. xix.

[143] The data on M.R. Jayakar poses a problem. He was born on 13 November 1873. M.R. Jayakar. 1958. *The Story of My Life*. Bombay: Asia Publishing House, p. 1; P. Rajeswar Rao. 1991. *The Great Indian Patriots*. New Delhi: Mittal. This is corroborated by the fact that on 10 March 1959, when he passed away, it was reported that he was 86 years old. *Times of India*. 1959. 'Dr. Jayakar Dead', *Times of India*, 11 March, p. 1. However, this would mean that by 13 November 1938, he would have reached the age of 65—and would have had to retire according

Not counting the two judges who continued on the Federal Court after 1947 (Kania and Fazl Ali), the average tenure on the court was 4.5 years. Sulaiman passed away early, and two judges (Khan and Spens) resigned before the natural completion of their terms.

Professionally speaking, four judges (Sulaiman, Varadachariar, Kania, and Fazl Ali) out of eight had been high court judges before getting to the Federal Court. Of these, only two (Sulaiman and Fazl Ali) had previously served as the chief justice of a high court[144] although one (Kania) had served as acting Chief Justice of the Bombay High Court. The remaining four Federal Court judges (that is, those who had not been high court judges) had some significant political experience, or other experience working in the government. In fact, both Gwyer and Jayakar, the first members of the court, had significant roles to play in drafting the Government of India Act, 1935 itself—Gwyer[145] as first Parliamentary Counsel to the Treasury, and Jayakar as an Indian representative consulted by the Joint Committee on Indian Constitutional Reform. Zafrulla Khan, who would join the court later, was also a delegate at the Round Table Conferences, and an Indian representative consulted by the

---

to the provisions of the Government of India Act, 1935. However, it is unclear if this actually happened. The 1939 volume of the *Federal Court Reports* still listed him as being a judge on the court until 6 January 1939, when he replaced Shadi Lal on the Privy Council. The Government of India Act, 1935 did not seem to have any provision by which an ad hoc judge could be appointed to the court, which might have explained Jayakar's continuance on the court after reaching retirement age. One of two scenarios is possible: he retired in November 1938 and there was no occasion for him to resign in January 1939, or his term was extended by the executive government. His autobiography is not helpful, since it deals with the period ending 1925. His biographer, V.B. Kulkarni, states that Jayakar 'withdrew from the Federal Court' before going to the Privy Council in January 1939. V.B. Kulkarni. 1976. *M.R. Jayakar*. New Delhi: Ministry of Information and Broadcasting, Government of India, p. 243. Accordingly, it is assumed here that he retired from the Federal Court in November 1938.

[144] Sulaiman was previously the Chief Justice of the Allahabad High Court, while Fazl Ali was the Chief Justice of the Patna High Court.

[145] Gwyer had also previously been legal adviser to the Ministry of Shipping (1916–19), legal adviser to the Ministry of Health (1919–26), and H.M. Procurator-General and Treasury Solicitor (1926–33). *Times of India.* 1943–4. *The Indian Yearbook and Who's Who*, vol. 30. Bombay: Bennett Coleman, p. 1021.

Joint Committee. Jayakar,[146] Zafrulla Khan,[147] and William Patrick Spens[148] were established politicians.

In terms of regions represented on the court, amongst eight judges, two were from Bombay (Jayakar and Kania), two from England (Gwyer and Spens), and one each from Allahabad (Sulaiman), Madras (Varadachariar), Lahore (Khan), and Bihar (Fazl Ali). No judge was appointed to the court from Calcutta, perhaps because the posts of Law Member of the Viceroy's Council since the late 1920s and Advocate General to the Federal Court had typically been occupied by lawyers from Bengal.[149]

All eight judges had practised as lawyers at some point in time, and both chief justices had been conferred silk (see Table 1.1). Educationally, five out of eight judges were barristers educated in England—only Jayakar, Varadachariar, and Kania had not studied in England.

FEDERAL COURT JUDGES (1947–50)

A day before India achieved independence, Harilal J. Kania took over as Chief Justice of India. Fazl Ali was the next most senior puisne judge on the court. Before the Constitution of India came into being

[146] Jayakar had an accomplished political career. He was elected to the Bombay Legislative Council in 1923 where he served as leader of the Swaraj Party, then member of Central Legislative Assembly (1926–30), leader of the opposition at the Simla Session (1930), and a delegate to the Round Table Conference in London. *Times of India, The Indian Yearbook*, vol. 30, p. 1034.

[147] Zafrulla Khan was a member of the Punjab Legislative Council (1926–35), a delegate to the Round Table Conferences, President of the All India Muslim League, and member of the Governor General's Council. *Times of India*. 1945–6. *The Indian Yearbook and Who's Who*, vol. 32. Bennett Coleman, pp. 1243–4. After resigning as a judge of the Federal Court in 1947, he went on to serve as Pakistan's foreign minister, and then as a judge on the International Court of Justice. See 'Sir Muhammad Zafrulla Khan (Pakistan): Elected President of The Seventeeth Session of the General Assembly', available online at http://www.un.org/ga/55/president/bio17.htm (last accessed on 19 March 2012).

[148] Spens was an MP belonging to the Conservative Party.

[149] Law Members of the Viceroy's Executive Council from Bengal between 1922 and 1946 were S.R. Das (1925), B.L. Mitter (1928), Nripendra Nath Sircar (1934), and Asoke Kumar Roy (1943). These data have been obtained by systematically mining the *Indian Yearbook and Who's Who* between 1922 and 1946. The Advocate General at the Federal Court of India was B.L. Mitter (Calcutta)

Table 1.1 Eight Judges Who Served on the Federal Court of India (1937–47)

Judge	Date of Birth	Start of Term	End of Term
Maurice Gwyer, Chief Justice	25 April 1878	1937	1943
Shah Muhammad Sulaiman	3 February 1886	1937	1941*
Mukund Ramrao Jayakar	13 November 1873	1937	1938
Srinivasa Varadachariar	20 June 1881	1939	1946
Zafrulla Khan	6 February 1893	1941	1947**
William Patrick Spens, Chief Justice	9 August 1885	1943	1947**
Harilal J. Kania	3 November 1890	1946	
Syed Fazl Ali	19 September 1886	1947	

Source: Author.
Notes:
* indicates death.
** indicates resignation.

on 26 January 1950, and consequently, before the Supreme Court for India came into being, four more judges would be appointed to the Federal Court. The six judges who served on the Federal Court of India in the period between 15 August 1947 and 26 January 1950 were a homogenous group of men (see Table 1.2). In 1947, Patanjali Sastri was appointed to the court, and the court had three members again, as it had always been. However, two appointments were made in quick succession in October 1948 (Mahajan and Mukherjea), and S.R. Das was appointed only six days before the new Constitution came into being, on 20 January 1950. They all served on the court simultaneously—the largest group that had ever been on the court until then.

Where only half the judges who served on the Federal Court during 1937–47 had previously been high court judges, now every single judge on the court was formerly a high court judge. There were

from 1 April 1937 to 31 March 1945, and from 1 April 1945 onwards it was Noshirwan P. Engineer (Bombay). These data have been obtained from the *Federal Court Reports*.

no appointments directly from the bar, and except for one,[150] none were involved in politics. Again, out of six judges, only two were chief justices of high courts.[151] None of these was the chief justice of the prestigious High Courts of Bombay, Madras, and Calcutta. On average, the judges had served 10.8 years on the high court before being appointed to the Federal Court,[152] and the mean age at which they were appointed to the high court was 46.9 years. The mean age of appointment to the Federal Court was 57.7 years—implying that they had served only 10 years on the high courts, on average. This was an older court than the Federal Court had previously been. The oldest was Fazl Ali (60), and the youngest was the last person to be appointed, S.R. Das (55).

The court had changed from what it used to be. The Chief Justice of India was Indian, for the first time. The most significant change was that all of the court's members had risen through the judiciary— none had been appointed from amongst lawyers or politicians. The number of barristers went down. Only two of them (Fazl Ali and S.R. Das) were barristers, where five of the eight who had served during 1937–47 had been barristers. The court now had five Hindus and one Muslim. The Muslim seat diminished in strength—though one out of three judges on the court used to be Muslim judges, now only one out of six judges was a Muslim.

CONSTITUENT ASSEMBLY OF INDIA

Even as new judges were being appointed to the Federal Court of India—more judges than had ever been seen on the court at the same time—the character and content of India's new Constitution were now being fashioned and extensively debated by the Constituent Assembly of India. The history of the enactment of the Indian

[150] Mahajan served as prime minister of Jammu and Kashmir in 1947–8, but he too was a high court judge. Syed Fazl Ali would later serve as Governor of Odisha (then 'Orissa') (1952–4) and Assam (1956–9), but that was after retirement.
[151] Fazl Ali was the Chief Justice of the Patna High Court, while S.R. Das was the Chief Justice of the Punjab High Court.
[152] However, the range was large, with the shortest term on a high court (Mahajan) being slightly over five years, and the longest term on a high court (Fazl Ali) being slightly over 19 years.

Table 1.2   Six Judges Who Served on the Federal Court of India (1947–50)

Judge	Start of Term
Harilal J. Kania	20 June 1946
Syed Fazl Ali	9 June 1947
M. Patanjali Sastri	6 December 1947
Mehr Chand Mahajan	4 October 1948
B.K. Mukherjea	14 October 1948
S.R. Das	20 January 1950

Source: Website of the Supreme Court of India (http://supremecourtofindia.nic.in).

Constitution, including some of the debates concerning the federal judiciary, have been impressively documented by other authors elsewhere.[153] For the purposes of this book, it is not necessary to comprehensively deal with this history, but only to recap key events in order to contextualize the debate surrounding judicial appointments. In this section I will focus more specifically on debates surrounding the selection criteria that were to be employed for judges who were to sit on India's new Supreme Court.

The Constituent Assembly was duly constituted in accordance with the proposals of the Cabinet Mission Plan in 1946.[154] On 30 April 1947, a 15-member committee (known as the 'Union Constitution Committee') was set up to prepare a report on the broad principles for the new union Constitution.[155] A special committee (sometimes also called an 'ad hoc Committee on the Supreme Court') was also

[153] See B. Shiva Rao. 1968. *The Framing of India's Constitution: A Study*. Bombay: Tripathi, pp. 480–510; Granville Austin. 1966. *The Indian Constitution: Cornerstone of a Nation*. New Delhi: Oxford University Press, pp. 164–85. See further M.P. Singh. 2000. 'Securing the Independence of the Judiciary: The Indian Experience', *Indiana International and Comparative Law Review*, 10(1): 245–92.
[154] The office of the Constituent Assembly was set up on 1 July 1946, with B.N. Rau in charge as Constitutional Adviser. See Rau, *India's Constitution*, p. 1. Its first session was held on 9 December 1946. *Constituent Assembly Debates*, vol. 1. See Holden Furber. 1949. 'Constitution-Making in India', *Far Eastern Survey*, 18(8): 86–9; Prime Minister Atlee. 1947. 'Statement by Prime Minister Atlee on the Transfer of Power in India', *Middle East Journal*, 20 February, 1(2): 210–12.
[155] *Constituent Assembly Debates*, vol. 3, pp. 471–3. A 25-member committee was also set up to prepare principles of a model provincial constitution.

set up to opine on the powers of the Supreme Court that was to be established. The committee's members included a former judge of the Federal Court (S. Varadachariar), and a former Advocate General to the Federal Court (B.L. Mitter), in addition to other noted jurists—Alladi Krishnaswamy Ayyar, K.M. Munshi, and B.N. Rau (Constitutional Adviser to the Constituent Assembly of India, and later, a judge on the International Court of Justice at the Hague).[156,157] On 21 May 1947, the ad hoc committee completed its report. In its report, the committee called for the creation of a court that would sit in two division benches, each consisting of five judges. More importantly, it suggested two alternative methods for making judicial appointments—(a) Supreme Court judges could either be appointed by the President of India in consultation with the Chief Justice, and then confirmed by at least seven out of a panel of 11 members—a panel composed of high court chief justices, members of the Central Legislature, and law officers of the union; or (b) the panel would recommend three names for appointment to the Supreme Court, out of which a judge would be appointed by the president in consultation with the chief justice. Judges of the Supreme Court were to continue to retire at age 65.[158] In a memorandum prepared by B.N. Rau, Constitutional Adviser to the Constituent Assembly, on 30 May 1947, Rau said that he substantially adopted the first of these alternatives, substituting the panel with the Council of State.[159] In Clause 50(2) (part 4, chapter 5) of Rau's draft, Supreme Court judges were to be appointed by the president with the approval of not less than two-thirds of the members of the Council of State.[160] Rau envisioned the Council of State as a kind of non-partisan Privy Council,[161]

---

[156] Rau, *India's Constitution*, p. v.

[157] See B. Shiva Rao. 1967. *The Framing of India's Constitution: Select Documents*, vol. 2. Bombay: Tripathi, p. 591.

[158] *Constituent Assembly Debates*, dated 21 July 1947, vol. 4, p. 733. See further, 'Report of the Ad hoc Committee on Supreme Court, 21 May 1947', paras. 13–15, in Rao, *Framing of India's Constitution: Select Documents*, vol. 2, p. 587. It was proposed that the composition of the panel would remain the same for 10 years, and then change.

[159] Rau, *India's Constitution*, p. 112.

[160] Rau, *India's Constitution*, p. 155.

[161] Rau, *India's Constitution*, p. 177.

and it was to consist of ex-officio members (for example, the Chief Justice of the Supreme Court, the Advocate General), former presidents, former prime ministers, former Supreme Court chief justices, and other members appointed by the president.[162] In another memorandum on the Provincial Constitution submitted to the Provincial Constitution Committee, Rau noted that 'High Court judges may be potential judges of the Supreme Court', and advocated that they too be appointed in the same manner as his proposal for the appointment of Supreme Court judges—by a two-thirds majority of the non-partisan Council of State.[163] Accordingly, like B.R. Puri in 1932, B.N. Rau too imagined that Supreme Court judges would be staffed by high court judges.

The Union Constitution Committee prepared a report on the principles of the Union Constitution, and submitted it to the Constituent Assembly of India on 4 July 1947.[164] Clause 18 of the report dealt with the federal judicature. The committee agreed with the proposals of the ad hoc committee on the Supreme Court, with one exception: judges were to be appointed 'by the President after consulting the Chief Justice and such other judges of the Supreme Court as also judges of the High Courts as may be necessary for the purpose'.[165] On 29 July 1947, the Constituent Assembly of India discussed Clause 18 of the Union Constitution Committee's report. As one member of the assembly would summarize,[166] five broad matters were discussed that day: (a) who would appoint Supreme Court judges, (b) who would remove Supreme Court judges, (c) qualifications for being appointed a Supreme Court judge, (d) who would determine the salary and emoluments of judges, and (e) the Court's jurisdiction. The only suggestion with respect to the qualifications for being appointed to the Supreme Court was that no judge could be appointed to the Supreme Court of India unless he was a citizen of India—a matter on which there

---

[162] Rau, *India's Constitution*, pp. 136–7.

[163] Rau, *India's Constitution*, p. 177.

[164] *Constituent Assembly Debates*, vol. 4, p. 716.

[165] *Constituent Assembly Debates*, vol. 4, p. 727. This appeared to be consistent with the recommendations of the Sapru Committee made in 1945. See Singh, 'Securing the Independence', p. 260.

[166] M. Ananthasayanam Ayyangar, *Constituent Assembly Debates*, vol. 4, p. 895.

was hardly any debate.[167] The strongest debate took place on how Supreme Court judges were to be removed. Alladi Krishnaswamy Ayyar proposed that they be removed by the president on an address from both Houses of Parliament, and he strongly argued in favour of the amendment.[168] The amendment was adopted—the only amendment on Clause 18 adopted that day.[169]

On 29 August 1947, a Drafting Committee was set up by the Constituent Assembly of India to carry out the task of drafting the Constitution.[170]

In October 1947, the first draft of a new Constitution for India was presented to the Constituent Assembly of India.[171] Articles 87–109 dealt with the federal judiciary. Article 87(1) provided for the establishment of a Supreme Court consisting of 10 judges, and one Chief Justice of India. Significantly, the provision dealt with how judges were to be appointed to the Supreme Court of India, largely based on Section 200 of the Government of India Act, 1935. Judges were to continue to retire at age 65. To be eligible for being considered a potential Supreme Court appointment, a person had to have spent either five years as a judge on a high court, or have been a duly licensed lawyer for 10 years, as before. Law professors could not be appointed as Supreme Court judges.

However, there were some key differences between the first draft of the Constitution and the Government of India Act, 1935, modelled along the lines of the Australian and Canadian constitutions. As the Constitutional Adviser, B.N. Rau, wrote in a note about the federal judiciary provisions of the first draft Constitution:

> These follow, for the most part, the corresponding provisions in the Government of India Act, 1935, as adapted by the India (Provisional Constitution) Order, 1947. Clause 87(4) relating to removal of judges follows section 72(ii)

---

[167] Shrimati G. Durgabai moved the amendment. *Constituent Assembly Debates*, vol. 4, p. 894.

[168] *Constituent Assembly Debates*, vol. 4, pp. 889–91.

[169] *Constituent Assembly Debates*, vol. 4, p. 904.

[170] B.R. Ambedkar, *Constituent Assembly Debates*, dated 25 November 1949, vols. 10 and 11, p. 972.

[171] For a copy of the text of the draft, see B. Shiva Rao. 1968. *The Framing of India's Constitution: Select Documents*, vol. 3. Bombay: Tripathi, p. 3.

of the Commonwealth of Australia Act. [The provision dealing with the appointment of ad hoc judges] is taken from section 30 of the Canadian Supreme Court Act.[172]

Most importantly, in keeping with Clause 18 of the report of the Union Constitution Committee, according to the first draft of the Constitution, Supreme Court judges were now to be appointed by the president, in consultation with Supreme Court judges and high court judges, and in consultation with the Chief Justice of India (except in the matter of appointing the Chief Justice of India).[173] The Government of India Act, 1935 had not envisaged 'consultation' with judges before judicial appointments, although apparently there may have been a convention back then that the Chief Justice of India was consulted on appointments.[174] Further, consequent to the acceptance of Alladi Krishnaswamy Ayyar's amendment, the process of removing judges had now changed. The Government of India Act, 1935 provided that a judge could be removed if the Judicial Committee of the Privy Council presented a report to the Crown in favour of his removal (upon a reference being made to the Privy Council), by the Crown.[175] Now, in order to remove a judge, an address was to be presented by both Houses of Parliament to the president in the same session for his removal.[176] The clause did not specify what sort of majority in Parliament was required to remove the judge.

B.N. Rau, Constitutional Adviser to the Constituent Assembly, then visited several countries—the United States, Canada, Ireland, and England[177]—in order to learn from their constitutional experiences.

---

[172] Rao, *Framing of India's Constitution: Select Documents*, vol. 3, p. 202.
[173] Article 87(2), first draft of the Indian Constitution. Rao, *Framing of India's Constitution: Select Documents*, vol. 3, p. 36.
[174] Singh, 'Securing the Independence', 260n94.
[175] Proviso (b) to Section 200(2), Government of India Act, 1935.
[176] Article 87(4), first draft of the Indian Constitution. B. Shiva Rao, *Framing of India's Constitution: Select Documents*, vol. 3, p. 37. The words 'misbehaviour' or 'infirmity of mind' in the Government of India Act, 1935 were replaced in the draft constitution by the words 'proved misbehaviour or incapacity'.
[177] He met the following people during his trip, amongst others: in Washington, ex-Chief Justice Hughes, Justice Felix Frankfurter, Justice Burton, and Justice Murphy; Mr. Boland, Irish Secretary for Foreign Affairs; in Ottawa, Justice Thorsen, President of the Exchequer Court, Mr. John Hearne, High Commissioner for Ireland, Mr. Wershof and Mr. Jackett, constitutional experts;

In the United States, he met Justice Felix Frankfurter, amongst others, who told him that the Supreme Court of India should convene and sit *en banc*, that 'the highest court of appeal in the land should not sit in divisions'.[178] In London, he met Sir John Beaumont, a judge of the Privy Council and former Chief Justice of the Bombay High Court. Beaumont told Rau that the retirement age of 60 years for High Court judges was not good enough.[179] As Rau wrote later:

> As regards the age-limit of High Court Judges, Sir John Beaumont said that, in his own experience, he had at least on two occasions failed to get the best men from the Bar for appointment to the Bench, because, with the present age-limit of 60, they had no chance of earning a full pension. He thought that the age-limit should at least be 65, and observed that if a judge was not too old for the Federal Court at the age of 65, there was no reason to think that he was too old for the High Court.[180]

In an appendix to his note, the Constitutional Adviser even suggested that the retirement age of high court judges be 65 years,[181] an amendment that was partially accepted by the Drafting Committee on 15 December 1947.[182] On 21 February 1948, the second draft

---

in New York, Justice Learned Hand of the Federal Circuit Court of Appeals. Rau, *India's Constitution*, p. 328. He met several other scholars, including Dr Jessup, Professor Mirkine, and Professor Dowling. Rau, *India's Constitution*, p. 334.

[178] Rao, *Framing of India's Constitution: Select Documents*, vol. 3, p. 219; Rau, *India's Constitution*, pp. 330–1.

[179] Beaumont was only repeating to Rau the views he had previously expressed at a meeting of the East India Association in May 1944. See Beaumont, 'Indian Judicial System', pp. 14–15. A high court judge, Beaumont had said, earned his full pension only after 11.5 years of service, and if the retirement age of high court judges was 60, then men above the age of 50 would be unwilling to accept high court judgeships since they would not be able to earn full pensions. Beaumont believed that the experience gained at the bar between the ages of 47 and 52 was invaluable for the bench, and that the age of retirement for high court judges should be 65, with the option of permitting the chief justice to force a judge to retire at the age of 62 if the chief justice felt that the judge was 'past his work'. Beaumont, 'Indian Judicial System', pp. 14–15.

[180] Rao, *Framing of India's Constitution: Select Documents*, vol. 3, p. 225; Rau, *India's Constitution*, pp. 338–9.

[181] Rao, *Framing of India's Constitution: Select Documents*, vol. 3, p. 228, para. 5.

[182] Rao, *Framing of India's Constitution: Select Documents*, vol. 3, p. 393. The Drafting Committee's draft provided that the retirement age of high court judges was 60, or such higher age fixed by state legislatures, not exceeding 65.

of the Constitution was placed before the Constituent Assembly of India.[183] Articles 103–27 dealt with the federal judicature. Very few changes had been made to these provisions after the first draft.[184] One of the most important changes was that now the address by Parliament to the president for the removal of a judge would require a two-thirds majority of the members present and voting.[185]

The second draft Constitution was submitted for public comments in February 1948. A significant event took place thereafter. A conference of the judges of the Federal Court, and chief justices of many high courts, was convened to discuss the provisions of the second draft Constitution. In their joint memorandum to the Constituent Assembly, the conference strongly advised against permitting high court and Supreme Court judges to retire at the same age. If the retirement age at high courts and the Supreme Court was to be the same, they opined, then high court judges and chief justices would not accept a position on the new Supreme Court of India. The 'honor and prestige' of being appointed to the Supreme Court would not offset the sacrifice that a senior high court judge or chief justice would have to make in order to give up his position of seniority on a prestigious high court, in return for a junior position on a relatively new court, with perhaps a lighter case load. Allowing Supreme Court judges to retire after high court judges would ensure that senior high court judges would have an incentive to serve on the Supreme Court—an enhanced term in service. This was very similar to the rationale adopted by the Joint Committee prior to the enactment of the Government of India Act, 1935 for maintaining a 'retirement age gap' between the Federal Court and high courts. The passage from the memorandum is worth quoting almost entirely:

> Some of the judges also expressed the view that the age of retirement of High Court judges should be raised to 65…. It was also pointed out that judges of the Supreme Court had ordinarily to be selected from among the

---

[183] For a copy of the text of the draft, see Rao, *Framing of India's Constitution: Select Documents*, vol. 3, p. 509.

[184] The number of judges the Supreme Court would initially have was lowered to seven, and there was a provision for the attendance of retired judges at sittings of the Court.

[185] Article 103(4), second draft of the Indian Constitution. Rao, *Framing of India's Constitution: Select Documents*, vol. 3, p. 555.

Chief Justices and senior puisne judges of the High Courts, or from the leading members of the Bar. The reduced scale of salaries fixed in the Draft Constitution, it was felt, was too low to attract the latter. *Nor would the Chief Justice of a High Court or a senior puisne judges with a normal expectancy of promotion to the Chief Justiceship have a sufficient inducement to accept a puisne judgeship in the Supreme Court if the age limit for retirement of the Supreme Court and the High Court judges is the same. The increase … in the salary would be wholly insufficient to offset the increased expenditure entailed in setting up a new household in Delhi* while continuing, as in most cases it would be found necessary for domestic reasons to continue, his establishment in his own place…. *The honor and prestige associated with a seat on the Supreme Court Bench have their limits as an attraction and it is the prospect of continuing in service for a period of five more years that chiefly attracts him to the new office. As this attraction would disappear if the age of superannuation for High Court judges also is raised to 65, judges for the Supreme Court will have to be selected from among junior and comparatively inexperienced judges of the High Court, and a court thus manned would hardly command the respect and confidence which the Supreme Court in the land ought to inspire.* On a careful balancing of these considerations we have come to the unanimous conclusion that—(1) it is essential that a difference of 3 to 5 years should be maintained between the retiring age of High Court judges and that of Supreme Court judges; (2) age limit for retirement should be raised to 65 for High Court judges and to 68 for Supreme Court judges.[186]

(emphasis supplied)

In addition, the memorandum asked that the Chief Justice of India not merely be 'consulted' in the matter of appointments, but that his 'concurrence' be obtained, that is, his recommendation should be binding on the executive. This was felt necessary in order to prevent judicial appointments from being made on political, communal, or partisan grounds, which was increasingly becoming prevalent.[187]

Several other suggestions were received by the Constituent Assembly. Amongst those considered was an amendment to fix a minimum age limit for appointment to the Supreme Court, that is, that judges should be appointed to the Supreme Court of India only after they have attained the age of 55;[188] one to make high court

[186] 'Memorandum Representing the Views of the Federal Court and of the Chief Justices Representing all the Provincial High Courts of the Union of India, March 1948', in B. Shiva Rao. 1968. *The Framing of India's Constitution: Select Documents*, vol. 4. Bombay: Tripathi, pp. 193, 198–9.

[187] *Framing of India's Constitution: Select Documents*, vol. 4, pp. 194–5.

[188] 'Proposed by R.R. Diwakar and S.V. Krishnamoorthy Rao, Comments and Suggestions on the Draft Constitution (February – October 1948)', in B. Shiva Rao,

chief justices ex-officio judges of the Supreme Court;[189] and one, perhaps the most prescient proposal, to allow the President of India to nominate 'distinguished jurists' as Supreme Court judges.[190]

On 4 November 1948, the second draft of the Constitution of India was introduced in the Constituent Assembly of India by B.R. Ambedkar, Chairman of the Drafting Committee.[191] On 24 May 1949, the Constituent Assembly discussed provisions of the draft Constitution relating to the appointment of the federal judiciary. A host of amendments were proposed to the provisions dealing with federal judges. In his speech, Ambedkar placed these into three categories: (a) amendments concerning how Supreme Court judges should be appointed, (b) amendments concerning the age of retirement of Supreme Court judges, and (c) amendments concerning the acceptance by retired judges of positions after retirement.

Three types of amendments were proposed on how to appoint judges to the Supreme Court of India: first, it was suggested that judges should be appointed with the concurrence of (and not merely after consulting with) the chief justice; second, it was suggested that the appointment of judges should be subject to confirmation by a two-thirds vote of Parliament; and third, it was suggested that judges be appointed by consulting with the Council of States. Each of these suggestions was rejected by Ambedkar. He recommended 'steering a middle course':

[I]t would be dangerous to leave the appointments to be made by the President, without any kind of reservation or limitation, that is to say, merely on the advice of the executive of the day. Similarly, it seems to me that to

---

Framing of India's Constitution: Select Documents, vol. 4, p. 142. Interestingly, the Constitutional Adviser, B.N. Rau, commented that this would prevent the president from appointing a person of 'outstanding merit' if he was less than 55 years of age.

[189] Proposed by Chief Justice Mallik of the Allahabad High Court, Framing of India's Constitution: Select Documents, vol. 4, p. 143.

[190] Proposed by A.B. Rudra, Principal, Jaipuria College, Calcutta, Framing of India's Constitution: Select Documents, vol. 4, p. 146. The proposal did not find favour with the Constitutional Adviser. He said, '[I]t would be hardly desirable to appoint as judge of the Supreme Court a person who is unacquainted with the practice and procedure of courts.'

[191] Constituent Assembly Debates, 1949, vol. 8 (Part A), pp. 31–44.

make every appointment which the executive wishes to make subject to the concurrence of the Legislature is also not a very suitable provision.... *With regard to the question of the concurrence of the Chief Justice, it seems to me that those who advocate that proposition seem to rely implicitly both on the impartiality of the Chief Justice and the soundness of his judgment.* I personally feel no doubt that the Chief Justice is a very eminent person. But after all, the Chief Justice is a man with all the failings, all the sentiments and all the prejudices which we as common people have; and I think, *to allow the Chief Justice practically a veto upon the appointment of judges is really to transfer the authority to the Chief Justice which we are not prepared to vest in the President or the Government of the day.* I therefore, think that that is also a dangerous proposition.[192]

(emphasis supplied)

There were two types of amendments proposed concerning the retirement age of Supreme Court judges, broadly speaking. On the one hand, it was proposed that they retire at age 60, like high court judges. On the other hand, it was proposed that no retirement age be fixed at all. Jawaharlal Nehru spoke against lowering the retirement age of Supreme Court judges. He cited the example of Albert Einstein and Oliver Wendell Holmes—arguing that just as Einstein or Holmes did their best work later on in their lives, 'first-rate' judges could be older than 65. However, he concluded by stating that 65 was 'by no means unfair'.[193] To this, Ambedkar added that he agreed that 65 years of age did not represent the 'zero hour in a man's intellectual ability', but he cited the fact that retired judges could be called back to the bench and argued that this would ensure that talent would not be lost on account of the retirement age—older, retired judges could always be called back to the Court.[194]

Ambedkar also spoke against the amendment which sought to bar judges from accepting positions in the government after retirement, arguing that the judiciary decided cases in which the government only had the remotest of interest, and that consequently, the chance of influencing the conduct of a member of the judiciary by the government was 'very remote'.[195]

---

[192] *Constituent Assembly Debates*, vol. 8, p. 258.
[193] *Constituent Assembly Debates*, vol. 8, pp. 246–7.
[194] *Constituent Assembly Debates*, vol. 8, p. 259.
[195] *Constituent Assembly Debates*, vol. 8, p. 259.

Importantly, H.V. Kamath suggested that the draft Constitution be amended to enable the President of India to appoint a 'distinguished jurist' as a Supreme Court judge. He argued that this would 'open a wider field of choice' for the president, and that his suggestion had been borrowed from provisions relating to judges of the International Court of Justice at The Hague:

> The House will see that the article as it stands restricts the selection of judges to only two categories. One category consists of those who have been judges of a high court or of two or more such courts in succession and the second category consists of those who have been advocates of a high court or of two or more high courts in succession. I am sure that the House will realize that it is desirable, nay *it is essential, to have men—or for the matter of that [sic] women—who are possessed of outstanding legal and juristic learning. In my humble judgment, such are not necessarily confined to Judges or Advocates.*[196]

(emphasis supplied)

Another member of the assembly, M. Ananthasayanam Ayyangar, spoke in support of the amendment, citing Frankfurter as a great example of the erudition that a law professor could bring to the Court:

> In various cases a Supreme Court has to deal with constitutional issues. A practicing lawyer barely comes across constitutional problems. A person may enter the profession of Law straightaway. He might be a member of a Law College or be a Dean of the Faculty of Law in an University. There are many eminent persons, there are many writers, there are jurists of great eminence. Why should it not be made possible for the President to appoint a jurist of distinction, if it is necessary? *As a matter of fact, I would advise that out of the seven judges, one of them must be a jurist of great reputation.* I am told, Sir, by my honourable Friend, Shri Alladi, whom I consulted, that some years ago President Roosevelt in the U.S.A. appointed one Philip [*sic*] Frankfurter. He was a Professor in the Harward [*sic*] University. That was a novel experiment that he made. Before that, barristers were being chosen and also persons from the judiciary. This experiment has proved enormously successful. He is considered to be one of the foremost judges, one of the most eminent judges in the U.S.A.[197]

(emphasis supplied)

[196] *Constituent Assembly Debates*, vol. 8, p. 241.
[197] *Constituent Assembly Debates*, vol. 8, p. 254.

The amendment was accepted by Ambedkar, although with some hesitation as to its language.[198]

All discussions on the draft Constitution ended on 17 October 1949. Notably absent in the debates was any substantial or significant discussion on other criteria that could be employed to appoint judges to the court—on whether regional representation could be followed while appointing judges to the court, whether gender, religion, or caste were to have a role to play in judicial appointments, whether educational or professional qualifications were important. Interestingly, in a speech made in London in 1944, Sir John Beaumont had criticized the Privy Council for being unrepresentative of the different regions of India. However, the Constituent Assembly of India did not seem to seriously apply itself to the question of the geographic representativeness or otherwise of the Supreme Court it was setting up. Beaumont had said:

> [T]here are so many races in India with so many habits and customs and ways of thought, that local knowledge in a Court of Appeal is desirable, and there cannot be much local knowledge in the Privy Council. For example, a Board of the Privy Council without any representative of Bombay might not appreciate the difference in mentality and habits between Gujerat and Kanara.[199]

On 3 November 1949, the draft Constitution, as revised by the Drafting Committee based on discussions in the Assembly, was submitted to the President of the Assembly.[200] It was enacted on 26 November 1949, but most of its provisions would come into force on 26 January 1950.[201] Article 124(1) provided for the establishment of a Supreme Court of India with a Chief Justice of India and not more than seven judges, although Parliament could prescribe a larger number. Judges were to be appointed by the president after consulting judges of the Supreme Court and High Courts, as the president deemed necessary for the purpose. The president was required to always 'consult' the Chief Justice of India before appointing judges

---

[198] He was unsure of whether the word 'eminent' should be used instead of 'distinguished'. *Constituent Assembly Debates*, vol. 8, p. 257.

[199] Beaumont, 'Indian Judicial System', p. 14.

[200] Rao, *Framing of India's Constitution: Select Documents*, vol. 4, p. 745.

[201] Article 394, Constitution of India.

(other than the Chief Justice of India) to the Supreme Court. Judges would retire at age 65. In order to be eligible for appointment to the Supreme Court, a person had to be a citizen of India, and a judge of a high court (or two or more such courts in succession) for five years, an advocate of a high court (or two or more such courts in succession) for ten years, or, in the opinion of the president, a 'distinguished jurist'.[202]

The Constitution did not say anything—and neither did those who drafted it—about what kind of judges were supposed to be appointed to the Court, except for the fact that they had to be 'first-rate' and of the 'highest integrity'.[203]

WAS 'ORIGINAL INTENT' IMPORTANT?

On 15 August 1948, B.N. Rau, Constitutional Adviser to the Constituent Assembly, wrote a special article for a prominent Indian newspaper, the *Hindu*, where he addressed the criticism that the Indian Constitution had borrowed extensively from the constitutions of other countries, and had nothing original in it. He argued that not merely had the constitutions of other countries been adapted to India's special circumstances, but also that learning from the experience of other countries was the 'path of wisdom'. He had a doctrinal argument which was less convincing—that borrowing the textual provisions of the constitutions of other countries would ensure that the courts of India would be able to interpret those provisions with less ambiguity:

> It is undoubtedly true that the draft has borrowed from other constitutions and notably from the Government of India Act, 1935. But so long as the borrowings have been adapted to India's peculiar circumstances, they cannot in themselves be said to constitute a defect. Most modern constitutions do make full use of the experience of other countries, borrow whatever is good from them and reject whatever is unsuitable. To profit from the experience of other countries or from the past experience of one's own is the path of wisdom. There is another advantage in borrowing not only the substance but even the language of established constitutions; for we obtain in this way the benefit of the interpretation put upon the borrowed provisions by the courts of the countries of their origin and we thus avoid ambiguity or doubt.[204]

---

[202] Article 124(3), Constitution of India.
[203] Jawaharlal Nehru, *Constituent Assembly Debates*, vol. 8, p. 247.
[204] Rau, *India's Constitution*, pp. 389–90.

Interestingly, Rau also advocated that the Indian Constitution should not be too rigid or unamendable in its initial years, for two reasons. First, because the Constituent Assembly of India itself had been elected by provincial legislative assemblies and other bodies not based on universal adult suffrage, and some of its members had been nominated instead of being elected. Second, conditions in India were changing rapidly, and the country was in a 'state of flux', politically and economically.[205] This article provides a significant insight into the value of the original text of the Indian Constitution. One of the chief draftsmen of the Constitution itself, B.N. Rau, believed that the Constitution was perhaps not as legitimate as it ought to have been. For this reason, its original text was entitled to lesser deference than is ordinarily accorded to constitutions generally—and he advocated that the Constitution's text should be amended easily.

This is important to keep in mind because it will be seen in Chapter 2 that in 1993,[206] the Supreme Court of India expressly rejected the value choices of the framers of India's Constitution, and seized the power to appoint judges, despite the textual commands of the Indian Constitution. B.N. Rau's article, where he questions the legitimacy of the Constituent Assembly of India, perhaps offers justification for ignoring original intent in the Indian Constitution.[207]

* * *

This historical backdrop to the establishment of the Supreme Court of India offers telling insights into practices that would gain prevalence in the Supreme Court later. It tells us that informal selection criteria were employed while making appointments to the Federal Court of India. First, the Government of India Act, 1935 did not prescribe any religious or racial 'quotas' for the court. Yet, its three members were always British, Hindu, and Muslim respectively. This was despite the fact that Tej Sapru, an Indian representative at the Third Round Table Conference, had specifically argued that religious and racial considerations should not prevail while making appointments to the court. The Act did not prohibit Indians from becoming the Chief Justice of

[205] Rau, *India's Constitution*, pp. 393–4.
[206] *Supreme Court Advocates on Record Association* v. *Union of India*, AIR 1994 SC 268.
[207] See Abhinav Chandrachud. 2011. *Due Process of Law*. Lucknow: Eastern Book Company, pp. 66–72.

the Federal Court. Yet, Varadachariar was overlooked for appointment as Chief Justice when Gwyer retired, and an outside British
lawyer was appointed to the post. Second, the Joint Committee on
Indian Constitutional Reform had hoped that ICS judges would be
appointed to the court, to bring 'diversity of perspectives' to the
court. This did not happen. Instead, informally, the court's judges
brought diversity of a different kind to the court—geographic
diversity. Third, after 1947, all of the court's judges were former
high court judges, despite the fact that the Act permitted lawyers
to be appointed to the court, and although previously, 50 per cent
of the court had consisted of lawyer-politicians. All this points to
the fact that informal selection criteria were employed in making
appointments to the Federal Court of India—the Supreme Court's
predecessor. It will be seen that many of these informal selection
criteria either continued on the Supreme Court or found their way
into the Court again, in the form of regional representation, the
appointment of minority judges, and the overwhelming dominance
of high court judges on the Supreme Court.

The tenure of judges who ended their judicial careers as Federal
Court judges[208] was remarkably short. At a mean of only 4.5 years,
the pre-independence Federal Court tenure would perhaps set the
tone for the length of terms that future judges on the Supreme Court
of India would serve in office.

History also enables us to ask questions of the present. The chief
architect of India's Constitution, B.R. Ambedkar, strongly criticized
a proposal to make the opinion of the Chief Justice of India in the
matter of appointing judges binding on the executive, calling this a
'dangerous proposition'. However, it will be seen in Chapter 2 that
in 1993,[209] the Supreme Court of India seized the power to appoint
judges, and in effect, accepted the proposal that was rejected by the
Constituent Assembly of India. The 1993 judgment of the Supreme
Court analysed in Chapter 2 (termed the Second Judges case) would
therefore be remarkable for its express rejection of the value choices
of the framers of India's Constitution. The political emergency of

[208] This does not include Harilal J. Kania, Fazl Ali, Patanjali Sastri, M.C. Mahajan,
B.K. Mukherjea, and S.R. Das, whose judicial careers ended as Supreme Court
judges or chief justices.
[209] *Supreme Court Advocates on Record Association* v. *Union of India*, AIR 1994 SC 268.

1975 taught the Supreme Court that the framers' express textual value choices were not capable of always offering the 'right' answers to constitutional questions, and the doctrine of 'original intent' has always been weak in India ever since.[210] The 1993 judgment of the Supreme Court contributes to a steady stream of jurisprudence which directly contradicts the value choices of the framers of India's Constitution, and virtually negates the theory of original intent in the Indian context.

One must also ask if some of the justifications offered in support of law enacted in 1950 still hold true today. For example, the retirement age of 65 for Supreme Court judges was adopted under vastly different circumstances than those that prevail today. Perhaps it is time for the retirement age of Supreme Court judges to be increased to 70, particularly when politicians in India typically serve in office until much later. It will also be shown in Chapter 4 that the 'retirement age gap' is no longer necessary, as the justification that was offered in its support is no longer empirically true—that senior high court judges and high court chief justices no longer need the 'inducement' or incentive of extra years of service as a judge in order to agree to serve on the Supreme Court of India. Further, it is doubtful if Ambedkar's justification concerning why Supreme Court judges should be permitted to secure post-retirement government employment still holds true today. Ambedkar argued that the Indian judiciary only decides cases in which the government has a 'remote' interest, and that therefore, the possibility of the government influencing the conduct of a judge was 'very remote'. However, the docket of the Supreme Court today contradicts this argument. Not merely is the government one of the largest litigants before the Court, but the 'high-stakes' nature of the cases brought by and against the government before the Supreme Court makes it necessary for India's legislators to reconsider whether judges should be entitled to secure post-retirement employment with the government.[211]

---

[210] See Chandrachud, *Due Process of Law*.
[211] Of course, the government could argue that offering judges post-retirement employment is important because it takes away any incentive that judges might have to accept bribes while on the Court in order to make provisions for their future after retirement.

2

THE JUDGES CASES

INDIA IS A FEDERAL[1] COUNTRY with a strong central government,[2] and 28 states with a unitary court structure[3] running through its fabric. India has not followed the Kelsenian 'continental model' of institutional design, where the power of constitutional judicial review is centralized in one constitutional court. Instead, the power of constitutional adjudication in India is dispersed, shared between

---

[1] For a discussion of early federalism in India, see Alice Jacob. 1968. 'Centre-State Governmental Relations in the Indian Federal System', *Journal of the Indian Law Institute*, 10(4): 583–636.
[2] The Central Government has the power to dissolve state legislative assemblies. Article 356, Constitution of India. But see *S.R. Bommai* v. *Union of India*, AIR 1994 SC 1918, holding that the power to dissolve state assemblies is subject to judicial review. See further, Soli Sorabjee. 1994. 'Decision of the Supreme Court in S.R. Bommai v. Union of India: A Critique', *Supreme Court Cases*, (available online at http://www.ebc-india.com/lawyer/articles/94v3a1.htm). India has been termed a 'prefectorial' federal country. H.M. Rajashekara. 1997. 'The Nature of Indian Federalism: A Critique', *Asian Survey*, 37(3): 245–53, p. 246.
[3] See George H. Gadbois, Jr. 1969. 'Selection, Background Characteristics, and Voting Behavior of Indian Supreme Court Judges, 1950–1959', in Glendon Schubert and David J. Danelski (eds), *Comparative Judicial Behavior: Cross-cultural Studies of Political Decision-making in the East and West*. New York: Oxford University Press, p. 221.

the Supreme Court of India, and the high courts of each state. Subordinate courts are not empowered to decide constitutional cases. High court decisions may, under certain circumstances,[4] be appealed before the Supreme Court, the court of last resort. The Supreme Court functions not merely as an appellate court but also as a court of first instance, particularly in cases involving violations of 'fundamental rights' contained in Part III of India's Constitution. Accordingly, individuals can file cases directly before the Supreme Court claiming a violation of fundamental rights.[5]

India's Constitution was designed to ensure that Supreme Court judges enjoy security of tenure. Once appointed to the Court, they cannot be removed except by a strenuously difficult impeachment process,[6] their tenures cannot be shortened[7] or renewed,[8] and their privileges and allowances cannot be altered to their disadvantage.[9] However, in the 1970s, the Indira Gandhi government attempted to interfere with this structural judicial independence by controlling 'promotions' on the Supreme Court of India, that is, by superseding senior judges who had decided cases against the government. Between 1973 and 1977, the Indira Gandhi government interfered with what is referred to here as the 'seniority norm', that is, an unwritten practice which dictates that when the Chief Justice of India retires, the most senior puisne judge on the Court at the time

[4] A high court decision can be appealed if: (a) the high court grants a certificate of appeal, (b) if the case is a criminal case, where the high court either reverses an order of acquittal and sentences the accused to death, or if the high court withdraws a case from a lower court to hear it itself and sentences the accused to death, or (c) if the Supreme Court grants special leave to appeal. Articles 132, 133, 134, 135, and 136, Constitution of India.

[5] Article 32, Constitution of India.

[6] Article 124(4), Constitution of India. See further, proviso (b) to Article 217(1), Constitution of India. So far, not a single judge has been successfully removed in this manner.

[7] Supreme Court judges retire at the age of 65. Article 124(2), Constitution of India.

[8] Retired Supreme Court judges can, however, be offered extensions, but not as permanent Supreme Court judges, only as retired judges. Article 128, Constitution of India.

[9] Proviso to Article 125(2), Constitution of India. See further, proviso to Article 221(2), Constitution of India.

becomes the next Chief Justice of India, where seniority is measured by length of service on the Supreme Court.[10] These and other attempts to tamper with judicial independence made the Indian judiciary suspicious of executive control over judicial appointments, and when political power at the centre weakened, the Supreme Court seized the power to appoint judges.

This chapter traces the political developments that led to the present system of appointing judges to the Supreme Court of India, under which the five most senior judges of the Supreme Court (including the chief justice) appoint Supreme Court judges. The chapter begins by analysing the seniority norm in the Supreme Court—its historical origins in the high courts of India, and two highly political derogations from this principle that precipitated the Court's subsequent usurpation of the power to appoint judges. This chapter will examine political attempts to tamper with the composition of the judiciary, and the Supreme Court's responses to these attempts—the three Judges cases. It will be demonstrated that this development, that is, the Court's usurpation of the power to appoint judges, coincided in time with the weakening of political power at the centre, which supports Mark Ramseyer's thesis that judicial independence comes into being under conditions of repeated elections and electoral competition.[11] I conclude by finding that the 1993 and 1998 decisions of the Supreme Court did not enhance the structural independence of Supreme Court judges—instead, it enhanced the structural independence of high court judges, while simultaneously enhancing the institutional independence of the Supreme Court of India from a separation of powers standpoint.

THE SENIORITY NORM

The Supreme Court of India came into being on 26 January 1950, when India's new Constitution came into force. Harilal J. Kania, Chief Justice of the Federal Court of India, now became Chief

---

[10] See Abhinav Chandrachud. 2012. 'Supreme Court's Seniority Norm: Historical Origins', *Economic and Political Weekly*, 47(8): 26–30.
[11] Mark J. Ramseyer. 1994. 'The Puzzling (In)dependence of Courts: A Comparative Approach', *Journal of Legal Studies*, 23(2): 721–47.

Justice of the Supreme Court.[12] Nearly three years before then, when William Patrick Spens had resigned from the post of Chief Justice of India, Kania had become the first Chief Justice of India to obtain office by the rule of seniority: he was the most senior puisne justice on the Federal Court on the eve of Spens' resignation from the court. However, at the time, the fact that the most senior judge was becoming the chief justice of a court would have been considered an aberration rather than accepted convention.[13] Kania's appointment took place despite the fact that Prime Minister Nehru, in a private letter to the home minister, had expressed doubts about whether Kania should become Chief Justice of the Supreme Court.[14] Kania's appointment as Chief Justice of India was significant for two reasons: (*a*) he was the first Indian Chief Justice of India and (*b*) he was appointed to the post as the most senior puisne judge on the Court on the eve of the resignation of the outgoing Chief Justice of India.

During that decade, the principle that the most senior judge should become Chief Justice of India crystallized into an informal norm or constitutional convention. When Kania passed away in November 1951,[15] bringing a premature end to his term, it was rumoured that the government was contemplating appointing somebody other than the next most senior justice on the court (Patanjali Sastri) to the post

[12] Article 374(1) of the new Constitution provided that the judges of the Federal Court holding office immediately before the commencement of the Constitution would automatically become judges of the Supreme Court. This provision also applied to the post of Chief Justice. *See* Second Schedule, Part D, Paragraph 9(3) (a), Constitution of India.

[13] It will be recalled that when the first Chief Justice of the Federal Court, Maurice Gwyer, retired in June 1943, the most senior puisne judge on the court, S. Varadachariar, was overlooked for appointment as Chief Justice of India. Therefore, when Spens resigned as Chief Justice in 1947, there was no convention that the post would devolve upon the next most senior judge on the Court, and anybody could have been appointed to the post. See further, Chandrachud, 'Supreme Court's Seniority Norm'.

[14] Letter dated 23 January 1950. Granville Austin. 2003. *Working a Democratic Constitution: A History of the Indian Experience.* New Delhi: Oxford University Press, pp. 125–6.

[15] *Times of India.* 1951. 'Mr. Harilal Kania Dead: First Indian Chief Justice at Center', *Times of India,* 7 November, p. 1.

of chief justice.[16] But all the judges who were on the Court at the time threatened to resign if Sastri were not appointed chief justice, and if the norm of seniority were not followed.[17] Accordingly, the post of Chief Justice of India next went to Sastri, the most senior judge on the Court. In that decade, six chief justices served on the Court, and each was the most senior puisne judge on the Court on the eve of his appointment as Chief Justice of India.[18] The sixth chief justice later wrote that it was 'unwritten law' that the 'Chief Justiceship would go to the seniormost Judge of the Supreme Court'.[19] The shortest

---

[16] In fact, the Home Minister, K.N. Katju, asked the Attorney General of India, M.C. Setalvad, whether he was interested in taking Kania's place as Chief Justice of India, referring to a custom prevalent in England where the Attorney General replaces the Lord Chief Justice. Setalvad reminded the home minister that he had already surpassed the retirement age. Motilal C. Setalvad. 1970. *My Life: Law and Other Things*. London: Sweet and Maxwell, p. 185. Apparently, Setalvad suggested to the home minister that M.C. Chagla, Chief Justice of the Bombay High Court, be considered for the post. M.C. Chagla. 1974. *Roses in December: An Autobiography*. Bombay: Bharatiya Vidya Bhavan, p. 171. See further Vijay Gupta. 1995. *Decision Making in the Supreme Court of India*. Delhi: Kaveri, p. 30. It is said that the government then intended to appoint a junior Supreme Court justice, possibly B.K. Mukherjea, to the post of chief justice. K.S. Hegde. 1973. 'A Dangerous Doctrine', in Kuldip Nayar (ed.), *Supersession of Judges*. New Delhi: Indian Book Company, p. 47.

[17] Chagla, *Roses in December*, p. 171. The Law Commission of India has referred to this incident in its 121st report. Law Commission of India. 1987. *One Hundred Twenty-First Report on a New Forum for Judicial Appointments*. New Delhi: Law Commission, Government of India, p. 4, para. 1.14.

[18] After the Law Commission's 14th report was published, a story began to do the rounds that the Attorney General, M.C. Setalvad, had recommended that the next two most senior judges after Sastri—Justices Mahajan and Mukherjea—be superseded after Sastri retired, although Setalvad later wrote that this was false. In response to the rumours at the time, Mahajan and Mukherjea each threatened to resign. Setalvad, *My Life*, p. 190. Another rumour which seemed to have done the rounds at the time was that Justice Mukherjea was going to be appointed chief justice over Mahajan, when Sastri resigned. Austin, *Working a Democratic Constitution*, p. 134. This might have been because of Nehru. Mukherjea resisted the attempt. See Fali S. Nariman. 2013. 'Remembering Justice H.R. Khanna', The 4th H.R. Khanna Lecture delivered at the Indian Institute of Public Administration, New Delhi, 3 July. Nariman says that Mukherjea's portrait hangs in the Supreme Court because he did not agree to supersede Mahajan.

[19] B.P. Sinha. 1985. *Reminiscences and Reflections of a Chief Justice*. Delhi: B.R. Publications, pp. 71–2.

term was served by M.C. Mahajan, at a little under a year, while the longest term was served by B.P. Sinha at over four years.

In September 1958, the Law Commission of India, an expert legal advisory body constituted by the government, submitted its 14th report to the government, which outlined suggestions for reform in the judicial administration of the country. The commission's members were distinguished legal scholars, and its opinion carried great weight. In fact, in March 1957, four judges of the Supreme Court of India, including the Chief Justice of India, testified before the commission as witnesses.[20] India's first Attorney General, M.C. Setalvad, was the commission's chairman, while M.C. Chagla (Chief Justice of the Bombay High Court), K.N. Wanchoo (Chief Justice of the Rajasthan High Court, and later, Chief Justice of India), and S.M. Sikri (Advocate General of Punjab, and later, Chief Justice of India) were some of its members. Amongst the various suggestions in its report, which spanned two volumes and over 1,200 pages, the Law Commission highlighted certain problems in the manner in which judges were being selected and appointed to the Supreme Court. First, the Law Commission noted that judges were being appointed to the Supreme Court of India on communal and regional grounds, despite the fact that Chief Justice Kania had, during his inaugural speech at the Supreme Court, mentioned that merit was to be the basis of selecting judges. It was hinted that such considerations were perhaps prevalent because of the exercise of executive influence in the appointment process:

> It is widely felt that communal and regional considerations have prevailed in making the selection of the Judges. The idea seems to have gained ground that the component States of India should have, as it were, representation on the Court. Though we call ourselves a secular State, ideas of communal representation which were viciously planted in our body politic by the British, have not entirely lost their influence. What perhaps is still more to be regretted is the general impression that now and again executive influence exerted from the highest quarters has been responsible for some appointments to the Bench.[21]

[20] Setalvad, *My Life*, p. 254.
[21] Law Commission of India. 1958. *Fourteenth Report: Reform of Judicial Administration*, vol. 1. New Delhi: Ministry of Law, Government of India, p. 34, para. 6.

Next, it was noted that although the Constitution of India prescribed wide eligibility criteria for appointment to the Supreme Court, no person had been appointed to the Supreme Court of India under the lawyer or 'distinguished jurist' categories, until then. The Law Commission noted that it was 'generally recognized' that India had not produced 'academic lawyers and jurists of note who could, as in the United States, be honoured with seats on the Supreme Court Bench'.[22] However, the Law Commission did not agree with the prevalent view which seemed to have gained ground in making judicial appointments that it was 'somewhat hazardous' to appoint judges to the Court without 'previous judicial experience'.[23]

> In our view, too great an emphasis seems to have been placed in the past on the need for judicial experience in the selection of Supreme Court Judges. Surely, if it was easy to know some distinguished members of the Bar who would have made thoroughly bad Judges it should be equally easy to recognize other distinguished members of the Bar who would have made extremely good Judges.[24]

The Law Commission recognized that the earnings of the 'leaders of the Bar' did not compare with the salaries paid to Supreme Court judges, but observed that this could be compensated by appointing lawyers to the court young, so that they would have a 'fairly long tenure on the Bench'.[25] Importantly, the Law Commission recommended that judges on the Supreme Court be given at least 10 years in office, a sufficiently lengthy tenure. However, the Law Commission did not feel justified in recommending an increase in the retirement age from 65 to 70, finding that this would be 'an experiment fraught with hazards'.[26] The recommendations of the Law Commission with respect to the age of appointment to the Supreme Court of India are especially prescient, and are reproduced below because they bear special relevance to the discussion in Chapter 3:

> It has frequently been observed, that both, in the selection to the Bench of the Supreme Court as well as to that of the High Court, age and a certain

---

[22] Law Commission, *Fourteenth Report*, p. 35, para. 8.
[23] Law Commission, *Fourteenth Report*, p. 35, para. 9.
[24] Law Commission, *Fourteenth Report*, p. 36, para. 10.
[25] Law Commission, *Fourteenth Report*, p. 37, para. 12.
[26] Law Commission, *Fourteenth Report*, p. 38, para. 16.

amount of maturity are essential. It appears to us that this view not unoften favours experience at the expense of ability. We have known of very distinguished Judges and Chief Justices who were called upon to occupy their offices at a fairly young age when they were but rising junior members of the Bar. There is no reason why younger Judges of the High Courts who have shown marked ability should not be appointed to the Supreme Court Bench.... It must not be forgotten that youth carries a freshness and vigour of mind which have their advantages as much as maturity and experience flowing from age.[27]

The Law Commission also noted that the practice of appointing senior high court judges to the Supreme Court of India had the potential of destabilizing the Court, because judges were consequently not getting to serve on the Supreme Court for sufficient lengths of time.

The selection, mainly of persons who have retired or are about to retire from the High Court Bench as Judges of the Supreme Court, has resulted in those chosen having a very short tenure on the Bench. In our view, it is undesirable that a person who would have a short tenure of office should be chosen as a Judge of the Court. It is imperative in the interests of the stability of the judicial administration of the country that a Judge of the Supreme Court should be able to have a tenure of office of at least ten years. Too frequent a change of personnel has its disadvantages in a Court whose decisions lay down the law of the land and are binding on all the Courts in India. Certainty in the law and a continuity in the approach to some basic questions are fundamental requisites and these tend to be impaired if judicial personnel is subject to frequent changes.[28]

The Law Commission also observed that the Chief Justice of India should get to serve a tenure of at least five to seven years, as continuity in the office of the Chief Justice of India was essential in the interests of judicial administration.

[The Chief Justice's] importance in the scheme of judicial administration outlined in our Constitution cannot be over-emphasized.... In the quick succession to the office at present in vogue, a Chief Justice who has succeeded in familiarizing himself with his many tasks becomes liable to retire before he can have time to put into force the principles and policies which he considers beneficial.[29]

[27] Law Commission, *Fourteenth Report*, p. 37, para. 13.
[28] Law Commission, *Fourteenth Report*, p. 37, paras. 13–14.
[29] Law Commission, *Fourteenth Report*, pp. 38–9, para. 17.

Most importantly, however, the Law Commission criticized the observance of the seniority norm in the Supreme Court of India.[30] It was suggested, both for the Supreme Court and for the high courts, that Chief Justices should be selected by keeping in mind the special needs of the office. The Law Commission believed that chief justices of India did not have to be the most senior puisne judges on the Court—they could be picked from amongst chief justices of high courts, 'puisne Judges of High Courts of outstanding merit', and 'distinguished senior members of the bar'.[31] The Law Commission observed:

> It has been a practice till now for the seniormost puisne judge to be pro-moted to be the Chief Justice on the occurrence of a vacancy.... It is obvious that succession to an office of this character cannot be regulated by mere seniority.... It is well accepted that the qualifications needed for a success-ful Chief Justice are very different from the qualifications which go to make an erudite and able judge.... It is, therefore, necessary to set a healthy con-vention that appointment to the office of the Chief Justice rests on special considerations and does not as a matter of course go to the senior-most puisne Judge.[32]

The Law Commission's report spurred considerable debate a few years later, in 1960, when the House of the People (Lok Sabha) con-sidered a bill to increase the number of judges on the Supreme Court of India.[33] The minister of state in the Ministry of Home Affairs made a statement in the House of the People that at least 'two experienced and competent advocates' had declined offers of direct judgeships on the Supreme Court.[34] Many members expressed their dissatisfaction with this state of affairs. Some argued that not enough lawyers had been offered direct judgeships on the Supreme Court. For example, Sadhan Gupta said that there were more than 'only two competent advocates ... throughout the country', and that other lawyers might have accepted judgeship offers, had they been asked.[35]

---

[30] Law Commission, *Fourteenth Report*, pp. 39–40.

[31] Law Commission, *Fourteenth Report*, p. 40, para. 18.

[32] Law Commission, *Fourteenth Report*, pp. 39–40, para. 18.

[33] Supreme Court (Number of Judges) Amendment Bill, *Lok Sabha Debates*, 10th Session, dated 27 April 1960, Second Series, vol. 43, no. 58, p. 14144.

[34] *Lok Sabha Debates*, 27 April 1960, p. 14151.

[35] *Lok Sabha Debates*, 27 April 1960, p. 14170.

Similarly, Easwara Iyer, hinted that not enough lawyers were being offered direct judgeships on the Supreme Court, and that the examples cited by the minister were 'two stray instances', which could be called 'exceptions to the rule, rather than the rule itself'[36]—the rule being that lawyers would consider it an 'honour' and a 'duty' to accept a judgeship on the Supreme Court. On the other hand, some members argued that only those lawyers, senior in age, were being offered judgeships on the Supreme Court, and were unwilling to accept judgeship offers because they would serve short terms in office,[37] and that young lawyers ought to be offered Supreme Court judgeships instead. For example, Ajit Singh Sarhadi felt that in ensuring that the 'talent of the bar' made its way to the Supreme Court, 'the age level should have no consideration'.[38] Sarhadi continued, '[T]he hon. Minister knows very well that judges have been appointed at a very young age in UK and USA.'[39] Another member, Satyendra Narayan Sinha, suggested to the minister of state that if he 'widens the area of selection and takes care to invite such persons as have already distinguished themselves at the Bar and *can look forward to a long career on the Bench*'[40] (emphasis supplied), then lawyers would not decline judgeship offers for the Supreme Court. There were, thus, two themes discernible from the debate on that day: first, that not enough lawyers were being offered Supreme Court judgeships, and second, that young lawyers (who would get to serve long terms on the Supreme Court on account of their age) were not being offered Supreme Court judgeships.

The minister responded by saying that high court judges were typically always former practising lawyers, so by appointing high court judges to the Supreme Court, the Supreme Court too had former lawyers on it. The minister added that since the Supreme Court was the 'highest court of justice' in India, appointments could not be made 'in a very general way', that appointments had to be

---

[36]   *Lok Sabha Debates*, 27 April 1960, p. 14211.

[37]   Since the age of retirement on the Supreme Court of India is 65, the older a person is on the eve of his appointment to the Supreme Court, the shorter his term on the Court will be.

[38]   Ajit Singh Sarhadi, *Lok Sabha Debates*, 27 April 1960, pp. 14202–3.

[39]   *Lok Sabha Debates*, 27 April 1960, p. 14203.

[40]   *Lok Sabha Debates*, 27 April 1960, p. 14217.

'confined to a select few', and that '[c]onsiderations of the highest merit, [and] considerations of the longest experience'[41] had to be taken into account before appointing judges to the Supreme Court.

Interestingly, many members expressed disagreement with some of the views of the Law Commission. For instance, Sarhadi argued in favour of regional representation on the Supreme Court of India:

> In the matter of recruitment to the Supreme Court, I respectfully submit that the Minister should consider one fact. Whereas efficiency, merit and talent should be the primary consideration for appointment of Supreme Court Judges, regional considerations also should be taken into account ... in a big country like ours, regional considerations cannot be overlooked ... we have to consider the interests of the sections of the people also while finalising the appointments.[42]

Similarly, disagreeing with the Law Commission's views on seniority, Iyer argued that seniority should not be ignored altogether, especially in staffing the positions of the chief justices of high courts, and he emphasized that ignoring seniority would 'invariably ... create a sense of frustration in the senior Judges'.[43]

The seniority norm in the Court made appointing judges to the Supreme Court more complicated. Since every judge on the Supreme Court retires at age 65, when a judge was appointed to the Supreme Court of India, it was possible to ascertain, on that very day, whether or not he would go on to become Chief Justice of India: the answer was usually[44] in the affirmative if he was younger than all the remaining judges on the Court. For this reason, the question of who became a Supreme Court judge was even more important, as it would, in all likelihood, determine who became Chief Justice of India.

In February 1964, the seniority norm was not observed for the first time in over a decade. When B.P. Sinha retired as Chief Justice of India, Syed Jaffer Imam was the next most senior puisne judge on

---

[41] *Lok Sabha Debates,* 27 April 1960, p. 14224.

[42] *Lok Sabha Debates,* 27 April 1960, pp. 14203–4.

[43] *Lok Sabha Debates,* 27 April 1960, p. 14210. On an unrelated note, Iyer also regretted that women were not being appointed judges on the Supreme Court.

[44] Assuming that the judge did not resign, or die in office, before becoming Chief Justice of India.

the Court. However, he was seriously ill,[45] having suffered repeated strokes, and having been 'incapacitated, physically and mentally'.[46] For this reason, the next most senior judge, P.B. Gajendragadkar, was made Chief Justice of India, and Imam was persuaded to resign by Prime Minister Nehru in February 1964.[47] Although Imam is reported as having resigned in January 1964, the decision to appoint Gajendragadkar as Chief Justice of India was announced 'nearly three months before Sinha was to retire',[48] which made it a supersession by any measure. This was the first 'supersession' in the Supreme Court of India.[49] However, the supersession went under the radar since it was not politically driven, but motivated only by reasons of expediency. Further, the Chief Justice of India was not picked from outside the Court, but from within the ranks of the Court itself, and even then, only the next most senior puisne judge was picked for the post. From February 1964 to April 1973, although there was 'persistent talk'[50] that two senior judges (J.C. Shah and S.M. Sikri) would be superseded,[51] especially after the 1969 split in the Congress party after which Mohan Kumaramangalam was rumoured to have been considered for the post of Chief Justice of India,[52] the next six chief justices of India were picked by the rule of seniority.

The Source of the Seniority Norm

The seniority norm, a 'simple, entirely objective, precisely measurable criterion',[53] had the potential to significantly impact the

---

[45] George H. Gadbois, Jr. 2011. *Judges of the Supreme Court of India: 1950–1989.* New Delhi: Oxford University Press, pp. 54–5.

[46] Hegde, 'Dangerous Doctrine'.

[47] Setalvad, *My Life*, p. 508.

[48] P.B. Gajendragadkar. 1983. *To the Best of My Memory.* Bombay: Bharatiya Vidya Bhavan, p. 159.

[49] Vijay Gupta has argued that this was not a supersession at all, since Imam was persuaded to resign a day before the outgoing chief justice retired. Gupta, *Decision Making*, p. 20. However, the fact that the announcement was made while Imam was still on the bench means that this could be termed a supersession.

[50] Hegde, 'Dangerous Doctrine', p. 47.

[51] Gupta, *Decision Making*, p. 21.

[52] Hegde, 'Dangerous Doctrine', p. 47.

[53] George H. Gadbois, Jr. 1982. 'Judicial Appointments in India: The Perils of Non-contextual Analysis', *Asian Thought and Society*, 7: 124–43.

Supreme Court's jurisprudence. The Supreme Court of India does not convene *en banc* or in plenary sessions. Its judges sit in benches or panels, usually of two judges. The Chief Justice of India is the one who determines how each bench is to be composed, and more importantly, he also determines the type of cases that each bench or panel will typically decide. The question of who becomes Chief Justice of India is, for this reason, very important.

But where did the seniority norm, or the norm that the post of Chief Justice of the Supreme Court of India should go to the most senior puisne judge, come from? In order to answer this question, I systematically went through law reports[54] published roughly between 1870 and 1950 for the High Courts of Bombay, Calcutta, Madras, and Allahabad—the first high courts established in India by letters patent consequent to the Indian High Courts Act, 1861, and also the High Court of Patna, another old and reputable court in British India. The law reports of these courts were examined to see if there was any evidence for the prevalence of the seniority norm.[55] Of the five high courts analysed,[56] there was evidence that the seniority norm was sparingly followed in some form only in two courts: Allahabad and Patna. Where the norm was in vogue, it was followed for a brief period of time only, and never too religiously. On both the Allahabad and Patna High Courts, three judges each were appointed as chief justice by the rule of seniority, that is, they were the most senior puisne judges on the court on the eve of their appointment as chief justice. In Allahabad this happened between 1932 and 1946, and in Patna between 1943 and 1950. In each case, the first person who became chief justice by virtue of his seniority on the court was an Indian judge, that is, he was not English, and he was the first Indian judge ever to have been appointed chief justice

[54] See Chandrachud, 'Supreme Court's Seniority Norm'. For information between 1870 and 1913, I went through the *Indian Law Reports*, *Indian Decisions*, and *Indian High Court Decisions*. For information between 1914 and 1950, I went through the *All India Reporter*.

[55] For a detailed note on the methodology used, see Chandrachud, 'Supreme Court's Seniority Norm'.

[56] It must be underscored that the analysis in this section relies on the accuracy of reporting in the law reports—the *Indian Law Reports*, *Indian Decisions*, *Indian High Court Decisions*, and *All India Reporter*.

of that court. However, one British judge on each of these courts became chief justice by virtue of the rule of seniority, so when and where the seniority norm was followed it was not confined only to Indian judges, although the appointment of an Indian judge as chief justice may have started the trend. Even on the Federal Court of India, the first chief justice to have been appointed by the rule of seniority (Kania) was an Indian. Thus, the seniority norm in three courts—the Federal Court, the Allahabad High Court, and the Patna High Court—was similar in that it began with the appointment of an Indian chief justice.

Approximately 15 per cent of the chief justice posts in five high courts were staffed by the most senior puisne judge on the court. Viewed as a cohesive whole, the seniority norm in the high courts of colonial India was an exception rather than a rule. The appointment in the 1950s of one Chief Justice of India after another on the rule of seniority, then, was an aberration.

SUPERSESSION OF JUDGES

Seniority Norm in the High Courts (1950–84)

After the new Constitution came into force in January 1950, though the executive technically had the power to appoint Supreme Court judges, and the Constitution only required the President of India to consult judges of the Supreme Court and high courts as he deemed necessary; in practice, appointments were almost always made with the consent of the Chief Justice of India.[57] With the coming into

---

[57] Gadbois, *Judges of the Supreme Court*, p. 7. Chief Justice B.P. Sinha wrote that he could 'personally testify to the fact' that the several home ministers who served on the cabinet between independence and 1964 consistently followed the policy of respecting the views of the Chief Justice of India in the matter of appointment and transfer of judges. Sinha, *Reminiscences and Reflections*, p. 98. Two Chief Justices of India, Gajendragadkar and Subba Rao, publicly declared that almost all appointments during their terms were made in accordance with their recommendations. S.P. Sathe. 1998. 'Appointment of Judges: The Issues', *Economic and Political Weekly*, 33(32): 2155–7. In his autobiography, Gajendragadkar wrote that the government would 'attach ... decisive importance' to the opinion of the Chief Justice of India and that this was a 'valid and basically sound' convention. Gajendragadkar, *To the Best of My Memory*, pp. 164–5.

force of the new Constitution, the unwritten seniority norm now became the rule, rather than the exception, on each of the high courts examined previously. Thus, in the High Courts of Bombay, Calcutta, Madras, Allahabad, and Patna, the most senior puisne judge on the eve of the retirement of the outgoing chief justice almost always became the next chief justice of the high court. Until the judges' transfer policy came into force in the mid-1980s (a policy by which the post of chief justice of a high court would only be staffed from amongst puisne judges at other courts) roughly between 1950 and 1985, the seniority norm was strictly followed on these courts.[58] A brief explanatory note on how seniority is measured is necessary: (a) When two lawyers are appointed to a high court on the same day, the lawyer who is 'senior', that is, who was registered with the

---

In 1959, the home minister, Govind Ballabh Pant, informed the Lok Sabha that 'since 1950, 17 judges have been appointed to the Supreme Court and each one of those Judges was nominated and recommended by the Chief Justice of India'. *Lok Sabha Debates*, 1959, 7th Session, Second Series, 28, col. 7521; Gadbois, 'Selection, Background Characteristics, and Voting Behavior', p. 222.

[58] I have arrived at my analysis in this section using the same methodology as the one used before, that is, by surveying the *All India Reporter* for each high court. This methodology would be unable to detect two kinds of peculiarities, and this section must therefore be understood in that context. First, assume that Justice X and Justice Y are appointed to High Court A on the same day, and Justice X is senior to Justice Y. Assume that the very next day, Justice X, the more senior judge, is transferred to High Court B. After several years, the *All India Reporter* for High Court A may show Justice Y as being the most senior puisne judge on High Court A at the time the outgoing chief justice retires. However, if Justice X has not retired from High Court B, Justice X may be considered the most senior judge for High Court A. Accordingly, if Justice Y is appointed Chief Justice of High Court A despite the fact that Justice X is a puisne judge on High Court B, Justice Y may be considered as having superseded Justice X. My methodology would be unable to detect such kinds of supersessions. However, I believe that such cases would be exceedingly rare because the judges' transfer policy had not yet come into being, so routine transfers were very rare, and 'punitive' transfers too were virtually unheard of until the Emergency. For this reason I do not believe this peculiarity poses a significant problem to the methodology I have adopted in this section. Second, it is important to remember that for high court judges, all-India seniority is not one of the defining criteria taken into account to make appointments to the Supreme Court. See for example, R.M. Sahai. 2005. *A Lawyer's Journey: An Autobiography*. New Delhi: Universal, p. 75.

state bar council prior in time, is considered the 'senior' judge. For this reason, in India, registering with the bar council is considered the single greatest priority after graduating law school. (*b*) If a lawyer and a judge are appointed to a court on the same day, the lawyer (called a 'bar judge') is considered senior.[59]

Consider the following example. Justice A is appointed to High Court X on 19 March 1991. Justice B is appointed to High Court Y on 22 February 1993. (My example draws on Justices D.K. Jain and R.V. Raveendran's appointment dates respectively. Despite being appointed to the high court after Justice D.K. Jain, R.V. Raveendran was appointed to the Supreme Court before Jain. However, for the reasons described, this would not be considered a supersession.) Intuitively, one would feel that Justice A is senior to Justice B, since he was appointed a high court judge first. However, this is not so, since all-India seniority is not overwhelmingly taken into account for appointing high court judges to the Supreme Court (cf. Interview 5). Accordingly, Justice B may become the senior-most puisne judge on High Court Y quicker than Justice A on High Court X, and Justice B may get appointed to the Supreme Court before Justice A, and this will not be considered a supersession. The seniority convention is relative to each high court and must be understood in that context. The methodology I am using will not be able to detect a judge's all-India seniority, but this would be unnecessary given that all-India seniority is not the single most relevant criterion taken into account while making appointments to the Supreme Court.

[59] Thus, for example, when Justices Santosh Hegde and R.P. Sethi were appointed to the Supreme Court of India on the same day, 8 January 1999, Santosh Hegde—the 'bar judge', was considered senior to R.P. Sethi, the Karnataka High Court Chief Justice. However, this seems to be a norm of convenience, which has at times been violated in the past. Thus, for example, when Kuldip Singh and four high court judges were appointed to the Supreme Court on the same day, 14 December 1988, all four high court judges were considered senior to Kuldip Singh, a 'bar' judge. This was particularly significant given that if Kuldip Singh were considered senior to the other four judges appointed on the same day as him, he would have become Chief Justice of India after M.N. Venkatachaliah retired. This did not happen, as Justice Ahmadi, one of the judges appointed on the same day as Kuldip Singh, considered 'senior' to Singh, retired as Chief Justice after Singh retired from the Court. See S.S. Sodhi. 2007. *The Other Side of Justice*. New Delhi: Hay House, pp. 294–8. Today, it is therefore unlikely that a lawyer appointed to the Supreme Court will be given 'seniority' over a high court judge appointed to the Supreme Court on the same day, if the lawyer and judge both have chances of becoming Chief Justice of India. Similar instances have been recounted to me by some retired Supreme Court judges when they were appointed to the high court, that is, although some were 'bar' judges, the subordinate court judge was given seniority (for example, Interview 5).

From 'Skirmishes' to Activism

Although the Supreme Court started out as a 'technocratic court'[60] in the 1950s, conflicts soon began to emerge between the executive and the judiciary, particularly in the area of property rights. S.P. Sathe elegantly documented the shift in the Court's stance from being a positivist court to an activist one.[61] Between 1950 and 1973, four confrontations took place between the executive and the judiciary, and with each confrontation the court grew increasingly estranged from the executive. The first confrontation took place in the case of *Sri Sankari Prasad Singh Deo* v. *Union of India*.[62] In a unanimous opinion the Court held in favour of the government. The second confrontation between the executive and the judiciary took place over a decade later, in the case of *Sajjan Singh* v. *Rajasthan*.[63] Once again, the Court unanimously dismissed the writ petitions filed against the government. However, this time, two judges[64] expressed doubts over the Sankari Prasad bench's reasoning. The Court's decision in the Sajjan Singh case was handed down on 30 October 1964, five months after Prime Minister Nehru's death. In the three national elections that independent India had seen under Nehru's leadership, the Indian National Congress party, Nehru's party, had never fallen to lower than 361 seats in the Lok Sabha, the lower house of Parliament. It controlled between 73.07 and 75.1 per cent of the Lok Sabha,[65]

---

[60] S.P. Sathe. 2002. *Judicial Activism in India: Transgressing Borders and Enforcing Limits.* New Delhi: Oxford University Press, p. 4.

[61] Sathe, *Judicial Activism in India.*

[62] AIR 1951 SC 458.

[63] AIR 1965 SC 845.

[64] Hidayatullah and Mudholkar.

[65] Election Commission of India. 1952. 'Statistical Report on General Elections, 1951, to the First Lok Sabha, Volume I', available online at http://eci.nic.in/eci_main/StatisticalReports/LS_1951/VOL_1_51_LS.PDF; (last accessed on 12 March 2012); Election Commission of India. 1958. 'Statistical Report on General Elections, 1957, to the Second Lok Sabha, Volume I', available online at http://eci.nic.in/eci_main/StatisticalReports/LS_1957/Vol_I_57_LS.pdf (last accessed on 12 March 2012); Election Commission of India. 1963. 'Statistical Report on General Elections, 1962, to the Third Lok Sabha, Volume I', available online at http://eci.nic.in/eci_main/StatisticalReports/LS_1962/Vol_I_LS_62.pdf (last accessed on 12 March 2012).

staggering majorities measured by any standard. Therefore, it is important to bear in mind that the doubts over the Court's previous unanimous opinion in the Sankari Prasad case were expressed by two judges at a time when the Central Government had lost one of its most credible and charismatic leaders. Granville Austin wrote that the first two confrontations between the executive and the judiciary were mere 'skirmishes'. The third was an out-and-out 'war'.[66] The case of *I.C. Golak Nath* v. *Punjab*[67] was heard by 11 judges. The Court ruled by a narrow majority of six to five: while reserving for the Court the power to investigate the legality of constitutional amendments on the one hand, the Court denied the petitioners in the case any relief on the other.[68]

The fourth general elections to the Lok Sabha in India were held during 15–21 February 1967.[69] The Court's decision in the Golak Nath case was pronounced on 27 February 1967, a week after the elections. In the 1967 elections, without the charismatic Prime Minister Nehru at its helm, the Congress party suffered a sizable loss of seats. It won 283 seats out of 520 in the Lok Sabha, and at 54.4 per cent of the house it still had a majority,[70] though its weakest majority in the history of independent India until then. E.P.W. da Costa, India's 'pioneer pollster'[71] would later term this the 'February, 1967, Revolution', noting that 'after 20 years of fairly barren political

---

[66] Austin, *Working a Democratic Constitution*, p. 198.

[67] AIR 1967 SC 1643.

[68] What made matters worse was that Subba Rao soon resigned from his position as chief justice and made an unsuccessful, though menacing, bid to become President of India. The Congress party's presidential nominee, Zakir Hussain, received fewer votes that year than any previous Congress presidential nominee had received, although he eventually won the election. Gadbois, *Judges of the Supreme Court*, p. 78.

[69] Norman D. Palmer. 1967. 'India's Fourth General Election', *Asian Survey*, 7(5): 275–91.

[70] Election Commission of India. 1968. 'Statistical Report on General Elections, 1967, to the Fourth Lok Sabha, Volume I', available online at http://eci.nic.in/eci_main/StatisticalReports/LS_1967/Vol_I_LS_67.pdf (last accessed on 12 March 2012).

[71] Ramachandra Guha. 2007. *India after Gandhi: The History of the World's Largest Democracy*. HarperCollins, p. 419.

stability' India had been 'launched on an uncertain sea'.[72] In 1969, a split occurred in the Congress party. The split was facilitated by a disagreement between Indira Gandhi and the old party leadership, the 'Syndicate', over who would succeed the recently deceased President of India, Zakir Hussain.[73] Indira Gandhi proposed the candidature of V.V. Giri, who eventually won. Soon after the schism in her party, Indira Gandhi called for national elections, and in 1971, her party, Congress (R), gained much of what it had lost in the 1967 election—a total of 352 seats out of 518, or 67.95 per cent of the house,[74] a two-thirds majority, which would be necessary to amend the Constitution. One of the planks of the Congress (R) party's manifesto during the 1971 election, an election in which Indira Gandhi used her famous '*Garibi Hatao*' (End poverty) slogan,[75] was that if elected, radical changes would be made to the Constitution.

The fourth and most momentous confrontation between the executive and the judiciary took place in 1972–3, in the case of *Kesavananda Bharati* v. *State of Kerala*.[76] Rumours had started to do the rounds that the government was preparing to 'pack' the Court in order to have the Golak Nath decision overruled.[77] On 24 April 1973,

---

[72] E.P.W. da Costa. 1967. 'Electoral Alliances, Not Voters, Swung Results against Congress', *Times of India*, 13 April, p. 10.

[73] Guha, *India after Gandhi*, pp. 437–40.

[74] Election Commission of India. 1973. 'Statistical Report on General Elections, 1971, to the Fifth Lok Sabha, Volume I', available online at http://eci.nic.in/eci_main/StatisticalReports/LS_1971/Vol_I_LS71.pdf (last accessed on 12 March 2012). However, the party won only 43.68 per cent of the votes polled. Upendra Baxi makes the argument that the majority of judges in the Kesavananda Bharati case denied the legitimacy of such a government. Upendra Baxi. 1980. *The Indian Supreme Court and Politics*. Lucknow: Eastern Book Company, p. 23.

[75] Guha, *India after Gandhi*, p. 543.

[76] AIR 1973 SC 1461.

[77] Austin, *Working a Democratic Constitution*, p. 269. At that point, the Court had 10 members on it. However, four judges (Bhargava, Mitter, Vaidialingam, and Dua) were due to retire very soon. Seven new judges were required on the Court. Five of these—S. Chandra Roy, Palekar, Khanna, Mathew, and Beg—were appointed to the Court very soon, during July–December 1971. Two more judges were appointed the following year—Dwivedi and Mukherjea, However, in the meantime, in November 1971, S. Chandra Roy suffered three heart attacks and passed away. Gadbois, *Judges of the Supreme Court*, p. 167. The Court now

a day before Chief Justice Sikri's last day on the Court, the Court virtually upheld every constitutional amendment under challenge.[78] However, the Court was deeply divided on the question of judicial review and the power of courts to test the constitutionality of statutes. By a slim seven-to-six[79] majority the Court held that the Constitution had an 'unamendable' or entrenched 'basic structure'.[80]

Punitive Supersession I

The next day it was announced on All India Radio that the next Chief Justice of India would be A.N. Ray—the fourth most senior puisne judge on the Court at the time, a judge who was not in the line of succession according to the seniority norm. At the time, the seniority norm was the rule rather than the exception, having been followed almost without exception for 23 years on the Supreme Court of India and the high courts. The three judges who had been superseded— Justices Shelat, Hegde, and Grover—had repeatedly held against the

---

needed an eighth appointment, and Chandrachud was the last member of the bench appointed to the Court, in August 1972. The Court now had 13 members. Seven of these—the new appointees—were supposedly hand-picked for the Court by cabinet ministers, S. Mohan Kumaramangalam, minister of steel and mines, S.S. Ray, minister of education, or H.R. Gokhale, minister of law. Austin, *Working a Democratic Constitution*, p. 269. A few days before the hearings began (31 October 1972), on 17 October 1972, a 14th member was added to the Court—A. Alagiriswami, presumably to help deal with the other cases on the Court at the time. Two of the four judges who retired that year (Vaidialingam and Dua) were also brought back to dispose of the other cases before the Court while 13 judges sat together for the first time in the history of the Court's existence.

[78] See Abhinav Chandrachud. 2011. *Due Process of Law*. Lucknow: Eastern Book Company.

[79] Justices Sikri, Shelat, Hegde, Grover, Mukherjea, Reddy, and Khanna were part of the majority on the question of the basic structure doctrine. Justices Ray, Palekar, Mathew, Beg, Dwivedi, and Chandrachud were part of the minority on the question.

[80] There was reason to believe that the government had expected this verdict in advance, and that some of its leaders had even secretly read drafts of the Court's opinions before they were declared. Austin, *Working a Democratic Constitution*, pp. 269–77.

government's position in many of the key confrontational cases. All three resigned.[81] The supersession of Justices Shelat, Hegde, and Grover created a national outrage.[82] The three superseded judges had clearly been punished by the government for holding against it.[83] In retrospect, however, the supersession was perhaps not all that unexpected to some of the judges on the Court.[84]

[81] Shelat heard the news first, and then contacted Hegde and Grover. Soon, all three of them met at Shelat's residence, where Sikri joined them. As a 'preliminary measure' the three judges applied for 10 days' leave (Hegde, 'Dangerous Doctrine', p. 47) but then each of the three superseded judges submitted their resignations to President V.V. Giri, a few hours after the new chief justice was sworn in at a 'simple ceremony' in the Ashoka Hall of Rashtrapati Bhavan. *Times of India.* 1973. '3 Superseded Supreme Court Judges Resign in Protest', *Times of India,* 27 April 27, p. 1. The three superseded judges boycotted the ceremony, as did the outgoing Chief Justice Sikri, who cited an illness in the family as his reason for being absent.

[82] See Kuldip Nayar. 1973. *Supersession of Judges.* New Delhi: Indian Book Company.

[83] Shelat had consistently held against the government starting with the Golak Nath case, in each of the defining confrontations between the executive and the judiciary. For the government, Hegde's crime was not merely the fact that he had held against the government in the cases enumerated above. In a case involving an election petition alleging corrupt practices against Prime Minister Indira Gandhi, Hegde had ruled that the evidence against her was admissible. Austin, *Working a Democratic Constitution,* p. 281. The supersession perhaps even had Hegde as its main target. Later, Hegde wrote that he had suspected that he might be superseded when it came his turn to be appointed Chief Justice of India, although he had not expected the same fate for his colleagues, Shelat and Grover. Hegde, 'Dangerous Doctrine', p. 46. The third superseded judge, A.N. Grover, had survived an attempt on his life in March 1968, in open court, when a deranged man with a knife luckily got no further than inflicting a few cuts on his scalp. M. Hidayatullah. 1981. *My Own Boswell.* New Delhi: Gulab, pp. 218–20. Now, five years later, this was perhaps the unkindest cut of all.

[84] State counsel appearing in the Kesavananda Bharati case had publicly alluded to 'the alternative of "political" action' if the court's rulings 'did not find favor with the Government'. N.A. Palkhivala. 1974. *Our Constitution: Defaced and Defiled.* New Delhi: Macmillan, p. 93. Justice K.K. Mathew, a judge even more junior than Ray, the eighth most senior puisne judge at the time, had apparently been offered the post of Chief Justice of India first, but he had declined. Gadbois, *Judges of the Supreme Court,* 193n7. A.N. Ray was likely to have known of his own appointment in advance. However, the outgoing Chief Justice Sikri and the three superseded judges were taken by surprise.

The 'driving force behind the supersession',[85] and its most vocal proponent, S. Mohan Kumaramangalam, wrote a book[86] justifying the government's position. Relying on the Law Commission's 14th report, which had criticized the seniority norm, Kumaramangalam argued that it was necessary to examine the 'philosophy' of judges, their 'outlook on life' and their 'conception of social needs'. In chapter 6 of his book (pp. 71–2), after quoting Justice Benjamin Cardozo, and citing President Franklin Delano Roosevelt's attempts to 'pack' the court during the New Deal era (though forgetting to mention that the attempts had failed, and had stirred outrage), he compared the philosophies of Justices Hegde and Ray, finding 'fundamental differences' in their approaches to adjudication. Kumaramangalam argued that Hegde's opinions demonstrated his beliefs—that 'only the courts are of importance', that the 'judiciary are the "last bulwark of democracy"', and that 'judges are the only check on the Executive'.[87] Hegde, Kumaramangalam said, was 'not prepared to recognize that Parliament even represents the people or the people's will', while Justice Ray was clearly of that view.[88]

---

[85] Austin, *Working a Democratic Constitution*, p. 283.

[86] S. Mohan Kumaramangalam. 1973. *Judicial Appointments: An Analysis of the Recent Controversy over the Appointment of the Chief Justice of India*. New Delhi: Gulab.

[87] Kumaramangalam, *Judicial Appointments*, pp. 71–2.

[88] Kumaramangalam, *Judicial Appointments*, pp. 64–5. He cited numerous instances of the seniority convention not having been followed whilst making appointments to the Supreme Court of India, and a few such instances where the convention had not been followed while appointing chief justices of high courts, using them to justify the appointment of A.N. Ray. While he was right that appointments to the Supreme Court had not always been made from amongst the most senior judges in the country, he failed to mention that the few instances when junior judges were appointed high court chief justices over senior judges were exceptions to the rule—the evidence pointed overwhelmingly to the fact that the seniority convention had metamorphosed into an unwritten constitutional convention in the matter of appointing high court chief justices. At the time, there was perhaps some scope for the government to ensure that favourable high court judges would be appointed to the Supreme Court—by picking young judges for appointment to the Supreme Court, it was possible for the government to pick potentially favourable future chief justices of India. But to interfere with the seniority convention on the Supreme Court, once judges were appointed to the Court, was unacceptable.

The Emergency: Punitive Transfers and Punitive Supersession II

A little over two years after the first supersession had taken place, on 26 June 1975, in exercise of the powers conferred by Article 352 of the Constitution, the President of India, on the advice of the prime minister alone,[89] but not her cabinet, made a proclamation of Emergency in India. During an Emergency, the fundamental rights guaranteed by the Indian Constitution could be extinguished, even the right to life, and the right not to be arbitrarily detained.[90] On 27 June, the president suspended the right to move the courts to enforce fundamental rights. A series of politically motivated arrests followed, and as many as 676[91] of the government's political opponents were arbitrarily sent to prison. Many of the prime minister's political opponents went underground and some fled the country. The detention orders issued during the Emergency were challenged by Indira Gandhi's political opponents. Several high courts held in their favour. In response, the government transferred 16 high court judges, some of whom were chief justices, to other high courts without their consent. A list of 56 judges who had either been transferred, or who were proposed to be transferred, was prepared by the government, and then leaked in order to rattle the judiciary.[92] The government claimed that the transfers were in the national interest—in 1955, the States Reorganisation Commission had recommended that one-third the judges of each high court be appointed from outside the state in order to foster interaction amongst communities and to promote national integration. The government justified its actions on the ground that it was only relying on this suggestion. In 1955, the commission had written:

> Guided by the consideration that the principal organs of State should be so constituted as to inspire confidence and to help in arresting parochial trends, we would also recommend that at least one-third of the number of Judges in a High Court should consist of persons who are recruited from

[89] Austin, *Working a Democratic Constitution*, pp. 305–7.
[90] Article 359, Constitution of India. After the Emergency was lifted, the provision was amended by the Constitution (Forty-Fourth Amendment) Act, 1978, as a result of which Articles 20 and 21 can no longer be suspended during an Emergency.
[91] Austin, *Working a Democratic Constitution*, p. 309.
[92] H.M. Seervai. 1996. *Constitutional Law of India*, 4th ed., vol. 3. Bombay: Tripathi, p. 2698.

outside that State. In making appointments to a High Court bench, professional standing and ability must obviously be the over-riding considerations. But the suggestion we have made will extend the field of choice and will have the advantage of regulating the staffing of the higher judiciary as far as possible on the same principles as in the case of the Civil Service.[93]

However, the transfers appeared to be politically motivated and punitive, that is, designed to punish judges for deciding cases against the government. For 26 years before this, when a judge was transferred to another court, the transfer seldom occurred without his consent. This mass transfer of judges was stark for how it was effected without obtaining consent from any of the transferred judges. One such judge, Sankal Chand Himatlal Sheth, transferred from the Gujarat to the Andhra Pradesh High Court on 27 May 1976, challenged his transfer before the Supreme Court of India, although he took up his place on the Andhra Pradesh High Court. His case, decided later on, would constitute the first step in the tussle between the executive and the judiciary for the power to control the Court's composition.

In the meantime, the state governments filed appeals before the Supreme Court of India challenging the decisions where high courts had freed the government's political enemies. By a majority of four to one, the Court held in favour of the government. The writ of habeas corpus would not be available to arbitrarily arrested and detained individuals during the Emergency, the Court said. The case of *ADM Jabalpur* v. *Shivakant Shukla*,[94] or the 'Habeas Corpus case' as it came to be known, would go down as one of the low points of India's constitutional history. The only dissenting judge, Justice H.R. Khanna, held that the state did not have the power to deprive a person of his life or liberty without the authority of law. Previously, as part of the majority, Khanna had held against the government in the Kesavananda Bharati case. Now, in a minority of one, he wrote a courageous dissent. A.N. Ray would not convene another bench involving detention cases with senior judges on the bench.[95]

---

[93] Government of India. 1955. *Report of the States Reorganisation Commission.* New Delhi: Government of India, p. 233, para. 861.

[94] AIR 1976 SC 1207.

[95] Baxi, *Indian Supreme Court*, pp. 44–5. However, Baxi notes that the senior judges on the Court made no apparent attempts to restrain the chief justice either.

Justice Khanna paid the price. The Habeas Corpus case was decided on 28 April 1976. Nine months later, on 18 January,[96] Indira Gandhi decided to call elections, and 11 days later, when A.N. Ray retired on 29 January 1977, Khanna, the next most senior judge on the court, was superseded. Instead of appointing him Chief Justice of India, the government appointed M.H. Beg, next in the line of seniority. The presidential order appointing Beg was issued on 28 January 1977.[97] Khanna resigned that night, requesting that his resignation take effect on 12 March, until which time he would be on leave.[98] The government sought to justify the supersession on the ground that had he been appointed Chief Justice, Khanna would have served a very short term in office—five months and five days, of which 70 days would fall within the court vacation, so it was effectively only three months and nine days or a total of about 99 days in office—an insufficient tenure for a Chief Justice of India—while Beg, on the other hand, would serve 13 months in office.[99] However, a term of five months would not have been unusually short. Two of the 14 Chief Justices of the Supreme Court of India until then, A.K. Sarkar[100] and J.C. Shah,[101] had served shorter terms in office.

The two instances of supersession had taken place one after the other—Ray had superseded three judges after Sikri retired, and now Beg was made to supersede Khanna when Ray retired. The government was only continuing its policy of overlooking unfavourable judges for appointment to the post of chief justice, 'fully in keeping with the declared policy of the government'.[102] The seniority norm had not been reverted to ever since S.M. Sikri became the Chief Justice of India in 1971. Unlike the practice on the high courts before independence, a departure from the seniority norm did not entail appointing a lawyer

[96] *Times of India.* 1977. 'Lok Sabha Elections in March: Prime Minister Announces Further Relaxation of Emergency', *Times of India*, 19 January, p. 1.
[97] *Times of India.* 1977. 'Beg Is Named Chief Justice; Khanna Quits', *Times of India*, 29 January, p. 1.
[98] *Times of India*, 'Beg Is Named Chief Justice'; see further, H.R. Khanna. 1987. *Neither Roses nor Thorns.* Lucknow: Eastern Book Company, p. 89.
[99] *Times of India*, 'Beg Is Named Chief Justice'.
[100] 16 March–29 June 1966.
[101] 17 December 1970–22 January 1971.
[102] *Times of India*, 'Beg Is Named Chief Justice'.

or an outsider to the post of chief justice—it meant that a junior judge on the Supreme Court would be appointed to the post of Chief Justice of India, or 'rewarded' for his good work.

THE (FIRST) JUDGES CASE

After 21 months of Emergency rule, in the general elections held in March 1977, the Congress party secured only 154 seats[103] out of 542 or 28.41 per cent of the composition of the Lok Sabha—losing power at the centre for the first time in the history of independent India. It had been 'reduced to a party confined to the southern and western states'.[104] The Janata Party, formed only that January by the merger of four opposition parties,[105] won over 290 seats, or approximately 54 per cent of the strength of the house. The *Times of India* called the election a 'second liberation struggle'.[106] With the Congress party now out of power, and a coalition government at the centre, a con-stitution bench of the Supreme Court of India convened that year to decide the case of Sankal Chand Himatlal Sheth—the Gujarat judge who had been transferred to the Andhra Pradesh High Court during the Emergency.

In Justice Sheth's case,[107] the various opinions written by the Court seemed to narrow down to three questions: (*a*) Is a high court judge's consent required before he can be transferred to another court? (*b*) Does the constitutional requirement under Article 222 that the President of India must 'consult' the Chief Justice of India

---

[103] Election Commission of India. 1978. 'Statistical Report on General Elec-tions, 1977, to the Sixth Lok Sabha, Volume 1', available online at http://eci.nic.in/eci_main/StatisticalReports/LS_1977/Vol_I_LS_77.pdf (last accessed on 13 March 2012).

[104] *Times of India.* 1977. 'The Great Defeat', *Times of India*, 22 March, p. 8.

[105] These were Bharatiya Lok Dal (Charan Singh), Congress (Organization) (Asoka Mehta), Socialist Party (George Fernandes), and Jana Sangh (Atal Bihari Vajpayee and L.K. Advani). After the elections, Congress for Democracy, led by Jagjivan Ram, also joined the coalition. See *Times of India.* 1977. '4 Opposition Groups Form Janata Party', *Times of India*, 20 January, p. 1; *Times of India.* 1977. 'Janata Party is Born', *Times of India*, 2 May, p. 1.

[106] *Times of India*, 'Great Defeat'.

[107] *Union of India* v. *Sankal Chand Himatlal Sheth*, (1978) 1 SCR 423; AIR 1977 SC 2328.

before making transfers mean that the Chief Justice's opinion is binding on the president, that is, does 'consultation' mean 'concurrence'? (c) For what reasons can a judge be transferred to another court?[108] The Court pronounced its decision on 19 September 1977, but this decision would not be as significant as others later: the order transferring Justice Sheth had been issued under a different regime, and the new Janata government did not vehemently contest the previous Indira Gandhi government's stand on the transfer of judges.[109]

The Court unanimously answered the second question in the negative.[110] It was held that in consulting the Chief Justice of India before making a transfer, the president was not bound by his advice. However, the Court held that consultation constituted an important built-in safeguard against arbitrary transfers, and that the consultation accordingly had to be meaningful. Consultation, wrote Justice Krishna Iyer, must be 'real, substantial and effective consultation based on full and proper materials placed before the Chief Justice by the Government'.[111] The Court also held that if the president chose to ignore the advice of the Chief Justice of India, the Court could always look into the question of whether 'extraneous circumstances'

---

[108] The bench was composed of the three most senior judges on the Court (Chandrachud, Bhagwati, and Krishna Iyer), and two junior judges (Untwalia and Fazal Ali). The chief justice was not on the bench.

[109] In fact, on 26 August 1977, the Court issued an order recording a statement made by the attorney general that the transfers were illegal. The Court also recorded that Sheth withdrew his petition with the consent of the court. See *Union of India v. Sankal Chand Himatlal Sheth*, (1978) 1 SCR 423, 456. Under the 'mootness' doctrine, there was no reason for the Court to pass judgment in this case. However, the former government's attempts to tamper with the composition and courage of the judiciary prompted the Court to hear the case and write judgments that would serve as guidelines later. For this reason, however, the opinions written in this case must be measured against the common law principle that only a true adversarial contest between competing parties generates good law. This was a one-sided contest.

[110] On the first question, three judges held that in order to transfer a judge from one high court to another, his consent was not required. Justice Krishna Iyer (with Fazal Ali) held that if this were not so, the object of the law would be defeated and the chief justice would be rendered 'powerless'. The contention that a transfer to another court constitutes a fresh appointment to that court, necessitating consent, was rejected. Justices Bhagwati and Untwalia dissented.

[111] *Union of India v. Sankal Chand Himatlal Sheth*, (1978) 1 SCR 423, p. 501.

had entered the verdict. As Justice Krishna Iyer wrote, there would then be a 'high legal risk of invalidation'.[112] Noted constitutional scholar, H.M. Seervai, found that the Sankal Chand Sheth bench had instituted two important safeguards against arbitrary transfer: (*a*) 'full, fair and complete discussion' or consultation and (*b*) the risk of invalidation if the president did not abide by the decision of the Chief Justice of India.[113] For now, the Court had built certain important safeguards into the process of consultation with the Chief Justice of India, reserving for itself the power of judicial review if the president went against the advice of the chief justice.

After the Janata Party came to power, it was debated whether the government should tamper with the seniority norm once again, even if these debates were only aimed at undoing the evils set up by Indira Gandhi's Congress party during the Emergency. Accordingly, it was debated whether Chief Justice Beg should be asked to step down, and the superseded judge, H.R. Khanna, be made Chief Justice, to restore what he lost on account of his courage in the Habeas Corpus case. Then, when it was time for Beg to retire, a group of 52 'public men and lawyers' submitted a memorandum to the government seeking that the next two judges in the line of seniority (Chandrachud

---

[112] *Union of India* v. *Sankal Chand Himatlal Sheth,* (1978) 1 SCR 423, p. 502.

[113] Seervai, *Constitutional Law,* p. 2708. In answering the third question, the Court unanimously agreed that transfers could only be made in the public interest, and could not be punitive. However, there appeared to be some disagreement over what the word 'punitive' meant in this context. Justice Chandrachud appeared to distinguish between two kinds of punitive transfers, though this was not spelled out in the judgment. On the one hand, he held that a transfer made in order to punish a judge for deciding against the government was impermissible. On the other hand, he held that a judge could be transferred from one court to another for misconduct, for example, for favouring certain sections of the bar, for being casteist, or dishonest. Both types of transfers fall under the umbrella term 'punitive' in the Court's language—the first type of transfer punishes a judge's courage (as Seervai wrote, 'not for doing anything wrong but for doing right', *Constitutional Law,* p. 2802), the second type of transfer punishes his misconduct. Justice Chandrachud held that what can be termed a 'courage-punitive' transfer was impermissible, while a 'misconduct-punitive' transfer was permissible. There did not seem to be agreement on this. Justice Untwalia, for example, held that even 'misconduct-punitive' transfers would still be 'punitive', although they would be permissible if they were made with consent, and after complying with the rules of natural justice. This issue would resurface later on.

and Bhagwati), who had held in favour of the government in the Habeas Corpus case, be superseded—to punish these two judges for holding in favour of the government.[114] However, the Janata Party stood firm on the seniority norm, and none of these proposals ever went through.

On 10 August 1979, the Law Commission of India submitted a report to the government on the appointment of judges. Though the report was submitted to the government by Justice S.N. Shankar, Chairman of the Commission, he wrote in his prefatory letter to the law minister that the report had mainly been prepared by Justice H.R. Khanna when he was the chairman, and though it did not bear his signature, it bore his 'full concurrence'. This report was therefore of considerable weight. In its report, the Law Commission recommended that judges of the Supreme Court of India should be of the highest calibre.[115] Importantly, the Law Commission recommended that the Chief Justice of India consult the three most senior judges on the Court before making any recommendations to the president for the appointment of Supreme Court judges. Significantly, the report made recommendations concerning the optimum age of proposed appointees to the Court, the seniority norm, and regional representation on the Court.

Concerning age, the commission recommended that Supreme Court judges be appointed between the ages of 54 and 60 in order to ensure that mature individuals were appointed to the Court. The commission recommended 60 as the 'upper age limit' in order to ensure that the minimum term of office would be five years.

> We are conscious of the fact that there have been judges who have been appointed in the past to the court at an age less than 54 years and who have distinguished themselves. Looking, however, to all the facts and keeping in view the general rule, we consider that in future no appointment should be made of a person to the bench of the Supreme Court at an age less than 54.[116]

---

[114] *Times of India.* 1978. 'Chief Justice: Govt. Move Queried: Plea to JP on Judge's Selection', *Times of India,* 7 January, p. 1. See further, Gadbois, *Judges of the Supreme Court,* pp. 254–6.
[115] Law Commission of India. 1979. *Eightieth Report on the Method of Appointment of Judges.* New Delhi: Law Commission of India, Government of India.
[116] Law Commission, *Eightieth Report,* p. 30, para. 7.8.

The commission recommended that the seniority norm be observed in the matter of appointing the Chief Justice of India. The commission's recommendations concerning the seniority norm were especially significant because the report had mainly been prepared by H.R. Khanna, a superseded judge. Even so, the commission recommended that the seniority norm could be departed from, but only if the majority of all the judges on the Supreme Court of India so agreed.

> We feel that the principle of seniority should be observed in the appointment to the office of the Chief Justice. Past experience tells us that whenever there has been a departure from this principle, the appointment has roused considerable controversy. It has thus affected the image of the office of Chief Justice. The vesting of unbridled power in the executive to depart from the principle of seniority in the matter of appointment to the office of Chief Justice is liable to be abused. It is also likely to make inroads into the independence of the judiciary and the approach of the judges. In case the Government considers it proper in some individual case to depart from the principle of seniority for appointment to the post of Chief Justice, in such an event, in our opinion, the matter should be referred by the Government to a panel consisting of all the sitting Supreme Court Judges. The principle of seniority should be departed from only if the above panel finds sufficient cause for such a course. In case of difference of opinion, the decision of the majority shall be taken to be the decision of the panel.[117]

The commission also took note of the fact that appointments were made to the Supreme Court of India on regional considerations. Rather than dismissing this practice, it suggested that it be tied together with merit. In the opinion of the commission, regional representation was all right so long as the best person from the region was selected for appointment to the Supreme Court. This was perhaps a tacit rejection of the seniority criterion for appointing judges to the Supreme Court, which will be examined in Chapter 4.

> We are conscious of the fact in the matter of appointment to the Supreme Court, despite the need for selection on the basis of merit, regard is also had for representation of different regions. Even so, consistently with that also, it can be ensured that the best person from the region is appointed to the court.[118]

---

[117] Law Commission, *Eightieth Report*, p. 30, para. 7.9.
[118] Law Commission, *Eightieth Report*, p. 30, para. 7.10. Similarly, in its 121st report, the Law Commission of India noted that diversity factors were taken into account while making appointments to the Supreme Court of India. See text accompanying note 175 in this chapter.

FIRST JUDGES CASE

Background

On 15 July 1979, Morarji Desai resigned as Prime Minister of India.[119] His government had lost its majority, having 'bled from massive defections'.[120] Later that month, on 28 July 1979,[121] Charan Singh became Prime Minister of India, backed, of all people, by Indira Gandhi, whom he had once called a 'congenital liar'.[122] Barely a month later, Indira Gandhi withdrew support from the government, and the president ordered national elections on 22 August 1979.[123] The general elections were held during 3–6 January 1980. Indira Gandhi's Congress party (Congress [I]) won 353 seats out of 529, or 66.7 per cent of the composition of the house,[124] a two-thirds majority once more, sufficient to be able to amend the Constitution. The Janata Party performed dismally, finishing fourth, with 31 seats.[125]

On constitutional issues the Supreme Court of India stood firm. A Canadian scholar, Bhagwan D. Dua, interviewed the law minister,

---

[119] Peter Niesewand. 1979. 'Desai Quits to Stave Off Defeat', *Guardian*, 16 July, p. 1.

[120] Austin, *Working a Democratic Constitution*, p. 466. This was ironic, because after winning a majority in the Lok Sabha, the Janata Party was in a minority in the Rajya Sabha, the upper house of Parliament, and had actively encouraged defections from Congress party members. Now, defections brought an end to the Janata government.

[121] Kasturi Rangan. 1979. 'Singh Takes Office in India and Pledges Nonaligned Policy', *New York Times*, 29 July, p. 1.

[122] *India Today*. 1979. 'Politics of Uncertainty', *India Today*, 1(16), p. 12.

[123] This was a controversial decision, as President Sanjiva Reddy did not invite the leader of the opposition, Jagjivan Ram, to form the government. Jagjivan Ram's Janata Party needed only 65 votes more to prove a majority—it had 205 supporters in the house. *India Today*. 1979. 'Distasteful Controversy', *India Today*, 1(17), p. 9.

[124] Election Commission of India. 1981. 'Statistical Report on General Elections, 1980, to the Seventh Lok Sabha, Volume I', available online at http://eci.nic.in/eci_main/StatisticalReports/LS_1980/Vol_I_LS_80.pdf (last accessed on 14 October 2011).

[125] Election Commission, 'Statistical Report on General Elections, 1980'. Spinning a charkha in a bedroom at his flat in Bombay, Morarji Desai said that the election was Indira Gandhi's personal victory, denying that he lost power on account of his policies of prohibition. *Times of India*. 1980. 'It Is Indira's Personal Victory: Morarji', *Times of India*, 10 January, p. 3. The Times of India

Shiv Shankar, six high court chief justices, and eleven high court judges, and wrote that the 'battle lines' had been clearly drawn between the executive and the judiciary, particularly between the executive and the Chief Justice of India, who had been 'the anathema of the Congress (I) party for strongly thwarting the moves of the Gandhi government to pack the courts'.[126] Dua wrote:

> Though the entire judicial system was pressured to conform, the ruling party zeroed its attack on the *pater familias*. Unlike Justice Bhagwati, who was labeled as a Congress (I) man for his laudatory letter to Mrs. Gandhi, Chief Justice Chandrachud had a very low rating with the ruling household. Appointed Chief Justice of the Supreme Court of India by the Janata government—a disqualification in itself under the new regime—Chandrachud had not exactly endeared himself to the Gandhis for sending Sanjay to jail in 1978 or for turning volte face during the Janata period. By mid-1981, the estrangement between Chandrachud and the ruling party was so great that Askoke [*sic*] Sen, a Congress (I) MP and the President of the Supreme Court Bar Association, even hinted at his impeachment by Parliament. Undaunted, the Chief Justice continued to defend the judiciary against executive interference and called upon the Bench and Bar to be united as this was 'the only way we could fight the provocation and attack on the judges'.... Throughout 1980, the Chief Justice had refused to submit to pressures and made the government appoint eight chief justices to High Courts (and five judges to the Supreme Court) according to well-established constitutional practices. However, the government was getting desperately anxious not only to appoint its own loyal supporters to the Bench but also to transfer or 'weed out' some 115 High Court judges, half of whom were temporary, appointed by the Janata government.[127]

The Decision

Against this backdrop, almost two years later, the Supreme Court of India decided a case which posed another, more serious, challenge to the independence of the judiciary. The case of *S.P. Gupta* v. *President*

---

wrote that it was 'carnival time at the sunlit 12 Willingdon Crescent', Indira Gandhi's residence since her defeat in the 1977 elections, 'on [that] winter morning, with cheers and smiles and flowers everywhere'. *Times of India*. 1980. 'Flowers & Cheers Showered', *Times of India*, 8 January, p. 1.

[126] Bhagwan D. Dua. 1983. 'A Study in Executive-Judicial Conflict: The Indian Case', *Asian Survey*, 23(4): 463–83, p. 464.

[127] Dua, 'Study in Executive-Judicial Conflict', 474–5.

of India[128] would come to be known as the first Judges case. Three incidents precipitated the Court's decision. First, on 19 January 1981, the President of India transferred Justice M.M. Ismail, Chief Justice of the Madras High Court, to the Kerala High Court as chief justice, and Chief Justice K.B.N. Singh of the Patna High Court to the Madras High Court as chief justice. This was ostensibly part of the government's new policy that the chief justice of a high court would not serve on the same court as the court on which he served as a puisne judge.[129] Second, in March 1981, Indira Gandhi hinted at 'a large scale reshuffling of administrative and judicial services' to undo appointments made during 1977–9.[130] As the two-year terms of three 'additional'[131] Delhi High Court judges (Kumar, Vohra, and Wad) were about to expire, the government only extended their terms by three months. One of these judges in particular, O.N. Vohra, had held against Sanjay Gandhi in the *Kissa Kursi Ka* case,[132] and was perhaps seen as a political enemy.[133] Third, on 18 March 1981,

---

[128]   (1982) 2 SCR 365; AIR 1982 SC 149.

[129]   This was not the first time that high court chief justices had been transferred to other courts. During the Emergency, the several judges who had been transferred by the government included three chief justices: Chief Justice S. Obul Reddy from Andhra Pradesh to Gujarat, Chief Justice B.J. Divan from Gujarat to Andhra Pradesh, and Chief Justice P. Govindan Nair from Kerala to Madras. Now, the fresh transfer of two chief justices was perceived as a troubling return to the past. See *Times of India*. 1977. 'Transfer of High Court Judges to Be Nullified', *Times of India*, 6 April, p. 15. Later that year, Justice M.M. Ismail resigned. *Times of India*. 1981. 'Madras Chief Justice Resigns', *Times of India*, 9 July, p. 1.

[130]   She said that the Janata and Marxist governments had made political appointments to the high courts, and in a speech, publicly asked, 'Can we expect justice from those who are so closely connected with the Janata and Marxist governments'? *Times of India*. 1981. 'Janata Made Partisan Appointments: PM', *Times of India*, 17 March, p. 7.

[131]   An 'additional' judge is appointed by the president to a high court under Article 224 of the Constitution of India, if there is a 'temporary increase in the business of a High Court', or if there are 'arrears of work' at a high court.

[132]   V.C. Shukla, former minister for information and broadcasting, and Sanjay Gandhi, Indira Gandhi's son, were involved in destroying a film critical of the Congress party, *Kissa kursi ka* (The Story of the Seat). See *State Through Delhi* v. *Sanjay Gandhi*, AIR 1978 SC 961.

[133]   Later, these short-term extensions would become a 'frequent phenomenon' (Justice Tulzapurkar in *S.P. Gupta* v. *President of India*, [1982] 2 SCR 365, p. 891)

a circular letter addressed by the law minister, Shiv Shankar, to the Governor of Punjab and the chief ministers of the other states (except the north-eastern states), a copy of which was sent to the chief justice of each state, outlined the government's new judges' transfer policy. The letter requested that consent be sought from additional judges and from persons who were going to be appointed additional judges of the high courts—consent to be appointed or transferred to another high court. The letter outlined the goal of the government's new transfer policy, a goal which was ostensibly in keeping with the recommendation of the States Reorganisation Commission several decades ago.

It was believed that the new judges' transfer policy was intended to undo the guidelines issued by the Supreme Court in the Sankal Chand Sheth case.[134] As Justice Tulzapurkar pointed out in his judgment later on, the circular letter was issued at a time when 'politicians and persons occupying high positions had been indulging in a campaign of denigrating the higher Judiciary, treating every Court

---

across the high courts of the country, and one Supreme Court judge would remark that judges were being treated 'worse than clerks'. See Dua, 'Study in Executive-Judicial Conflict', pp. 472–6. This was particularly troubling given the fact that the system of appointing additional judges was now in vogue— before being appointed a permanent judge on a high court, a judicial candidate was first appointed an additional judge. As Justice Venkataramiah pointed out in his judgment (S.P. Gupta v. President of India, [1982] 2 SCR 365, p. 1285), this became a 'gateway' for entering the cadre of permanent judges. Justice Venkataramiah also wrote that ever since the seventh amendment to the Constitution (Constitution [Seventh Amendment] Act, 1956), nearly 500 high court judges were appointed in the country, and four-fifths of them were first appointed as additional judges, while only one-fifth were first appointed permanent judges (p. 1303). It was normal to expect that additional judges would be confirmed as permanent judges barring exceptional circumstances, and if they were not confirmed, their terms as additional judges would be extended—even the extensions were typically sufficiently long. Now, the growing prevalence of short-term extensions caused concern that the executive was creating disincentives against deciding cases against the government at the high court level. After all, if the government were given the discretion not to confirm an additional judge, the judge would have an incentive to hold in favour of the government.

[134] This was because of two reasons: (a) Where an additional judge was confirmed as a permanent judge but shifted to a high court other than the one on which he had served as an additional judge, there was some reason to believe that the transfer would be considered a fresh 'appointment', since the judge

decision adverse to Government as a deliberate and motivated attack on the Executive'.[135] A chief minister of a 'prominent state' had deprecated the 'Dictatorship of the Court'.[136] A cabinet minister in the Central Government had 'bracketed' the judiciary with opposition parties.[137] 'The highest executive head at the center' had said that the previous Janata government had made a number of political appointments.[138] This created an atmosphere of 'fear psychosis' in the 'not-so-sterner stuff' in the judiciary.[139]

Writ petitions were filed by lawyers in Bombay, Delhi, Madras, Allahabad, and Patna, on behalf of the judiciary, challenging the government's policy.[140] The seven judgments issued by the Court in the last week of December 1981 occupied 956 pages in the Supreme Court Reports—and qualified as the longest decision ever written by the Supreme Court of India.[141] In answering the questions[142]

would be considered as having been 'appointed' a permanent judge on the new court, as opposed to being considered 'transferred' to the new court. This was a clever way of circumventing the existing norms on judicial transfers, since Sankal Chand Sheth's case only applied to transfers of judges, but not to appointments. (b) By instituting a policy on the transfer of judges, it was believed that the government wanted to reduce the discretion of the Chief Justice of India in making recommendations concerning transfers.

[135] *S.P. Gupta* v. *President of India*, (1982) 2 SCR 365, p. 959.

[136] *S.P. Gupta* v. *President of India*, (1982) 2 SCR 365, p. 959. See further, *Times of India*. 1982. 'Judge Transfers: Nani Regrets Court Decision', *Times of India*, 22 January, p. 15.

[137] *S.P. Gupta* v. *President of India*, (1982) 2 SCR 365, p. 959.

[138] *S.P. Gupta* v. *President of India*, (1982) 2 SCR 365, p. 959.

[139] *S.P. Gupta* v. *President of India*, (1982) 2 SCR 365, p. 960.

[140] A bench of seven judges was constituted to hear the case. Again, the Chief Justice of India was not on the bench. Instead, the bench was composed of the six most senior judges on the Court at the time (Bhagwati, Gupta, Fazal Ali, Tulzapurkar, Desai, and Pathak), two (Bhagwati and Pathak) of whom were in the line of succession to the post of Chief Justice of India by the seniority convention; the seventh was a junior judge (Venkataramiah) on the Court, who was next in the line of succession to the post of Chief Justice of India, after the two prospective chief justices on the bench retired. Only two judges (Bhagwati and Fazal Ali) had served on the Sankal Chand Sheth bench. Bhagwan Dua wrote that the Court at the time was 'badly disunited', and 'backbiting' amongst judges had gained notoriety in legal circles. Dua, 'Study in Executive-Judicial Conflict', p. 477.

[141] Seervai, *Constitutional Law*, p. 2707.

[142] Stripped of its complex dimensions, there were essentially three questions before the Court: (a) whether the circular letter issued by the Law Ministry was

presented by the case, the Court deliberated upon six questions, broadly speaking: (*a*) whether transfers could only be made in the 'public interest', and whether 'public interest' included what has been termed in this study as 'misconduct-punitive' transfers, that is, transfers designed to punish a judge for misconduct, as distinguished from courage,[143] (*b*) whether the opinion of the Chief Justice

---

valid, (*b*) whether the fact that S.N. Kumar, (the Court did not consider the other two Delhi High Court judge's cases; Vohra did not appear before the court and Wad was given an extension of a year) an additional judge of the Delhi High Court, was not confirmed as a permanent judge, was valid, despite the fact that the Chief Justice of India was against the move, and (*c*) whether the transfer of Chief Justice K.B.N. Singh was valid, a question for which the Chief Justice of India was made to file an affidavit before the Supreme Court. All three questions were answered in the affirmative. There were two blocks of judges—Justices Bhagwati, Fazal Ali, and Desai held that the circular was valid, that the move to drop S.N. Kumar was valid, and the move to transfer K.B.N. Singh was invalid, while Justices Gupta, Tulzapurkar, and Pathak held that the circular was invalid, the move to drop S.N. Kumar was invalid, and the decision to transfer K.B.N. Singh was valid. Justice Venkataramiah tilted the scales, and answered all three questions in the affirmative. The result was that Justices Gupta, Tulzapurkar, and Pathak dissented on the first two questions (circular and S.N. Kumar), while Justices Bhagwati, Fazal Ali, and Desai dissented on the third question (K.B.N. Singh). However, in the process the Court issued important guidelines concerning the appointment and transfer of judges. Justices Bhagwati and Desai also expressed opinions concerning appointment criteria to be employed in the appointment of judges to the Supreme Court of India.

[143] The Court unanimously answered the first question in the affirmative. As in Sankal Chand Sheth's case, it was held that transfers could only be made in the 'public interest', and 'punitive' transfers were outside the ambit of public interest. However, there was a strong debate as to what transfers were 'punitive'. The majority seemed to agree that all kinds of punitive transfers—transfers punishing either courage or misconduct—were impermissible. Justices Tulzapurkar (*S.P. Gupta* v. *President of India*, [1982] 2 SCR 365, p. 942) and Pathak (p. 1193) each held that impeachment was the only way to remove a judge for misconduct. Referring to a speech made by B.R. Ambedkar in the Constituent Assembly, Justice Tulzapurkar (pp. 943–4) added that transfers were only permissible if they were designed towards, (*a*) bringing better talent to a court, (*b*) bringing chief justices from outside who were unaffected by local politics, (*c*) relocating judges who were unable to get along with the chief justice or his colleagues on account of their temperament, or (*d*) 'remedying unsatisfactory conditions obtaining in a High Court'. Similarly, Justice Bhagwati (pp. 673–4) held that whenever a judge was transferred on account of his conduct or behaviour, it would be by way

of India was to be given 'primacy' amongst the opinions of other constitutional functionaries (that is, the Chief Justice of a high court, and the governor of a state) by the president, while making an appointment to the High Court (this question arose because Justice S.N. Kumar at the Delhi High Court was dropped despite the opinion of the Chief Justice of India),[144] (c) whether the president was bound by the advice of the Chief Justice of India on the question of judicial appointments, that is, whether 'consultation' amounted to 'concurrence', (d) whether short-term extensions for additional judges were permissible,[145] (e) whether an additional judge had the right to be considered for confirmation as a permanent judge,[146] and (f) whether at the stage of appointment of an additional judge for a further term, the judge had to go through the test of 'suitability'.[147]

---

of punishment, and that this was consequently impermissible. Justice Gupta (pp. 705–6) seemed to agree with this proposition when he held that transferring a judge for his 'parochial tendencies' was a punitive transfer. Justice Desai (pp. 1111–15) too seemed to agree when he held that a judge transferred for being involved in a 'local factious atmosphere' would be punished and stigmatized, and that this sort of transfer was impermissible. The majority also agreed that the consent of a judge was not required before transferring him, and that transfers were not 'punitive' merely because a high court judge's consent had not been obtained. Justice Bhagwati dissented on this point, sticking to his stand in the Sankal Chand Sheth case, and he held that a judge could only be transferred with his consent, but he held in the alternative that 'punitive' transfers were impermissible.

[144] Dua, 'Study in Executive–Judicial Conflict', p. 477.

[145] On the fourth question, there was general agreement that short-term extensions for additional judges were impermissible. Justices Bhagwati (*S.P. Gupta* v. *President of India*, [1982] 2 SCR 365, pp. 566–7) and Desai (pp. 1058–60) held that extensions of less than two years were impermissible, unless the arrears of cases were such that on an honest assessment, it could be said that they could be disposed of in less than two years, although this was implausible. Justice Tulzapurkar (pp. 930–2) held that an extension should be for a period of at least one year, whether the arrears justified this or not.

[146] On the fifth question, the Court unanimously (see Seervai, Constitutional Law, p. 2720) agreed that an additional judge had the right to be considered for being appointed a permanent judge, and could therefore challenge his non-confirmation, unlike a person whose candidature was considered for the first time by the president, and who had no such right.

[147] On the sixth question, five judges (Justices Bhagwati, Fazal Ali, Desai, Pathak, and Venkataramiah) agreed that an additional judge had to go through

By a majority of five to two,[148] the Court answered the second question in the negative, that is, that the Chief Justice's opinion was not to be given 'primacy' by the President of India. In making appointments to high courts, the President of India is required to consult three constitutional functionaries: (*a*) the Chief Justice of India, (*b*) the chief justice of a high court, and (*c*) the governor of the state. At times, differences of opinion could arise amongst these functionaries, and in such cases the question was: whose opinion should the president accept? Five judges held that the opinion of the chief justice did not trump the opinions of the other two functionaries— that it was up to the president to decide what to do if any of the three constitutional functionaries disagreed.[149]

The Court unanimously answered the third question in the negative. Accordingly, it was held that the President of India was not bound by the advice of the Chief Justice of India, and that 'consultation' did not amount to 'concurrence'. This was perhaps the most heavily criticized aspect of the decision. If the chief justice's opinion were not binding on the president, then the executive could ride

---

the test of 'suitability' while being considered for reappointment (see Seervai, *Constitutional Law*, p. 2755), that is, that the president would consider whether the judge was 'suitable' for reappointment or confirmation—however, as Justice Pathak articulated, no account was to be taken of the 'merits of judgments, decrees and orders' rendered by the judge, and there would be a presumption that the judge was fit for service. *S.P. Gupta* v. *President of India*, (1982) 2 SCR 365, p. 1173.

[148] Justices Gupta (*S.P. Gupta* v. *President of India*, [1982] 2 SCR 365, pp. 703–4) and Tulzapurkar (pp. 927–9) dissented.

[149] However, Justice Pathak added the caveat that it was hard to say that the Chief Justice of India and the chief justice of a high court were at the same level, that the advice of the Chief Justice of India enjoyed 'mere parity'—perhaps indicating that the opinion of the Chief Justice deserved slightly more weight, though not 'primacy'. *S.P. Gupta* v. *President of India*, (1982) 2 SCR 365, 1165–7. Justices Bhagwati and Venkataramiah held that each of the three constitutional functionaries played an important role in the consultation process—the chief justice of the high court assessed the competence, character, and integrity of a candidate, the governor could assess the character, integrity, social philosophy, antecedents, and value system of a judge (though not other technical matters), and the Chief Justice of India would 'stand outside the turmoil of local passions and prejudices'. *S.P. Gupta* v. *President of India*, (1982) 2 SCR 365, pp. 541–4 (per Bhagwati J.).

roughshod over the judiciary once more, as it had done during the Emergency. The Court would be unable to assert its independence and control over its own composition, facing a daunting executive with a large two-thirds majority in Parliament. One newspaper termed this a 'New Year's Gift' for the executive.[150] However, Justice Desai held that the opinion of the chief justice was to be given 'great weight'.[151]

It can be seen that the first Judges case did not entail any questions about appointing judges to the Supreme Court of India. The case only concerned the confirmation and extension of additional high court judges, and the transfer of judges and chief justices of high courts. However, while deciding the case, Justices Bhagwati and Desai made certain observations about criteria to be employed in selecting and appointing judges. Justice Bhagwati held that while appointing judges, one needed to look not merely at the judge's professional competence, but also at his 'social philosophy'.[152] He wrote:

> The appointment of a Judge of a High Court or the Supreme Court does *not depend merely upon the professional or functional suitability* of the person concerned in terms of experience or knowledge of law though this requirement is certainly important and vital and ignoring it might result in impairment of the efficiency of administration of justice, but also on several other considerations such as *honesty, integrity* and general pattern of behaviour which would ensure *dispassionate and objective adjudication* with an open mind, free and fearless approach to matters in issue, *social acceptability of the person concerned to the high judicial office in terms of current norms and ethos of the society, commitment to democracy* and the rule of law, *faith in the constitutional objectives* indicating his approach towards the Preamble and the Directive Principles of State Policy, *sympathy or absence thereof with the constitutional goals and the needs of an activist judicial system.* These various considerations, apart from professional and functional suitability, have to be taken into account while appointing a Judge of a High Court or the Supreme Court and it is presumably on this account that the power of appointment is entrusted to the Executive.[153]

(emphasis supplied)

---

[150] Dua, 'Study in Executive-Judicial Conflict', p. 464.
[151] *S.P. Gupta* v. *President of India*, (1982) 2 SCR 365, p. 1063.
[152] *S.P. Gupta* v. *President of India*, (1982) 2 SCR 365, p. 544.
[153] *S.P. Gupta* v. *President of India*, (1982) 2 SCR 365, p. 546.

Further, while appointing judges, Justice Bhagwati advocated that 'no power should be vested in a single individual howsoever high and great he may be and howsoever honest and well meaning'.[154] Accordingly, Justice Bhagwati advocated the establishment of a 'collegium'—holding that the Chief Justice of India should consult 'wider interests'. However, he did not specify who was to be a part of the collegium.

> We would rather suggest that there must be a collegium to make recommendation to the President in regard to appointment of a Supreme Court or High Court Judge. The *recommending authority should be more broad-based* and there should be *consultation with wider interests*. If the collegium is composed of persons who are expected to have knowledge of the persons who may be fit for appointment on the Bench and of qualities required for appointment and this last requirement is absolutely essential—it would go a long way towards securing the right kind of Judges, who would be truly independent in the sense we have indicated above and who would invest the judicial process with significance and meaning, for the deprived and exploited sections of humanity.[155]
>
> (emphasis supplied)

Justice Desai listed out criteria to be considered in making appointments to high courts. Importantly, he spoke of judges being of a 'sufficiently mature age', considered a 'good guide for a sombre approach in a law court'.

> (i) does he satisfy the *qualifications* prescribed in Article 217(2), (ii) whether he is of *sufficiently mature age which is generally considered a good guide for a sombre approach in a law court*; (iii) is he of *unimpeachable integrity*; (iv) has he a *spotless character* (v) is he a man of *reliable habits*; (vi) what is his *equipment in law*; (vii) does he subscribe to the *social philosophy* and values enshrined in the Constitution; (viii) does he suffer from *any insurmountable aberrations*; (ix) does he disclose a *capacity to persuade and be persuaded*; (x) would he have a *team spirit*; (xi) has he a *quick grasp*, a smart intellect and a compassionate heart. These are only illustrative and not exhaustive.[156]
>
> (emphasis supplied)

Of the criteria prescribed by these judges, 'social philosophy' and 'mature age' seemed to be the most striking. After all, it is obvious

---

[154] *S.P. Gupta* v. *President of India*, (1982) 2 SCR 365, p. 548.
[155] *S.P. Gupta* v. *President of India*, (1982) 2 SCR 365, p. 548.
[156] *S.P. Gupta* v. *President of India*, (1982) 2 SCR 385, p. 1064 B.

that judges must be honest, but the fact that they must subscribe to certain social philosophies, or that they must be senior/of a mature age, was not as intuitively ascertainable.

On the whole, the first Judges case was seen as striking a blow to judicial independence, largely on account of the fact that the opinion of the Chief Justice of India would not be binding on the president, that is, that 'consultation' did not amount to 'concurrence'. Although this case only dealt with high court judges and chief justices, the decision would have important consequences for the manner in which even Supreme Court judges would be appointed.

SECOND JUDGES CASE

Background

The second Judges case would be decided by the Supreme Court of India nearly 12 years after the first case had been decided. Between December 1981 (the first Judges case) and October 1993 (the second Judges case), the political landscape of India would drastically change. During this time, the Supreme Court would see nine new chief justices preside over Court No. 1,[157] and over the span of three national general elections, government would change hands twice, and four new prime ministers would serve in office.[158] At the same time, the higher judiciary would face its most serious crisis of credibility.

Prime Minister Indira Gandhi was assassinated on 31 October 1984. The All India Radio announced the prime minister's death at 6 pm, and eight hours later, Rajiv Gandhi, her elder son, was sworn in as the new Prime Minister of India.[159] Later that year, India held its eighth national general elections. On an overwhelming wave of sympathy, the Congress party under Rajiv Gandhi won 404 seats[160]—as

---

[157] Chief Justices Bhagwati, Pathak, Venkataramiah, Mukharji, Misra, Singh, Kania, Sharma, and Venkatachaliah.

[158] Prime Ministers Rajiv Gandhi, V.P. Singh, Chandra Shekhar, and P.V. Narasimha Rao.

[159] *Times of India.* 1984. 'Nation Mourns Indira', *Times of India*, 1 November, p. 1.

[160] Election Commission of India. 1985. 'Statistical Report on General Elections, 1984, to the Eighth Lok Sabha, Volume I', available online at http://eci.nic.in/eci_main/StatisticalReports/LS_1984/Vol_I_LS_84.pdf (last accessed on 15 March 2012).

Ramachandra Guha points out, far more than it had ever won under Nehru or Indira Gandhi.[161] The party controlled 78.59 per cent of the house, comfortably over the two-thirds majority necessary to amend the Constitution.

Court Packing

In May 1985, a bench of three judges of the Supreme Court of India accused the Rajiv Gandhi government of packing the high courts with 'sycophant judges'.[162] The government had resorted to interesting tactics to push through its appointments. In Madhya Pradesh, for example, after the outgoing chief justice retired, the next most senior judge was only made an 'acting' chief justice, until he cleared the government's 10 names recommended for appointment to the court. As Prabhu Chawla wrote, '[T]he message was clear: keep a judge in an acting position so that he concurs with the Government's recommendations on appointments to the bench in the hope of getting confirmed himself.'[163] *India Today* reported that of the 53 appointments made to high courts in India roughly during 1984–5, 32 had been made by acting chief justices, of which 25 were in Allahabad and Madhya Pradesh, and the remaining in Kerala and Jammu and Kashmir.[164]

Two months later, on 12 July 1985, the 16th Chief Justice of India retired from office. In an interview with the *India Today* magazine, he said that the 'appointment of judges is too much of a clandestine affair', and he recommended 'wider consultation' and 'freer discussion' on the question of judicial appointments.[165] The outgoing chief justice's successor, Chief Justice P.N. Bhagwati, would engage in an 'unprecedented tug of war'[166] with the law minister, Asoke Sen, on

---

[161] Guha, India after Gandhi, p. 571.
[162] Prabhu Chawla. 1985. 'Flouted Guidelines', *India Today*, 15 June, 10(11), p. 78.
[163] Chawla, 'Flouted Guidelines', p. 78.
[164] Ibid.
[165] *India Today*. 1985. 'We Are Not Spineless', *India Today*, 31 July, 10(14), p. 42.
[166] Sumit Mitra. 1986. 'Tug of War', *India Today*, 15 January, 11(1), p. 47. During Bhagwati's term, the government also contemplated increasing the retirement age of the Chief Justice of India—but Rajiv Gandhi was against making a constitutional amendment for the purpose, and Bhagwati retired at the age

appointing judges to the Supreme Court of India. Justice Bhagwati wanted to bring 'activist' judges to the Court, who shared his social philosophy, but the government resisted his appointments.[167] In turn, Chief Justice Bhagwati declined to accept the government's suggestion that the Delhi High Court Chief Justice be appointed to the Supreme Court.[168] Similarly, appointments to the Calcutta, Patna, and Punjab and Haryana High Courts had taken on a political tenor.[169]

The judges' transfer policy was being applied by the executive in a selective and arbitrary manner. The transfer policy required that a high court chief justice come from the outside, but the policy was selectively applied.[170] As Prabhu Chawla wrote at the time, the

---

of 65. The decision not to extend the chief justice's retirement age seemed to have caused some strains in the relationship between the chief justice and the executive. Perhaps for this reason, Bhagwati did not respond in time to the government when it asked him for his recommendation on the next Chief Justice of India, and Bhagwati had to speak to the president personally before his successor, Justice Pathak, was appointed chief justice. *India Today*. 1986. 'Presidential Tact', *India Today*, 15 December, 11(23), p. 67.

[167] One of these judges was Justice P.B. Sawant—a judge on the Bombay High Court, who was seventh in seniority at the time. In the first week of March 1986, Sawant was told by Chief Justice Bhagwati that on 6 March 1986, he would have to be present in Delhi, as his name was going to be declared for appointment to the Supreme Court that night—a Thursday—and on 10 March 1986 he would be sworn in as a Supreme Court judge. Sawant had a prior speaking engagement in Madurai, which Justice Bhagwati requested him to cancel. Justice Sawant arrived in Delhi and was present on the specified date, but his name was not declared. As it turned out, Justices M.M. Dutt, K.N. Singh, and Sivasanker Natarajan were appointed to the Court on 10 March 1986. Sawant's appointment took three years more. Had he been appointed a Supreme Court judge at that time, he would have been Chief Justice of India for approximately three years. The *India Today* magazine (Mitra, 'Tug of War') reported that the law minister, Asoke Sen, had politely declined Sawant's appointment.

[168] Mitra, 'Tug of War'.

[169] See Prabhu Chawla. 1986. 'Controversial Appointments', *India Today*, 30 November, 11(22), p. 38. Further, the executive–judiciary tussle was not limited to judicial appointments alone. Bhagwati wanted Justice Desai, a retired Supreme Court judge, to succeed Justice Mathew as chairman of the Law Commission. Though the law minister opposed this move, Desai became the commission's chairman. See Mitra, 'Tug of War'.

[170] For example, Yogeshwar Dayal was made Delhi High Court Chief Justice and K.N. Saikia was made Gauhati High Court Chief Justice, and both these

government's judges' transfer policy seemed to be one of 'pick and choose'.[171]

Chief Justice R.S. Pathak had suggested six names for appointment to the Supreme Court of India, but three were not acted on by the government.[172] In six[173] states 'serious differences' arose between the chief minister and the chief justice of the respective high court about appointments to vacant high court posts. A senior lawyer commented that all this pointed to the fact that 'Rajiv Gandhi [believed] in his mother's philosophy of packing the judiciary with favorites and committed judges' and that state governments had been 'encouraged to tinker with the judiciary'.[174]

In July 1987, the Law Commission of India in its 121st report made certain observations as to the criteria employed in appointing judges to the Supreme Court of India. The Law Commission noted that regional and minority representation was a criterion taken into account in making judicial appointments to the Supreme Court:

> [T]he constituency from which selection is made is a limited constituency of High Court Judges who have put in more than five years' service as a Judge of the High Court and about whose credentials no enquiry is required to be made as he is a sitting Judge of the High Court. If there are roughly 450 High Court Judges and the selection is confined to those who qualify and are not about to retire, the selection is to be made from roughly about

---

judges had served as puisne judges on these courts respectively. Debi Singh Tewatia, Chief Justice of the Punjab and Haryana High Court, was transferred to the Calcutta High Court only a day after he took over as chief justice of his own court. Tewatia had made a pro-communist speech during the Emergency, which some felt might have influenced the decision to transfer him. Prabhu Chawla. 1987. 'Shuffling the Pack', *India Today*, 15 November, 12(21), p. 76. The fact that not all Chief Justices were transferred to other courts attached a certain stigma to those who were transferred.

[171] Chawla, 'Shuffling the Pack', p. 76.

[172] These included the Delhi High Court Chief Justice T.P.S. Chawla, and the Punjab and Haryana High Court Chief Justice, H.N. Seth. Chawla, 'Shuffling the Pack', p. 76.

[173] Maharashtra, Tamil Nadu, Bihar, Uttar Pradesh, Andhra Pradesh, and Assam. Chawla, 'Shuffling the Pack'.

[174] Chawla, 'Shuffling the Pack', p. 76.

150 to 200 Judges. Again, federal principle is generally kept in view which would dictate a choice limited to High Courts which are not represented in the Supreme Court. More often, the question of minority representation is also kept in view. The scope, thus, for selection of talent is so limited that the choice sometimes dictates itself.[175]

Early in 1989, there were signs of government interfering with judicial appointments at the high courts once more. At the Madhya Pradesh High Court, once again, the acting Chief Justice G. Sohani was not confirmed as permanent chief justice by the government for 18 months, to use this potentially as a ploy to coerce him into accepting the government's appointments.[176] An additional judge at that court, Brij Mohan Lal, was not confirmed as a permanent judge for several years, despite having been recommended for confirmation by three high court chief justices (Oza, Verma, and Sohani), and three Chief Justices of India (Chandrachud, Bhagwati, and Pathak).[177] This was allegedly done because Lal had struck down the government's liquor policy.[178] In June 1989, *India Today* reported that '[u]nless the chief justice of [a] high court displays a high degree of independence and integrity, many of the judges end up being appointed because of their political affiliations'.[179]

An Era of Uncertainty, a Crisis of Credibility

Then, all of a sudden, things dramatically began to change. In the November 1989 general elections, no single party won a clear majority—the first time in India's history that this happened. The Congress party won 197 seats out of 529,[180] or 37.24 per cent of the house. V.P. Singh's Janata Dal party (formed by a merger of the Jan Morcha and the old Janata Party), an 'inchoate mix of

[175] Law Commission, *One Hundred Twenty-First Report*, p. 19, para. 3.14.
[176] N.K. Singh. 1989. 'Injudicious Actions', *India Today*, 30 June, 14(12), p. 52.
[177] Singh, 'Injudicious Actions'.
[178] Singh, 'Injudicious Actions'.
[179] Singh, 'Injudicious Actions', p. 52.
[180] Election Commission of India. 1990. 'Statistical Report on General Elections, 1989, to the Ninth Lok Sabha, Volume I', available online at http://eci.nic.in/eci_main/StatisticalReports/LS_1989/Vol_I_LS_89.pdf (last accessed on 15 March 2012).

irreconcilable opposites',[181] won 143 seats, and formed the government (the 'National Front' government, a minority government formed between the Janata Dal and a coalition of regional parties), supported from the outside by the Bharatiya Janata Party (BJP) and the Left.[182] Vir Sanghvi called this the 'inauguration of an era of uncertainty'.[183]

In the meantime, the judiciary was suffering from a crisis of credibility. A day before retiring from the Court, the outgoing Chief Justice of India, E.S. Venkataramiah, told a prominent news reporter, Kuldip Nayar, that the 'judiciary in India has deteriorated in its standards because such Judges are appointed, as are willing to be "influenced" by lavish parties and whisky bottles'.[184] In fact, a petition was later filed before the Bombay High Court alleging that the former Chief Justice of India had committed contempt of court,[185] although the petition was eventually dismissed.[186] Then, in the Bombay High Court, allegations of impropriety were levelled by the advocate general of the state against a sitting high court judge.[187] Allegations of corruption were also beginning to emerge against a sitting Supreme Court judge, something that had not happened since the inception of the Court—V. Ramaswami, a sitting Supreme Court judge, was being accused of misusing his office as Chief Justice of the Punjab and Haryana High Court. *India Today* reported that Soli Sorabjee, a noted Supreme Court senior lawyer, said that the 'standard of judicial integrity' had 'fallen alarmingly'.[188] Chief Justice Sabyasachi Mukharji said that the judiciary was facing a 'crisis of credibility'.[189]

---

[181]   A.S. Abraham. 1989. 'The Next Election: Country at the Crossroads', *Times of India*, 11 September, p. 16.

[182]   Guha, *India after Gandhi*, p. 591.

[183]   Guha, *India after Gandhi*, p. 591.

[184]   See *Vishwanath v. E.S. Venkataramiah*, (1990) 92 Bom LR 270.

[185]   *Vishwanath v. E.S. Venkataramiah*, (1990) 92 Bom LR 270.

[186]   See Anil Divan. 2007. 'Contempt of Court and the Truth', *Hindu*, 29 October, available online at http://www.hindu.com/2007/10/29/stories/2007102956041000.htm (last accessed on 15 March 2012).

[187]   Raj Chengappa and M. Rahman. 1990. 'Crisis of Credibility', *India Today*, 15 July, 15(13), p. 18.

[188]   Chengappa and Rahman, 'Crisis of Credibility', p. 18.

[189]   Raj Chengappa. 1990. 'I Feel Very Sorry and Perturbed', *India Today*, 15 July, 15(13), p. 22.

At the same time, the conflict between the executive and the judiciary over the matter of appointing judges had not abated. Chief Justice Sabyasachi Mukharji objected to the National Judicial Commission bill which sought to take the power of appointing judges away from the Chief Justice of India, and in a letter to the Law Ministry he argued that it would undermine judicial independence.[190] The transfer of Justice P.S. Mishra, a Patna High Court judge, at a time when the Chief Minister of the state, Laloo Prasad Yadav, had threatened that unfavourable judges would be transferred out of state, was seen by many as 'smack[ing] of political vendetta and executive bias'.[191] The V.P. Singh government had stalled the appointment of 67 judicial nominees.[192]

Then, V.P. Singh's National Front government collapsed, no more than a year into its reign.[193] As a consequence, on 5 November 1990, the Janata Dal split, with one faction being led by Chandra Shekhar. A day later, the Congress party decided to support Chandra Shekhar's Janata Dal from the outside. The very next day, V.P. Singh lost the vote of confidence (by 346–142 votes) in the lower house, and resigned as prime minister. The President, R. Venkataraman, invited Chandra Shekhar to form the government, and after being sworn in as prime minister on 10 November, he won a vote of confidence (by 280–214 votes) on 16 November.[194]

As V.P. Singh's government was falling at the centre, the Supreme Court of India was hearing a public interest case filed, amongst others, by the Supreme Court Advocates on Record Association, which requested the Court to staff judicial vacancies at the Supreme Court and high courts. On 26 October 1990, a three-judge bench of the

---

[190] Chengappa, 'I Feel Very Sorry'.

[191] Chengappa, 'I Feel Very Sorry', p. 22.

[192] Rahul Pathak. 1992. 'Crumbling Citadel', *India Today*, 30 June, 17(12), p. 51.

[193] BJP president, L.K. Advani had commenced a rath yatra, a tour of India which proposed to arrive in Ayodhya, the site of the Babri Masjid, conflagrating communal tensions. This created an irreconcilable conflict between the two major supporting planks of the National Front government—the BJP and the Left, and each threatened to withdraw support if the rath yatra were either not permitted to take place (BJP) or permitted to take place (Left). See *Times of India*. 1990. 'Pressure Mounts on VP', *Times of India*, 23 October, p. 1.

[194] *Times of India*. 1991. '117 Crisis-Ridden Days', *Times of India*, 7 March, p. 16.

Court (Chief Justice Ranganath Misra, and Justices Venkatachaliah and Punchhi) felt that the first Judges case needed to be reconsidered. The Court recorded that recommendations made for judicial appointments were often reopened by the executive if there had been a 'change in the personnel of the Chief Justice of the High Court or the Chief Minister of the State'. The question was referred to a larger bench.[195]

Then, only 117 days after he came to power, Chandra Shekhar resigned on 6 March 1991,[196] and upon the president's request, continued as a caretaker prime minister until the general elections were held. Barely a few weeks later, on 21 May 1991, Rajiv Gandhi was assassinated.[197] Riding a second sympathy wave following the assassination of one of its leaders, the Congress party won 232 seats in the 1991 general elections,[198] or 44.52 per cent of the house, and formed a government with the support of independents, with P.V. Narasimha Rao sworn in as prime minister on 21 June 1991.

In the meantime, there were troubling rumours, though unsubstantiated, that a Chief Justice of India had misused his 18 days in office,[199] the shortest term served by a Chief Justice of India in office. More pressingly, allegations against V. Ramaswami grew serious. *India Today* reported that he had been appointed Chief Justice of the Punjab and Haryana High Court because he had 'promised to be "strict" in granting bail to militants'.[200] The allegation against him, however, was that he exorbitantly spent state funds, especially to furnish his residence.[201] Impeaching a judge requires a two-thirds

[195] *Subash Sharma* v. *Union of India*, AIR 1991 SC 631.

[196] *Times of India*, '117 Crisis-Ridden Days'. Serious disagreements arose between the Congress party and the Janata Dal when it was learned that two Haryana intelligence personnel were secretly observing Rajiv Gandhi's residence. See *Times of India*. 1991. 'Spies Set on Rajiv', *Times of India*, 5 March, p. 1.

[197] *Times of India*. 1991. 'Rajiv Gandhi Assassinated', *Times of India*, 22 May, p. 1.

[198] Election Commission of India. 1992. 'Statistical Report on General Elections, 1991, to the Tenth Lok Sabha', available online at http://eci.nic.in/eci_main1/ElectionStatistics.aspx (last accessed on 17 October 2011).

[199] Pathak, 'Crumbling Citadel', p. 52.

[200] Pathak, 'Crumbling Citadel', p. 52.

[201] See Manoj Mitta. 1991. 'Move to Impeach Justice Ramaswami', *Times of India*, 3 March, p. 24; Kanwar Sandhu and W.P.S. Sindhu. 1991. 'Edgy Ethics', *India Today*, 28 February, 16(4), p. 41.

majority in Parliament.[202] It was not clear if the Congress party would support the impeachment, if the alleged 'quid pro quo' between Ramaswami and the Congress party were true.

The tussle between the executive and the judiciary now began taking place increasingly at the high court level. The law minister, Vijaya Bhaskara Reddy, claimed that state governments were trying to 'pack' the high courts with 'their own men'.[203] The Chief Justice of the Patna High Court, B.C. Basak, had a strong disagreement with the Chief Minister of Bihar, Laloo Prasad Yadav, over judicial appointments to the High Court, so much so that the chief justice even requested additional security at his residence.[204] In Madhya Pradesh, the chief minister stalled the appointment of one judge, suggested by the chief justice, for over four months.[205] The tussle between the executive and the judiciary no longer seemed to take place at the federal level; the weak central executive could no longer afford to tinker with the judiciary. However, stronger state governments tried to interfere with judicial appointments.

In the years leading up to the second Judges case, there was no significant 'skirmish' or 'war' between the executive and the judiciary on substantive principles of law. There was no Basic Structure case, no Habeas Corpus case in this era, no Emergency, and after the end of Rajiv Gandhi's term as prime minister, no substantial attempt to arm-twist the Chief Justice of India or the federal judiciary. Tussles between the executive and the judiciary over judicial appointments at the high courts did take place, and formed an important backdrop to the second Judges case. The executive at the centre was weak and had to weather several trust votes in Parliament. P.V. Narasimha Rao survived trust votes on 17 July 1992,[206] and 28 July 1993.[207]

The crisis of credibility in the judiciary reached its peak on 10 May 1993. After an embarrassing period of two years, during which time the Supreme Court had to face the blemish of serious allegations levelled against one of its judges, V. Ramaswami, the motion for his

---

[202] Article 124(4), Constitution of India.
[203] Pathak, 'Crumbling Citadel', p. 52.
[204] Pathak, 'Crumbling Citadel', p. 52.
[205] Pathak, 'Crumbling Citadel', p. 52.
[206] *Times of India*. 1992. 'Rao Wins Trust Vote', *Times of India*, 18 July, p. 1.
[207] *Times of India*. 1993. 'Rao Survives No Confidence', *Times of India*, 29 July, p. 1.

impeachment failed in the Lok Sabha, because the Congress party issued a 'surreptitious whip' directing its members of Parliament to abstain from the vote.[208] Noted constitutional scholar, H.M. Seervai, called this '[o]ne of the most disgraceful episodes in the history of the [Supreme Court]'.[209]

The Decision

Against this backdrop, on 6 October 1993, a bench of nine judges of the Supreme Court of India decided the second Judges case. The number nine here is significant. Sankal Chand Sheth's case, the prelude to the first Judges case, was decided by a bench of five judges, and S.P. Gupta's case, the first Judges case, was decided by a bench of seven judges. Now, in October 1993, these nine judges of the Supreme Court were not bound by either of the Court's two decisions in the Judges cases, on account of the norm that a bench of a larger strength can overrule previous decisions, even by a slimmer majority.[210] Justice Venkatachaliah was Chief Justice of India at the time, and a weak Congress government was in power, which had weathered several votes of confidence on the floor of the house. This was not the strong Congress government of the Indira Gandhi years or even the Rajiv Gandhi years which could harass or tinker with the federal judiciary.

The bench was composed of every single future Chief Justice of India on the Court, that is, there were five judges on the Court at the time who, by the norm of seniority, were due to become Chief Justice of India in the ordinary course of things—each of these judges[211] was assigned to the second Judges case bench by the Chief Justice of India. Out of the four most senior puisne judges on the Court at

[208] *Times of India.* 1993. '70 Cong MPs in Favour of Motion', *Times of India,* 13 May, p. 1.

[209] Seervai, *Constitutional Law,* p. 2909.

[210] For example, a bench of nine judges of the Supreme Court which decides a case by a five-to-four majority can overrule a unanimous decision of seven judges of the Supreme Court. See Chintan Chandrachud. 2010. 'The Supreme Court of India's Practice of Referring Cases to Larger Benches: A Need For Review', *Supreme Court Cases* 1: 37–48.

[211] Ahmadi, Verma, Punchhi, Anand, and Bharucha.

the time, two[212] were not likely to be Chief Justice of India by the seniority norm, but they were also included in the bench by the chief justice.[213] Two judges[214] were junior judges. The bench composition reflected the greatest possible degree of regional diversity—each judge hailed from a different state in India.[215]

In the second Judges case, *Supreme Court Advocates on Record Association* v. *Union of India*,[216] the Court considered two questions: (*a*) whether the Chief Justice of India had 'primacy'[217] with respect

---

[212]   Pandian and Kuldip Singh.

[213]   T.K. Thommen retired on 25 September 1993, and would not have been around when the case was decided.

[214]   Dayal and G.N. Ray.

[215]   Gujarat, Madhya Pradesh, Punjab and Haryana, Jammu and Kashmir, Maharashtra, Tamil Nadu, Delhi, and West Bengal. Kuldip Singh was a 'bar' judge, and for this purpose is left out of the analysis. If he is counted as a Punjab and Haryana judge, then there would have been two judges on the bench from the High Court of Punjab and Haryana. The Judges cases offer a glimpse into the basis upon which the Chief Justice of India made bench assignments in these cases. The Chief Justice of India never sat to hear these cases, perhaps because it would not have seemed appropriate for him to adjudicate upon his own powers vis-à-vis the president and other constitutional functionaries in matters of judicial appointment. The bench always had amongst its members all future Chief Justices of India by the seniority convention on the Court. A large number of the judges, if not most of them, were the most senior judges on the Court at the time. The benches were always regionally diverse, and very rarely were there two judges on a bench who came from the same region. This only happened in the S.P. Gupta case, where Bhagwati and Desai both came from the state of Gujarat—as it turned out, both voted in the same way in that case. On the face of it, bench assignments did not appear to affect the manner in which the judges voted.

[216]   AIR 1994 SC 268. The four most junior judges on the bench (Dayal, Ray, Anand, and Bharucha) voted along with J.S. Verma, who wrote the majority opinion. Pandian and Kuldip Singh wrote concurring opinions, while Ahmadi and Punchhi, two future chief justices of India, wrote dissenting opinions.

[217]   At the outset it must be pointed out that the word 'primacy' used in this case tends to be confusing when read in the light of the previous decisions, as Justice Ahmadi pointed out in his dissent. In the S.P. Gupta case, when the Court used the word 'primacy' it was asking itself whether the Chief Justice was to be given 'primacy' over other constitutional functionaries (that is, the governor of a state and the chief justice of a high court) in the matter of transferring high court judges. On the other hand, in that case, the question of whether the chief justice's opinion was binding on the President of India was not framed as a 'primacy' question. The word 'primacy' in that case dealt only with the

to judicial appointments and transfers and (*b*) whether these matters were justiciable.[218] For the purposes of this book, the Court's 'primacy' analysis in the Supreme Court Advocates on Record case will be examined from the point of view of three questions that the Court seemed to ask itself: (*a*) does the opinion of the Chief Justice of India bind the president (that is, does consultation amount to concurrence)? (*b*) does the opinion of the Chief Justice of India trump the opinion of the high court chief justice (that is, does the Chief Justice of India have 'primacy', in the S.P. Gupta sense, over the chief justice of a high court)? and (3) does the opinion of the Chief Justice of India trump the opinion of the Supreme Court judges he consults before making appointments?[219]

---

relationship amongst the Chief Justice of India, the chief justice of a high court, and the governor of a state. The word 'concurrence' (that is, does consultation amount to concurrence?) was used to describe the interaction between the Chief Justice of India and the president. In the Supreme Court Advocates on Record Association case, the word 'primacy' was compendiously used to encapsulate both the 'primacy' and 'concurrence' debates in the S.P. Gupta case.

[218] It was held that:

> Except on the ground of want of consultation with the named constitutional functionaries or lack of any condition of eligibility in the case of an appointment, or of a transfer being made without the recommendation of the Chief Justice of India, these matters are not justiciable on any other ground, including that of bias, which in any case is excluded by the element of plurality in the process of decision making.

Supreme Court Advocates on Record Association v. *Union of India*, AIR 1994 SC 268, p. 441 (per Verma J.).

[219] The third question arose out of the majority's holding in this case that in making recommendations for judicial appointments to the Supreme Court of India, the Chief Justice of India was required to consult the two most senior judges on the Court, and to consult the most senior judge on the Court whose opinion was 'likely to be significant in adjudging the suitability of the candidate', either because the judge hailed from the high court whose judge was being considered, or 'otherwise'. *Supreme Court Advocates on Record Association* v. *Union of India*, AIR 1994 SC 268, p. 436 (per Verma J.).

The majority also considered the process of transferring judges from one high court to another. Importantly, the Court held that a transfer made by the Chief Justice of India would not be considered 'punitive'. It will be recalled that in S.P. Gupta's case it was held that both 'courage-punitive' and 'misconduct-punitive' transfers (terms coined in this book for the sake of convenience) were prohibited by the Constitution. In the Supreme Court Advocates on

The Court prescribed a new procedure for appointing judges. For appointments to the Supreme Court, the Chief Justice of India would have to consult (a) the two most senior judges on the Supreme Court and (b) the most senior judge on the Supreme Court whose opinion was 'likely to be significant in adjudging the suitability of the candidate', either because the judge hailed from the same high court as the candidate, or 'otherwise'.[220] For appointments to a high court, the Chief Justice of India would have to seek (a) the views of his colleagues on the Supreme Court 'likely to be conversant with the affairs of the concerned High Court', (b) the opinion of the chief justice of the high court (formed after ascertaining the views of at least the two most senior judges on that high court)—an opinion entitled to the 'greatest weight', (c) the opinion of the 'other functionaries', that is, the governor of the state acting on the aid and advice of his council of ministers—an opinion entitled to 'due weight', and (d) if the Chief Justice of India so wished, the opinion of one or more senior judges of that high court whose opinions were 'likely to be significant' in the formation of the opinion of the Chief

---

Record Association case, however, the Court held that no transfer would be considered 'punitive' if it was initiated by the Chief Justice of India. In other words, so long as the transfer was not made by the executive, it would be permissible, even if it was designed to punish the misconduct of a judge (or perhaps even the courage of a judge). The Court's decision in S.P. Gupta's case, on this point, was also overruled, and the decision of the Court in the second Judges case seemed to revert to the Sankal Chand position, or perhaps to even go beyond it.

The Court also specified the process for transferring a high court judge. Before transferring a high court judge (the initiative could only come from the Chief Justice of India), the Chief Justice of India was to take into account the views of (a) the chief justice of the high court from which the transfer was to be made, (b) any Supreme Court judge whose opinion may be significant, and (c) at least one other senior high court chief justice, or other person whose views are considered relevant. Personal factors relating to the judge being transferred were to be taken into account. It was held that a transfer made in accordance with the opinion of the Chief Justice of India would not be justiciable. *Supreme Court Advocates on Record Association* v. *Union of India*, AIR 1994 SC 268, p. 440 (per Verma J.).

[220] *Supreme Court Advocates on Record Association* v. *Union of India*, AIR 1994 SC 268, p. 436 (per Verma J.).

Justice of India. All opinions were to be expressed in writing to avoid ambiguity.[221]

The first question was answered in the affirmative. It was held that the opinion of the Chief Justice of India would bind the president, that is, that consultation amounted to 'concurrence'.[222] For this reason, the majority decision in the S.P. Gupta case was overruled. For the first time in India's constitutional history, against the backdrop of a weak central government, and against the history of court packing during the Indira Gandhi and Rajiv Gandhi years, the Supreme Court of India asserted its 'primacy' over the executive, and its power to control its own composition. Unlike Article II of the US Constitution, which prescribes that the president seek both the 'advice' and 'consent' of the Senate before making judicial appointments, the Indian Constitution did not explicitly require the president to obtain the consent of the Chief Justice of India while making appointments—in this decision, the Court read consent into the Constitution.

However, the Court's answers to the next two questions created exceptions to its answer to the first question. In answering the second question, the Court found that if the Chief Justice of India and the chief justice of a high court disagreed in their opinions as to the suitability of a candidate for appointment to the high court, then the President of India would have the option of refusing to accept the opinion of the Chief Justice of India.[223] In other words, the opinion of the Chief Justice of India would not 'trump' or have 'primacy' over the opinion of the chief justice of a high court, and when there was a disagreement between the two chief justices, the opinion of the Chief Justice of India would not bind the president—that is, in that limited circumstance, consultation would not amount to 'concurrence'.

The third question was also answered in the negative. It was held that if there were a difference of opinion between the Chief Justice of India and the 'senior judges consulted', then the president would

---

[221] *Supreme Court Advocates on Record Association* v. *Union of India*, AIR 1994 SC 268, p. 436 (per Verma J.).

[222] *Supreme Court Advocates on Record Association* v. *Union of India*, AIR 1994 SC 268, p. 437 (per Verma J.).

[223] *Supreme Court Advocates on Record Association* v. *Union of India*, AIR 1994 SC 268, p. 438 (per Verma J.).

not be bound by the opinion of the Chief Justice of India—that is, in that limited circumstance as well, consultation would not amount to 'concurrence'. Going a step further, it was held that if the president did not consider a candidate recommended by the Chief Justice of India (in consultation with the senior judges) suitable for appointment, on account of the candidate's 'antecedents and personal character', the president could ask the Chief Justice of India to reconsider his recommendation in favour of that candidate. If the Chief Justice of India and the senior judges consulted all agreed that the appointment should be made anyway, then the president would be bound to make the appointment, as a matter of 'healthy convention'. However, if a difference of opinion then emerged between the Chief Justice of India and the senior judges consulted, for example, if a senior judge found that the recommendation in favour of the candidate should be withdrawn in the light of the evidence presented by the president, the president would be justified in not making the appointment, notwithstanding that the Chief Justice of India may continue to insist that the appointment be made.[224] Interestingly, the Court also enumerated certain additional grounds upon which the president could refuse to make an appointment—for example, if the tenure of the judge was likely to be 'unduly short', if the candidate had 'doubtful antecedents', or if his health and fitness were in question.[225]

In short, no appointment could be made to the Supreme Court of India, or to a high court, contrary to the advice of the Chief Justice of India. However, not every candidate recommended by the Chief Justice of India had to be appointed by the president. The Court distinguished between making an appointment in conformity with the opinion of the Chief Justice of India and not making an appointment at all.

Interestingly, several members of the bench offered insights into appointment criteria to be employed while selecting and appointing judges to courts. In his majority opinion, Justice J.S. Verma wrote that the seniority of a high court judge both on his own high court

---

[224] *Supreme Court Advocates on Record Association* v. *Union of India*, AIR 1994 SC 268, p. 438 (per Verma J.).
[225] *Supreme Court Advocates on Record Association* v. *Union of India*, AIR 1994 SC 268, p. 438 (per Verma J.).

and on an all-India basis ought to be considered while making appointments to the Supreme Court, and that seniority should not be departed from unless there were exceptional reasons for doing so. Senior judges, he wrote, had the 'legitimate expectation' of being appointed to the Supreme Court, and deference to this expectation meant compliance with the constitutional rule of non-arbitrariness:[226]

> *Inter se seniority amongst Judges in their High Court* and *their combined seniority on all India basis* is of admitted significance in the matter of future prospects. Inter se seniority amongst Judges in the Supreme Court, based on the date of appointment, is of similar significance. It is, therefore, reasonable that this aspect is kept in view and given due weight while making appointments from amongst High Court Judges to the Supreme Court. *Unless there be any strong cogent reason to justify a departure, that order of seniority must be maintained between them while making their appointment to the Supreme Court.* Apart from recognising *the legitimate expectation of the High Court Judges to be considered for appointment to the Supreme Court according to their seniority,* this would also lend greater credence to the process of appointment and would avoid any distortion in the seniority between the appointees drawn even from the same High Court. The likelihood of the Supreme Court being deprived of the benefit of the services of some who are considered suitable for appointment, but decline a belated offer, would also be prevented. Due consideration of every legitimate expectation in the decision making process is a requirement of the rule of non-arbitrariness and, therefore, this also is a norm to be observed by the Chief Justice of India in recommending appointments to the Supreme Court. Obviously, this factor applies only to those considered suitable and at least equally meritorious by the Chief Justice of India, for appointment to the Supreme Court. *Just as a High Court Judge at the time of his initial appointment has the legitimate expectation to become Chief Justice of a High Court in his turn in the ordinary course, he has the legitimate expectation to be considered for appointment to the Supreme Court in his turn, according to his seniority.*[227]

(emphasis supplied)

The majority in the second Judges case advocated the application of the seniority norm not merely in the matter of promoting judges to the post of chief justice of a court, but also in appointing judges to the Supreme Court of India. Justice Ahmadi, however, disagreed with

---

[226] For an account of the evolution of this principle under Indian constitutional law, see Chandrachud, *Due Process of Law.*

[227] *Supreme Court Advocates on Record Association* v. *Union of India,* AIR 1994 SC 268, p. 437 (per Verma J.).

the majority. He held that the seniority norm ought to be deviated from while appointing judges to the Supreme Court in order to achieve a more representative court. Applying only the seniority norm in appointing judges to the Supreme Court, wrote Justice Ahmadi, would disturb the representative character of the Court:

> Take for example, the first four judges in the all-India seniority are from a single High Court. If you appoint all of them the *'representative' character of the Court will be disturbed*. Take for example the senior most judge of High Court X is at serial No. 50 in the all-India seniority and there is no judge in the apex court from that High Court which is one of the major High Courts. The Chief Justice of India will find it difficult to nominate him for appointment and if he does there is every possibility of his seniors questioning the decision of the Chief Justice of India in Court. In order *to maintain the representative character of the High Courts and the Supreme Court so that people of all hues have confidence in the institution,* the rule of seniority, which may be valid for civil Services (even in civil Services the higher posts are filled on merit), can have no application to constitutional functionaries. So also the 'legitimate expectation' doctrine can have no relevance in determining the suitability of the appointee. *The seniority principle and the legitimate expectation doctrine are incapable of realistic application as they would destroy the representative character of the superior judiciary, which is absolutely essential* for every segment of society to have confidence in the system. The seniority principle and the legitimate expectation doctrine would only push merit to the second place. Appointments to the superior judiciary should be solely on merit and other suitability factors.... We must hasten to add that where both the candidates under consideration are of equal merit, inter se seniority may have a role to play, subject to other requirements for maintaining the representative character, etc. being satisfied.[228]
>
> (emphasis supplied)

In addition to seniority, the majority also advocated taking into account other criteria like regional representation and merit. The process of appointing judges was to be initiated by the Chief Justice of India while appointing judges to the Supreme Court, and by the chief justice of a high court while appointing judges to a high court. The majority held:

> This legitimate expectation has relevance on the ground of longer experience on the Bench, and is a factor material for determining the suitability

[228] *Supreme Court Advocates on Record Association* v. *Union of India,* AIR 1994 SC 268, p. 389 (per Ahmadi J.).

of the appointee. *Along with other factors, such as, proper representation of all sections of the people from all parts of the country,* legitimate expectation of the suitable and equally meritorious Judges to be considered in their turn is a relevant factor for due consideration while making the choice of the most suitable and meritorious amongst them, *the outweighing consideration being merit,* to select the best available for the apex court.[229]

(emphasis supplied)

The majority strongly supported the seniority norm in the matter of appointing the Chief Justice of India. It held:

[A]ppointments to the office of Chief Justice of India have, by convention, been of the senior-most Judge of the Supreme Court considered fit to hold the office; and the proposal is initiated in advance by the outgoing Chief Justice of India. The provision in Article 124(2) enabling consultation with any other Judge is to provide for such consultation, if there be any doubt about the fitness of the senior-most Judge to hold the office, which alone may permit and justify a departure from the long standing convention. For this reason, no other substantive consultative process is involved. There is no reason to depart from the existing convention and, therefore, any further norm for the working of Article 124(2) in the appointment of Chief Justice of India is unnecessary.[230]

(emphasis supplied)

Justice Kuldip Singh, however, disagreed with the Court on the application of the seniority norm in appointing the Chief Justice of India,[231] criticizing the seniority norm:

There are instances where the recommendee of the Chief Justice of India was not the seniormost puisne Judge of the Supreme Court. The very

---

[229] *Supreme Court Advocates on Record Association* v. *Union of India,* AIR 1994 SC 268, p. 437 (per Verma J.).

[230] *Supreme Court Advocates on Record Association* v. *Union of India,* AIR 1994 SC 268, pp. 439–40 (per Verma J.).

[231] It is important to recall that Justice Kuldip Singh was appointed to the Supreme Court of India on the same day as four other high court judges were appointed to the Court. By the conventional norm that the 'bar judge' should get seniority under such circumstances, Kuldip Singh ought to have been the most senior judge amongst those appointed on that day. However, this norm was not followed. In fact, it was for this reason that Justice Kuldip Singh missed out on becoming Chief Justice of India—Justice Ahmadi, a judge appointed to the court on the same day as Kuldip Singh—retired as Chief Justice of India after Justice Kuldip Singh retired.

fact, that the recommendation of the outgoing Chief Justice of India has come to stay as a standing practice, goes to show that there is no existing convention of appointing the seniormost puisne Judge as the Chief Justice of India.... The seniority rule stagnates the system due to lack of enterprise; merit on the other hand does justice to the selected and brings vigour to the system. In any case, to follow 'seniority alone' rule, there has to be some objective basis for reckoning seniority. Method of appointment and seniority are inextricably-linked [*sic*]. Often, High Court Judges with lower seniority in the same High Court are selected for appointment to the Supreme Court. Many a time appointment is of a High Court Judge, to the Supreme Court, who is much lower in all India seniority. There are many instances where a junior High Court Judge was elevated earlier and sometime later the senior from the same High Court was also brought to the Supreme Court. *When Judges are appointed to the Supreme Court from two sources, and they take oath the same day, no one knows how the inter-se seniority is fixed. On an earlier occasion appointee from the Bar was placed senior but on a later occasion the process was reversed.* These instances are not by way of criticism but only as a pointer with a view to straighten the exercise of discretion in the future. It may be that the High Court Judges, lower in seniority, are preferred on the basis of their merit in the process of selection. Even on that premises [*sic*] *there is no justification to apply 'seniority alone' rule to the office of the Chief Justice of India.* Needless to say that the duties and responsibilities of the office of the Chief Justice of India are much more onerous than that of a Judge of the Supreme Court. The responsibility of toning-up the Judiciary in the country rests on the shoulders of the Chief Justice of India.... *It is thus obvious that with these manifold duties, functions and responsibilities attached to the high and prestigious office of the Chief Justice of India, the appointment to the said office must be by selection based on objective standards and not by mere seniority.* If proper emphasis has to be given to initiative, dynamism and speedy action, the criterion of seniority which relies only on the quality of the person at the time of his recruitment, will unhesitatingly have to be pushed to the background.[232]

(emphasis supplied)

In his concurring opinion, Justice Pandian wrote that judges should be appointed from diverse backgrounds. He was astonished that as on 1 January 1993, of the 18 high courts in the country, as many as 12 did not have a single judge belonging to a Scheduled Caste or an Other Backward Class, and 14 did not have a single judge belonging to a Scheduled Tribe. However, he also sounded a

---

[232] *Supreme Court Advocates on Record Association* v. *Union of India*, AIR 1994 SC 268, p. 415 (as per Kuldip Singh J.).

note of caution against appointing judges on regional, communal, or caste-based grounds. He held:

> It is essential and vital for the establishment of real participatory democracy that all sections and classes of people, be they backward classes or scheduled castes or scheduled tribes or minorities or women, should be afforded equal opportunity so that the judicial administration is also participated in by the outstanding and meritorious candidates belonging to all sections of the society not by any selective or insular group.[233]

Justice Pandian also noted that there could be 'meritorious and suitable candidates practicing in forums other than the High Courts',[234] and the Chief Justice of the state would not know who these candidates were. Justice Pandian found that for this reason, the government would be in a position to bring such candidates to the attention of the Chief Justice.

Noted constitutional scholar, H.M. Seervai, later wrote, 'Never has a majority judgment of the [Supreme Court] reached a lower level of judicial incompetence.'[235] However, against the backdrop of a weakening executive, the judiciary had now started to assert itself, and to assert control over its own composition.

THIRD JUDGES CASE

Between 6 October 1993, the date of the Supreme Court's decision in the second Judges case, and 28 October 1998, the Court's decision in the third Judges case, India continued on its path of political instability at the centre. Two general elections were held within the span of these five years, one in 1996, and the other in 1998. Each time, the electorate picked no clear winner—weak minority governments came to power on the back of tenuous coalitional alliances. During this period, India witnessed its shortest ever term for a government—the BJP government lasted all of 13 days in office after the 1996 general elections. The post of prime minister changed

---

[233] *Supreme Court Advocates on Record Association* v. *Union of India*, AIR 1994 SC 268, p. 348 (per Pandian J.).
[234] *Supreme Court Advocates on Record Association* v. *Union of India*, AIR 1994 SC 268, p. 348 (per Pandian J.).
[235] Seervai, *Constitutional Law*, p. 2928.

four times during this period.[236] Against this backdrop, the Court continued to assert itself and its power seemed to grow, almost in inverse proportion to the decline of executive power. The Court's most visible assertions of political power came in the famous *Vineet Narain* v. *Union of India*, (1996) 2 SCC 199 'Jain diaries' case where it took upon itself the task of supervising corruption investigations, and in the Bommai case[237] where the Court seemed to enter the political thicket. All this took place against the backdrop of rising allegations of corruption against the higher judiciary.[238] It was in this context that the third Judges case was decided.

The 'wider consultation' that the Court called for in the third Judges case was perhaps an indication of the Court's distrust of its own members—the fewer the members of the judiciary who made judicial appointments, the Court seemed to hold, the greater the chances of arbitrariness and error. The fear of judicial arbitrariness, in the context of the Court's rising power and the executive's tottering at the centre, was perhaps the motive force of the Court's decision in the third Judges case.

Background

The 15 March 1996 issue of *India Today* magazine had a Supreme Court judge on its cover, for perhaps the first time in its history. The caption read 'Mr. Justice'. The issue detailed a Supreme Court judge's role in the investigation against corruption in India. The Court's overtures in the Jain diaries case were a clear indicator of its rising assertiveness in this era, against the backdrop of weak political institutions. The Court used the writ of 'continuing mandamus'[239]

---

[236] The following served as prime ministers in succession: A.B. Vajpayee, H.D. Deve Gowda, I.K. Gujral, and A.B. Vajpayee.

[237] *S.R. Bommai* v. *Union of India*, AIR 1994 SC 1918. See Sorabjee, 'Decision of the Supreme Court'; Gary Jeffrey Jacobsohn. 2008. 'Bommai and the Judicial Power: A View from the United States', *Indian Journal of Constitutional Law*, 2: 38–66.

[238] See for example, note 240.

[239] In the Court's words, '[I]t was advantageous not to hear the matter through and issue a writ of mandamus, leaving it to the authorities to comply with it, but to keep the matter pending while the investigations were being carried on, ensuring that this was done by monitoring them from time to time and issuing orders in this behalf.' *Vineet Narain* v. *Union of India*, (1998) 1 SCC 226, p. 226.

in the Jain diaries case, and periodically supervised the enforcement of its own orders. But while the judiciary was taking on the executive in a crusade against corruption on the one hand, its members were not immune from allegations of corruption on the other. In March 1995, the Chief Justice of the Bombay High Court resigned, facing allegations of corruption.[240]

At around the same time, there was also dissatisfaction in the bar as to how judges were being appointed to the Supreme Court of India.[241]

---

[240] It had been alleged that he had received money from a London-based publisher for a book he had written on Muslim law, and that this payment had served as a proxy for a bribe. Manoj Mitta. 1995. 'Judges Under Fire', *India Today*, 31 March, 21(6), p. 58. Later, this became the subject of contempt proceedings filed against the Bar Council of Maharashtra and others, where the petitioner claimed that the chief justice had been coerced into resigning. In the contempt proceedings, the Supreme Court issued guidelines on how such cases should be treated in the future, in order to avoid the 'needless embarrassment of contempt proceedings against the office bearers of the Bar Association'. *C. Ravichandran Iyer v. Justice A.M. Bhattacharjee*, (1995) 5 SCC 457, p. 481.

[241] During Chief Justice Ahmadi's term, the two most senior judges, Kuldip Singh and J.S. Verma had agreed to the appointment of S.S. Sodhi, a judge of the Punjab and Haryana High Court (and then Chief Justice of the Allahabad High Court), to the Supreme Court of India. Yet, he had not been appointed. Ahmadi chose to consult two other judges, Punchhi and Sahai, who had expressed their reservations. Without mentioning any names, Fali S. Nariman mentions this incident in his autobiography. Fali S. Nariman. 2010. *Before Memory Fades: An Autobiography*. Hay House, pp. 397–8. In his autobiography, Justice Sodhi writes that Chief Justice Ahmadi asked Justices Punchhi and Sahai for their views about Justice S.S. Sodhi 'without the knowledge or consent' of Justices Kuldip Singh and J.S. Verma. According to Justice Sodhi, Punchhi was opposed to Sodhi's appointment because Punchhi had aligned himself with V. Ramaswami when he was Chief Justice of the Chandigarh High Court, while Sodhi 'stood out prominently amongst the judges who were opposed to his doings'. Justice Sahai, Sodhi writes, was 'unhappy' with him because (*a*) he 'did not agree to recommend his son for appointment as judge of the Allahabad High Court', and (*b*) he 'transferred Justice S.N. Sahay, his son's father-in-law, from Lucknow to Allahabad despite Justice Sahai's asking [him] not to do so'. See Sodhi, *Other Side of Justice*, pp. 294–8. In 1996, S. Marimuthu, a district court judge, was appointed to the Madras High Court, despite representations made to Chief Justice Ahmadi by senior lawyers like V.M. Tarkunde, Shanti Bhushan, and Ram Jethmalani that he should not be appointed. Manoj Mitta. 1996. 'Above the Law', *India Today*, 31 December, 21(24), p. 52.

The old system of executive interference had now been replaced by 'politicking' among judges.

In April–May 1996, India held its 11th general election—one of the cleanest elections ever held, on account of the efforts of Chief Election Commissioner T.N. Seshan.[242] No party gained a clear majority in the Lok Sabha. The BJP won the most seats—161 out of 543,[243] or 29.66 per cent of the house. The Congress party finished second with 140 seats. President Shankar Dayal Sharma invited the BJP to form the government, and on 16 May 1996, Atal Bihari Vajpayee was sworn in as Prime Minister of India.[244] However, his minority government lasted only 13 days, and he resigned, facing the prospect of a no-confidence vote in the house.[245] Following this failed experiment, another minority government came to power—the 'National Front-Left Front' coalition, which came to be called the 'United Front' coalition, a conglomeration of 13 ideologically disparate regional parties[246] backed from the outside by the Congress party—the 'main electoral opponent' of many of its constituents.[247] Together, the 13 regional parties of the United Front government had only 178 seats[248] in the house—roughly translating to about 32 per cent of seats, and together with Congress' support, it accounted roughly for only 58 per cent of seats. Gone were the Indira Gandhi and Rajiv Gandhi years where one party could dominate the agenda of the government. A commentator wrote at the time that with 'the

[242] Sumit Ganguly. 1997. 'India in 1996: A Year of Upheaval', *Asian Survey*, 37(2): 126–35.

[243] Election Commission of India. 1997. 'Statistical Report on General Elections, 1996, to the Eleventh Lok Sabha, Volume I', available online at http://eci. nic.in/eci_main/StatisticalReports/LS_1996/Vol_I_LS_96.pdf (last accessed on 22 October 2011).

[244] Janak Singh. 1996. 'Vajpayee Sworn In as PM', *Times of India*, 17 May, p. 1.

[245] Arun Subramaniam. 1996. 'Walking a Tightrope', *India Today*, 15 June, 21(11), p. 22.

[246] The parties were: Janata Dal, Communist Party of India (Marxist), Communist Party of India, Dravida Munnetra Kazhagam (DMK), Tamil Maanila Congress, Samajwadi Party, Telegu Desam Party(N), Asom Gana Parishad, INC(T), FB, Revolutionary Socialist Party, Madhya Pradesh Vikas Congress, and Karnataka Congress Party. Arun Subramaniam, 'Walking a Tightrope', p. 22.

[247] Subramaniam, 'Walking a Tightrope', p. 22.

[248] Subramaniam, 'Walking a Tightrope', p. 22.

breakdown of the dominant party system, India [had] entered a transition period characterized by fluid, fragmented political formations and unstable coalition governments'.[249] The Chief Minister of Karnataka, and president of the Janata Dal party in Karnataka, H.D. Deve Gowda, was sworn in as Prime Minister of India on 1 June 1996.[250]

In April 1997, the Congress party forced the resignation of Deve Gowda as Prime Minister of India—Congress party president, Sitaram Kesari, withdrew support from the government.[251] On 11 April 1997, Deve Gowda lost a trust vote on the floor of the house (by 158–292 votes).[252] Inder Kumar Gujral was sworn in as Prime Minister of India on 21 April 1997.[253]

In the meantime, V.N. Gadgil, a Congress party member, moved a bill to make judicial appointments political once more, because the courts were going 'too far',[254] a telling indicator of the Court's rising power at the time. The move did not succeed. Similarly, a bill to amend the Constitution was drafted by the law minister, Ramakant D. Khalap, to take the power of appointing judges away from the Chief Justice of India. However, this too did not material-ize, reportedly because the BJP changed its mind over the issue.[255] A bill to limit the public interest litigations that the Court could hear was also drafted at the time, but the BJP and the Left opposed it.[256] All this points to the fact that the weak central executive at the time, with its disparate interests, perhaps speaking in incoherent

[249] Sudha Pai. 1996. 'Transformation of the Indian Party System: The 1996 Lok Sabha Elections', *Asian Survey*, 36(12): 1170–83.

[250] *Times of India*. 1996. 'Chidambaram Gets Finance, Mulayam Defence', *Times of India*, 2 June, p. 1.

[251] See Sumit Mitra. 1997. 'Gowda's Gaffes and Kesri's Curse', *India Today*, 30 April, 22(8), p. 14.

[252] Janak Singh. 1997. 'Deve Gowda Resigns after Losing Confidence Vote', *Times of India*, 12 April, p. 1.

[253] *Times of India*. 1997. 'I.K. Gujral Will Be Sworn In as PM Today', *Times of India*, 21 April, p. 1.

[254] *India Today*. 1997. 'Crossfire: Judges' Appointments', *India Today*, 21 July, 22(17), p. 48.

[255] Sumit Mitra and Sayantan Chakravarty. 1997. 'Locking Horns', *India Today*, 28 July, 22(18), p. 22.

[256] Mitra and Chakravarty, 'Locking Horns', p. 22.

voices, was unable to tether the judiciary, although it was piqued by it.

The new minority government would be short-lived too. That year, a retired Chief Justice of the Rajasthan High Court, Milap Chand Jain, submitted his official report following an investigation into the circumstances surrounding Rajiv Gandhi's assassination. He concluded that the assassination would not have been possible without the support of the state government in Tamil Nadu—a government formed by the DMK, a member of the United Front coalition. The Congress party threatened to withdraw support if the DMK were not ousted from the United Front coalition. The coalition refused to budge. After the Congress party withdrew its support from the government, both the BJP and the Congress party staked claims to forming the government, but the President of India rejected them both, and called for elections to be held in February–March 1998.[257]

Again, in the midst of the 'Jain diaries' case, fresh allegations of corruption were levelled against the higher judiciary.[258] The results of the general elections to the 12th Lok Sabha were expected—no single party won a clear majority. The BJP won the most seats

[257] Sumit Ganguly. 1998. 'India in 1997: Another Year of Turmoil', *Asian Survey*, 38(2): 126–34.

[258] On 7 May 1997, all the judges of the Supreme Court of India reportedly adopted a set of guidelines for probity in public life applicable to themselves. At around the same time, a judge of the Rajasthan High Court, B.J. Sethna, alleged that Chief Justice J.S. Verma had illegally drawn allowances during his stint as chief justice in Jodhpur between 1986 and 1989. Other allegations surfaced. J.S. Verma's retirement was around the corner, and his successor by the seniority convention, Justice Punchhi, the 'darling of the bar' (*India Today*. 1997. 'Judicial Dissensions', *India Today*, 6 October, 22[28], p. 38) had unwittingly become controversial. A representation was made to the Chief Justice of India by the Committee on Judicial Accountability (CJA), which included senior lawyers like V.M. Tarkunde, Shanti Bhushan, and Ram Jethmalani, that the judge be super-seded. However, the view that Punchhi was unfit for the post of Chief Justice of India was not unanimously held and it divided the bar. The Supreme Court Bar Association suspended the senior lawyers who had made representations against Punchhi, calling the allegations against him 'irresponsible' (*Times of India*. 1997. 'SC Bar Association Suspends 5 Top Lawyers over Punchhi Issue', *Times of India*, 30 September, p. 1). The Chief Justice of India, J.S. Verma, set up a committee of three judges (M.K. Mukherjee, S.C. Sen, and S.P. Bharucha) to

again—182 out of 543, or 33.5 per cent of the house.[259] The Congress party won 141 seats, approximately, 25.9 per cent of the house. With the memory of its failed 13-day government at the back of its mind, the BJP carried out intensive efforts to form a government. On 19 March 1998, Atal Bihari Vajpayee was sworn in as Prime Minister of India once more.[260] Then, on 28 March 1998, a BJP-led 18-party[261] coalition won a confidence vote on the floor of the house (by 274–261 votes).[262]

---

probe the allegations against Punchhi (*India Today*. 1997. 'A Benchmark for Bar Brawls', *India Today*, 24 November, 22[35], p. 36). If Punchhi were to be superseded, the next most senior judge, S.C. Agrawal, would become Chief Justice of India. Finally, two months after the controversy first erupted, on 5 January 1998, days before he was due to retire, J.S. Verma drove to Rashtrapati Bhavan to inform the president that he would be recommending Punchhi as his successor (*India Today*. 1998. 'Punchhi At Last', *India Today*, 19 January, 23[3], p. 40). However, I.K. Gujral, who was Prime Minister of India at the time, states in his autobiography that Justice Verma had suggested that Justice Punchhi's recommendation be held back, on 5 January 1998, out of worry that a public interest case may be filed by CJA challenging the appointment. I.K. Gujaral. 2011. *Matters of Discretion: An Autobiography*. New Delhi: Hay House, pp. 478–9.

[259] Election Commission of India. 1999. 'Statistical Report on General Elections, 1998, to the 12th Lok Sabha, Volume I', available online at http://eci.nic.in/eci_main/StatisticalReports/LS_1998/Vol_I_LS_98.pdf (last accessed on 24 October 2011).

[260] Janak Singh. 1998. 'Yashwant Sinha Gets Finance', *Times of India*, 20 March, p. 1.

[261] The members of the coalition were: All India Anna Dravida Munnetra Kazhagam, Telegu Desam Party, Samata Party, Biju Janata Dal, Shiromani Akali Dal, Trinamul Congress, Shiv Sena, Marumalarchi Deravida Munnetra Kazhagam, Pattali Makkal Katchi, Lok Shakti, Haryana Vikas Party, Tamizhaga Raji Congress, Janata Party, and five smaller regional parties. Janak Singh. 1998. '12 Ministers May Take Oath', *Times of India*, 19 March, p. 10.

[262] *Times of India*. 1998. 'Vajpayee Sails Home on TDP Support', *Times of India*, 29 March, p. 1. The coalition's most hard-fought and valued members included Jayalalitha's All India Anna Dravida Munnetra Kazhagam, which had 27 members in the house (Swapan Dasgupta and Vaasanthi. 1998. 'The Odd One Out', *India Today*, 23 March, 23[12], p. 12), and the Telegu Desam Party, a former member of the United Front government, which had 12 members in Parliament (*Times of India*. 1998. 'SP Will Boycott Swearing-in of New Cabinet', *Times of India*, 18 March, p. 7), and whose leader, Chandrababu Naidu, had even served as convener of the United Front.

The Decision

The Chief Justice of India, M.M. Punchhi, recommended three names[263] for appointment to the Supreme Court of India. One of the three judges recommended, Bhawani Singh, was very young at the time, and would have become Chief Justice of India for five years had the recommendation been accepted.[264] In making these recommendations, Punchhi had only consulted the two most senior judges on the Court: S.C. Agrawal and G.N. Ray, but no other judges. His predecessor, J.S. Verma, had claimed that he would consult five judges, and members of the bar, before making such recommendations.[265]

By May 1998, Punchhi had already made his recommendations. Under the second Judges case, the appointments were binding on the president, unless, amongst other reasons, a disagreement arose between the Chief Justice of India and one of the senior judges he consulted. In order to buy time, the president requested the Supreme Court of India for an advisory opinion on the nature of the consultation that was required to take place between the Chief Justice of India and his colleagues. By the time the case was decided—on 28 October 1998—the Chief Justice of India, Punchhi, and the two senior judges he had consulted, Agrawal and Ray, had each retired. On the face of it, therefore, the president appeared to have made this reference seeking an advisory opinion from the Supreme Court in order to circumvent Punchhi's recommendation,[266] in the words of Fali S. Nariman, 'simply to avoid a possibly ugly situation

---

[263] U.C. Bannerjee, R.C. Lahoti, and Bhawani Singh. Sumit Mitra. 1998. 'Nudge the Judge', *India Today*, 4 May, 23(18), p. 22.

[264] Punchhi also recommended that the following high court chief justices be transferred: M.M. Singh Liberhan (Madras) to Gauhati, A.B. Sahariya (Punjab and Haryana) to Rajasthan, R.P. Sethi (Karnataka) to Kerala, and Om Prakash (Kerala) to Punjab and Haryana. The CJA alleged that these judges were being punished for having crossed Punchhi's path in the past—*India Today* reported that the allegation was that some of them had objected to the appointment of Suresh Amba, one of Punchhi's juniors, to the High Court, on separate occasions. Mitra, 'Nudge the Judge', p. 22.

[265] Mitra, 'Nudge the Judge', p. 22.

[266] U.C. Banerjee and R.C. Lahoti were subsequently appointed to the Court on 9 December 1998.

from developing'.[267] However, the Court seized this opportunity to shed some light on its decision in the second Judges case.

A bench of nine judges heard the case. The fact that this was a bench of nine judges, and not 11 judges, meant that the Court could not overrule its decision in the second Judges case, but merely interpret it. Even the government did not want a reconsideration of the second Judges case.[268] The bench was composed of the nine most senior judges on the Court.[269] The president had posed nine questions to the Supreme Court of India. The Court consolidated these questions into three groups of issues: (*a*) the nature of the consultation process between the Chief Justice of India and other judges, (*b*) judicial review, and (*c*) the relevance of seniority in making appointments to the Court.

Only one opinion was written for the Court and as a result the Court's decision in the third Judges case was the shortest amongst all the Judges cases. Justice S.P. Bharucha, the author of the Court's opinion, was also the only member of the Court at the time who had served on the bench in the second Judges case. In its decision in the third Judges case, the Supreme Court made three significant departures from its decision in the second Judges case.[270]

---

[267] Nariman, *Before Memory Fades*, p. 398. He called it 'one of most futile presidential references ever filed by the Government of India', and an 'Anti-Justice Punchhi Reference'. Nariman, *Before Memory Fades*, pp. 398–9.

[268] *In re Presidential Reference*, AIR 1999 SC 1, p. 15, para. 9.

[269] Bharucha, Mukherjee, Majmudar, Manohar, Nanavati, Ahmed, Venkataswami, Kirpal, and Pattanaik. The Chief Justice of India, A.S. Anand, did not sit on this bench, as had always been the case in the previous Judges cases. However, the reference was made by the president on 23 July 1998, at a time when Justice Anand was not the Chief Justice of India—he was perhaps not assigned to the bench anticipating that he would become Chief Justice of India by the time the case was decided. However, significantly, two junior judges who were due to become Chief Justice of India later by the seniority convention, V.N. Khare and Rajendra Babu, who were serving on the Court at the time, were not assigned to this bench. This was unlike every single one of the previous Judges cases before this, where future Chief Justices of India were always on the bench, even though they may have been very junior judges. As a result of the emphasis on seniority in composing this bench, regional diversity was perhaps sacrificed. Consequently, two judges each from the states of Maharashtra (Bharucha and Manohar) and Gujarat (Majmudar and Nanavati) sat on the bench.

[270] Besides these three significant departures from the second Judges case, the Court issued some clarifications concerning the second Judges case—reiterating

The first departure was that the Court increased the number of judges the Chief Justice of India would have to consult before making an appointment to the Supreme Court of India. Under the second Judges case, the Chief Justice of India was only required to consult the two most senior judges on the Court. Now, before making appointments to the Supreme Court, he would have to consult the four most senior judges on the Court. The Court called this body, namely, the Chief Justice of India and the four most senior judges, the collegium. As discussed earlier, the term collegium had previously been used by Justice Bhagwati in the first Judges case,[271] although he had not

---

the previous decision on the one hand, and adding more process on the other. Thus, for example:

1. It was clarified that while appointing judges to high courts, the Chief Justice of India was only required to consult the two most senior judges of the Court, as usual. *In re Presidential Reference*, AIR 1999 SC 1, p. 19, para. 27.

2. While transferring a high court judge from one state to another, the Chief Justice of India was required to consult the four most senior judges on the Supreme Court of India, the Chief Justice of the transferor high court, and the chief justice of the transferee high court, along with other Supreme Court judges who would be 'in a position to provide material which would assist in the process'. *In re Presidential Reference*, AIR 1999 SC 1, p. 21, paras. 33–4. The same applied to the transfer of high court chief justices, except that for this only the views of one or more knowledgeable Supreme Court judges had to be ascertained. *In re Presidential Reference*, AIR 1999 SC 1, p. 21, para. 36.

3. It was clarified that where the president returned a file containing a recommendation to the Chief Justice of India, asking him to reconsider the suitability of the candidate, the Chief Justice of India could, in his discretion, ask the person whose candidature was being considered for his response, in which case the collegium would have to consider the response. *In re Presidential Reference*, AIR 1999 SC 1, p. 18, para. 21.

4. The Court reiterated that judicial review in the matter of appointments would only be available on the limited grounds of (*a*) absence of consultation or (*b*) lack of eligibility. *In re Presidential Reference*, AIR 1999 SC 1, p. 19, para. 29. In the matter of transfers, judicial review would only be available if the transfer was not made in accordance with the prescribed process. *In re Presidential Reference*, AIR 1999 SC 1, p. 21, para. 35.

[271] See further, Law Commission of India. 2008. 'Proposal for Reconsideration of Judges cases I, II and III, Report No. 214', 21 November, available online

specified in detail, back then, who the collegium ought to consist of. In the third Judges case, the term collegium was used to describe the Chief Justice of India and the four most senior judges on the court.[272]

The Court clarified who was, and who was not, to be a part of the collegium. First, it was held that even if the next Chief Justice of India by the seniority norm were not one of the four most senior judges on the Court, he would nonetheless 'invariably' be made part of the collegium.[273] Second, it was held that any other senior judge (that is, besides the four most senior judges on the Court) consulted by the Chief Justice of India would not be part of the collegium. According to the second Judges case, the Chief Justice of India was required to additionally consult the most senior judge on the Supreme Court from the high court of the candidate being considered for appointment. In the third Judges case, the Court clarified that this judge would not be made part of the collegium, unless he was already a part of the collegium by virtue of his seniority.[274] It was clarified that it was of no consequence that the judge being so consulted did not belong to the same parent high court as the candidate being considered—a senior Supreme Court judge could be consulted for

---

at http://lawcommissionofindia.nic.in/reports/report214.pdf (last accessed on 17 March 2012), p. 43. In this report, the Law Commission recommended an 'urgent and immediate review' of the present method of appointing judges.

[272] *In re Presidential Reference*, AIR 1999 SC 1, p. 16, para. 14.

[273] *In re Presidential Reference*, AIR 1999 SC 1, p. 16, para. 15. In fact, the only time before this decision that it had ever come to pass that at least one of the four most senior judges on the Court was not in line to become Chief Justice of India by the seniority convention was in 1956, when S.R. Das was Chief Justice of India, and the four most senior judges (Bose, Bhagwati, Jagannadhadas, and Ayyar) were not in the line of succession. At that time, the collegium system of appointments was not in vogue. Later, this would only come to pass once again, during Chief Justice K.G. Balakrishnan's term, when the four most senior judges on the Court (Agrawal, Bhan, Pasayat, and Singh) were not in line for the post of Chief Justice of India.

[274] *In re Presidential Reference*, AIR 1999 SC 1, p. 17, para. 16. Thus, for example, if an Allahabad High Court judge were being considered for appointment to the Supreme Court, the most senior Supreme Court judge who had served in the Allahabad High Court would have to be consulted by the Chief Justice of India. Such judges would not be considered part of the collegium, unless they were one of the four most senior judges on the Court.

a candidate even if the judge only knew the candidate because he had been transferred to the candidate's high court, whether as chief justice or as puisne judge.[275] It was also clarified that if the most senior judge from the candidate's high court on the Supreme Court of India was not in a position to assess the candidate's worthiness, the next most senior Supreme Court judge from the candidate's high court could be consulted.[276] Third, the Court addressed the contingency that a member of the collegium may cease to be a part of the Court before the president asks the Chief Justice of India to reconsider a recommendation made by the collegium. In the second Judges case, it was held that the president could request the Chief Justice of India to reconsider a recommendation, if the president did not find the candidate suitable. The Court had held that if the Chief Justice of India along with the senior judges unanimously agreed that the appointment should be made anyway, despite the president's objections, then the president would have to make the appointment as a matter of 'healthy convention'. In the third Judges case, it was clarified that if, in the meanwhile, one or more members of the collegium retired or were 'otherwise unavailable' at the time that the president requested the Chief Justice to reconsider a recommendation, the decision as to that candidate's suitability could be made by a collegium consisting of the remaining members of the original collegium, and other judges who had reached the required seniority, that is, those who had reached the position of the four most senior puisne judges of the Court.[277]

The second significant departure that the Court made from the second Judges case was that it limited the president's discretion when there was a difference of opinion between the Chief Justice of India and the judges he consulted. According to the second Judges case, if one or both of the two most senior judges on the Court disagreed with the opinion of the Chief Justice of India, the president had the option of either accepting the chief justice's recommendation for appointment or rejecting it. It has been discussed how this demonstrated that the Chief Justice of India did not have 'primacy' over

[275] *In re Presidential Reference*, AIR 1999 SC 1, p. 17, para. 18.
[276] *In re Presidential Reference*, AIR 1999 SC 1, p. 17, para. 17A.
[277] *In re Presidential Reference*, AIR 1999 SC 1, p. 18, para. 20.

the other judges he consulted, since the president had the option of refusing to accept the Chief Justice's recommendation in that limited circumstance. However, now, in the third Judges case, the Court held that the president had no option but to refuse the Chief Justice's recommendation if it was not in agreement with the views of a majority of the members of the collegium, that is, if at least three judges of the collegium disagreed with the Chief Justice of India.[278] In other words, it was now beyond doubt that the Chief Justice of India did not have 'primacy' over his other senior colleagues on the Court—the president no longer had the discretion to accept the chief justice's view when it was in conflict with the views of a majority of the members of the collegium. Perhaps in order to appear not to be overruling the second Judges case, the Court in the third Judges case held that its decision in the second Judges case had only dealt with this matter 'delicately', that in sum and substance this was exactly what the Court had intended to hold in the second Judges case.

The third significant departure that the Court made from the second Judges case was that it watered down its previous emphasis on seniority while making appointments to the Supreme Court of India. Judges of outstanding merit, it was held, could be appointed to the Supreme Court irrespective of seniority. Judges equally placed, in terms of merit, could be appointed to the Court based on other criteria, like seniority or regional representation.[279] It was held that the collegium did not have to record 'strong cogent reasons' for deviating from the norm of seniority in making appointments to the Supreme Court, when a judge of outstanding merit was being appointed to the Court.

Merit … is the predominant consideration for the purposes of appointment to the Supreme Court. Where, therefore, there is outstanding merit the possessor thereof

---

[278] *In re Presidential Reference*, AIR 1999 SC 1, p. 17, para. 19.
[279] *In re Presidential Reference*, AIR 1999 SC 1, p. 18, paras. 23–4. While reading this, it must be kept in mind that the author of this opinion was appointed to the Bombay High Court at the age of 40, and then to the Supreme Court of India at the age of 55. It will be seen in Chapter 3 that judges are very rarely appointed to High Courts before the age of 45, and to the Supreme Court before the age of 55. Had seniority been the only ground for appointment to the Supreme Court, and had merit not been taken into account at all, this would perhaps not have been possible.

deserves to be appointed regardless of the fact that he may not stand high in the all India seniority list or in his own High Court. All that then needs to be recorded when recommending him for appointment is that he has outstanding merit. *When the contenders for appointment to the Supreme Court do not possess such outstanding merit but have, nevertheless, the required merit in more or less equal degree, there may be reason to recommend one among them because, for example, the particular region of the country in which his parent High Court is situated is not represented on the Supreme Court bench.* All that then needs to be recorded when making the recommendation for appointment is this factor.... It is only when, for very strong reasons, a collegium finds that, whatever his seniority, some High Court Judge should never be appointed to the Supreme Court that it should so record. This would then be justified and would afford guidance on subsequent occasions of considering who to recommend.

(emphasis supplied)

Interestingly, the Court clarified what it had meant while using the phrase 'legitimate expectation' in the second Judges cases, in the context of judicial appointments to the Supreme Court. The phrase 'legitimate expectation' was now replaced with the word 'hope'—phraseology that no longer conveyed entitlement: '[A]ll that was intended to be conveyed was that it was very natural that senior High Court Judges should entertain hopes of elevation to the Supreme Court and that the Chief Justice of India and the collegium should bear this in mind.'[280]

*   *   *

Constitutional court judges in independent India have enjoyed security of tenure since the Constitution came into being, that is, they cannot be removed except by a strenuously difficult impeachment process, upon a showing of 'proved misbehaviour or incapacity'.[281] So far, not a single judge has been successfully removed in this manner, though a few attempts have been made. Once a judge is appointed as a permanent judge on a high court or as a judge on the Supreme Court, he is thus guaranteed security of tenure. His benefits cannot be altered to his disadvantage once he is appointed.[282] Accordingly, the mere fact that a judge is appointed to a high court or to the

---

[280] *In re Presidential Reference*, AIR 1999 SC 1, p. 19, para. 25.

[281] Article 124(4) and proviso (b) to Article 217(1), Constitution of India.

[282] Proviso to Article 125(2) and proviso to Article 221(2), Constitution of India.

Supreme Court by the executive does not take away from the judge's independence from executive influence, since the judge has security of tenure, and can decide cases according to his own conscience once on the court, even against the party that was responsible for his appointment. He may feel a sense of obligation or gratitude towards the political party that appointed him to the court, but from a structural standpoint, he is independent because he has security of tenure.

However, before the second Judges case in 1993, the executive could interfere with the independence of the judiciary by tampering with judicial promotions and transfers or by offering judges post-retirement rewards for deciding cases favourably. The executive primarily controlled four kinds of 'promotions'[283] prior to 1993: (a) the promotion of a subordinate court judge as a high court judge, (b) the promotion of an additional high court judge as permanent high court judge, (c) the promotion of a high court judge to the post of high court chief justice, and (d) the promotion of a high court judge or chief justice to the post of Supreme Court judge. Additionally, the Indira Gandhi government seized control of a fifth kind of promotion in order to control the judiciary: the promotion of a Supreme Court judge to the post of Chief Justice of India. The Supreme Court of India seized control of the first four kinds of promotions in its 1993 and 1998 decisions in the second and third Judges cases respectively, and by doing so, it enhanced the independence of the judiciary in India. However, these four kinds of promotions only impact the independence of the high court (and subordinate court) judiciary, and not the Supreme Court judiciary. Once a person is appointed to the Supreme Court, the only 'promotion' that can be offered as a reward or punishment for judicial decisions is his promotion to the post of Chief Justice of India—and except for the Indira Gandhi years, it has been seen that the seniority norm was followed in the Court almost without exception. Therefore, the 1993 and 1998 decisions of the Court in the second and third Judges cases did not impact the independence of Supreme Court judges, or structural independence. Instead, what these decisions did do was to enhance the Court's

---

[283] In some cases, constitutionally speaking, these may be considered fresh appointments, though that does not take away from their essential character of being in the nature of promotions.

institutional independence—in other words, rather than making Supreme Court judges independent, these cases made the Supreme Court itself independent of executive checks and balances, not in a structural sense impacting individual justices, but in an institutional sense from a separation of powers standpoint.

The same can be said about transfers. The executive could interfere with the independence of high court judges by transferring them from one court to another, whether as a puisne judge or chief justice. By seizing this power in the 1993 and 1998 decisions, the Supreme Court of India enhanced the independence of the high court judiciary, but not that of the Supreme Court judiciary. This is because, once appointed to the Supreme Court, judges cannot be transferred. For this reason, the 1993 and 1998 decisions enhanced the structural independence of high court judges, while enhancing the institutional independence of the Supreme Court.

Despite the 1993 and 1998 decisions of the Supreme Court of India in the second and third Judges cases, the executive can still offer incentives or rewards to judges, that would accrue to them post-retirement, if they decide cases favourably (for example, post-retirement employment).[284]

One of the central themes of this chapter has been that the Supreme Court of India usurped the power to appoint judges against the backdrop of an increasingly weak central government. The 1993 and 1998 Judges cases were not decided during the powerful Indira Gandhi government era, but at a time when political power was weakening at the centre. It is beyond the scope of this book to enter into any substantial normative discussion as to whether the present method of appointing judges, that is, the collegium system, is constitutionally appropriate or adequate. This book concerns itself not with the process of the collegium system, but its outcome: subsequent chapters will assess the collegium system from the standpoint of the

---

[284] However, there are no simple answers to the question of whether judges ought to be able to accept post-retirement employment from the government. The government could argue that post-retirement employment gives judges incentives not to take bribes. If they have no prospects of employment after retirement, they may be incentivized to make money while on the court. The government could argue that by offering judges the safety net of post-retirement employment, it diminishes that incentive.

criteria used to appoint judges to the Supreme Court. Though I did not ask most judges for their appraisal of the collegium system, it may be worth mentioning here that one of the judges I interviewed, who served on the collegium in the mid-2000s, informed me that the collegium system in its present form was 'rubbish', that the collegium was not equipped with the knowledge necessary to make judicial appointments (Interview 4). The judge informed me that the Chief Justice of India overruled the collegium in one instance and confirmed the name of an additional judge as a permanent judge on a high court. Scholarly appraisals of the process of the collegium system have likewise been quite critical of it.[285] Criticisms of the collegium system include: it conflicts with the intent of the framers of India's Constitution;[286] it 'detract(s) the judges of the collegium from their principal judicial work of hearing and deciding cases';[287] the collegium resorts to 'ad hoc informal consultations' with other judges, which consultations do not significantly investigate criteria such as work, standing, integrity, and so on;[288] the collegium lays too heavy an emphasis on seniority in making appointments to the Supreme Court;[289] assessments offered by judges during the consultations are sometimes 'warped or tainted';[290] and 'sometimes better judges are overlooked or ignored'.[291] Additionally, the collegium system puts the Court outside the sphere of legitimate checks and balances. The legitimacy of counter-majoritarian judges in a democracy is hinged on their appointment by popularly elected representatives.

---

[285]   T.R. Andhyarujina. 2009. 'Appointment of Judges by Collegium of Judges', *Hindu*, 18 December, available online at http://www.thehindu.com/opinion/op-ed/article66672.ece (last accessed on 21 April 2012); Nariman, *Before Memory Fades*, pp. 399–405.

[286]   Andhyarujina, 'Appointment of Judges'.

[287]   Andhyarujina, 'Appointment of Judges'.

[288]   Andhyarujina, 'Appointment of Judges'.

[289]   Andhyarujina, 'Appointment of Judges'.

[290]   Nariman, *Before Memory Fades*, p. 401.

[291]   Nariman, *Before Memory Fades*, p. 400. Nariman cites the example of Justice M.L. Pendse who was not appointed to the Supreme Court, despite being, in the opinion of one Supreme Court judge, 'the best high court judge in the country', because he was 'disobedient', and because the 'Bombay Lobby' (that is, 'judges from Bombay then in the Supreme Court') was against his appointment. Nariman, *Before Memory Fades*, p. 401.

Intuitively, the fact that popularly elected officials appoint and remove judges makes counter-majoritarian courts legitimate in a democracy. However, in India, though the appointment of judges is theoretically made by the president, for all practical purposes the collegium appoints judges. Given that no judge in independent India has successfully been removed by the process of impeachment so far, the collegium system illegitimately insulates the Supreme Court and the judiciary from vibrant democratic checks and balances.[292] One jurist has suggested that the 'image of the court has gravely suffered' as a consequence of the present method of selecting judges.[293,*]

NOTE

* This book was written before the Fourth Judges Case, that is, *Supreme Court Advocates-on-Record Association* v. *Union of India*, (2016) 5 SCC 1, was decided. In that case, the Supreme Court rejected the National Judicial Appointments Commission and reaffirmed the collegium system. This book was cited by Justice Chelameswar in his dissenting judgment in that case.

---

[292] See Abhinav Chandrachud. 2010. 'The Insulation of India's Constitutional Judiciary', *Economic and Political Weekly*, 45(13): 38–42.

[293] Nariman, *Before Memory Fades*, p. 405.

3

AGE OF APPOINTMENT

THIS CHAPTER ANALYSES THE AGE at which judges have been appointed
to the Supreme Court of India between 1950 and 2011.[1] Since
Supreme Court judges retire at the age of 65,[2] the age at which a
judge is appointed to the Court automatically determines the length
of time that the judge will serve on the Court. My interviews with
former judges of the Supreme Court suggest that a person's age is
taken into account before he is appointed to the Supreme Court.
One gets the feeling that judges are sought to be appointed to the
Supreme Court when they are old enough so that they do not serve
very long tenures in office. A former Chief Justice of India, and a
former member of the collegium, said that it has almost become an
informal convention that senior high court judges are not appointed
to the Supreme Court until after they reach 'at least' the age of 55, if
they happen to be young while at a position of seniority (Interviews
9, 26). Some judges said that it is informally understood that barring a few exceptions no person is appointed to the post of high

---

[1] The study described here ends with the appointment of Justices S.J. Mukhopadhaya, Ranjana Desai, and J.S. Khehar to the Supreme Court on 13 September
2011. See also note 71 below.
[2] Article 124(2), Constitution of India.

court judge until he reaches the age of 45,[3] and since it takes 12–14 years for a person to climb the seniority ladder on a high court, and since Supreme Court judges are almost exclusively appointed from amongst the ranks of high court judges or chief justices, a person will naturally be of a relatively advanced age before he can be appointed to the Supreme Court (Interviews 17, 18). Other judges who answered this question agreed that there was a minimum age below which a judge would not be appointed to the Supreme Court (for example, Interviews 15, 16), and one termed it an 'unwritten rule' (Interview 24). One judge suggested that there is no age limit for appointment to the Supreme Court, but that 'usually 3-4 years are needed' to be appointed to the Court (Interview 25), that is, that a length of three–four years is considered a sufficient term in office. One judge said that there is a 'convention', 'rightly so', which has emerged more recently, that judges will not be appointed until after the age of 55—this ensures that Supreme Court judges have some maturity, which 'comes invariably with age' (Interview 28). This chapter seeks to demonstrate that these qualitative findings generally prove to be quantitatively true—that judges are appointed to the Supreme Court within a certain age bracket, and that consequently the tenure of judges on the Supreme Court is short in comparison with constitutional courts the world over, though similar to the tenure of justices in Asian countries like Japan, South Korea, and Indonesia.

In this chapter, it will be quantitatively demonstrated that the 1993 and 1998 Judges cases discussed in Chapter 2 have counterintuitively been followed by an increase in the age of appointment to the Court, with the result that judges appointed to the Supreme Court of India in the last two decades are older, on average, than those appointed in any previous decade. Using my findings, I will hypothesize that despite the institutional independence of the Supreme Court (measured in terms of the ability of senior Supreme Court judges to appoint Supreme Court judges, and freedom from executive checks and balances from a separation of powers

---

[3] In his autobiography, Fali S. Nariman mentions that when he was offered a high court judgeship in 1966, there was a convention that an offer of judgeship to anyone below the age of 40 required the approval of the Chief Justice of India. Nariman. 2010. *Before Memory Fades: An Autobiography*. Hay House, p. 136. The age criterion may therefore have been around for a while.

standpoint) the judiciary has imposed a norm of restraint upon itself by limiting the tenure (and therefore the influence) of each individual judge, as a compromise offered to the political branch of government in order to compensate for its independence and to make its independence less unpalatable for political actors.

In a seminal paper published in 1994, Mark Ramseyer argued that an independent judiciary comes into being when political actors expect: (a) elections to continue indefinitely and (b) to win elections only erratically.[4] Under such circumstances, political parties have an interest in ensuring an independent judiciary that may enforce long-term bargains they made with their constituents. An independent judiciary may also protect political actors now in power from persecution by state machinery once they are out of power—for which they will have to appoint independent, and not subservient, judges.[5] The age at which a judge is appointed to the Supreme Court of India does not materially affect his independence. This is because once a judge is appointed to the Court, he has security of tenure for the rest of his term on the Court, no matter how long or short the term may be.[6] However, intuitively, for reasons that will be discussed in detail below, the longer a judge serves in office, the more influential or powerful he may become. If a judge is both independent and

[4] Mark J. Ramseyer. 1994. 'The Puzzling (In)dependence of Courts: A Comparative Approach', *Journal of Legal Studies*, 23(2): 721–47. See further Matthew C. Stephenson. 2003. '"When the Devil Turns…": The Political Foundations of Independent Judicial Review', *Journal of Legal Studies*, 32(1): 59–89; William M. Landes and Richard A. Posner. 1975. 'The Independent Judiciary in an Interest-Group Perspective', *Journal of Law and Economics*, 18(3): 875–901.

[5] If the party in power was to appoint subservient judges that would only hold in its favour, the opposition party that comes to power subsequently may choose not to obey the subservient judges or to replace them with its own judges. Instead, the opposition party might be more amenable to accepting decisions of independent judges once it comes to power. A party in power that expects to lose power (but to potentially regain it later on) and that expects elections to continue indefinitely, therefore, has incentives to appoint independent judges.

[6] It is arguable that a political actor may strike a deal with a judge to appoint the judge to the court young only if he favours that political actor's policies. However, this argument falls through because once the judge is so appointed to the court, he has security of tenure, and cannot be removed from the court for any reason, and so the deal struck between the political actor and the judge cannot be enforced.

influential, there is greater scope for him to become an activist judge. This is all the more so if the Court is institutionally independent. Judicial activism, as distinguished from judicial independence, is a threat to political actors even in competitive electoral democracies where parties expect to win elections erratically. Using the empirical findings of this chapter I will hypothesize that in the last 20 years, although the Court's institutional independence has increased (since senior judges have the power to appoint judges after the 1993 and 1998 Judges cases), the judiciary itself has compensated for its increased independence by diminishing the influence of judges on the Court (that is, by shortening their tenures), as a compromise to make political actors more amenable to accept their independence.

Specifically, using the empirical findings of this chapter I will hypothesize that: (*a*) the high number of judges on India's Supreme Court has the effect of diffusing the influence wielded by each judge, (*b*) Supreme Court judges in India typically serve short three-to-seven-year terms in office, which reduces their ability to bring change to the Court or to materially impact the docket of the Court in any way, and their ability to be activist, much like in Japan, (*c*) the tenure of the Chief Justice of the Supreme Court—arguably, the single most powerful actor in India's judiciary—is incredibly short, which has the effect of limiting his influence, and (*d*) before the 1993 and 1998 Judges cases were decided, the political leadership of India was increasingly content with appointing judges older, so that they would exercise a limited influence while serving on the Court.[7] I will also hypothesize that following the 1993 and 1998 Judges cases, as a compromise for securing the power to appoint judges, the collegium appoints judges even older than they were before, to compensate for the Court's institutional independence.

THE TENURE DEBATE

The process of appointing judges in liberal democracies seeks to achieve some semblance of balance between democratic accountability

[7] One of the few exceptions to this occurred during the reign of the Janata Party, which appointed judges very young so that they could last longer on the Court, and potentially serve as safeguards against civil rights abuses of the kind committed during the Emergency under the watch of a pliant judiciary.

and judicial independence,[8] although the two often bear an inverse relationship with one another—as accountability decreases, independence increases and vice versa.[9] Such debates typically focus on how judges should be appointed,[10] how they should be removed,[11] the length of the term they should serve in office,[12] and what they should be able to do after leaving office.[13] Conventional wisdom dictates that counter-majoritarian courts in democracies derive their legitimacy from the elected representatives of the people, and that the pockets of 'undemocratic' counter-majoritarianism we call courts are especially legitimate when their members are appointed by elected officials. In the Indian context, we have seen that as political power at the centre weakened in the 1990s, judges of the Supreme Court of India asserted their power to determine their own composition—and the Court devised a system of co-option (*cooptación*)[14] where its most senior judges seized the power to appoint judges. This is problematic

---

[8] See for example, Lee Epstein, Jack Knight, and Olga Shvetsova. 2001. 'Comparing Judicial Selection Systems', *William and Mary Bill of Rights Journal*, 10(1): 7–36, pp. 19–20; Donald P. Kommers. 1976. *Judicial Politics in West Germany: A Study of the Federal Constitutional Court*. Beverly Hills: SAGE, p. 114; Peter D. Webster. 1995. 'Selection and Retention of Judges: Is There One "Best" Method?', *Florida State University Law Review*, 23(1): 1–42.

[9] Nicholas L. Georgakopoulos. 2000. 'Discretion in the Career and Recognition Judiciary', *Chicago Law School Roundtable*, 7(1): 205–26.

[10] See for example, Stephen J. Ware. 2009. 'The Missouri Plan in National Perspective', *Missouri Law Review*, 74(3): 751–75; Mary L. Volkcansek. 2009. 'Exporting the Missouri Plan: Judicial Appointment Commissions', *Missouri Law Review*, 74(3): 783–800; Justice Robert L. Brown. 1998. 'From Whence Cometh Our State Appellate Judges: Popular Elections Versus the Missouri Plan', *University of Arkansas Little Rock Law Journal*, 20(2): 313–26; James E. Lozier. 1996. 'The Missouri Plan A/K/A Merit Selection: Is It the Best Solution for Selecting Michigan's Judges?', *Michigan Bar Journal* 75(9): 918–27.

[11] See for example, Michael J. Gerhardt. 2000. *The Federal Impeachment Process: A Constitutional and Historical Analysis*. Chicago: University of Chicago Press.

[12] See for example, Philip D. Oliver. 1986. 'Systematic Justice: A Proposed Constitutional Amendment to Establish Fixed, Staggered Terms for Members of the United States Supreme Court', *Ohio State Law Journal*, 47(4): 799–834; Saikrishna B. Prakash. 1999. 'America's Aristocracy', *Yale Law Journal*, 109(3): 541–86, pp. 568–84, reviewing Mark Tushnet. 1999. *Taking the Constitution Away from the Courts*. Princeton: Princeton University Press.

[13] See Chapter 1.

[14] This term was used especially in Colombia—a system designed in 1957 to 'preserve the independence of the highest level judiciary'. Justice Manuel

from the standpoint of the Court's democratic legitimacy. Although judicial appointments are formally made by the executive in India, the recommendations of the collegium of senior judges are binding upon the executive, and for this reason, judges appointed in India today are arguably democratically illegitimate, on account of their heavy political insulation.[15] However, from a political science standpoint, judicial independence in India (in terms of the judiciary's heavy insulation from elected officials) might be democratic in that it is a tacitly accepted compromise by political actors who expect continuing elections and erratic electoral victories.

This chapter focuses on the tenure of judges of the Supreme Court of India. Judicial independence requires that once a judge is appointed to office, his or her tenure should not be capable of being either shortened (except for serious incapacity or misconduct) or extended—each of which would create incentives for judges to please the executive. For this reason, the question of the length of time judges ought to serve in office is an important one, as little can be done by way of correction once a judge is appointed to a court in a vibrant democracy. Constitutional systems of major liberal democracies the world over have converged on four constructs of tenure: (a) life tenure, probably the rarest system prevalent in the world,[16] supported famously by Alexander Hamilton,[17] and still prevalent in

---

José Cepeda-Espinosa. 2004. 'Judicial Activism in a Violent Context: The Origin, Role, and Impact of the Colombian Constitutional Court', *Washington University Global Studies Law Review*, 3(Special Issue): 529–700, 540n22.

[15] See Abhinav Chandrachud. 2010. 'The Insulation of India's Constitutional Judiciary', *Economic and Political Weekly*, 45(13): 38.

[16] Steven G. Calabresi and James Lindgren. 2006. 'Term Limits for the Supreme Court: Life Tenure Reconsidered', *Harvard Journal of Law and Public Policy*, 29(3): 769–877. See further, Paul D. Carrington and Roger C. Cramton. 2006. 'The Supreme Court Renewal Act: A Return to Basic Principles', in Roger C. Cramton and Paul D. Carrington (eds), *Reforming the Court: Term Limits for Supreme Court Justices*, pp. 467–71. Durham: Carolina Academic Press.

[17] Alexander Hamilton. n.d. 'The Federalist Papers No. 78', available online at http://avalon.law.yale.edu/18th_century/fed78.asp (last accessed on 19 November 2011). See Henry Paul Monaghan. 1988. 'The Confirmation Process: Law or Politics', *Harvard Law Review*, 101(6): 1202–12. For a more recent defence of life tenure, see Ward Farnsworth. 2005. 'The Regulation of Turnover on the Supreme Court', *University of Illinois Law Review*, (2): 407–53.

the United States, where judges serve on constitutional courts for the rest of their lives after appointment, and their terms end only upon resignation, death, or impeachment, (*b*) mandatory retirement, where constitutional court judges mandatorily retire at a specified age, typically seen in common law countries (for example, the United Kingdom,[18] Canada,[19] Australia,[20] Israel,[21] and India), though not always in common law countries alone (for example, Brazil[22]), and embodied in the Syracuse Draft Principles on the Independence of the Judiciary,[23] (*c*) term limits, where a judge serves on a constitutional court for a fixed, typically non-renewable term, usually seen in civil law countries that follow Hans Kelsen's 'continental model' of constitutional design, where powers of constitutional adjudication are centralized and concentrated in one constitutional court, and not

[18] Supreme court judges retire at the age of 70, under Section 26(1) read with Schedule 5, Judicial Pensions and Retirement Act, 1993, c. 8, read with Section 35(3), Constitutional Reform Act, 2005, c. 4.

[19] Judges of the Supreme Court of Canada retire at the age of 75. See the website of the Supreme Court of Canada, http://www.scc-csc.gc.ca/court-cour/judges-juges/about-apropos-eng.aspx (last accessed on 19 November 2011).

[20] Following a change in the law in 1977, high court judges in Australia retire at the age of 70. Andrew Leigh. 2006. 'System Works in Australia', *National Law Journal*, 2 June, available online at http://andrewleigh.org/pdf/SupremeCourt RetirementNLJ.pdf (last accessed on 16 November 2011).

[21] Israel combines characteristics of both common law and civil law systems. However, on the whole, Israel resembles a common law country more than a civil law country. Judges of the Supreme Court of Israel retire at the age of 70. See the website of the Judicial Authority of Israel, http://elyon1.court.gov.il/eng/system/index.html (last accessed on 19 November 2011).

[22] Judges of the Supreme Federal Court of Brazil retire at the age of 70. See the website of the Supreme Court of Brazil at http://www2.stf.jus.br/portalStfInternacional/cms/verConteudo.php?sigla=portalStfSobreCorte_en_us&idConteudo=120283 (last accessed on 19 November 2011).

[23] Article 12 says, 'All judges, whether selected by appointment or elected, should have guaranteed tenure until a mandatory retirement age, subject only to removal for incapacity or serious illness.' These principles, popularly called the 'Syracuse Principles', were drafted by a committee of experts brought together by the International Association of Penal Law and the International Commission of Jurists, at Syracuse, Sicily, in May 1981. See the text of the 'Syracuse Draft Principles on the Independence of the Judiciary', in Shimon Shetreet and Jules Deschênes (eds). 1985. *Judicial Independence: The Contemporary Debate*, pp. 414–21. Dordrecht: Martinus Nijhoff.

dispersed amongst various courts (for example, France, Italy, Spain, and Portugal),[24] and (d) a hybrid system of term limits and mandatory retirement, where a judge serves on a constitutional court for a fixed, usually non-renewable term, subject to early mandatory retirement upon reaching a certain age (for example, Germany and South Africa).[25]

The question of how long judges should serve in office has engendered great debate.[26] Two central arguments advanced by those who support limited tenure are that such limits would make courts more accountable, and bring newer social perspectives to the bench. Arguing against life tenure in the United States, Steven Calabresi and James Lindgren[27] found that the principle that judges should be democratically accountable requires a 'frequent and regular' turnover of judges. They posited that the appointment of a judge by elected representatives of the people constitutes the only real democratic check on the unelected judiciary in the United States, and in order for this check to be effective, it has to be exercised frequently. On the other hand, Andrew Leigh[28] pointed to the debate prevalent at the time life tenures were abolished in the High Court of Australia. There, when Edward McTiernan retired from the high court in 1976 after serving on the court for nearly 46 years, the following year, in 1977, the Australian Constitution was amended to make high court judges retire mandatorily at age 70, and in the consequent referendum, the proposal won 80 per cent of the vote—becoming one of the most popular reforms in Australia's history. In support of the amendment, the Senate Standing Committee on Legal and Constitutional Affairs had found that a mandatory

[24] Judges of the Constitutional Court of these countries serve nine-year terms (typically non-renewable) in office. See Vicki Jackson and Mark Tushnet. 2006. *Comparative Constitutional Law*, 2nd ed. New York: Foundation, pp. 498–9.

[25] Jackson and Tushnet, *Comparative Constitutional Law*, pp. 489–9.

[26] See for example, Vicki C. Jackson. 2007. 'Packages of Judicial Independence: The Selection and Tenure of Article III Judges', *Georgetown Law Journal*, 95(4): 965–1039, pp. 1000–7.

[27] Calabresi and Lindgren, 'Term Limits'.

[28] Andrew Leigh. 2001. 'Tenure', in Tony Blackshield, Michael Coper, and George Williams (eds), *The Oxford Companion to the High Court of Australia*, pp. 664–5. Sydney: Oxford University Press, pp. 664–5.

retirement age would make courts dynamic, as younger judges would have an opportunity to come to the bench, and bring fresh social perspectives to the court. A possible third argument in favour of shorter tenures, seen particularly in Asian countries like Japan, is that shortening the tenure of a constitutional court judge reduces the amount of time he has to be able to make a difference—keeping judicial activism at bay.[29]

However, there is a possible counterargument—that longer tenures ensure certainty and predictability in the articulation and application of constitutional norms, and therefore bolster the rule of law itself.[30] If the tenure that judges serve on a constitutional court is too short, it would threaten to make the court institutionally incoherent, and consequently ineffective, as newer judges might be more willing to break from the past. It is not inconceivable that judges who do not serve long periods of time on the court together do not develop a sense of collegiality with regard to one another, and are less unwilling to overrule the decisions of their brethren.[31] Further, if judges on constitutional courts serve terms that are too short, that would limit their ability to wield any substantial influence on the system, as is said to be the case in Japan.[32] Scholars have suggested that judges do their best work when they serve sufficiently long tenures in office.[33] DiTullio and Schochet[34] suggested that shorter terms (for example, six-year terms) create an added risk that the

---

[29] See David M. O'Brien. 2006. 'The Politics of Judicial Selection and Appointments in Japan and Ten South and Southeast Asian Countries', in Kate Malleson and Peter H. Russell (eds), *Appointing Judges in an Age of Judicial Power: Critical Perspectives from around the World*, pp. 355–74. Toronto: University of Toronto Press, pp. 359–60; David S. Law. 2009. 'The Anatomy of a Conservative Court: Judicial Review in Japan', *Texas Law Review*, 87(7): 1545–94.

[30] But see Justin Driver. 2011. 'Judicial Inconsistency as Virtue: The Case of Justice Stevens', *Georgetown Law Journal*, 99(5): 1263–78, arguing that Justice Stevens was inconsistent during his long career.

[31] See Georgakopoulos, 'Discretion in the Career'.

[32] See Law, 'Anatomy of a Conservative Court', p. 1574.

[33] James E. DiTullio and John B. Schochet. 2004. 'Saving This Honorable Court: A Proposal to Replace Life Tenure on the Supreme Court with Staggered, Nonrenewable Eighteen-Year Terms', *Virginia Law Review*, 90(4): 1093–149, p. 1128.

[34] DiTullio and Schochet, 'Saving This Honorable Court'.

judges may be more worried about post-court employment, and may try to 'curry favour' with potential employers, which includes the government. Interestingly, in an affidavit filed before the Ontario Superior Court of Justice in a case decided in 2008, Professor Carl Baar cited India as an example of a country where the tenure of judges was too short, and where the perceptions of the bar were that this encouraged judges to curry favour with the executive to secure increases in the retirement age or post-retirement jobs.[35]

The life tenure and mandatory retirement systems have two key similarities: first, they create similar incentives to appoint younger judges, and second, they discriminate between different judges. Not unlike the life tenure system, the mandatory retirement system creates incentives for the executive to appoint judges young. After all, the younger a judge is appointed to the court, the more time he will take to reach the age of retirement, and the more time he will serve on the court. An ambitious political authority eager to control the court would therefore have an incentive to appoint judges younger, so that they could last longer on the court, both in mandatory retirement systems and life tenure systems. Both life tenure and mandatory retirement have the additional disadvantage that they do not ensure that judges will serve equal terms in office—in that sense they are discriminatory. The length of time that a judge will serve in office

---

[35] *Association of Justices of the Peace of Ontario* v. *Ontario (Attorney General)*, 2008 CanLII 26258 (ON SC), available online at http://canlii.ca/t/1x3ld (last accessed on 9 March 2012). In paragraphs 10–11 of his affidavit (on file with the author), Professor Carl Baar wrote:

> [N]o judge in India may serve beyond age 65. This has led to perceptions by the practicing bar that judges may seek to curry favour from governments in order to secure further increases in the age of mandatory retirement, or secure post-retirement appointments.... The lesson that we can draw in Ontario from these findings is that even though mandatory retirement of judges is generally consistent with judicial independence and is found throughout the world, the age can be set so low as to lead to a perception that the impartiality of judicial officers might be compromised.

Further, interestingly, in 2003, the Allahabad High Court dismissed a case filed by a lawyer who claimed, amongst other things, that the tenure of the Chief Justice of India should not be lower than five years, and that high court and Supreme Court judges should have life tenure. It was held that the court was not the appropriate forum for that discussion, and the court advised the lawyer to select another forum, 'if he so likes'. *Ashok Pandey* v. *Satish Chandra*, MANU/UP/1116/2003.

in a life tenure system will vary depending upon the age at which
the judge is appointed, and the health and longevity of each judge.
Different judges are likely to serve different terms in office. Similarly,
mandatory retirement age systems also foster discrimination, since
judges appointed to the court at different ages will serve different
lengths of terms in office, as they will all retire at the same age.

Both life tenure and mandatory retirement systems have the
potential of undermining judicial independence at the lower appellate courts. If judges are appointed to the supreme court largely from
amongst the appellate court judiciary, then these judges may have
incentives to curry favour with the executive to ensure that they
get appointed younger. A system where the age at which a judge
is appointed to the supreme court determines the length of his or
her term in office may encourage judges to aspire to be appointed
young.[36]

The mandatory retirement system has been criticized in the
United States principally by citing examples of judges whose stellar
terms on the court would have been cut short had they been required
to retire mandatorily; for example, Justice William J. Brennan, who
retired at age 84.[37] Such a system would also have cut short the
terms of several distinguished judges who were appointed to the
court relatively later on in their lives, and scholars have suggested
that these judges may not have even been appointed to the court in
the first place had a mandatory retirement system been in place;
for example, Justices Benjamin Cardozo (nominated at 61), Earl
Warren (at 62), Harry Blackmun (at 61), Lewis Powell (at 64), and
Ruth Bader Ginsburg (at 60).[38] Further, at the time that the statute

[36] Arguably, all appellate court judges may have incentives to curry favour with
the executive so that they can earn a nomination to the supreme court, no matter which system is prevalent. Not all appellate court judges may be appointed
to the supreme court, and this may create incentives for them to seek nominations in the first place. However, I would argue that life tenure and mandatory
retirement systems create an additional incentive for appellate court judges to
curry favour with the executive, in order to be appointed younger and serve on
the court longer.

[37] Epstein, Knight, and Shvetsova, 'Comparing Judicial Selection Systems', p. 26.

[38] DiTullio and Schochet, 'Saving This Honorable Court', p. 1136. But see
Epstein, Knight, and Shvetsova, 'Comparing Judicial Selection Systems', arguing that some 'failures' would not have made it to the court either.

of the International Criminal Court (ICC) was being debated, there was a proposal that the tribunal's judges should retire at age 65— however, the proposal was dropped because the retirement age was arbitrary and not supported by international or national practice.[39] Instead, judges of the ICC have a fixed, nine-year, non-renewable term.[40]

By contrast, fixed-term limits such as those seen in France ensure that judges serve equal lengths of terms in office, and are more egalitarian. There is no inappropriate incentive to appoint unusually young judges, and no discrimination amongst judges. Fixed-term systems can also be used to engineer a certain optimum tenure, which ensures the predictability of constitutional rules on the one hand, and political and social accountability on the other.

There is no cross-national consensus on what the optimum term for a judge on a constitutional court ought to be. In the United States, between 1789 and 1970, the average tenure of a supreme court judge was 14.9 years, but thereafter it went up to 25.6 years.[41] Several presidents in the 20th century preferred their nominees to be in their mid-50s, so that they could have sufficient legal experience but could also remain 'sufficiently vigorous' for the supreme court.[42] In recent times, Justice Clarence Thomas was appointed at the age of 43.[43] In Europe, term lengths range from 6–12 years, with a mean of 9.3, and 8–10 year terms being the most common.[44] Tenures in mandatory retirement countries are determined by the difference between the age at which judges are appointed and the mandatory retirement age. In the Supreme Court of the United Kingdom and High Court of Australia the retirement age is 70, and it is 75 in the

---

[39] Medard R. Rwelamira. 1999. 'Composition and Administration of the Court', in Roy S. Lee (ed.), *The International Criminal Court: The Making of the Rome Statute*, pp. 153–74. The Hague: Kluwer, p. 157.

[40] Article 36(9)(a), Rome Statute of the ICC.

[41] Calabresi and Lindgren, 'Term Limits', 795n75.

[42] Barbara A. Perry. 1991. *A "Representative" Supreme Court? The Impact of Race, Religion, and Gender on Appointments.* New York: Greenwood Press, p. 12.

[43] Joel Jacobsen. 2002. 'Remembered Justice: The Background, Early Career, and Judicial Appointments of Justice Potter Stewart', *Akron Law Review*, 35(2): 227–50, n149.

[44] Epstein, Knight, and Shvetsova, 'Comparing Judicial Selection Systems', p. 31.

Supreme Court of Canada.[45] The average age of appointment on the Australian High Court between 1981 and 2000 was 54 years,[46] and according to one study the typical tenure of high court judges there was 14 years.[47] According to another study, in 1996, the average age of appointment of the judges who were on the Canadian Supreme Court at the time was 56 years,[48] which would mean that the judges would serve about 19 years in office. Countries with the hybrid model of term limits and mandatory retirement typically have shorter fixed terms. For example, in Germany[49] and South Africa,[50] the tenure on the constitutional court is 12 years, subject to mandatory retirement at the age of 68 and 70 respectively. It remains to be empirically determined whether the mandatory retirement age typically inhibits the tenure on these courts, although intuitively, it would be logical that judges would be appointed young enough in these countries that they would serve their full terms, barring rare exceptional circumstances.[51] Countries where only term limits are prevalent typically seem to have even shorter terms than the mandatory retirement or hybrid countries. For example, in France, Italy, Spain, and Portugal, the term limit on the constitutional court is nine years.[52]

[45] See text in notes 18–20 above.

[46] Leigh, 'Judicial Tenure', pp. 664–5.

[47] Leigh, 'System Works in Australia'.

[48] Ian Greene, Carl Baar, Peter McCormick, George Szablowski, and Martin Thomas. 1998. *Final Appeal: Decision-making in Canadian Courts of Appeal.* Toronto: James Lorimer, p. 101.

[49] Article 4, Federal Constitutional Court Act, available online at http://www.gesetze-im-internet.de/bundesrecht/bverfgg/gesamt.pdf (last accessed on 10 March 2012).

[50] Section 176(1), Constitution of South Africa. However, in South Africa, if a judge's 12-year term expires before he completes 15 years as a judge, he must continue for another three years, but not beyond the age of 75. Section 4, Judges' Remuneration and Conditions of Employment Act, 2001. See further, *Justice Alliance of South Africa* v. *President of Republic of South Africa and Others,* 2011 (5) SA 388 (CC), available online at http://www.saflii.org/za/cases/ZACC/2011/23.html#sdfootnote2anc (last accessed on 9 March 2012).

[51] For example, a study concluded in 1976 found that the median age of appointment to the Federal Constitutional Court in Germany was 53, suggesting that a large proportion of the judges would serve full terms. See Kommers, *Judicial Politics in West Germany,* p. 146.

[52] See text in note 24 above.

Asian countries at times seem to have very short tenures for their constitutional court judges. The Supreme Court of Japan, called the 'Saiko Saibansho', known for its remarkable exercise of judicial restraint, follows the mandatory retirement system, where judges retire at age 70.[53] However, the age at which judges are appointed to the court ensures that they typically do not serve more than six years on the bench.[54] There, the age of appointment to the court increased over the decades, much in the same way as it did in India, from 61.2 in the 1950s, 62.9 in the 1960s, 63.7 in the 1970s, to 64 in the 1980s and 1990s.[55] This has resulted in a greater turnover of judges on the court. The Constitutional Court of South Korea follows the hybrid model—its judges serve for fixed six-year terms (which may be extended, although this is said to be rarely done) and retire at age 65 (the president retires at age 70).[56] In the Constitutional Court of Indonesia, judges serve for fixed, five-year terms, but again, the terms may be renewed.[57]

It is in this context that the age at which judges are appointed to the Supreme Court of India, and their consequent length of terms in office, must be understood.

SIZE OF THE SUPREME COURT OF INDIA

The Supreme Court of India has 31 judges,* including the Chief Justice.[58] At the time of its inaugural session on 28 January 1950, two days after India's new Constitution came into force, the maximum permissible strength of the Court was eight judges (including the chief justice), but it was later increased to 11, 14, 18, 26, and 31

---

[53] O'Brien, 'Politics of Judicial Selection', p. 359.
[54] O'Brien, 'Politics of Judicial Selection', p. 359.
[55] O'Brien, 'Politics of Judicial Selection', p. 359.
[56] Information obtained from the website of the Constitutional Court of South Korea, available online at http://english.ccourt.go.kr (last accessed on 19 November 2011).
[57] See Harjono. n.d. 'The Indonesian Constitutional Court', available online at http://www.ccourt.go.kr/home/history/world/pdf/05.pdf (last accessed on 9 March 2012).
[58] Article 124(1), Constitution of India, read with the Supreme Court (Number of Judges) Amendment Act, 2008 (5 February 2009).

judges (including the chief justice) in 1956,[59] 1960,[60] 1977,[61] 1986,[62] and 2009[63] respectively.[64] At 31 judges, the Supreme Court is perhaps one of the largest apex constitutional courts in the world. Consider that the apex constitutional courts of the following countries are significantly smaller than that in India: Australia (7), Brazil (11), Canada (9), France (9), Germany (16), Indonesia (9), Israel (15), Italy (15), Japan (15), Portugal (13), South Africa (11), South Korea (9), Spain (12), Taiwan (15), United Kingdom (12), and United States (9).[65] Except for the constitutional court of Germany, the number of judges on the Supreme Court is at least double the size of the supreme constitutional judiciaries of each of these countries. The Supreme Court falls only one judge short of doubling the number of judges in the Federal Constitutional Court of Germany.

The large size of the Supreme Court of India may serve the purpose of diffusing the political strength of the judges. For example, assuming that cases are democratically distributed by the Chief Justice amongst all judges on the Court, no single judge will carry too much weight, and no opinion too much importance. Used a certain way, this can create a greater diffusion of power amongst the justices. There is empirical evidence to demonstrate that the Supreme Court is increasingly deciding cases using benches of only two judges.[66]

---

[59] Supreme Court (Number of Judges) Act, 1956 (16 September 1956).

[60] Supreme Court (Number of Judges) Amendment Act, 1960 (6 May 1960).

[61] Supreme Court (Number of Judges) Amendment Act, 1977 (31 December 1977).

[62] Supreme Court (Number of Judges) Amendment Act, 1986 (9 May 1986).

[63] Supreme Court (Number of Judges) Amendment Act, 2008 (5 February 2009).

[64] See further, K.K. Venugopal. 2010. 'Towards a Holistic Restructuring of the Supreme Court of India', R.K. Jain Memorial Lecture, 30 January, available online at http://www.hindu.com/nic/venugopal_lecture.pdf (last accessed on 10 March 2012).

[65] Each of these countries has been picked, either on account of the size of the economy of the country or the activism of the court, from amongst the countries listed by Freedom House as being free in its 2011 rankings. Freedom House. 2011. 'Freedom in the World 2011: The Authoritarian Challenge to Democracy', available online at http://www.freedomhouse.org/report/freedom-world/freedom-world-2011 (last accessed on 18 November 2011).

[66] See Nick Robinson, Anjana Agarwal, Vrinda Bhandari, Ankit Goel, Karishma Kakkar, Reeba Muthalaly, et al. 2011. 'Interpreting the Constitution: Supreme

The Court's large size can serve to offset the concentration of power that may result from the proliferation of these small two-judge benches. However, the large size of India's Supreme Court and the numerous panels[67] it sits in exacerbates the risk that it will articulate incoherent and inconsistent norms, and that the institution will spark unpredictability and the absence of the rule of law. The large size of the Court also undermines the prestige of the office of a Supreme Court judge. Greater diffusion of power amongst more judges tends to make the office of a Supreme Court judge less prestigious, and the office may consequently attract less talent.

The large size of the Supreme Court of India serves to weaken the power, status, and prestige of each individual judge on the court. It is more likely that on a larger court, different cases of constitutional significance will be decided by different judges and not the same ones, with the result that each individual judge will be less powerful than he would ordinarily have been on a smaller court. The diffused status of each individual Supreme Court judge arguably makes judicial independence more palatable for political actors, as it ensures that no single individual rises to a menacing level of excessive political power.

AGE AND TENURE ON THE SUPREME COURT OF INDIA

The age at which a judge is appointed to the Supreme Court is one of the most crucial factors that will determine the fate of his career. First, since Supreme Court judges mandatorily retire at age 65,[68] the age at which a judge is appointed to the Court determines his tenure, that is, the number of years he will serve on the Court. Second, the

---

Court Constitution Benches since Independence', *Economic and Political Weekly*, 46(9): 27–31; Abhinav Chandrachud. 2012. 'Speech, Structure and Behavior on the Supreme Court of India', *Columbia Journal of Asian Law*, 25(2): 222–74.

[67] The Court does not convene in plenary sessions. See Chapter 2.

[68] Article 124(2), Constitution of India. The term of a Supreme Court judge is non-renewable. Retired Supreme Court judges can, however, be offered extensions (Article 128, Constitution of India), though as retired judges and not as permanent Supreme Court judges. Extensions are typically offered for a brief period of time only. The practice of offering extensions has gradually declined and is now virtually non-existent.

age at which a judge is appointed to the Court also determines, in most cases, whether or not the judge will become the Chief Justice of India. On account of the seniority norm[69] discussed earlier, a judge who is younger than everyone else on the Court at the time he is appointed to the Court is almost always likely to eventually become the Chief Justice of India. Given that chief justices of India control the process of appointing judges, that they determine the composition of panels, and assign cases to panels, the question of how young a judge is appointed to the Court is one which can fundamentally influence the trajectory and docket of the Court itself.

On account of the mandatory retirement age, the earlier a person is appointed to the Court, the longer his tenure on the Court will be. But what is the earliest that a person can be appointed to the Court? According to the Indian Constitution, the answer depends upon the person's professional background. Article 124(3) of the Indian Constitution prescribes the qualifications for Supreme Court judges. It will be recalled that under this provision a person is not qualified for appointment as a judge of the Supreme Court unless he is a citizen of India and (*a*) has been a high court judge for at least five years, or (*b*) has been an advocate practising before a high court for at least 10 years, or (*c*) is a 'distinguished jurist' in the opinion of the President of India. Using these indicators it is possible to calculate the earliest age at which a person might theoretically be appointed a Supreme Court judge, assuming that a person graduates law school and registers with a Bar Council at the age of 23, which is typical in India.

High court judges can be appointed to the Supreme Court of India only after they have served for at least five years on a high court (or on two or more high courts). A person cannot be appointed a high court judge, in turn, unless he is a citizen of India and (*a*) has held a judicial office in India for 10 years or (*b*) has practised as an advocate in a high court for 10 years.[70] There is no space for 'distinguished jurists' to be appointed to the high courts. Accordingly, the earliest that a high court judge can be appointed to the Supreme Court is

---

[69] See further, Abhinav Chandrachud. 2012. 'Supreme Court's Seniority Norm: Historical Origins', *Economic and Political Weekly*, 47(8): 26–30.
[70] Article 217(2), Constitution of India.

at the age of 38. This is because, assuming that a person graduates law school at the age of 23, and is appointed as a high court judge after 10 years, at the age of 33, he must then wait five years before being appointed to the Supreme Court, until he turns 38. For this reason, a high court judge appointed to the Supreme Court can serve a maximum term of approximately 27 years, that is, 65 minus 38.

Alternatively, a person can be appointed to the Supreme Court as early as at the age of 33. This is because, assuming that the person graduates law school at the age of 23, he must wait for 10 years, until he turns 33, before he can be appointed to the Supreme Court. For this reason, an advocate appointed directly to the Supreme Court can serve a maximum term of approximately 32 years, that is, 65 minus 33.

Finally, the Indian Constitution prescribes no minimum age of appointment for a 'distinguished jurist'. Although there is no standard duration within which a professor can acquire tenure in India, it is assumed here, for the sake of argument, that it takes 20 years for a person to acquire tenure at a law school in India and a status of academic distinction. Accordingly, assuming that a person graduates law school at 23, the maximum term that a 'distinguished jurist' can serve on the Supreme Court is about 22 years, that is, 65 minus 43. A 'distinguished jurist' has never been appointed to the Supreme Court of India in its entire history.

In practice, however, judges tend to be much older, and do not even come close to the maximum terms that they can theoretically serve in office.

Between 1950 and 2011, 196 judges[71] were appointed to the Supreme Court of India, of whom only four[**] were not previously high court judges or chief justices. The mean age of appointment to the high court, for judges who made it to the Supreme Court, was approximately 46.34 years (median: 46.02 years; standard deviation: 3.57 years). The mean tenure of judges on the high courts before they were elevated to the Supreme Court was approximately 12.85 years (median: 13.23 years; standard deviation: 3.18 years). This is broadly consistent with the mean in European countries—Lee Epstein *et al.*

[71] For the purposes of these figures, the analysis ends with the appointment of Justices S.J. Mukhopadhaya, Ranjana Desai, and J.S. Khehar to the Supreme Court of India on 13 September 2011. The rest of the chapter does not use figures for judges appointed to the Court from 2010 onwards.

found that of 21 European nations mandating some form of prior legal experience for supreme court judges, the mean was 12 years.[72] The mean age of appointment to the Supreme Court of India was 59.19 years.[73] The mean tenure[74] of judges on the Supreme Court was 5.53 years (median: 5.25 years; standard deviation: 2.36 years). Chief Justice P.N. Bhagwati served the longest tenure on the Supreme Court (13.43 years) and was also the youngest judge to be appointed to the Court (51.57 years). The oldest judge to be appointed to the Court was Justice K.N. Saikia (62.79 years). However, the judge who served the shortest tenure on the Court was S.C. Roy, who passed away in office after serving for a few months.

The data indicates that before arriving on the Supreme Court of India, candidates typically serve as judges for 10–16 years in the high courts, but on the Supreme Court they typically serve for only about three–seven years in office. The tenure on the Supreme Court is perhaps one of the shortest in the world, and perhaps only consistent with the tenure prevalent in some Asian countries, such as South Korea or Indonesia.

The age of appointment to the Supreme Court of India has not remained constant, and the mean age of appointment to the Court has steadily increased over the years. Judges appointed to the Court in the first decade of its existence were the youngest on average, at a mean age of 57.67 years.[75] There was a spike in the age of appointment in the 1960s (mean: 58.89 years), but younger judges were appointed once again in the 1970s (mean: 57.92 years). In fact, although the mean age of appointment in the 1970s was slightly higher than in the 1950s, some of the youngest judges in the Court's history were

[72] Epstein, Knight, and Shvetsova, 'Comparing Judicial Selection Systems', p. 18.
[73] In calculating this figure, the age of appointment of the first six members of the Court (Justices Kania, Fazl Ali, Sastri, Mahajan, Mukherjea, and Das) was taken to be the age at which they were appointed to the Federal Court of India.
[74] In some cases, judges may have resigned early or died prior to the natural completion of their terms. In such cases, the age at which the judge was appointed would not tell us the length of term he served in office.
[75] The first six judges of the Court were counted as having been appointed to the Federal Court, since they all only carried over into the Supreme Court of India. If this was not done, the mean age of appointment would spike a little, and the judges in the 1970s would become the youngest judges appointed in the country. I followed the latter methodology in Abhinav Chandrachud. 2011. 'The Age Factor', *Frontline*, 8–21 October, 28(21).

appointed in the 1970s. The age of appointment increased thereafter, across the 1980s (mean: 59.64 years) and the 1990s (mean: 59.79 years). The decade of the 1990s was one in which the oldest judges in the court's history were appointed to the Court on average, followed by the 2000s, where the age of appointment remained high (mean: 59.7 years).

At first blush, these changes might seem small, almost inconsequential. After all, the difference between the mean age of appointment to the Court in the 1950s and that in the 1990s was only two years, a figure which, standing by itself, seems hardly worth writing about. However, it is important to understand that given that the term of Supreme Court judges in India is itself so short, even a difference of one year can be substantial. The archetypical judge appointed to the Court in the 1950s would serve on the Court for a term of eight years. However, the archetypical judge appointed to the court in the 1990s would suffer a substantial 25 per cent decrease in the length of his term—at six years. Given that the mean tenure on the Supreme Court of India is very short, a difference of even one year can be substantial. Therefore, although changes in the mean figures analysed in the previous paragraph might seem inconsequential at first, it must be underscored that in the Indian context, given the short length of terms, they are substantial.

Figure 3.1 is a box plot in which each 'box' depicts the interquartile range (that is, the range between the 25th and 75th percentile) of the sample, the line running through the box represents the median age of appointment to the Court during that decade, and the 'whiskers' reflect the range between the highest and lowest values of appointments made during that period within 1.5 times the interquartile range. Outliers, if any, are indicated by dots.

In brief, Figure 3.1 tells us that over 75 per cent of the judges appointed to the Court during the last three decades were typically between 58 and 62 years of age, unlike before, when they were younger. The median age of appointment to the Court exceeded 60 years in the last two decades, for the first time ever, indicating that 50 per cent of the judges appointed to the Court in these last two decades were over the age of 60, and that the oldest judges in the Court's history were therefore appointed in the last two decades, during a period which coincided with the Court's 1993 and 1998 Judges

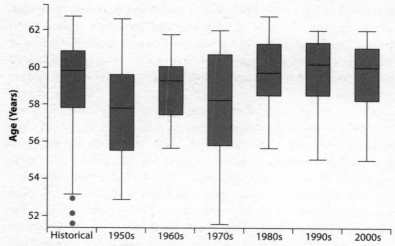

Figure 3.1   Age of Appointment to the Supreme Court of India
Source: Author.
Note: 'Historical' indicates the appointments made to the Supreme Court between 1950 and 2009.

cases discussed in Chapter 2. The data also tell us that between 1950 and 2011, there were three 'outliers' who were appointed to the Court unusually young. These were Justice Hidayatullah (52.96 years) in the 1950s, and Justices Chandrachud (52.13 years) and Bhagwati (51.57) in the 1970s, whose age of appointment is more than one-and-a-half times below the inter-quartile range for the period between 1950 and 2009.

Figure 3.2 is a histogram which reflects the most frequent age at which judges were appointed to the Supreme Court of India between 1950 and 2009. Figure 3.2 tells us that judges were most commonly appointed to the Supreme Court between the ages of 58 and 62 years. Since Supreme Court judges retire at the age of 65, this would confirm that the average tenure for a Supreme Court judge is three–seven years in office.

While the mean age of appointment to the Supreme Court of India has gone up over the decades, the mean age of appointment to the high courts has gone down. Judges are appointed to the Supreme Court older, and judges who make it to the Supreme Court were appointed to the high courts younger than their predecessors on the

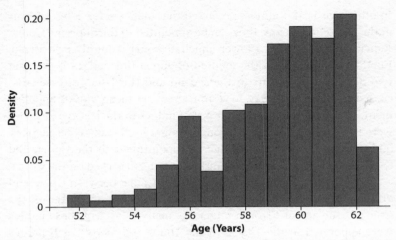

Figure 3.2 Age at Which Judges Were Most Frequently Appointed to the Supreme Court of India (1950–2009)
Source: Author.

Supreme Court. Judges in the 1950s and 1970s served the longest terms in office at the Supreme Court, at a mean tenure of 6.81 years and 6.44 years respectively. Interestingly, although the mean age of appointment of judges to the Supreme Court in the 1960s was lower than in the 1980s and 2000s, the mean tenure that a judge appointed to the Court in the 1960s served on the Court (5.28 years) was lower than in these two decades (5.30 years in both the 1980s and 2000s). This is because five of the 16 judges appointed to the Court in the 1960s had their terms unnaturally shortened. One died (P. Satyanarayana Raju), one resigned to go on to pursue other ambitions (Mudholkar), but three (Shelat, Hegde, and Grover) resigned because they were superseded by A.N. Ray during Indira Gandhi's government after the Basic Structure case. Supreme Court judges appointed to the Court in the 1990s served the shortest tenure in office, at a mean tenure of 4.92 years. The data indicate that the tenure on the Supreme Court is diminishing, while judges who make it to the Supreme Court are increasingly serving longer tenures on the high courts.

The upshot is that there seems to be a greater emphasis on experience as a criterion for appointment to the Supreme Court today.

In other words, it is almost preferred that judges serve longer terms in the high court before they can be appointed to the Supreme Court. Judicial experience on a lower appellate court is highly prioritized. Further, the change in the method of appointing judges in the last two decades consequent to the second and third Judges cases discussed in Chapter 2 may have impacted the mean age of appointment. It will be seen in Chapter 4 that judges in the last two decades were increasingly appointed from amongst high court chief justices. This naturally increases the age of appointment to the Court, and consequently diminishes the length of the term served on the Court.

Out of 189 judges appointed to the Court between 1950 and 2009, only 24 judges (that is, 12.7 per cent) were appointed to the Court at the age of 55 or younger. As many as 10[76] of these judges were appointed in the 1950s. In the 1960s, only two[77] such judges were appointed to the Court. In the 1970s there were seven[78] such judges appointed to the Court at the age of 55 or younger. Between 1980 and 2009, in three decades, only five[79] judges were appointed to

---

[76] Justices H.J. Kania, S.R. Das, B.P. Sinha, S.J. Imam, P.B. Gajendragadkar, A.K. Sarkar, K. Subba Rao, K.N. Wanchoo, M. Hidayatullah, and J.C. Shah. In Chandrachud, 'Age Factor', I had not counted Justices Kania and Das in this calculation because they had been appointed to the Federal Court of India at the age of 55 or younger, but were much older at the time the Supreme Court of India came into being. However, I believe that it would perhaps be unfair to attribute to these judges their age at the time the Supreme Court came into being for the purposes of this calculation. For this reason, for judges who served on both the Federal Court and the Supreme Court, the age at which they were appointed to the Federal Court has been counted here for the purposes of ascertaining whether or not they were of the age of 55 or less at the time of their appointment to the Court.

[77] Justices S.M. Sikri and A.N. Grover. In Chandrachud, 'Age Factor', I had not mentioned A.N. Grover, since he was appointed to the Court only four days prior to his 56th birthday. However, in the interest of preciseness, he has been included in this calculation.

[78] Justices Y.V. Chandrachud, P.N. Bhagwati, Murtaza Fazal Ali, R.S. Pathak, O. Chinnappa Reddy, A.P. Sen, and E.S. Venkataramiah.

[79] Justices Sabyasachi Mukharji, M.M. Punchhi, A.S. Anand, S.P. Bharucha, and K.G. Balakrishnan. In Chandrachud, 'Age Factor', I had not included Justice M.M. Punchhi in this calculation, since he was appointed to the court only four days prior to his 56th birthday. However, in the interest of preciseness, he has been included in this calculation.

the Court at the age of 55 or younger. In many of the semi-structured qualitative interviews I conducted with judges, I was told that it was an informal norm that a judge would not be appointed to the Supreme Court until after he had reached the age of 55 (for example, Interview 9). The quantitative evidence tends to support this claim.

In fact, a number of judges were appointed to the Supreme Court after having retired from the high court. The age of retirement of high court judges was increased from 60 years to 62 years in 1963.[80] Until then, there had been four judges who had been appointed to the Court after retiring from a high court (Aiyar, Hasan, Ayyar, and Ayyangar), and as many as three of these came from Madras. Thereafter, four[81] more judges were appointed after retiring from the high court (Alagiriswami,[82] Islam, Saikia, and Beevi). One (Alagiriswami) was from the Madras High Court, two (Islam and Saikia) from the Gauhati High Court, and one (Beevi) was the first woman judge to be appointed to the Supreme Court.

CHIEF JUSTICES OF INDIA

Between 1950 and 2009, India had 37 chief justices on the Supreme Court. The mean age at which they were appointed to the Supreme Court (56.34 years) was nearly three years lower than the general mean age of appointment of judges to the Supreme Court during that time. In order to become Chief Justice of India, a judge has to be younger than everyone else senior to him on the Court on the date of his appointment to the Court, or in rare cases, just lucky (for example, if a senior judge younger than him dies, or resigns prematurely consequent to a supersession or otherwise). So far, there has been no female Chief Justice of India. The mean term that a Chief Justice of India served in the office of chief justice was just 1.63 years

---

[80] Constitution (Fifteenth Amendment) Act, 1963.

[81] Some judges came very close to retiring from the high court, prior to their appointment to the Supreme Court. Jaswant Singh was appointed two days before, V. Khalid six days before, N.D. Ojha one day before, N.G. Venkatachala two days before, B.L. Hansaria eleven days before, K.S. Paripoornan one day before, P.K. Balasubramanian one day before, and Swatanter Kumar thirteen days before, their respective 62nd birthdays.

[82] Justice Alagiriswami was appointed on his 62nd birthday.

(median: 1.16 years; standard deviation: 1.49 years). Only six[83] chief justices served terms in the office of the chief justice for three years or more. Chief Justice Y.V. Chandrachud served the longest tenure as Chief Justice of India at 7.38 years, which made him the only 'outlier' amongst the chief justices of the Supreme Court—his term as chief justice was more than 1.5 times the inter-quartile range of the terms served by all the chief justices of the Supreme Court. The shortest term was served by Justice K.N. Singh at 18 days.

The incredibly short tenure of Supreme Court chief justices is significant from the point of view that it diffuses the power of the single most important actor in the Indian judiciary. The Chief Justice of India has the power to constitute benches (that is, panels), and to assign cases to benches. He leads the process of appointing judges to the Supreme Court of India and high courts, especially after the second Judges case in 1993, discussed in Chapter 2. The fact that the Chief Justice of India serves such a remarkably short tenure in office limits the ability of the most important judicial actor in India to materially alter the Court's jurisprudence. Consider that the US Supreme Court, on account of life tenure, has had only 17 chief justices in over two centuries (between 1789 and 2011), while India has had more than double (37 chief justices) in less than a third of that time (between 1950 and 2009).

Of the 37 chief justices, 31 made appointments during their term. Only 14,[84] that is, less than half of those who made appointments to the Supreme Court during their terms as chief justices, appointed judges younger than the mean age of appointment between 1950 and 2011, that is, judges younger than 59.19 years, on average. For example, Chief Justice Mahajan appointed two judges during his tenure: Ayyar (age: 60.1) and Sinha (age: 55.83). The mean age of appointment during Chief Justice Mahajan's term was consequently 57.97—lower than the mean age of appointment to the Court between 1950 and 2011. Only three of these 14 chief justices (Misra,

---

[83] Chief Justices S.R. Das, B.P. Sinha, A.N. Ray, Y.V. Chandrachud, A.S. Anand, and K.G. Balakrishnan.

[84] Chief Justices M.C. Mahajan, B.K. Mukherjea, S.R. Das, B.P. Sinha, P.B. Gajendragadkar, K.N. Wanchoo, S.M. Sikri, A.N. Ray, M.H. Beg, Y.V. Chandrachud, Sabyasachi Mukharji, Ranganath Misra, K.N. Singh, and V.N. Khare.

Singh, and Khare) served on the Court in the last two decades, that is, between 1990 and 2009. Accordingly, between 1950 and 2009, the majority of India's 37 chief justices made appointments whose mean age of appointment was higher than 59.19 years.

On average, Chief Justice B.K. Mukherjea[85] made the youngest appointments to the Supreme Court, while Chief Justice H.J. Kania made the oldest appointments. Chief Justice K.G. Balakrishnan appointed the highest number of judges to the Court (20).

POLITICAL ESTABLISHMENT

Chapter 2 charted the course of the political history of India and situated the Supreme Court of India in a political context. Using that construct, it is possible to decipher eight key phases in India's political history relevant for the purposes of studying appointments to the Supreme Court: (*a*) the Nehru years (January 1950 to 27 May 1964), when Prime Minister Nehru was at the helm of affairs, (*b*) the post-Nehru years (28 May 1964 to March 1971) before Indira Gandhi successfully asserted herself and broke free of the 'Syndicate' in her party, (*c*) the Indira Gandhi years (March 1971 to March 1977), when Prime Minister Indira Gandhi was in power, but before the Congress party lost power, (*d*) the Janata Party interregnum (March 1977 to January 1980), when the Congress party lost power at the centre for the first time in India's history, (*e*) Indira Gandhi's return to power (January 1980 to 31 October 1984), (*f*) the Rajiv Gandhi years (31 October 1984 to November 1989), when Indira Gandhi's elder son

---

[85] In Chandrachud, 'Age Factor', I calculated that B.K. Mukherjea was amongst those who made the oldest appointments to the Court. This is because I had taken into account the fact that during his term, Chandrasekhara Aiyar, a judge who had retired from the Supreme Court of India, was appointed on a temporary basis to the Court. To calculate the mean age of the judges appointed by Mukherjea, I had taken into account the age of Aiyar. After giving this some thought, I believe that it is perhaps not fair to take into account the age of judges appointed temporarily: chances are that they were appointed to fill a temporary need on the Court, and that their appointment in all likelihood may not have deprived another judge of appointment to the Court. For this reason, the analysis in this chapter does not take into account temporary appointments made during the term of a chief justice.

Table 3.1 Thirty-seven Chief Justices of the Supreme Court of India (1950–2009)

No.	Chief Justice of India	Start of Term as Chief Justice	End of Term as Chief Justice	Tenure as Chief Justice (Years)	Age at Which Appointed	Mean Age of Judges Appointed	Number of Judges Appointed
1.	H.J. Kania	26 January 1950	6 November 1951	1.78	55.63	61.2	2
2.	Patanjali Sastri	7 November 1951	4 January 1954	2.16	58.92	59.63	3
3.	Mehr Chand Mahajan	4 January 1954	23 December 1954	0.97	58.78	57.97	2
4.	B.K. Mukherjea	23 December 1954	31 January 1956	1.11	57.17	54.73	1
5.	S.R. Das	1 February 1956	1 October 1959	3.66	55.3	56.87	9
6.	B.P. Sinha	1 October 1959	1 February 1964	4.34	55.84	58.12	4
7.	P.B. Gajendragadkar	1 February 1964	16 March 1966	2.12	55.84	58.17	5
8.	A.K. Sarkar	16 March 66	29 June 66	0.29	55.68	N/A	0
9.	K. Subba Rao	30 June 1966	11 April 1967	0.78	55.55	59.9	3
10.	K.N. Wanchoo	12 April 1967	25 February 1968	0.87	55.46	57.04	2
11.	M. Hidayatullah	25 February 1968	17 December 1970	2.81	52.96	59.62	3
12.	J.C. Shah	17 December 1970	22 January 1971	0.1	53.72	N/A	0
13.	S.M. Sikri	22 January 1971	26 April 1973	2.26	55.77	58.93	9
14.	A.N. Ray	26 April 73	29 January 77	3.76	57.51	58.21	10
15.	M.H. Beg	29 January 1977	22 February 1978	1.07	58.8	55.73	3

No.	Name						
16.	Y.V. Chandrachud	22 February 1978	12 July 1985	7.38	52.13	58.8	14
17.	P.N. Bhagwati	12 July 1985	21 December 1986	1.44	51.57	60.37	5
18.	R.S. Pathak	21 December 86	18 June 1989	2.49	53.24	59.35	12
19	E.S. Venkataramiah	19 June 1989	18 December 89	0.5	54.22	59.51	6
20.	Sabyasachi Mukharji	18 December 1989	25 September 1990	0.77	55.79	58.8	3
21.	Ranganath Misra	25 September 1990	25 November 1991	1.17	56.3	59.01	5
22.	K.N. Singh	25 November 1991	13 December 1991	0.05	59.24	56.35	1
23.	M.H. Kania	13 December 1991	18 November 1992	0.93	59.45	59.21	3
24.	L.M. Sharma	18 November 1992	12 February 1993	0.24	59.64	N/A	0
25.	M.N. Venkatachaliah	12 February 1993	25 October 1994	1.7	57.94	61.07	6
26.	A.M. Ahmadi	25 October 1994	25 March 1997	2.41	56.72	59.76	11
27.	J.S. Verma	25 March 1997	18 January 1998	0.82	56.37	59.99	4
28.	M.M. Punchhi	18 January 1998	10 October 1998	0.73	55.99	N/A	0
29.	A.S. Anand	10 October 1998	1 November 2001	3.06	55.04	59.33	18
30.	S.P. Bharucha	1 November 2001	6 May 2002	0.51	55.15	59.95	3
31.	B.N. Kirpal	6 May 2002	8 November 2002	0.51	57.84	60.33	3
32.	G.B. Pattanaik	8 November 2002	19 December 2002	0.11	57.73	N/A	0
33.	V.N. Khare	19 December 2002	2 May 2004	1.37	57.89	58.96	3

(continued)

Table 3.1 (*continued*)

No.	Chief Justice of India	Start of Term as Chief Justice	End of Term as Chief Justice	Tenure as Chief Justice (Years)	Age at Which Appointed	Mean Age of Judges Appointed	Number of Judges Appointed
34.	S. Rajendra Babu	2 May 2004	1 June 2004	0.08	58.32	N/A	0
35.	R.C. Lahoti	1 June 2004	1 November 2005	1.42	58.1	59.78	8
36.	Y.K. Sabharwal	1 November 2005	14 January 2007	1.2	58.04	60.13	6
37.	K.G. Balakrishnan	14 January 2007	12 May 2010	3.32	55.07	60.2	20

Source: Author.

Notes:

1. The last column ('Number of Judges Appointed') refers to the total number of judges appointed to the Supreme Court of India during the term of the chief justice.

2. N/A denotes 'not applicable'.

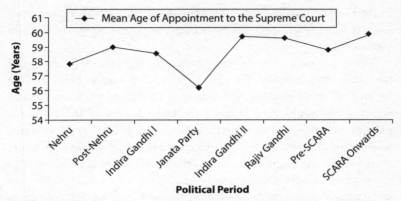

Figure 3.3   Mean Age of Appointment to the Supreme Court of India
Source: Author.

was prime minister, with the largest majority at the centre that India had ever seen, (*g*) the years after Rajiv Gandhi lost the national election, leading up to the second Judges case (termed the 'Pre-SCARA' years) (November 1989 to 5 October 1993) defined by weak coalition governments at the centre, and (*h*) the years following the second Judges cases (termed 'SCARA Onwards') where the Court seized power to appoint its own members (starting 6 October 1993).

Figure 3.3 sets out the mean age of appointment to the Supreme Court during each of these eight key political phases in India's history. Strikingly, the oldest judges in the country were appointed in the political period termed in Figure 3.3 as 'SCARA Onwards', that is, the period starting with the Supreme Court's decision in the second Judges case in 1993, discussed in Chapter 2. After the second Judges case, the Court seized power to appoint its own members. In a two-sample mean comparison test between the mean age of appointment before the second Judges case and the mean age of appointment after the second Judges case, the difference in means was statistically significant.[86] In other words, the age of appointment

[86]   The difference in the means between the age of appointment before October 1993 and after October 1993 was −1.289311, and the p value was 0.0000. However, since the data were not normally distributed, I ran a two-sample Wilcoxin rank-sum (Mann–Whitney) test, to compare the median age of appointment

to the Court after the second Judges case in 1993 has increased from what it was before 1993, and this increase proves to be statistically significant.

There are many reasons why judges in the last 20 years might have been appointed to the Court older than before. First, India's history of 'supersessions' and attempts to tamper with the Court's composition might have induced the Chief Justice of India and his judicial consultees to eliminate discretion in judicial appointments, to emphasize seniority, and to grant nearly every senior high court chief justice the right to be considered eligible for appointment to the Supreme Court. Consequently, as senior high court chief justices increasingly began to be appointed to the Court by the collegium during this time, the mean age of appointment to the Court naturally increased. This phenomenon will be examined in greater detail in Chapter 4. Second, by appointing older judges to the Supreme Court, the collegium reduced the power and influence of individual justices appointed to the Court. Judges in the post-SCARA period were appointed even older than the judges appointed by Indira Gandhi (after the Janata interregnum) and by Rajiv Gandhi. It is possible that this phenomenon, namely, the appointment of older judges to the Supreme Court in the post-SCARA period, was potentially offered as a compromise to political actors in order to ensure that the judicial independence usurped by the judiciary consequent to the second and third Judges cases, examined in Chapter 2, was less unpalatable to political actors.

Figure 3.4 explains the interaction between the institutional independence of the Supreme Court and the judicial influence of individual judges. It will be recalled that Chapter 2 concluded with the observation that the 1993 and 1998 decisions of the Supreme Court enhanced its institutional independence from a separation of powers standpoint, that is, it freed the Court of checks and balances, but did not necessarily enhance the independence of individual Supreme Court judges. The term 'institutional independence' in Figure 3.4 must be understood in this context. The term 'judicial influence' in

---

before October 1993 and after October 1993. Again, the null hypothesis (that is, that the two variables have the same median) was rejected at a statistically significant level (p value: 0.0004).

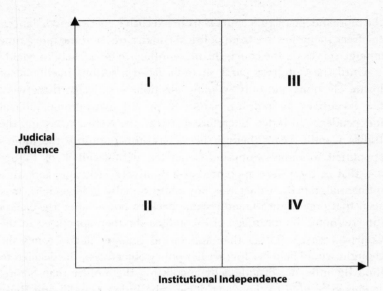

Figure 3.4 Judicial Activism
Source: Author.

Figure 3.4 refers to the length of time a judge serves on the Supreme Court. It has been proposed in this chapter that the longer a judge serves on a court, the more the time he will have remaining on the court once he rises to a senior position, and the more influential he can consequently become.

Institutional independence and judicial influence can each make a judge activist. Figure 3.4 sets out that: (*a*) a judge may be influential, but the court may not be institutionally independent (cell 'I' in Figure 3.4), (that is, the judge serves on the court for a lengthy tenure, but judicial appointments are still controlled by the executive), (*b*) a judge may not be influential, and the court may not be institutionally independent (cell 'II' in Figure 3.4), (*c*) a judge may be influential and the court may be institutionally independent (cell 'III' in Figure 3.4), or (*d*) the court may be institutionally independent, but a judge may not be influential (cell 'IV' in Figure 3.4). It is hypothesized that cell 'III' produces the highest degree of judicial activism, cell 'II' produces the highest degree of judicial restraint, whereas cells 'I' and 'IV' produce moderate degrees of judicial activism. This is because the more independent a court is from executive checks and balances, the freer its judges are from political constraints, and the more time a judge serves on the court, the more influence he is likely to wield.

Until the Congress party in India faced a serious likelihood of losing elections and only winning elections erratically, there were few incentives for political actors to permit institutional judicial independence in India. Therefore, between the Nehru years and the Indira Gandhi years (before the Janata interregnum), the judges appointed to India's Supreme Court fell within cell 'I' of Figure 3.4, that is, they were appointed at a relatively early age, and were influential, but the Court was not institutionally independent. It is seen that once Indira Gandhi came back to power after the Janata interregnum, the mean age of the judges she then appointed to the Court increased. Rather than appointing younger judges (ones she thought would help her further her policy objectives), she decided to limit the influence of judges by appointing them older than before. Judges appointed to the court during the Indira Gandhi and Rajiv Gandhi years fell within cell 'II' of Figure 3.4, that is, they were less influential, and the Court lacked institutional independence.

Figure 3.3 indicates that the youngest judges in the country were appointed during the Janata Party interregnum—the first time in India's history that a non-Congress party was controlling the centre. Although only seven[87] judges were appointed during the reign of the Janata Party, the average age of these judges was far below the mean age of judges appointed during any other political period. The judges were appointed by the Janata Party during the period immediately following the Emergency. The Supreme Court had failed the country in the Habeas Corpus case.[88] Many of the Janata Party leaders had been arbitrarily imprisoned during the Emergency. Therefore, the Janata Party had a strong interest in shaping the composition of the judiciary. Perhaps in a bid to control the composition of the Court for a long period of time, it appointed younger judges to the Court, who would consequently serve longer terms in office. It was seen

---

[87] Justices V.D. Tulzapurkar, D.A. Desai, R.S. Pathak, A.D. Koshal, O. Chinnappa Reddy, A.P. Sen, and E.S. Venkataramiah.
[88] See Abhinav Chandrachud. 2011. *Due Process of Law*. Lucknow: Eastern Book Company.

in Chapter 2 that Indira Gandhi even suggested, upon her return to power, that the Janata Party had tried to control the composition of the courts. The judges appointed by the Janata Party fell within cell 'I' of Figure 3.4: they were appointed young, and were therefore more influential, but at the same time the Court lacked institutional independence. Interestingly, the Janata Party also increased the size of the Court by adding four more judges in 1977. This may potentially have created the space for them to ensure that younger judges would be appointed to the Court during their watch.

After the second Judges case, the Court was institutionally independent for the first time in its history. However, during this phase, the oldest judges in the country were appointed to the Court, on average. Accordingly, these judges fell within cell 'IV' of Figure 3.4, in that although the Court was institutionally independent, its judges had limited influence because of their short tenures, and therefore moderate potential for judicial activism.

Therefore, counter-intuitively, when the Supreme Court of India gained institutional independence, it compensated for this independence by limiting the influence wielded by individual Supreme Court judges, by limiting their tenure. This was perhaps done in order to make the institutional independence of the judiciary seem less unpalatable to political actors. However, this promises to produce a moderate level of judicial activism as compared to the Rajiv Gandhi years or Indira Gandhi's years in power following the Janata interregnum. In no period of India's history have judges fallen within cell 'III' of Figure 3.4, that is, institutional independence coupled with judicial influence.

* * *

The large size of the Supreme Court of India and the short tenure of its judges serve to diffuse the influence that any judge can wield on the Court. As an institution that wields 'enormous power in every sphere of human activity',[89] the Supreme Court has been termed one of the world's most powerful courts[90] and is well known for its

---

[89] Venugopal, 'Towards a Holistic Restructuring'.
[90] S.P. Sathe. 2002. *Judicial Activism in India: Transgressing Borders and Enforcing Limits*. New Delhi: Oxford University Press.

judicial activism. The Court's most activist judges were appointed in the 1950s and the 1970s, and they were appointed young. For example, Justice K. Subba Rao was appointed to the Court in 1958 at the age of 55, and he ended up being one of the most influential judges on the Court, a prolific dissenter,[91] whose decisions began the end of the 'Gopalan era' on the Court.[92] Thereafter, Justice P.N. Bhagwati was appointed in 1973 at the age of 51—the youngest judge ever to have been appointed to the Court—and was perhaps one of the most activist judges the Court has ever seen. Justice Bhagwati is credited with the 'public interest litigation' movement in the Supreme Court, which fundamentally altered the trajectory of the Court's jurisprudence, by relaxing standing rules, and making it possible for ordinary citizens to bring cases on behalf of disadvantaged members of society, and later to agitate 'diffused' rights. Bhagwati is also credited with the 'Maneka Gandhi' era on the Court, which finally ended the influence of a case[93] that had limited the ability of the Court to widely interpret the Indian Constitution—a phenomenon that K. Subba Rao had set in motion. Similarly, Justice Krishna Iyer was appointed to the Court in 1973 at the relatively young age of 57, and he too was remarkably influential on the Court. Even in the decades that followed, key figures of judicial activism were typically those who had been appointed to the Court young. Appointed at the young age of 56 in 1988, Kuldip Singh took charge of the Court's environmental docket, while J.S. Verma, appointed to the Court in 1989 at the age of 56, spearheaded the Court's crusade against corruption in the 'Jain diaries' case discussed in Chapter 2.[94]

---

[91] See George H. Gadbois, Jr. 1970. 'Indian Judicial Behavior', *Economic and Political Weekly*, 5(3/5): 149, 151, 153–5, 157, 159, 161, 163, 165–6; Rajeev Dhavan. 1977. *The Supreme Court of India: A Socio-legal Critique of Its Juristic Techniques.* Bombay: Tripathi, p. 35.

[92] See Chandrachud, *Due Process of Law*.

[93] *A.K. Gopalan* v. *State of Madras*, AIR 1950 SC 27.

[94] Of course, judicial activism is not necessarily the province of the young. Chief Justice Patanjali Sastri, Justice H.R. Khanna, and more recently, Justice A.K. Ganguly, were all appointed to the Court at a relatively late age, but each managed to influence the outlook of the Court. However, the impact that these judges would have had on the Court would perhaps have been even greater had they been able to serve longer terms in office. See Chandrachud, 'Age Factor'.

Judicial activism in India has typically (though perhaps not always) been led by judges who were appointed to the Court at an age lower than the mean. Limiting the tenure of a judge in India may therefore have the effect of limiting the activism of the Court's members, by reducing their influence on the Court. Evidence of this was seen in Chapter 2, where judges were not appointed to the Court despite being recommended by chief justices of India, because they were too young. A judge who serves a longer term on the Court has more years left when he has reached a senior position on the Court, and can therefore better influence its jurisprudence and docket.[95] The studied persistence in keeping the age of appointment to the Court high and the tenure served on the Court consequently low perhaps had as its aim the goal of keeping judicial activism at bay, especially during the Rajiv Gandhi years.

In the past two decades the judiciary has inflicted the wound of shorter tenures upon itself. The mean age of appointment to the Supreme Court actually increased in the last two decades—at a time when judges of the Supreme Court had co-opted the power to appoint themselves. Ironically, despite being independent, the judiciary in India has subjected itself to a diminishing tenure. However, it has been suggested in this chapter that this was possibly a compromise offered by the judiciary to the executive in order to make the Supreme Court's institutional independence following the 1993 and 1998 decisions less unpalatable to the executive. Although judicial terms might be shorter today, the enhanced institutional independence of the Court might produce similar levels of judicial activism as those seen prior to 1993 when judicial tenures were longer.

However, it is also likely that the practice of reducing the tenures of judges on the Supreme Court of India was motivated by a desire to ensure that more judges got to serve on the Court, rather than a

[95] It may be argued that a shorter term on the Supreme Court may actually produce the opposite effect and may actually stimulate judicial activism through a sense of abandon. However, this is difficult to argue in the Indian context because cases are assigned to judges by the chief justice. Accordingly, if a judge wants to be activist contrary to the wishes of the chief justice, he may be 'penalized' by being given non-essential cases. By the time a judge becomes senior enough to be Chief Justice of India, he has a very short period of time in which he can change the system, which is difficult to achieve.

privileged few. It is possible that judges, senior in age, are being appointed to the Court so that they will retire quickly, and more judges will be able to serve on the Court. As the discussion in Chapter 2 indicated, serving on the Supreme Court has almost become a 'legitimate expectation' for high court judges—the short tenure on the Supreme Court ensures that no judge occupies the position of a Supreme Court judge for too long a period of time, and almost everybody eligible gets a chance to serve on the Court. Perhaps this serves as an incentive that can be offered to get talented people to agree to become high court judges. If more high court judges reach the Supreme Court, more lawyers may be willing to give up their lucrative practices in order to take up a high court judgeship. However, the shorter tenure on the Supreme Court arguably reduces the prestige of serving as a Supreme Court judge, not merely by itself, but also as a result of the consequential high turnover of judges on the Court. This, in turn, may dilute the incentive in favour of accepting a high court judgeship.

It is also very likely that the high age of appointment to the Supreme Court (and the consequent diminishing tenure of the Court's judges) is attributable to the emphasis on appointing high court chief justices to the Court, which will be examined in greater detail in Chapter 4.

NOTES

* In 2019, the strength of the Supreme Court was increased to 34 judges (including the Chief Justice).
** Between 2014 and 2018, four more judges were appointed directly from the Bar.

4

SENIORITY

THIS CHAPTER ANALYSES WHETHER 'SENIORITY' is an informal criterion taken into account in making appointments to the Supreme Court of India. In other words, this chapter seeks to determine whether only 'senior' high court judges can be appointed to the Supreme Court— whether seniority is an informal prerequisite or eligibility criterion for appointment to the Court. Amongst 198 judges appointed to the Supreme Court between 1950 and 2011, only four were not high court judges or high court chief justices prior to their appointment to the Supreme Court—in other words, an overwhelming 97.9 per cent of the judges appointed to the Supreme Court had prior judicial experience. The Supreme Court is therefore characterized by a high degree of career homogeneity, which is particularly stark given its diversity (especially its geographic diversity), analysed in Chapter 5. However, it is not merely prior judicial experience that matters for appointment to the Supreme Court, but also the tenure served on a high court, measured against the other judges on that court. Stated simply, high court judges will be considered for appointment to the Supreme Court only once they have attained a certain level of seniority on their high court.

A number of judges I interviewed indicated that seniority was the dominant criterion employed in appointing candidates to the

Supreme Court of India (Interviews 1, 2, 5, 19). One judge said that judges are appointed to the Supreme Court based on the rule of 'seniority-cum-merit' (Interview 2), while another added that judges are appointed based on 'seniority, ability and suitability including integrity' (Interview 19). A retired judge informed me that his appointment to the Supreme Court was stalled by several years, and that he was not appointed to the Court earlier because his appointment at a time when he was a relatively junior judge on a high court would have resulted in the supersession of seven–eight judges, that this would have a caused a 'commotion' (Interview 5). One judge said that there is no constitutional rule that only high court chief justices should be appointed to the Supreme Court, but that this has increasingly been done in the last 10–15 years (Interview 24). One judge told me during an interview that although there is no formal preference for high court chief justices over ordinary puisne high court judges, high court chief justices are 'more in number' on the Supreme Court, because they are experienced (Interview 28). This chapter quantitatively analyses the claim that seniority is an informal criterion used to appoint judges to the Supreme Court, and concludes by finding that the claim is generally true.

THE 'PRIOR JUDICIAL EXPERIENCE' DEBATE

There is a vast scholarly literature in the United States concerning whether judges of the Supreme Court ought to have prior judicial experience. In a paper published in 1959,[1] John R. Schmidhauser noticed that judges who served on the US Supreme Court between 1789 and 1957 were mostly either involved in politics as lawyers, or state or federal court judges. Schmidhauser found that the 'most important change' after 1862 was that increasingly, judges who primarily had judicial careers were being selected for appointment to the US Supreme Court. By 2003, Lee Epstein et al. found that prior service on the federal bench was a 'near prerequisite' for appointment

[1] John R. Schmidhauser. 1959. 'The Justices of the Supreme Court: A Collective Portrait', *Midwest Journal of Political Science*, 3(1): 1–57. See further, John R. Schmidhauser. 1979. *Judges and Justices: The Federal Appellate Judiciary*. Boston: Little, Brown, pp. 92–5.

to the US Supreme Court.[2] In fact, before Elena Kagan was appointed to the US Supreme Court in 2010, the court was composed entirely of former appellate court judges for the first time in its history.[3] This phenomenon is not necessarily limited to the United States alone. Kate Malleson found that in the United Kingdom, starting with the second half of the 20th century, all Court of Appeal judges came from the high court, and all law lords on the House of Lords starting from 1876 came from the Court of Appeal, with only 12 exceptions (seven appointed from the bar, five from the high court).[4] A study found that 'high-level national judges' were considered the most suitable candidates for positions on international judicial bodies, especially when states compete with one another for judgeships, that academics were accused of drawing out legal proceedings and writing lengthy dissents.[5] The norm of prior judicial experience can have benefits

[2] Lee Epstein, Jack Knight, and Andrew D. Martin. 2003. 'The Norm of Prior Judicial Experience and Its Consequences for Career Diversity on the U.S. Supreme Court', *California Law Review*, 91(4): 903–65. This may not be so on other national supreme courts. For example, in Japan, there is a convention that supreme court judges must be appointed equally from three groups: (*a*) inferior court judges, (*b*) practising lawyers, and (*c*) public prosecutors, law professors, or others. David M. O'Brien. 2006. 'The Politics of Judicial Selection and Appointments in Japan, and Ten South and Southeast Asian Countries', in Kate Malleson and Peter H. Russell (eds), *Appointing Judges in an Age of Judicial Power: Critical Perspectives from around the World*, pp. 355–74. Toronto: University of Toronto Press, p. 359. By contrast, there is a constitutional requirement that at least four judges of the Constitutional Court of South Africa should be judges prior to their appointment. Section 174(5), Constitution of South Africa. See François Du Bois. 2006. 'Judicial Selection in Post-Apartheid South Africa', in Kate Malleson and Peter H. Russell (eds), *Appointing Judges in an Age of Judicial Power: Critical Perspectives from around the World*, pp. 280–312. Toronto: University of Toronto Press.
[3] John W. Whitehead and John M. Beckett. 2009. 'A Dysfunctional Supreme Court: Remedies and a Comparative Analysis', *Charleston Law Review*, 4(1): 171–222.
[4] Kate Malleson. 2009. 'Appointments to the House of Lords: Who Goes Upstairs', in Louis Blom-Cooper, Brice Dickson, and Gavin Drewry (eds), *The Judicial House of Lords: 1876–2009*. Oxford: Oxford University Press, pp. 112–21.
[5] Erik Voeten. 2009. 'The Politics of International Judicial Appointments', *Chicago Journal of International Law*, 9(2): 387–406, p. 396. By contrast, there is no norm of what a suitable judicial candidate is on the European Court of

and drawbacks, but, for reasons that will be discussed in greater detail below, Epstein *et al.* found that the benefits were limited, and the drawbacks formidable.[6] Henry J. Abraham wrote that 'many of the most illustrious members of the Court were judicially inexperienced',[7] a list which includes justices like John Marshall, Earl Warren, Joseph Story, Louis D. Brandeis, and Felix Frankfurter.

Those in favour of prior judicial experience argue that such appointments are likely to be less politically contentious, and once appointed, such judges are likely to be more restrained on the supreme court than judges without prior judicial experience,[8] and more willing to adhere to precedent or neutral sources of law, although these claims have been contested by Epstein et al.[9] Another benefit of picking a supreme court judge from amongst a pool of existing appellate court judges is that these judges are tried and tested—their political philosophies can be readily ascertained, their capability as judges can be objectively measured, their ethics and integrity may be known, they may already have been investigated by intelligence agencies,[10] and they have considerable experience in deciding cases.

On the other hand, a norm of prior judicial experience for supreme court judges can be problematic for several reasons. Epstein et al. have argued that 'circuit effects' constitute one of the most serious

---

Human Rights, where states do not compete with one another to make judicial appointments. Allison Danner and Erik Voeten. n.d. 'Who is Running the International Criminal Justice System?', available online at http://ebooks.cambridge.org/chapter.jsf?bid=CBO9780511845369&cid=CBO9780511845369A013 (last accessed on 21 January 2012).

[6] Lee Epstein, Andrew D. Martin, Kevin M. Quinn, and Jeffrey A. Segal. 2009. 'Circuit Effects: How the Norm of Federal Judicial Experience Biases the Supreme Court', *University of Pennsylvania Law Review*, 157(3): 833–80.

[7] Henry J. Abraham. 1999. *Justices, Presidents, and Senators: A History of the U.S. Supreme Court Appointments from Washington to Clinton.* Lanham: Rowman and Littlefield, p. 36.

[8] Schmidhauser, *Justices of the Supreme Court*, p. 41, noticing that supporters of prior experience argue that such judges are 'more likely to develop attitudes of restraint'.

[9] Epstein, Martin, Quinn, and Segal, 'Circuit Effects'.

[10] However, a former judge of the Supreme Court of India indicated to me during an interview that the intelligence investigation conducted during his appointment was superficial (Interview 24).

drawbacks of the norm of prior judicial experience—there is a predisposition on the US Supreme Court for judges with prior judicial experience to affirm the decisions of their home circuit courts.[11] 'Circuit effects' may be less likely in India, where the Supreme Court of India does not convene in plenary sessions, and where there is empirical evidence to suggest that panels or benches are so composed by the Chief Justice of India that a judge rarely hears an appeal against a decision issued by his home high court.[12] However, Epstein et al. have pointed out that another drawback of the norm of prior judicial experience is that it tends to make a court less career diverse: supreme court judges all tend to have the same professional background, and bring the same set of career experiences to the cases they decide. Epstein et al. have argued that as a result of career homogeneity, the court may not make optimal decisions, since the range of inputs and ideas that judges bring to the decisions of the court may be limited. Further, as a result of career homogeneity, the court may not get appropriate gender or racial diversity since minorities are less likely to be on the appellate courts from whose ranks supreme court vacancies are staffed.

Vicki Jackson has pointed out that if lower court positions are viewed as 'stepping stones' rather than 'capstones', lower court judges may have higher incentives to decide cases with a view to getting promoted to the supreme court.[13] This ties into the debate surrounding the merits and demerits of European model career judiciaries and common law model 'recognition'[14] judiciaries. Nicholas L. Georgakopoulos has pointed out that in a career judiciary, judges have a reasonable expectation of being promoted to higher courts, and consequently, career judges tend to be less innovative, since they hope to please appellate courts in order to earn promotions.[15]

---

[11] Epstein, Martin, Quinn, and Segal, 'Circuit Effects'.

[12] See Abhinav Chandrachud. 2012. 'Speech, Structure and Behavior on the Supreme Court of India', *Columbia Journal of Asian Law*, 25(2): 222.

[13] Vicki Jackson. 2007. 'Packages of Judicial Independence: The Selection and Tenure of Article III Judges', *Georgetown Law Journal*, 95: 965–1008.

[14] The term 'recognition judiciary' was coined by Georgakopoulos. See Nicholas L. Georgakopoulos. 2000. 'Discretion in the Career and Recognition Judiciary', *Chicago Law School Roundtable*, 7: 205.

[15] Georgakopoulos, 'Discretion in the Career'.

By contrast, since the chance of being promoted to a higher court is very low in a recognition judiciary, common law judges are less subservient. Chief Justice Rehnquist of the US Supreme Court feared that the norm of prior judicial experience would result in the US Supreme Court resembling the judiciary in civil law countries, and that it would consequently not be able to command respect.[16]

It was seen in Chapter 2 that the Supreme Court of India at times found that high court judges were entitled to a 'legitimate expectation' (a term used in the second Judges case) of being promoted to the Supreme Court, not unlike the expectation of promotion to higher courts in civil law countries. As one judge I interviewed said, lawyers are not, barring 'exceptional cases', appointed directly to the Supreme Court, '[s]ince large number [sic] of suitable Judges of High Court having had judicial training are available and to meet their expectations to reach Supreme Court. Otherwise there would be frustration' (Interview 19). Against the backdrop of this legitimate expectation, a norm of prior judicial experience in the Supreme Court would threaten to make high court judges less innovative and more conservative in a bid to curry favour with the Supreme Court and earn a promotion. The norm of prior judicial experience in India also prevents other professionals with diverse experiences from getting to the bench. Broadly speaking, the Indian Constitution provides that judges, lawyers, or jurists (including law professors) can become Supreme Court judges.[17] However, only four lawyers* have ever made it directly to the Supreme Court (S.M. Sikri, S. Chandra Roy, Kuldip Singh, and Santosh Hegde), one in each decade, barring the 1950s and 2000s.[18] No full-time law professor has ever made it to

[16]   See Epstein, Knight, and Martin, 'Norm of Prior Judicial Experience', p. 910.
[17]   Article 124, Constitution of India.
[18]   Other lawyers were invited for appointment to the Court, but they declined. The list of lawyers who declined includes M.C. Setalvad, S.V. Gupte, H.M. Seervai, Lal Narayan Sinha, N.A. Palkhivala, Fali Nariman, K. Parasaran, S.N. Kacker, and K.K. Venugopal. Motilal C. Setalvad. 1970. *My Life: Law and Other Things.* Bombay: Tripathi, pp. 185, 508; Fali S. Nariman. 2010. *Before Memory Fades: An Autobiography.* Hay House, p. 198 (Nariman had previously declined a high court judgeship for 'financial reasons'. Nariman, *Before Memory Fades*, p. 137); George H. Gadbois, Jr. 2011. *Judges of the Supreme Court of India: 1950–1989.* New Delhi: Oxford University Press, pp. 62, 105–6n4, 137, 157, 264. Further, Chief Justice S.M. Sikri had attempted to appoint between one and two lawyers to the Court,

the Supreme Court. The norm of prior judicial experience prevents these professionals, recognized by the Constitution, from getting to the bench. Further, although lawyers can still get to the Supreme Court by first earning an appointment to a high court, law professors cannot be appointed to high courts directly, and as a consequence,

---

and Chief Justice A.N. Ray had attempted to appoint one senior advocate from Calcutta to the Court, but these lawyers had declined too. Gadbois, *Judges of the Supreme Court*, pp. 157, 201. In his autobiography, Somnath Chatterjee mentions that he was offered a Supreme Court judgeship by Law Minister Shiv Shankar, but that he declined. Somnath Chatterjee. 2010. *Keeping the Faith: Memoirs of a Parliamentarian*. New Delhi: HarperCollins. Had Chatterjee accepted the offer, it is not clear whether he would have been appointed under the lawyer category or the 'distinguished jurist' category, although he would presumably have met the criteria necessary for eligibility under the lawyer category. In more recent times, Harish Salve, Iqbal Chagla, and Goolam Vahanvati were offered direct Supreme Court judgeships, but they declined.

However, even if a vast number of lawyers were invited to be appointed to the Court—lawyers who declined—it is by no means evident that it was intended that there should be an overwhelming majority of lawyers serving on the Supreme Court of India at the same time. First, it is very likely that the number of lawyers who were offered Supreme Court judgeships was only a small proportion of the strength of the Court at any given point in time—it was perhaps always intended that the majority of judges on the Supreme Court would be judges with prior judicial experience. Evidence in favour of this hypothesis was seen in the Lok Sabha debates of 1960, discussed in Chapter 2. Second, it is perhaps more plausible to hypothesize that when a lawyer turned down an offer for a judgeship on the Supreme Court, another lawyer was made the same offer, who, in turn, declined the offer, and so on. For example, in his autobiography, M.C. Setalvad mentions that the incoming chief justice, P.B. Gajendragadkar, was anxious to appoint a member of the bar as a Supreme Court judge; that S.V. Gupte, the Additional Solicitor General of India, was asked by Setalvad, at Gajendragadkar's suggestion, whether he would have liked to accept a Supreme Court judgeship; and that it was only when Gupte 'declined for personal reasons' that Gajendragadkar 'then mentioned Sikri'. Setalvad, *My Life*, p. 508. Thus, the fact that many lawyers were asked whether they were interested in Supreme Court judgeships cannot be cited as evidence in favour of the proposition that many lawyers would have been appointed to the Court had the decliners accepted their offers—instead it is likely that when a lawyer accepted a Supreme Court judgeship offer, the search for a lawyer-appointee ended there. Third, one gets the feeling that it is especially unlikely, though there is no hard evidence to back this claim, that many lawyers were offered direct judgeships on the Supreme Court in the last 20 years.

law professors are entirely excluded from being appointed to the Supreme Court. Women, and religious and caste minorities might be less prevalent on high courts in India, and as a consequence of the norm of prior judicial experience, such candidates too may tend to be excluded from appointment to the Supreme Court, although it will be seen in Chapter 5 that this is sought to be compensated by means of an informal quota system.

However, the debate of prior judicial experience in India is more nuanced because the Supreme Court is not merely staffed with former appellate court judges, but with *senior* former appellate court judges. The emphasis in India is not merely on prior judicial experience, but on lengthy prior judicial experience. This limits the career diversity of Indian Supreme Court judges even further, since senior high court judges would have had the opportunity to participate in less diverse professional pursuits prior to their appointment to the high court bench.

THE SENIORITY CRITERION

Seniority has always been a criterion for appointment to the Supreme Court of India, but its definition has changed in the last 20 years.[19] Figure 4.1 plots the trajectory of the proportion of Supreme Court judges, who were high court chief justices, appointed to the Court during each decade between 1950 and 2011.[20] It is seen that around 50 per cent of the judges appointed during the 1950s and 1960s were previously high court chief justices, but the rest were previously only puisne high court judges.[21] The proportion of high court chief justices on the Supreme Court remained under 50 per cent during the next two decades. Accordingly, over four decades, the Supreme Court was composed of judges amongst whom at least half, if not more, had not served as high court chief justices. Of course, the puisne high court judges who were appointed to the Supreme Court

[19] An acting chief justice is not counted as a chief justice for the purposes of this book, but he is counted as the most senior puisne judge on the high court on which he serves.

[20] See further Gadbois, *Judges of the Supreme Court*, pp. 366–7.

[21] Only one judge, appointed to the Court in the 1960s (S.M. Sikri), was a lawyer directly appointed to the Supreme Court.

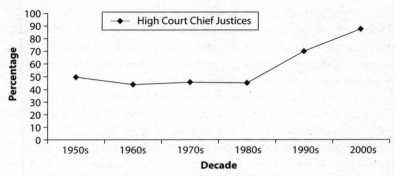

Figure 4.1 Proportion of Judges on the Supreme Court of India Who Were High Court Chief Justices
Source: Author.

were also typically fairly senior on their respective high courts prior to their appointment to the Supreme Court—in many instances, they served as acting high court chief justices, and junior[22] high court judges were seldom, if ever, appointed to the Supreme Court. Gadbois writes that over 80 per cent of the judges appointed to the Court between 1950 and 1989 were fourth or higher in seniority.[23] However, in the next two decades, between 1990 and 2009, the proportion of high court chief justices appointed to the Supreme Court went up significantly, so that in the 1990s, approximately 70 per cent of the judges appointed to the Court were former high court chief justices, and in the 2000s, approximately 88 per cent of those appointed to the Court were former high court chief justices.

Broadly speaking, until 1997, the percentage of former high court chief justices serving on the Supreme Court of India by the end of the term of each Chief Justice of India hovered around 50 per cent, with a few exceptions. However, by the end of Chief Justice A.M. Ahmadi's term in 1997, the percentage of judges serving on the Supreme Court who had previously served as high court chief justices went up to 73.9 per cent, the highest ever proportion of high

---

[22] In other words, judges appointed to the Supreme Court were seldom at the bottom of the list of seniority on high courts. Those who were not high court chief justices were typically always at the senior end of the high court judiciary.
[23] Gadbois, *Judges of the Supreme Court*, p. 366.

court chief justices on the Court in its history.[24] The proportion of high court chief justices on the Court continued along this trajectory, such that by the end of Chief Justice K.G. Balakrishnan's term in 2010, a staggering 93.3 per cent of the Court consisted of judges who had served as high court chief justices.

In the first four decades of the Court's existence, the seniority criterion for appointment to the Supreme Court of India meant that only senior puisne high court judges, or high court chief justices, could be considered for appointment to the Supreme Court. However, in the last two decades of the Court's existence, coinciding with the era of the second and third Judges cases analysed in Chapter 2, the seniority criterion overwhelmingly dictates that in almost all cases, in order to be considered for appointment to the Supreme Court, a candidate must be a high court chief justice. There has been a statistically significant increase in the mean number of high court chief justices appointed to the Supreme Court after its decision in the second Judges case in 1993.[25]

There is also a discernible trend in the last 20 years that judges appointed to the Supreme Court of India have served on more than one high court as chief justice. In the two decades beginning with the 1990s, around one-third of the high court chief justices appointed to the Supreme Court had served on more than one high court as chief justice. In many of these instances, a puisne judge serving on a high court (either because that was his parent high court or because he was transferred to that high court) would be made chief justice of that high court and then transferred to another high court as chief justice. During an interview, a judge informed me that the judge

[24] By the end of Chief Justice Ahmadi's term, three judges who had not served as high court chief justices (Kuldip Singh, P.B. Sawant, and R.M. Sahai) and two who had only served as acting high court chief justices (N.G. Venkatachala and Faizanuddin) had retired; 11 judges were appointed to the Supreme Court, of whom only one (K.T. Thomas) had not served as a high court chief justice.

[25] I ran a two-sample proportion test between the total number of high court chief justices appointed to the Supreme Court before the second Judges case in 1993, and the total number of high court chief justices appointed to the Supreme Court after the second Judges case (a puisne high court judge was assigned a value of 0, and a high court chief justice was assigned a value of 1). The difference in means was statistically significant (difference: −.36; p value: 0.0000).

was appointed chief justice of the judge's parent high court because there were no vacancies on other high courts, but on the understanding that as soon as a vacancy arose on another high court, the judge would be transferred there as chief justice—sure enough, this was what happened (Interview 3). However, from available sources of data, it appears that such cases are not always the cause of the multiple high court phenomenon,[26] and many Supreme Court judges formerly served on more than one high court as chief justices despite not having served as puisne judges in those high courts. Data suggest that no Supreme Court judge served as chief justice of his parent high court between 2000 and 2009, and yet a high proportion of judges served as chief justices of more than one high court during that decade.

RATIONALE FOR THE SENIORITY CRITERION

It is worth asking why there has been a shift in the application of the eligibility criterion of seniority in the appointments made to the Supreme Court of India in the last 20 years. In other words, why has the focus shifted from appointing senior high court judges and high court chief justices to the Supreme Court, to almost exclusively appointing high court chief justices?[27] There are at least four reasons why high court chief justices might be finding their way more often to the Supreme Court over puisne high court judges, although it is likely that the rationale is an amalgam of these reasons.

First, intuitively, high court chief justices would necessarily have lengthier experience as judges on one or more high courts than senior puisne high court judges, and lengthy high court experience

[26] Approximately 19 per cent of the Supreme Court judges who served as chief justices of more than one high court between 1950 and 2011 served as chief justice on the high court where they were originally appointed as puisne judges, that is, on their parent high courts.

[27] The number of high courts in India has increased over the years, but this does not explain why there are more high court chief justices appointed to the Supreme Court today. For nearly four decades, approximately between 1970 and 2009, the number of high courts in India remained the same (18 in number), but the number of high court chief justices appointed to the Supreme Court rose exponentially during that time. Further, although the number of high courts in

might be valued in a system which prizes prior judicial experience. High court chief justices who were appointed to the Supreme Court have served a statistically significant longer term—2.7 years more on average on a high court—than ordinary puisne high court judges appointed to the Supreme Court.[28] Further, judges appointed to the Supreme Court after the second Judges case in 1993 have served a statistically significant longer term—1.9 years more on a high court, on average—than those appointed before then.[29] Judges appointed to the Supreme Court in the last 20 years have lengthier prior judicial experience than before, and this is likely a consequence of the policy of appointing high court chief justices. Figure 4.2 plots the mean years of high court service of judges appointed to the Supreme Court between 1950 and 2011. If prior judicial experience is considered necessary for appointment to the Supreme Court, as it is, then judges who have longer high court experience would naturally be prized over those with shorter experience, and high court chief justices, having served on a high court for the longest time amongst the other judges

India (and consequently, the number of high court chief justice posts in India) has increased over the years, the number of Supreme Court judgeships has increased at a higher rate. Accordingly, the ratio of the number of high courts in India to the number of Supreme Court judgeships has gone down over the years, while the ratio of the number of high court chief justices appointed to the Supreme Court in each decade to the total number of Supreme Court judges appointed in each decade has gone up over the years. Consequently, the new definition of the eligibility criterion of seniority, that is, the increasing appointment of high court chief justices to the Supreme Court, cannot be attributed to the rise in the number of high courts in India.

[28] In a two-sample mean comparison test, comparing the mean length of term served on a high court by high court chief justices appointed to the Supreme Court with that of puisne high court judges appointed to the Supreme Court, there was a statistically significant difference in means (difference: 2.71; p value: 0.0000).

[29] Another two-sample mean comparison test, comparing the mean length of term served on a high court by judges appointed to the Supreme Court prior to the second Judges case in 1993, and that of judges appointed to the Supreme Court after the second Judges case in 1993, reveals a statistically significant difference in means (difference: −1.90; p value: 0.0000).

on their parent high courts, would necessarily have significantly lengthy high court experience under their belt.[30] However, this does not explain why there has been a shift towards appointing more high court chief justices to the Supreme Court only in the last 20 years. Seniority has always been a criterion for appointment to the Supreme Court—it was seen in Chapter 1 that the conference of Federal Court judges and high court chief justices in 1948 placed a high premium on the appointment of senior high court judges and high court chief justices to the Supreme Court. If seniority has always been an informal eligibility criterion for appointment to the Supreme Court, why is it that, only in the last 20 years, high court chief justices have overwhelmingly been appointed to the Supreme Court over senior puisne high court judges? One possible explanation is that the value attributed to lengthy judicial experience by the collegium is higher than the value it was attributed prior to the second Judges case. Another explanation could be that lengthy high court experience is only a side effect of the policy of appointing high court chief justices to the Supreme Court, rather than the desired effect, which could be any one of the three reasons discussed below.

Second, it may be that the post of Supreme Court judge is more prestigious today than it was in earlier years, as a result of which more high court chief justices who are offered the post of Supreme Court judge are willing to give up their senior positions on high courts for junior positions as Supreme Court judges. As discussed in Chapter 1, Gadbois[31] found that after independence, the practice was to offer Supreme Court judgeships to the chief justice of a high court, but the fact that no Bombay High Court Chief Justice or Madras High Court Chief Justice was eventually appointed to the

---

[30] This may not always be so. For example, it may take less time to become a senior judge, or to be eligible for appointment as a high court chief justice, on a smaller high court (that is, a court with fewer judges) than a larger one. However, broadly speaking, it is true that high court chief justices are the most experienced judges from amongst those on their respective parent high courts.

[31] George H. Gadbois, Jr. 1969. 'Selection, Background Characteristics, and Voting Behavior of Indian Supreme Court Judges, 1950–1959', in Glendon Schubert and David J. Danelski (eds), *Comparative Judicial Behavior: Cross-cultural Studies of Political Decision-making in the East and West*. New York: Oxford University Press, p. 223.

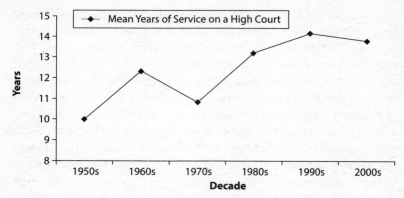

Figure 4.2   Length of High Court Experience of Judges Appointed to the Supreme Court of India
Source: Author.

Supreme Court during 1950–9 pointed to the fact that 'the Chief Justices of these High Courts considered their position to be one of greater prestige and importance than an associate judgeship on the Supreme Court'.[32] The position of chief justice of a high court was a prestigious one, even more so on the old and reputable high courts of India. A high court chief justice would have been less willing in earlier times to give up his position of pre-eminence on his high court, in exchange for a position as a junior Supreme Court judge on a court which was new and untested. It was seen in Chapter 1 that the Joint Committee on Indian Constitutional Reform had recommended in the 1930s that there should be a 'retirement age gap' (a term coined in this book) between the age at which Federal Court

---

[32] Gadbois, 'Selection, Background Characteristics, and Voting Behavior', p. 223. Gadbois points out that the following high court chief justices (or judges at the threshold of being appointed chief justices) declined offers to be elevated to the Supreme Court: M.C. Chagla, P.B. Chakravartti, P.V. Rajamannar, P.N. Mookerjee, S.P. Mitra, V.S. Malimath, M.M. Ismail, Satish Chandra, Bhimiah, and Sarwar Ali. Gadbois, *Judges of the Supreme Court*, pp. 17, 59, 61n16, 137, 157, 264, 314. To be sure, not all of these judges declined Supreme Court judgeship offers because they considered their high court positions to be superior to the Supreme Court. Many declined for personal reasons. However, many, especially in earlier times, declined because they considered their positions in their respective high courts to be preferable to junior positions on the Supreme Court.

of India judges and high court judges retire, for precisely this reason—in order to offer an inducement to high court judges to accept a position on the Federal Court. It was seen in Chapter 1 that even in the recommendations made by the conference of the judges of the Federal Court and chief justices of high courts, it was suggested that the retirement age of Supreme Court judges should be later than that of high court judges, so that high court chief justices or senior high court judges would have an incentive to accept the post of a Supreme Court judge, as they would get several additional years of service upon accepting. In earlier times, despite the retirement age gap inducement, high court chief justices perhaps did not consider it worthwhile to sacrifice their positions of seniority and pre-eminence on their high courts in favour of a junior Supreme Court appointment. Further, since the salaries and pensions payable to high court chief justices and puisne Supreme Court judges were the same, there were few financial incentives for high court chief justices to give up their positions in order to accept Supreme Court judgeships.[33] In more recent times, the Supreme Court of India has metamorphosed into an unquestionably prestigious court, and the post of high court chief justice has almost been reduced to a stepping stone to get to the Supreme Court.[34] Under these circumstances, high court chief

[33] In terms of the salaries they earn, the chief justice of a high court is considered to be at the same level as a Supreme Court judge. When India's Constitution came into being, Supreme Court judges and high court chief justices each earned Rs. 4,000 per month. See Second Schedule, Constitution of India. This understanding continues to this day. Today, Supreme Court judges and high court chief justices still earn an equal amount, Rs. 90,000 per month. See Section 12A, Supreme Court Judges (Salaries and Conditions of Service) Act, 1958, and Section 13A, High Court Judges (Salaries and Conditions of Service) Act, 1954. Supreme Court judges and high court chief justices are also treated to be at the same level with regard to pensions. See Clause 3, Part 1, Schedule, Supreme Court Judges (Salaries and Conditions of Service) Act, 1958.**

Thus, a high court chief justice has little or no financial incentive to accept a Supreme Court judgeship. Even a senior high court judge has few financial incentives to accept a Supreme Court judgeship when the increase in salary is weighed against the inconvenience of moving to a different geographic region, and displacing one's family.

[34] See Abhinav Chandrachud. 2010. 'Supreme, but Not Superior', *Indian Express*, 23 February.

justices may be more willing to sacrifice their tenures and positions of pre-eminence on the high courts in favour of a position on the Supreme Court. As one judge, appointed to the Supreme Court in the 1990s, told me during an interview, he was not asked by the erstwhile Chief Justice of India whether he wanted to become a Supreme Court judge—instead, he was told by the Chief Justice of India that he was being appointed to the Supreme Court and that he should make himself available in Delhi on the appointed date (Interview 10). The spike in the number of high court chief justices on the Supreme Court may accordingly be a function of the greater prestige associated with being a Supreme Court judge today. However, it is doubtful if the Supreme Court has only become prestigious in the last 20 years—its enhanced status does not explain why high court chief justices have, only over the last 20 years, found their way to the Supreme Court more often than puisne high court judges. After all, why were more high court chief justices not being appointed to the Supreme Court in the late 1970s and in the 1980s, when the Court was unquestionably a powerful and prestigious institution?

Third, there has perhaps been an overwhelming increase in the number of high court chief justices appointed to the Supreme Court of India in the last 20 years because the seniority criterion works to reduce discretion and arbitrariness in selecting judges for appointment to the Supreme Court. The spike in the number of high court chief justices appointed to the Supreme Court coincides and begins with the second Judges case decided in October 1993, after which the proportion of high court chief justices on the Court increased dramatically. It is plausible that the collegium of judges responsible for making Supreme Court appointments has increasingly resorted to appointing only high court chief justices to the Supreme Court because the pool of high court chief justices in the country is much smaller than the pool of senior high court judges. By reducing the number of candidates eligible for appointment to the Supreme Court, the collegium potentially reduces its discretion in selecting judges for the Supreme Court, consequently making Supreme Court appointments seem less subjective, or ideologically or politically motivated, and more objectively driven. In this sense, the seniority criterion seen on the Supreme Court in the last 20 years is a legitimacy-building measure. Appointing high court chief justices to the Court makes the process of appointing judges seem less arbitrary and more objective.[35] However, at least one judge I interviewed disagreed that the system of appointing high court chief justices to the Supreme Court makes the process of appointments less arbitrary (the judge himself was a high court chief justice subsequently appointed to the Supreme Court) (Interview 24). This norm also works to satisfy the legitimate expectation of high court chief justices that they would be appointed to the Supreme Court owing to their seniority.

Fourth, and perhaps most compellingly, since high court chief justices are also typically older judges on their respective courts, appointing high court chief justices to the Supreme Court of India also ensures that tenure on the Supreme Court will be shorter. As discussed in Chapter 3, this may make the Supreme Court's power to appoint judges seem less unpalatable to the political branches of government in India. In other words, the appointment of high court chief justices to the Supreme Court in the last 20 years might be a compromise measure offered by the Court to the political branches of government, in order to make the Court's power to appoint judges, following the second and third Judges cases, seem less unpalatable. This rationale is explored in the following section.

POLICY IMPLICATIONS OF THE SENIORITY CRITERION

This section deals with four potential policy implications of the seniority criterion of eligibility for in appointing judges to the Supreme Court of India, especially as it has played out in the last 20 years.

Tenure of Supreme Court Judges

What impact, if any, does the policy of appointing high court chief justices to the Supreme Court of India have on the average length of a judge's term on the Supreme Court? High court chief justices appointed to the Supreme Court are, on average, older than

[35] As Gadbois points out, the policy of appointing senior judges to the Supreme Court between 1950 and 1989 'reduce[d] the possibility of "extraneous considerations"—political or caste considerations ... being promotion criteria'. Gadbois, *Judges of the Supreme Court*, p. 367.

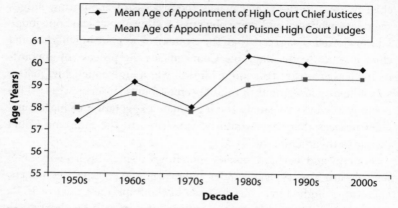

Figure 4.3   Mean Age of High Court Chief Justices and Puisne Judges Appointed to the Supreme Court of India
Source. Author.

ordinary puisne high court judges appointed to the Supreme Court.[36] Figure 4.3 demonstrates that in every decade except the 1950s, high court chief justices were appointed to the Supreme Court older than puisne high court judges. Accordingly, the policy of appointing high court chief justices to the Supreme Court results in an increase in the mean age of appointment to the Supreme Court, and it results in a reduction in the mean length of term served on the Supreme Court. The consequences of a shorter tenure on the Supreme Court have already been discussed in Chapter 3.

One might ask whether the higher mean age of appointment to the Supreme Court of India (and the consequent lower mean tenure) is an unintended side effect of the policy of appointing high court chief justices to the Supreme Court, or whether it is the policy's desired effect. This question can perhaps only be answered in a nuanced manner—high court chief justices have lengthy experience and an expectation of being appointed to the Supreme Court on account of their seniority; the Supreme Court is a prestigious institution, and an offer made to a high court chief justice to serve on the Supreme

[36] In a two-sample mean comparison test, comparing the mean age of appointment of high court chief justices to the Supreme Court, against that of puisne high court judges appointed to the Supreme Court, there was a statistically significant difference in means (difference: 0.77; p value: 0.0210).

Court is less likely to be turned down in today's world; a policy of appointing high court chief justices reduces the number of eligible candidates for appointment to the Supreme Court and makes the process seem less subjective; and the policy of appointing high court chief justices to the Supreme Court reduces the average tenure served on the Court, it feeds into the informal norm of only appointing judges to the Supreme Court after they reach the age of 55, consequently reducing the tenure, power, and influence wielded by each individual judge on the Court, and making the present system of collegium-based judicial appointments seem less unpalatable to the political branches of government in India. It is perhaps an amalgam of these reasons that forms the basis of the existence of the seniority criterion today.

Career Homogeneity

Is the seniority eligibility criterion for appointments to the Supreme Court of India limiting the professional career diversity of judges who get appointed to the Court? As discussed, amongst 198 judges appointed to the Court between 1950 and 2011, only four were not high court judges or high court chief justices prior to their appointment to the Court. Accordingly, in terms of professional background, an overwhelming majority of Supreme Court judges previously served as high court judges or chief justices, and could consequently boast of only one type of experience in the years leading up to their Supreme Court appointment, that is, experience on a high court. But what type of careers did these judges have prior to getting appointed to a high court? From available sources of information it can be gathered that the overwhelming majority of these judges worked as practising lawyers before becoming high court judges. A small proportion of them (approximately 9.5 per cent) served in the subordinate judiciary before becoming high court judges, while an even smaller proportion of them (approximately 3 per cent) served as bureaucrats in the civil service or administrative service before getting appointed to a high court.

Available data suggests that a relatively small proportion of the lawyers were active in politics (approximately 11 per cent), while approximately a fourth of them taught law on a part-time basis at a university for some period of time. Nearly half of the lawyers served as government lawyers in some capacity (for example, as standing counsel for the state, assistant government pleaders or government pleaders, assistant public prosecutors or public prosecutors, deputy/ additional advocates general or advocates general, and so on) prior to getting appointed as judges of high courts. The remaining lawyers were presumably in private practice.

However, it is safe to assume that an overwhelming majority (if not all) of the judges who were previously lawyers, worked as litigators and practised before a high court. In other words, judges appointed to the Supreme Court seldom include transactional lawyers, solicitors, or other lawyers whose practice does not take them regularly to a high court (for example, arbitration counsel, subordinate court trial lawyers, and so on). Consequently, the best trial court lawyers who regularly practise before subordinate civil or criminal courts, or the best securities or tax lawyers who regularly appear before the securities or tax tribunals, may never get offered judgeships on high courts, even though they may be as competent as high court lawyers who do get offered judgeships. This 'self-selection'[37] or 'cloning'[38] occurs because high court judges are appointed by senior judges themselves, who, consciously or unconsciously, seek out candidates that replicate their own former credentials—typically, frequent appearances in high court cases. This is not unlike the United Kingdom—a Law Lord of the House of Lords there commented that that is 'almost the only country in the world where the only lawyers who are thought fit to serve in [the] highest courts are those who have excelled as advocates in those courts'.[39] This problem can only be overcome if the collegium seeks out unconventional candidates for appointments to the high courts, or if a judicial appointments commission[40] with a wider composition is constituted to appoint judges to high courts.

[37] See Rachel Davis and George Williams. 2003. 'Reform of the Judicial Appointments Process: Gender and the Bench of the High Court of Australia', *Melbourne University Law Review*, 27(3): 819–63, p. 835.

[38] Davis and Williams, 'Reform of the Judicial Appointments Process', p. 835.

[39] Lady Hale. 2005. 'Making a Difference? Why We Need a More Diverse Judiciary', *Northern Ireland Legal Quarterly*, 56(3): 281–92, p. 282.

[40] For more on a judicial appointments commission in India, see Law Commission of India. 1987. *One Hundred Twenty-First Report on a New Forum for*

Only four lawyers have ever directly been appointed to the Supreme Court of India (that is, without having previously served as a high court judge or chief justice).[41,†] However, these four lawyers, each appointed to the Court during a different decade, were all from comparable professional backgrounds in that each of them had served as a high-ranking government lawyer. S.M. Sikri was the first lawyer appointed directly to the Supreme Court in February 1964, and he served as Assistant Advocate General of Punjab and then as Advocate General of Punjab for 13 years (1951–64). S. Chandra Roy was the next lawyer to be appointed directly to the Court in July 1971, and he served as a Senior Counsel to the Union of India before the Calcutta High Court for many years. Next, Kuldip Singh was appointed to the Court in December 1988, and he served as Senior Standing Counsel to the Central Government in the Punjab and Haryana High Court for 11 years (1971–82), then as Advocate General of Punjab for a few months in 1987, and finally as Additional Solicitor General of India from August 1987 onwards. Finally, Santosh Hegde, who was appointed to the Court in January 1999, served as Advocate General of Karnataka for four years (1984–8), then as Additional Solicitor General of India (1989–90), and finally as Solicitor General of India starting April 1998. Accordingly, each of the four lawyers appointed to the Supreme Court served as senior government lawyers—typically in prestigious, high-ranking positions. Based on this discussion it may be concluded that a very high level of distinction is necessary in order to earn a direct appointment to the Supreme Court—whereas the same level of accomplishment and achievement may not be necessary for appointment to a high court.

Why have more lawyers not directly been appointed to the Supreme Court of India? One gets the sense that too few lawyers are offered direct judgeships on the Supreme Court, and the ones who are offered judgeships decline their offers.[42] There are three possible explanations for why these offers might be declined.

Judicial Appointments. New Delhi: Law Commission, Government of India; Nirmalendu Bikash Rakshit. 2004. 'Judicial Appointments', *Economic and Political Weekly*. 39(27): 2959–61.

[41] See note 18 of this chapter.
[42] Ibid.

First, the term of Supreme Court judges is too short. It has been discussed so far that in order to get appointed to the Supreme Court, one has to be senior (typically between 58 and 62 years of age) such that one would get to serve between three and seven years in office before mandatorily retiring at the age of 65. Highly qualified and distinguished lawyers might not consider it worthwhile to give up their lucrative careers in private practice, or their positions of pre-eminence as high-ranking government lawyers (or their remaining years of private practice after completing their terms as government lawyers), in return for only a short three-to-seven-year term on the Supreme Court. A less qualified (and younger) lawyer who might be willing to accept a high court appointment would not get appointed directly to the Supreme Court because of the high level of distinction necessary for a direct appointment to the Supreme Court. But at the same time, high-ranking government lawyers and top private counsel may not find it worthwhile to trade their remaining years of lucrative practice in return for a short Supreme Court assignment. Evidence in favour of this hypothesis was seen in the Lok Sabha debates in 1960, discussed in Chapter 2. Second, the number of judges on the Supreme Court is too large, and arguably, the post is consequently less prestigious than it should be. There are as many as 30 puisne[‡] Supreme Court judges, whereas there is only one Attorney General of India, one Solicitor General of India, one Advocate General of a state, and so on. A high-ranking government lawyer like a solicitor general or an attorney general might not find it worthwhile giving up his position in exchange for becoming one out of 30 puisne[§] Supreme Court judges, who do not get to decide all cases, who might not get assigned to constitution benches or to benches deciding important cases, and who sit in fractured benches of two judges. Third, it is highly unlikely in today's world that lawyers offered direct judgeships on the Supreme Court would rise to the post of Chief Justice of India. After S.M. Sikri's appointment in 1964, no lawyer directly appointed to the Supreme Court has ever become Chief Justice of India.[43,¶] As discussed in Chapter 2, Kuldip

[43] Appointed to the Supreme Court in the 1970s, S.C. Roy could have become Chief Justice of India, but he passed away early. Gadbois, *Judges of the Supreme Court*, pp. 166–7.

Singh could have become Chief Justice of India had the conventional norm of seniority been followed, but this did not happen. Top lawyers might perhaps consider it worthwhile giving up their careers as lawyers if their appointment to the Supreme Court would make it possible for them to become Chief Justice of India by the seniority norm discussed in Chapter 2. However, it is highly unlikely that this will ever happen, because it would frustrate the aspirations of high court chief justices. As discussed in Chapter 2, high court chief justices in India have a legitimate expectation that they will be appointed to the Supreme Court, especially so in the last 20 years of the Court's existence. This legitimate expectation is an incentive which works to staff high courts with capable judges—after all, talented, younger lawyers (who lack the formal distinctions and accomplishments necessary to earn a direct Supreme Court appointment) will accept high court appointments if they know that they can make it to the Supreme Court after they attain a senior position as high court judges or chief justices. If this legitimate expectation is thwarted by the appointment of lawyers directly to the Supreme Court, then it may become more difficult to find talented lawyers to staff the high courts, all the more so if a lawyer is appointed directly to the Supreme Court young enough to become Chief Justice of India. Further, the incredibly short term of the Chief Justice of India might offer an additional explanation—high-ranking lawyers might not even find it worthwhile giving up their positions of prominence in exchange for the promise of becoming Chief Justice of India for a few months or so. Accordingly, even if a lawyer is offered a judgeship when he is young enough to become the Chief Justice of India by the seniority norm seen in Chapter 2, he might still decline because his tenure as Chief Justice of India would be inadequately short. For these reasons, even though several lawyers might have been offered direct Supreme Court judgeships,[44] they might have declined.

Full-time law professors cannot get appointed to a high court in India. This is because although the Constitution of India allows a 'distinguished jurist' to be appointed to the Supreme Court of India,[45]

[44] See note 18.
[45] Article 124(3)(c), Constitution of India.

there is no comparable provision for the appointment of a distinguished jurist to a high court. Since seniority is an informal eligibility criterion for appointments to the Supreme Court, and since there is now a policy of appointing high court chief justices to the Supreme Court, full-time law professors stand a very low chance of ever making it to the Supreme Court. It is small wonder therefore, that no full-time law professor has ever been appointed to the Supreme Court despite the constitutional provision enabling the appointment of distinguished jurists. A policy recommendation can be formulated based on this discussion—if full-time law professors are desired to be appointed to the Supreme Court, a constitutional amendment is necessary enabling full-time law professors to be appointed to high courts—thus permitting them to rise up the ranks as high court judges and to eventually get appointed as Supreme Court judges. As one judge informed me, law professors are not appointed to the Supreme Court because they have not been 'tested' as judges in the high courts (Interview 18). The present seniority norm makes the appointment of full-time law professors to the Supreme Court close to impossible, and this naturally affects the status and prestige of being a law professor in India. If law professors were appointed to the Supreme Court, lawyers would pay more attention to academic writing, and legal academia would be more valued in India than it is today.

Unequal Prior Judicial Experience

The seniority criterion of appointment to the Supreme Court empha-sizes that only senior judges (in the last two decades—typically only high court chief justices) will be eligible for appointment to the Supreme Court. However, seniority is defined relative to each high court, and since high courts in India are of different sizes, it takes less time on some courts to become a senior judge. This drawback arises on account of the interaction between the seniority criterion and the criterion of geographic representation discussed in Chapter 5. Consequently, when a senior judge from one high court becomes eligible for appointment to the Supreme Court, he may not have served the same length of time on that high court as another judge from a different high court who is also eligible for appointment to the Supreme Court. Consider the Patna and Karnataka High Courts. Judges who were appointed to the Supreme Court of India from the High Court of Patna were appointed at a median age of 42.79 years to the high court, and then went on to get appointed at a median age of 59.30 years on the Supreme Court. By contrast, judges from the Karnataka High Court were appointed at a median age of 46.36 years on the high court, but went on to get appointed to the Supreme Court at a median age of 58.34 years.[46] Judges from both the Patna and Karnataka High Courts served comparable terms on the Supreme Court, but the Bihar judges were more experienced (that is, they had longer prior judicial experience) than the Karnataka judges. This breeds unfairness in a system that values objectivity, and also undermines the requirement of prior judicial experience.

Incentives

There are at least three additional problems with the seniority eligibility criterion, each associated with the incentives that it generates.

First, the seniority criterion of appointing judges to the Supreme Court of India does not incentivize merit. Assume that Lawyer 1 is offered a judgeship on High Court A, and that he is 45 years old. Assume that High Court A has no other judge on it at the moment who is younger than Lawyer 1. Lawyer 1 knows that he has approximately 13–17 years before he will be senior enough on High Court A to be appointed a high court chief justice, after which he will be eligible for being considered for a Supreme Court appointment. Lawyer 1 knows that he cannot be removed for slacking off—the independence of the judiciary gives him security of tenure. So long as he is honest and in good health, and so long as he performs his job with a reasonable degree of competence, he stands a good chance of being promoted to the Supreme Court. The incentives for Lawyer 1 to perform well as a high court judge are therefore limited

---

[46] For the purpose of this analysis, Justice Santosh Hegde is not counted as a 'Karnataka judge', since he was appointed to the Supreme Court directly. If his appointment to the Supreme Court were counted with the lot of Karnataka High Court judges, the median age of appointment of Karnataka judges to the Supreme Court would rise to 58.4 years.

to the extent that he knows that he cannot jump the queue if his performance as a high court judge surpasses all expectations. This is beneficial because it ensures that he does not try to curry favour with the executive in order to jump the seniority queue, but it is also problematic because it does not incentivize merit. Lawyer 1 has no institutional incentives to go the extra mile as a high court judge— to get into court early, to stay late, to write quality decisions that will be cited by other courts and the academic world, to extensively read legal materials other than what is necessary for court work, and so on.[47]

Second, the seniority criterion creates disincentives against accepting judgeships on larger high courts where the process of becoming a senior judge takes longer. Since seniority is defined relative to a judge's high court, a judge appointed to a smaller court can become senior quicker, and becomes eligible for appointment to the Supreme Court quicker. Using the same hypothetical, assume that High Court A is a court of 100 judges, all of whom are between 46 and 61 years of age. For Lawyer 1 to get to a position of seniority on High Court A, he will have to wait for 100 judges to retire at age 62, some of whom are only a few years older than him. Assume that Lawyer 2, who is also 45 years old, is offered a judgeship on High Court B which has only 30 judges, all of whom are in their 50s. Lawyer 1 knows that if he accepts a judgeship on High Court A, it will take much longer for him to become a high court chief justice as opposed to his contemporary, Lawyer 2, who will become a senior judge on High Court B much quicker, and consequently, a high court chief justice eligible for Supreme Court appointment much sooner. Therefore, Lawyer 1 naturally has a disincentive against accepting the judgeship on High Court A, because he knows that he cannot climb the seniority ladder as quickly as Lawyer 2. Sometimes this problem may be overcome because the high court with fewer judges might generally appoint judges to the court older than on other courts with more judges. For example, judges from the Gauhati High Court who made it to the Supreme Court were appointed to the high court at a mean age of

---

[47] Many high court judges in India may choose to go the extra mile anyway, and it is by no means suggested here that high court judges do not work hard. The only argument here is that they do not have the appropriate institutional incentives to work hard, even though they may have personal incentives to do so.

50 years, and consequently served only a mean term of 3.4 years on the Supreme Court. Contrast this against the larger Bombay High Court, whose judges on the Supreme Court were appointed to the high court at a mean age of 44.8 and who served a mean term of 6.6 years on the Supreme Court. However, this may not always be so, especially on a 'premier' or reputable high court of a smaller size. For example, consider the appointment of Justices K.S. Paripoornan and S.P. Kurdukar to the Supreme Court in the 1990s. Paripoornan was appointed to the Kerala High Court in December 1982, whereas Kurdukar was appointed to the Bombay High Court about four years before, in April 1978. Kurdukar was accordingly more 'senior' to Paripoornan. However, both Paripoornan and Kurdukar became chief justices of high courts in January 1994, and Paripoornan was appointed to the Supreme Court two years before Kurdukar.

Third, when age is brought into the seniority equation, it creates additional disincentives against accepting judgeships. Recall that Lawyer 1 has been offered a judgeship on High Court A and that Lawyer 1 is 45 years old. Now assume that High Court A has five judges on it who are 44 years old. Lawyer 1 now knows that he will retire at the sixth position in seniority on High Court A and that he will never make it to the Supreme Court of India. This is because the retirement age at high courts in India is 62 years,[48] and on the day that Lawyer 1 turns 62, there will be five judges belonging to High Court A, who will be 61 years old. Since there is a limit on the number of judges from any high court that can serve on the Supreme Court or as high court chief justices, Lawyer 1 will not, in the normal course of things, become a high court chief justice, nor, consequently, will he ever be eligible for appointment to the Supreme Court. Lawyer 1 therefore has a disincentive against accepting the judgeship.

Diversity

Besides career homogeneity, the policy of exclusively appointing high court chief justices to the Supreme Court of India can impact the Court's minority and gender composition. The representation

[48]   Article 217(1), Constitution of India.

of religious minority communities, backward castes, and women on the Supreme Court will be examined in Chapter 5. However, the seniority criterion examined in this chapter limits the pool of candidates from which Supreme Court vacancies can be staffed, and makes it less probable that 'nontraditional'[49] candidates, like women, or candidates belonging to religious minority communities or backward castes, will be appointed to the Supreme Court. If such candidates are not appointed to the high courts young, they may not become senior enough on the high courts to be considered eligible for appointment to the Supreme Court. The appointment of non-traditional candidates to the high courts may consequently impact the religious, caste, and gender diversity of the Supreme Court, which may detrimentally impact its legitimacy. Attempts made to remedy this problem, and their efficacy, will be examined in Chapter 5.

* * *

This chapter has quantitatively and qualitatively demonstrated that seniority is an informal eligibility criterion taken into account while appointing judges to the Supreme Court of India. Supreme Court judge-ships are overwhelmingly staffed from amongst the ranks of senior high court judges, and in the last 20 years coinciding with the Supreme Court's decision in the second Judges case, from amongst the ranks of high court chief justices. The Indian Constitution provides that a high court judge becomes eligible for appointment to the Supreme Court only after serving five years in office.[50] However, in practice, over the last 20 years, judges get appointed to the Supreme Court after serving significantly longer terms on a high court—close to 13–14 years. The Constitution does not provide that only high court chief justices are eligible for appointment to the Supreme Court, nor does it provide that high court chief justices are to be given preference while making appointments to the Court. The Constitution also does not provide that seniority is to be taken into account while making appointments

---

[49] Elliot E. Slotnick. 1983–4. 'The Paths to the Federal Bench: Gender, Race and Judicial Recruitment Variation', *Judicature*, 67(8): 371–88; Sheldon Goldman and Matthew D. Saronson. 1994–5. 'Clinton's Nontraditional Judges: Creating a More Representative Bench', *Judicature*, 78(2): 68–73.

[50] Article 124(3)(a), Constitution of India.

to the Supreme Court. However, the seniority of judges is taken into account nevertheless, and a policy has informally evolved over the last 20 years that only high court chief justices will overwhelmingly be considered eligible for appointment to the Supreme Court.

It must be emphasized that seniority is only an eligibility criterion for appointment to the Supreme Court; it does not necessarily dictate the order of appointments amongst senior judges, or even guarantee that an appointment to the Supreme Court will follow (cf. Interview 24). For example, assume that Justice A, Justice B, and Justice C are Chief Justices of High Court 1, High Court 2, and High Court 3 respectively, and that they were all appointed as chief justices of their respective high courts on the same day. Justice A was previously appointed as a puisne judge on High Court 4 on 1 January 1999; Justice B was previously appointed as a puisne judge on High Court 5 on 2 January 1999; and Justice C was previously appointed as a puisne judge on High Court 6 on 3 January 1999. Although Justice A is the most senior judge amongst the three chief justices, this does not guarantee that he will be appointed to the Supreme Court before Justices B and C, or at all. Justice A's seniority only guarantees that he will be considered eligible for appointment to the Supreme Court. Thus, the collegium may decide to appoint Justice C first, then Justice B, and finally Justice A, or it may ignore all these judges and not appoint any of them to the Supreme Court altogether. Thus, seniority is only an eligibility criterion for appointment to the Supreme Court. Although the Indian Constitution prescribes eligibility criteria for appointment to the Supreme Court,[51] seniority is therefore an informal, unwritten eligibility criterion which supplements the express, written criteria prescribed by the Constitution.

The discussion in this chapter offers a policy justification for scrapping the difference in the retirement age between high court judges and Supreme Court judges—what has been termed the retirement age gap in this study. It will be recalled that as prescribed by the Indian Constitution, Supreme Court judges retire at the age of 65, and high court judges retire at the age of 62. This was specifically engineered to offer an incentive to high court chief justices and senior high court judges—the three additional years of service were

[51] Article 124(3), Constitution of India.

meant to encourage these coveted judges to give up their positions of seniority on high courts in return for a junior position on a new and untested Supreme Court of India. Salary and pension structures provided little or no incentives for high court chief justices to give up their positions in favour of Supreme Court appointments.[52] The fact that the Supreme Court today is overwhelmingly composed of high court chief justices is perhaps indicative that the retirement age gap now deserves to be scrapped. It is perhaps empirically true that high court chief justices no longer need the inducement of three additional years on the Supreme Court to serve on the Court, whose prestige and status is now unquestionable. The reasons that existed back in 1935 and 1948, discussed in Chapter 1, to ensure that able judges served on the newly established Federal Court and Supreme Court, no longer hold true today.[53]

NOTES

* Between 2014 and 2018, four more lawyers (R.F. Nariman, U.U. Lalit, L. Nageswara Rao, and Indu Malhotra) were appointed to the Supreme Court directly.

** Though the salaries of judges have been increased since this book was published, High Court Chief Justices and Supreme Court judges still draw the same salaries as each other.

† Between 2014 and 2018, four more lawyers were appointed directly to the Supreme Court.

‡ In 2019, the number of puisne Supreme Court judges was increased to 33.

§ In 2019, the number of puisne Supreme Court judges was increased to 33.

¶ However, Justice U.U. Lalit is likely to become the Chief Justice of India in 2022.

[52] See note 33.

[53] However, if the retirement age gap is scrapped, then there is a risk that older judges might be appointed to the Supreme Court (since the pool of high court judges from amongst whom Supreme Court appointments can be made will be older), as a result of which the tenure on the Supreme Court may diminish. Therefore, if the retirement age gap is scrapped, then that must be accompanied by a corresponding policy on the minimum tenure which Supreme Court judges should serve in India. See Abhinav Chandrachud. 2010. 'Protecting the Lawgivers', *Times of India*, 29 September.

5

DIVERSITY

THIS CHAPTER INVESTIGATES WHETHER 'DIVERSITY' is a criterion for appointing judges to the Supreme Court of India. The Indian Constitution does not require that the Court's judges be appointed by taking into account any form of diversity. In fact, in response to a request for information that I filed under the Right to Information Act, 2005, the Ministry of Law and Justice (Department of Justice) of the Government of India wrote to me that since judges are appointed under Article 124 of the Indian Constitution, 'which does not provide for reservation for any caste or class of persons', no information concerning the religion or caste of judges of the Supreme Court is maintained by the government.[1] However, my interviews with former judges of the Supreme Court indicated that there is an informal norm of diversity governing judicial appointments to the Supreme Court.

In particular, four kinds of diversity are taken into account while making appointments to the Supreme Court of India, with varying degrees of intensity.

First, an attempt is made to ensure that judges of the Supreme Court of India represent the different geographic regions of India.

---

[1] Letter dated 23 November 2011, 162/DS(J)/2011-RTI; on file with me.

A judge is considered to belong to a region or state where he was first[2] appointed as a high court judge, irrespective of where he was born, where he lived for most of his life, or what his mother tongue is. A former Chief Justice of India informed me that an attempt is made to appoint judges from 'all over the country', though perhaps not from all the states, but at least from 'all regions' (Interview 5), while other judges informed me that this has been a 'consistent practice', which is 'normally' followed (Interviews 15, 19, 28), though 'not always' (Interview 26). One judge said that this kind of diversity is necessary from the viewpoint of the Court's legitimacy, that 'India being a Federal Republic it is advisable to have Judges from different regions' (Interview 16). Others suggested that the geographic diversity norm was more pronounced—that states, not regions, were represented on the Supreme Court. One judge said that the 'general principle is for giving representation to each State so that expertise in local laws of each State is available' (Interview 13). One said that when a judge from one high court retires, an effort is made to appoint another judge from the same state to the Court (Interview 18), while another said that he was 'preferred' for appointment to the Supreme Court because there was a vacancy on the Supreme Court created by the retirement of a judge from his state (Interview 25). One judge said that while a 'regional balance' is sought to be maintained on the Court, larger states are entitled to have two of their judges on the Court (Interview 22). Another said that there is a system of 'proportional representation' on the Supreme Court, such that premier high courts get two judges on the Supreme Court, while smaller high courts get one judge on the Court (Interview 24). Not all judges expressed satisfaction or agreement with this norm. One said that he disagreed with the geographic diversity norm, but that there was 'no alternative' (Interview 17).

Second, an attempt is made to appoint members of religious minority communities to the Supreme Court of India. A Chief Justice of India informed me that the government wanted to 'take into account'

[2] If a person is first appointed to the post of additional judge on a high court, and is later appointed as a permanent judge while serving on another high court, he is typically still considered as belonging to the state or region in which he was he was initially appointed as an additional judge on a high court.

whether the Muslim community was represented on the Court, that the other communities were not as important on the government's list of priorities (Interview 23). Another Chief Justice of India, who served on the Court after the year 2000, said that an effort is made to appoint somebody from the Muslim community (Interview 9) to the Court. However, one judge said that there is a system of 'unofficial reservation' prevalent in the Supreme Court for minority religious communities, including Muslim, Christian, and Sikh communities (Interview 12). A former judge of the Supreme Court informed me that the Government of India routinely writes to the chief justices of high courts requesting them to appoint persons of minority communities as high court judges, that there is an informal 'quota' for minority judges (Interview 10). Another judge informed me that as chief justice of a high court, he received a request from the chief minister to appoint a person from a particular community to the high court, and an effort was made to honour the request (Interview 12), although others said that they did not face any such interference (for example, Interviews 24, 27). It is doubtful whether any conscious attempt is made to ensure representation to the Jain and Zoroastrian communities on the Supreme Court, to other religious communities (for example, the Veerashaiva religion), or to Agnostics, although judges belonging to these communities have made it to the Supreme Court. One judge agreed that there was a convention of having at least one Muslim judge on the Court (Interview 3), and one agreed that religion and caste are taken into account 'to an extent' (Interview 16). One judge said that there is 'no question' of any reservation for minorities or women in judicial appointments, but that that the collegium 'does consider' such matters (Interview 28). On the other hand, one judge said that religion and caste would only be taken into account if the Chief Justice of India gave weight to such considerations (Interview 5), while others said that religion and caste had nothing to do with appointments to the Supreme Court (Interviews 7, 8).

Third, an attempt is made to ensure representation to 'backward castes' on the Supreme Court of India. One judge (who was a former member of the collegium) informed me that caste was never openly discussed by the collegium, although there was an informal understanding that a backward caste judge would be appointed to the Court (Interview 3). A former member of the collegium said that there was never any direct pressure to appoint members of backward castes to the Court, but if a judge from a backward caste was available, his appointment would be considered (Interview 26). A Chief Justice of India said that caste was only a factor at the high court level (Interview 9), and others seemed to emphasize the importance of caste at the time of making appointments to the high courts. But since Supreme Court appointments are invariably made from the high courts, the caste considerations of high court appointments may percolate into judicial appointments to the Supreme Court. One judge said that it was a 'known factor prevailing in all High Courts' that priority is given to 'people of caste' so that they can 'become Chief Justice of a High Court' and 'get elevated to the Supreme Court' (Interview 20). One judge said that law ministers would send confidential letters to high court chief justices requesting them to appoint members of backward castes as judges and that this was an 'informal quota system' not prescribed by the Constitution (Interview 24), while another agreed that there was an informal 'quota' for judges of Scheduled Castes at the high courts (Interview 10), where 'every caste is represented' (Interview 6). Others did not think that caste was taken into account while making appointments to the Supreme Court (Interviews 7, 8, 22). The interviews generally indicate that caste is not uniformly a criterion having the same level of intensity on every high court, and that different weight is given to caste considerations for judicial appointments in different high courts (for example, Interview 1).

Finally, an attempt is made to appoint women to the Supreme Court of India, especially in more recent times. A former member of the collegium informed me that a female puisne high court judge was appointed to the Supreme Court directly (that is, without her having first served as a high court chief justice) possibly because she was a woman, although she was a 'strong candidate' irrespective of her gender (Interview 3). When a judge was asked why a (female) puisne high court judge was elevated to the Supreme Court before him, although he was a high court chief justice at the time, and despite the fact that he was senior to her (having been appointed to a high court prior in time), he remarked, 'ladies' quota' (Interview 2). Another judge said that 'if there are competent female Judges, they are

appointed even if they have not been Chief Justices' (Interview 13).
Two judges said that there was a convention that high courts should
have at least one female judge (Interviews 5, 12). One judge said that
as chief justice of a high court, he was requested by the governor of
the state (who happened to be a woman) to appoint a woman judge
to the high court, that they looked around for women to appoint,
but found nobody competent (Interview 12). Another said that law
ministers would send confidential letters to chief justices of high
courts requesting them to appoint women judges and that this was
an 'informal quota system' (Interview 24). Others agreed that an
attempt was made to ensure that women received some form of
representation on the Supreme Court (Interviews 17, 18).

This chapter analyses whether these qualitative findings prove to
be quantitatively true, and whether diversity is taken into account
for judicial appointments to the Supreme Court.

THE DIVERSITY DEBATE

Proponents of diversity argue that it enhances a court's legitimacy,
builds public confidence in the court, remedies past inequalities, and
improves the quality of decision-making on the court by bringing a
diversity of perspectives to its opinions.[3] A court that fairly reflects[4]
different religious, ethnic, geographic, gender, or racial components
of society may signal that it is 'open to all'.[5] Scholars have suggested
that diversity on courts may have symbolic or descriptive value on
the one hand, or substantive value on the other.[6] At the symbolic or

---

[3] See for example, Mark S. Hurwitz and Drew Noble Lanier. 2001. 'Women and
Minorities on State and Federal Appellate Benches, 1985 and 1999', *Judicature*,
85(2): 84–92.

[4] See Shimon Shetreet. 1985. 'Judicial Independence: New Conceptual Dimensions and Contemporary Challenges', in Shimon Shetreet and Jules Deschênes
(eds), *Judicial Independence: The Contemporary Debate*, pp. 590–681. Dordrecht:
Martinus Nijhoff.

[5] Barbara L. Graham. 2004. 'Toward an Understanding of Judicial Diversity
in American Courts', *Michigan Journal of Race and Law*, 10(1): 153–94.

[6] Hanna Pitkin used the terms 'descriptive' and 'substantive' to describe representation. Hanna Fenichel Pitkin. 1967. *The Concept of Representation*. Berkeley:
University of California Press.

descriptive level, a judge from a 'nontraditional'[7] background may become an inclusive symbol, or stand for something he or she physically resembles, despite not necessarily holding the same viewpoints of members of the community that he or she stands for or appears to represent. For example, Clarence Thomas, an African American judge on the US Supreme Court, did not share the views held by members of the African American community in civil liberties cases,[8] although he stood for or symbolized members of that community on the US Supreme Court because he physically resembled them.

At the substantive level, a non-traditional judge is more than a mere 'cosmetic symbol'[9] on a court. By his or her very presence on a bench, a judge may remove the prejudices that his or her colleagues may have about members of his or her community.[10] A judge from a non-traditional background may also bring 'traditionally excluded' perspectives to the cases being decided by the court. For example, feminist 'difference theorists' argue that women bring different values (caring, empathy, community, and so on) to cases as opposed to men (abstraction, individualism, and so on).[11] There is empirical evidence, for example, to suggest that women judges are harsher on women defendants.[12] Minority judges might bring 'special sensitivity' or 'unique perspectives' to decision-making.[13] However, viewed through this prism, appointing a judge to a court on diversity considerations may enhance the legitimacy and public appeal of the court, but it may simultaneously strike a pejorative blow to the community sought to be represented by the appointment. After all, how

---

[7] Elliot E. Slotnick. 1984–5. 'The Paths to the Federal Bench: Gender, Race and Judicial Recruitment Variation', *Judicature* 67: 371; Sheldon Goldman and Matthew D. Saronson. 1994–5. 'Clinton's Nontraditional Judges: Creating a More Representative Bench', *Judicature* 78(2): 68–73.

[8] Sherrilyn A. Ifill. 2000. 'Racial Diversity on the Bench: Beyond Role Models and Public Confidence', *Washington and Lee Law Review*, 57(2): 405–95.

[9] Ifill, 'Racial Diversity'.

[10] Sarah Westergren. 2004. 'Gender Effects in the Courts of Appeals Revisited: The Date since 1994', *Georgetown Law Journal*, 92(3): 689–708.

[11] Westergren, 'Gender Effects'.

[12] John Gruhl, Cassia Spohn, and Susan Welch. 1981. 'Women as Policymakers: The Case of Trial Judges', *American Journal of Political Science*, 25(2): 308–22; Westergren, 'Gender Effects'.

[13] Goldman and Saronson, 'Clinton's Nontraditional Judges', p. 68.

can one unelected person 'symbolize' or even 'represent' the views of an entire community? This form of diversity representation presupposes unanimity of opinions within the community sought to be represented, and undermines the very system of diversity it attempts to create. An unelected judge from a certain racial, religious, ethnic, geographic, or gender background cannot conceivably represent the diverse values and opinions within the community. For this reason, appointing a minority judge to a court purely on diversity grounds would undermine the diversity of opinion which prevails within the community that the judge belongs to.

Some critics of diversity on courts typically argue that it conflicts with the principle of merit in selecting judges. One scholar calls this the 'merit/diversity paradox',[14] an apparent conflict between either selecting the best judges to a court or selecting judges that best reflect the members of the society in which the court is situated. However, there are at least three reasons why diversity considerations for judicial appointments do not conflict with the merit principle. First, scholars have suggested that merit is not necessarily compromised when judges from diverse backgrounds are selected to courts. Judges selected to the US Supreme Court on diversity considerations always met a minimum standard of merit, and a few of them even went on to become some of the greatest judges the court had ever seen.[15] Second, merit cannot be defined in a social or contextual vacuum. In the Indian context, George H. Gadbois, Jr and M.P. Singh have suggested that the idea of merit is contextual.[16] The diversity of a non-traditional judge might well be considered an element of his or her own individual merit. Third, the very idea

[14] Leny E. De Groot-Van Leeuwen. 2006. 'Merit Selection and Diversity in the Dutch Judiciary', in Kate Malleson and Peter H. Russell (eds), *Appointing Judges in an Age of Judicial Power: Critical Perspectives from around the World*, pp. 145–58. Toronto: University of Toronto Press.

[15] Barbara A. Perry. 1991. *A "Representative" Supreme Court? The Impact of Race, Religion, and Gender on Appointments*, p. 4.

[16] George H. Gadbois, Jr. 1982. 'Judicial Appointments in India: The Perils of Non-contextual Analysis', *Asian Thought and Society*, 7: 124; M.P. Singh. 1999. 'Merit in the Appointment of Judges', *Supreme Court Cases*, (8): 1. See further, M.P. Singh. 2000. 'Securing the Independence of the Judiciary: The Indian Experience', *Indiana International and Comparative Law Review*, 10: 245.

of merit may be 'self-reflective',[17] 'self-selecting',[18] or 'self-cloning'. In other words, the definition of merit varies with the persons who judge merit—a judge of merit, consciously or unconsciously, may seek a replication of his or her own credentials in the candidate he or she seeks out. The judge of merit may seek out a candidate who is least likely to challenge the establishment.[19] Some scholars have suggested that it is a 'myth' that merit is a neutral standard.[20] The conflict between merit and diversity has also been categorized as one between traditionalists and behaviouralists—the former want judges to objectively and neutrally find the law, the latter recognize that judging is inherently a political process.[21]

Other critics of diversity argue that it conflicts with democratic theory, in that judges are not meant to 'represent' constituents, unlike legislators. In this sense, a judge from a non-traditional background who brings the perspectives of his or her community to cases threatens to make himself less impartial to his community's viewpoint in a case.[22] However, much of the scholarly literature acknowledges that judges are seldom neutral adjudicators—judging, in constitutional cases, is a political process, and personal value choices often colour decisions. For this reason, non-traditional or traditionally excluded judges on a panel may ensure that no single set of people or values dominates a court's opinions.[23] In this sense, diversity enhances the 'structural impartiality' of the court.[24] There is also the criticism that

---

[17]   Chief Justice Elias. 2008. 'Address to the Australian Women Lawyers' Conference', 13 June 2008, available online at http://www.courtsofnz.govt.nz/speechpapers/13-06-08.pdf/at_download/file. See further, Kate Malleson. 2009. 'Diversity in the Judiciary: The Case for Positive Action', *Journal of Law and Society*, 36(3): 376–402.

[18]   See Rachel Davis and George Williams. 2003. 'Reform of the Judicial Appointments Process: Gender and the Bench of the High Court of Australia', *Melbourne University Law Review*, 27: 819, 835.

[19]   Lady Hale. 2005. 'Making a Difference? Why We Need a More Diverse Judiciary', *Northern Ireland Legal Quarterly*, 56(32): 281 (2005).

[20]   Davis and Williams, 'Reform of the Judicial Appointments Process'.

[21]   Perry, *"Representative" Supreme Court*.

[22]   See for example, Hale, 'Making a Difference', p. 287.

[23]   Ifill, 'Racial Diversity'.

[24]   Sherrilyn A. Ifill. 1997. 'Judging the Judges: Racial Diversity, Impartiality and Representation on State Trial Courts', *Boston College Law Review*, 39(1): 95–149.

allowing judicial appointments to be made on considerations other than merit, like diversity, will inappropriately afford a backdoor entry for political influence to enter the system of judicial appointments.[25] However, this argument once again assumes that diversity candidates appointed to courts are non-meritorious—ensuring that such candidates meet a certain threshold level of merit may serve to exclude political influence.

There is a particularly large volume of literature on geographic diversity in international bodies.[26] Article 23 of the United Nations Charter calls on the General Assembly to elect non-permanent members to the Security Council, keeping in mind the principle of 'equitable geographic distribution'. This principle seems to have percolated into international judicial bodies as well, even though judges nominated by states are not state representatives and do not represent national interests. International judicial bodies have formal mechanisms for ensuring geographic diversity. Although judges on the International Court of Justice (ICJ) are required to be appointed regardless of their nationality,[27] the statute of the ICJ formally provides that no two judges can belong to the same nationality.[28] Similar formal provisions exist on the International Criminal Tribunal for the former Yugoslavia (ICTY),[29] the International Criminal Tribunal for Rwanda (ICTR),[30]

[25] See Malleson, 'Diversity in the Judiciary'.

[26] See for example, Amber Fitzgerald. 2000. 'Security Council Reform: Creating a More Representative Body of the Entire U.N. Membership', *Pace International Law Review*, 12(2): 319–65; Michael J. Kelly. 2000. 'U.N. Security Council Permanent Membership: A New Proposal for a Twenty-first Century Council', *Seton Hall Law Review*, 31(2): 319–99.

[27] Article 2, Statute of the ICJ. See United Nations. 1946. Statute of the International Court of Justice, 18 April, available online at http://www.unhcr.org/refworld/docid/3deb4b9c0.html (last accessed on 22 January 2012).

[28] Article 3(1), Statute of the ICJ.

[29] Article 12(1), Statute of the International Tribunal for the Prosecution of Persons Responsible for Serious Violations of International Humanitarian Law Committed in the Territory of the Former Yugoslavia since 1991, U.N. Doc. S/25704 at 36, annex (1993) and S/25704/Add.1 (1993), adopted by Security Council on 25 May 1993, U.N. Doc. S/RES/827 (1993).

[30] Article 11(1), Statute of the ICTR. See UN Security Council. 1994. 'Statute of the International Criminal Tribunal for Rwanda (as last amended on 13 October 2006), 8 November', available online at http://www.unhcr.org/refworld/docid/3ae6b3952c.html (last accessed on 22 January 2012).

and the International Criminal Court (ICC).[31] In fact, judges are to be appointed to the ICC in a manner that ensures representation for the principal legal systems of the world, equitable geographic representation, and fair representation for female and male judges— the first 'major international agreement' to emphasize gender representation.[32] However, informal norms determine geographic representation on these bodies, and state representation on these bodies is not always equal. Accordingly, a judge from each of the five permanent members of the Security Council (P5 countries), except China, has sat on the ICJ since its inception, and the remaining 10 seats on the ICJ are distributed regionally, such that Africa gets three seats (one seat each for north Africa, francophone sub-Saharan Africa, and anglophone sub-Saharan Africa), two seats each go to western Europe/other, Latin America/Caribbean, and Asia, and one seat goes to eastern Europe.[33] This arrangement matches the distribution of non-permanent seats on the Security Council.[34] Judges of P5 countries have also consistently held seats on either the ICTY or the ICTR.[35] However, judgeships on the ICTY are dominated by Western judges, while judgeships on the ICTR are dominated by African judges,[36] indicating that geographic representation on these bodies is organized in such a manner that the region that has the most interest in the tribunal's outcomes, or in the stability of the area the tribunal deals with, gets the most representation on

[31] Article 36(7), Rome Statute of the ICC. See UN General Assembly 1998. 'Rome Statute of the International Criminal Court (last amended January 2002), 17 July', A/CONF. 183/9, available online at http://www.unhcr.org/refworld/docid/3ae6b3a84.html (last accessed on 22 January 2012).

[32] William J. Aceves. 2001. 'Critical Jurisprudence and International Legal Scholarship: A Study of Equitable Distribution', *Columbia Journal of Transnational Law*, 39(2): 299–394, pp. 384–5.

[33] Jacob Katz Cogan. 2009. 'Representation and Power in International Organization: The Operational Constitution and Its Critics', *American Journal of International Law*, 103(2): 209–63.

[34] Cogan, 'Representation and Power'.

[35] Cogan, 'Representation and Power'.

[36] Allison Danner and Erik Voeten. n.d. 'Who is Running the International Criminal Justice System?', available online at http://www.gwu.edu/~igis/conferences/who_rules_the_globe/Danner_Voeten_IGIS.pdf (last accessed on 21 January 2012).

the tribunal.[37] It seems apparent that 'equitable' geographic distribution on these bodies does not mean 'equal' representation, and, in this sense, state representation on international judicial bodies does not comport with the principle of the sovereign equality of states, especially on account of the dominance of powerful states on these bodies. On the other hand, an informal norm dictates that each member state of the European Court of Justice (ECJ) gets to appoint a judge to the ECJ.[38] Geographic representation is perceived as being necessary for the legitimacy of these international judicial bodies.[39]

Geographic representation was an important consideration in staffing appointments to the US Supreme Court until the late 19th century. The convention of seeking to achieve a geographically balanced court began with President George Washington himself, who emphasized 'geographic suitability' on the court because he wanted to be 'president of *all* the states of the fledgling nation', and who consequently rewarded a strategic state with a supreme court appointment, on occasion.[40] Barbara Perry notes that the convention of balancing the US Supreme Court's membership by state or region was meant to make the court an 'inclusive symbol'.[41] This convention was said to be especially relevant until the late 19th century,[42] when US Supreme Court justices rode circuit and knowledge of local

[37] Danner and Voeten, 'Who is Running the International Criminal Justice System'.

[38] Cogan, 'Representation and Power'.

[39] See Medard R. Rwelamira. 1999. 'Composition and Administration of the Court', in Roy S. Lee (ed.), *The International Criminal Court: The Making of the Rome Statute*, pp. 153–74. The Hague: Kluwer; Aceves, 'Critical Jurisprudence'.

[40] Henry J. Abraham. 1999. *Justices, Presidents, and Senators: A History of the U.S. Supreme Court Appointments from Washington to Clinton*, Lanham: Rowman and Littlefield, p. 59.

[41] Perry, *"Representative" Supreme Court*.

[42] F.L. Morton. 2006. 'Judicial Appointments in Post-Charter Canada: A System in Transition', in Kate Malleson and Peter H. Russell (eds), *Appointing Judges in an Age of Judicial Power: Critical Perspectives from around the World*, pp. 56–79. Toronto: University of Toronto Press; Barbara A. Perry. 1989–90. 'The Life and Death of the "Catholic Seat" on the United States Supreme Court', *Journal of Law and Politics*, 6(1): 55–92.

laws was necessary,[43] and when regional disputes were 'the foremost conflict of the era'.[44] There was an informal practice that New England, Virginia, Pennsylvania, and New York would get seats on the US Supreme Court.[45] The 1999 edition of Henry J. Abraham's classical work on US Supreme Court justices records that the states of New York, Virginia, Ohio, Massachusetts, Pennsylvania, and Tennessee had seen the highest number of judges appointed to the US Supreme Court (in that order), and that judges had been appointed to the court from 31 of the 50 states of the United States.[46] Perry attributes three reasons to the demise of the convention of geographic balance in staffing appointments to the US Supreme Court: first, the Circuit Court of Appeals Act, 1891 ended the practice of circuit riding, and with it the practical necessity of having supreme court justices with knowledge of local laws;[47] second, with the end of the American Civil War, the 'old order' came to an end, and the forces of regionalism diminished in strength; third, other 'representative' factors, such as religion, race, ethnicity, and gender, put geography at the bottom of the list. However, geographic considerations were still given some weight until the mid-20th century,[48] and Nixon was the last president to seriously take into account geographic considerations.[49] When it existed, the norm of geographic diversity granted

[43] See Paul A. Freund. 1975. 'The New England Seat on the Supreme Court', *Proceedings of the Massachusetts Historical Society*, 87: 32–44. See further, Perry, *"Representative" Supreme Court*, p. 5.

[44] Jeffrey Toobin. 2009. 'Diverse Opinions', *New Yorker*, 8 June, available online at http://www.newyorker.com/talk/comment/2009/06/08/090608taco_talk_toobin (last accessed on 26 January 2012).

[45] Toobin, 'Diverse Opinions'. See further, John W. Whitehead and John M. Beckett. 2009. 'A Dysfunctional Supreme Court: Remedies and a Comparative Analysis', *Charleston Law Review*, 4: 171.

[46] Abraham, *Justices, Presidents, and Senators*, p. 46 (1999). See further, Henry J. Abraham. 1992. *Justices and Presidents: A Political History of Appointments to the Supreme Court*, 3rd ed. New York: Oxford University Press, p. 62.

[47] See further, John Benjamin Ashby. 1972. 'Supreme Court Appointments since 1937', Unpublished doctoral dissertation, University of Notre Dame, Political Science, General, 15–16.

[48] See Abraham, *Justices, Presidents, and Senators*, p. 191, stating that even President Dwight Eisenhower considered 'geographic balance' on the US Supreme Court to be important.

[49] Joel K. Goldstein. 2011. 'Choosing Justices: How Presidents Decide', *Journal of Law and Politics*, 26(4): 425–95.

legitimacy to the US Supreme Court's decisions—one scholar argues that the fact that the court's desegregation decision was issued by a court that included a justice each from Alabama (Hugo L. Black), Kentucky (Stanley F. Reed), and Texas (Tom C. Clark) bolstered the legitimacy of the decision.[50] Now, geographic representation is said to be irrelevant for judicial appointments to the US Supreme Court. For example, little was made of the fact that Justices Sandra Day O'Connor and William Rehnquist served on the same court despite both being from the state of Arizona.[51]

Judges are appointed to the Supreme Court of Canada by taking into account an informal norm of geographic representation, although formal law only requires that three judges be appointed to the court from Quebec.[52] Informally, three judges are appointed to the court from Ontario, one from Atlantic Canada, and two from the western provinces[53]—possibly one from British Columbia and one from the three prairie provinces.[54] Ontario's strength on the court fell to two judges in 1979, with the appointment of McIntyre (British Columbia) to replace Spence, although this was rectified in 1982 with the appointment of Wilson (Ontario) following Martland's retirement.[55] There is some debate as to whether at least one of the non-Quebec

---

[50] Freund, 'New England Seat', p. 44.

[51] Toobin, 'Diverse Opinions'. In fact, interestingly, they had briefly dated each other as students at Stanford Law School. Lou Cannon. 2005. 'When Ronnie Met Sandy', *New York Times*, 7 July, available online at http://www.nytimes.com/2005/07/07/opinion/07cannon.html (last accessed on 28 April 2012).

[52] James C. Hopkins and Albert C. Peeling. 2004. 'Aboriginal Judicial Appointments to the Supreme Court of Canada', 6 April, available online at http://www.indigenousbar.ca/pdf/Aboriginal%20Appointment%20to%20the%20Supreme%20Court%20Final.pdf (last accessed on 22 January 2012); Ian Greene, Carl Baar, Peter McCormick, George Szablowski, and Martin Thomas. 1998. *Final Appeal: Decision-making in Canadian Courts of Appeal*. Toronto: James Lorimer. See further, Richard Devlin, A. Wayne Mackay, and Natasha Kim. 2000. 'Reducing the Democratic Deficit: Representation, Diversity and the Canadian Judiciary, or Towards a "Triple P" Judiciary', *Alberta Law Review*, 38(4): 734–866.

[53] Hopkins and Peeling, 'Aboriginal Judicial Appointments'; Green et al., *Final Appeal*.

[54] Peter McCormick. 2005. 'Selecting the Supremes: The Appointment of Judges to the Supreme Court of Canada', *Journal of Appellate Practice and Process*, 7: 1.

[55] McCormick, 'Selecting the Supremes'.

judges should be francophone, and whether one of the Quebec judges should be anglophone.[56] By convention, the post of chief justice has also typically alternated between a judge from Quebec and a judge from the rest of Canada, since the 1930s.[57] This form of regional representation on the Canadian Supreme Court is meant to reassure provinces that their special circumstances will receive a 'fair hearing'.[58] Peter McCormick has said that though regional representation on the Canadian Supreme Court is a 'very strong convention', it 'complicate(s) the professionalism of a merit-based system'—after all, 'what if the objectively best judges at the occasion of any vacancy, over and over again, are sitting on the Ontario Court of Appeal, easily and always the country's strongest provincial court of appeal?'[59] In the United Kingdom, there was a convention of ensuring 'an appropriate ethnic balance' in the House of Lords, by conferring representation to all three constituent parts of the United Kingdom[60] (two judges would hail from Scotland,[61] and one from Northern Ireland[62], although the convention of having one judge from Northern Ireland serving on the court was not as firmly followed).[63] There is also a debate in the United Kingdom as to whether one judge should be appointed from Wales. There is some indication that judgeships on the Federal Constitutional Court of Germany are 'distributed proportionately on the basis of geographical origin and party affiliation',[64] that seats are evenly distributed on the court

---

[56] McCormick, 'Selecting the Supremes'.

[57] Hopkins and Peeling, 'Aboriginal Judicial Appointments'.

[58] Morton, 'Judicial Appointments'.

[59] McCormick, 'Selecting the Supremes'.

[60] Hale, 'Making a Difference', p. 291.

[61] Kate Malleson. 2009. 'Appointments to the House of Lords: Who Goes Upstairs', in Louis Blom-Cooper, Brice Dickson, and Gavin Drewry (eds), *The Judicial House of Lords: 1876–2009*. Oxford: Oxford University Press.

[62] Shetreet, 'Judicial Independence'.

[63] See Graham Gee. 2005. 'Devolution and the Courts', in Robert Hazell and Richard Rawlings (eds), *Devolution, Law Making and the Constitution*, pp. 252–94. Exeter: Imprint Academic.

[64] Donald P. Kommers. 2001. 'Autonomy versus Accountability: The German Judiciary', in Peter H. Russell and David M. O'Brien (eds), *Judicial Independence in the Age of Democracy: Critical Perspectives from around the World*, pp. 131–54. Charlottesville: University Press of Virginia, p. 147.

between the four regions of Germany: Bavaria, Rhineland, north-east Germany, and south-west Germany.[65] The 1814 Constitution of the Netherlands provided that judges of its supreme court should be picked from 'all provinces and landscapes',[66] although this was 'last referred to' in 1902.[67] Geographic considerations are irrelevant on the High Court of Australia, where appointments are driven by considerations of merit,[68] but where, consequently, some states see better representation than others.[69]

Religion was an informal factor considered while making appointments to the US Supreme Court starting with the late 19th century, although its role substantially, if not entirely, diminished by the late 20th century.[70] The US Constitution prohibits religious tests for public office, and the practice of appointing justices to the court for the religion they represent could therefore only be an

[65] Donald P. Kommers. 1976. *Judicial Politics in West Germany: A Study of the Federal Constitutional Court.* Beverly Hills: SAGE, p. 147.

[66] Leeuwen, 'Merit Selection and Diversity', p. 148.

[67] Leeuwen, 'Merit Selection and Diversity', p. 148.

[68] George Williams. 2008. 'High Court Appointments: The Need for Reform', *Sydney Law Review*, 30(1): 163–9.

[69] John M. Williams. 2001. 'Judicial Independence in Australia', in Peter H. Russell and David M. O'Brien (eds), *Judicial Independence in the Age of Democracy: Critical Perspectives from around the World*, pp. 173–93. Charlottesville: University Press of Virginia. However, one scholar has claimed that the requirement that the attorney general consult state attorneys general before making recommendations for judicial appointments briefly increased state representation. Elizabeth Handsley. 2006. '"The Judicial Whisper Goes Around": Appointment of Judicial Officers in Australia', in Kate Malleson and Peter H. Russell (eds), *Appointing Judges in an Age of Judicial Power: Critical Perspectives from around the World*, pp. 122–44. Toronto: University of Toronto Press.

[70] See Perry, *"Representative" Supreme Court*; Perry, 'Life and Death'; Philippa Strum. 1992. 'Book review of A 'Representative' Supreme Court? The Impact of Race, Religion, and Gender on Appointments', *Journal of American History*, 79(3): 1207–8; Abraham, *Justices, Presidents, and Senators*; John Benjamin Ashby, 'Supreme Court Appointments', p. 16; Thomas Karfunkel and Thomas W. Ryley. 1978. *The Jewish Seat: Anti-Semitism and the Appointment of Jews to the Supreme Court.* Hicksville: Exposition; Sheldon Goldman. 2006. 'The Politics of Appointing Catholics to the Federal Courts', *University of St. Thomas Law Journal*, 4(2): 193–220; Paul Horwitz. 2006. 'Religious Tests in the Mirror: The Constitutional Law and Constitutional Etiquette of Religion in Judicial Nominations', *William and Mary Bill of Rights Journal*, 15(1): 75–146.

informal one.[71] Presidents who appointed justices belonging to religious minority communities often did so to reward their core constituency or to attract members of that constituency as voters.[72] Members of the religious community may have viewed a supreme court appointment as confirmation of their integration into American public life.[73] In 1836, Roger B. Taney was the first Roman Catholic appointed to the US Supreme Court (he was later appointed Chief Justice by President Andrew Jackson), but religion had little to do with his appointment, and no Catholic served on the court for 30 years after his death. The 'Catholic seat' is said to have begun on the US Supreme Court with the appointment of Edward D. White in 1894, who was subsequently appointed chief justice in 1910 by President William H. Taft, who, some say,[74] wanted to attract the Catholic vote. Religion played a definite role in the appointment of Joseph McKenna to the court by President William McKinley in 1898,[75] consequent to which two Catholic justices served simultaneously on the court for the first time in its history. The appointments of Pierce Butler[76] by President Warren Harding in 1922 and Frank Murphy[77] by President Franklin Delano Roosevelt in 1940 were similarly coloured by considerations of religion. When Frank Murphy died in 1949, President Harry S. Truman did not replace him with another Catholic justice, but President Dwight D. Eisenhower restored the Catholic seat by appointing William Brennan to the court in 1956. Religion had a marginal role, if any, in the appointments of subsequent Catholic justices to the court,[78] as other diversity factors, such as race and gender, took precedence.

---

[71] Goldman, 'Politics of Appointing Catholics'. But see Horwitz, 'Religious Tests'.
[72] Goldman, 'Politics of Appointing Catholics'; Karfunkel and Ryley, *Jewish Seat*.
[73] Karfunkel and Ryley, *Jewish Seat*.
[74] See Perry, *"Representative" Supreme Court*, pp. 30–1.
[75] Cf. Perry, *"Representative" Supreme Court*, p. 29; Abraham, *Justices, Presidents, and Senators*, p. 116.
[76] Cf. Perry, *"Representative" Supreme Court*, pp. 32–3.
[77] Cf. Perry, *"Representative" Supreme Court*, pp. 37–8.
[78] These were the appointments of Antonin Scalia and Anthony Kennedy by President Ronald Reagan in 1986 and 1988 respectively, of Clarence Thomas by President George H.W. Bush in 1991, of John Roberts and Samuel Alito by President George W. Bush in 2005 and 2006 respectively, and of Sonia Sotomayor by President Barrack Obama in 2009.

The 'Jewish seat' was established on the US Supreme Court with the appointment of Louis D. Brandeis to the court by President Woodrow Wilson in 1916. Benjamin N. Cardozo was later appointed to the court in 1932 by President Herbert Hoover, followed by Felix Frankfurter (President Franklin Delano Roosevelt, in 1939), Arthur J. Goldberg (President John F. Kennedy, in 1962), and Abe Fortas (President Lyndon B. Johnson, in 1965). With the resignation of Abe Fortas from the court in 1969, President Nixon chose not to continue the tradition of the Jewish seat on the court, appointing a Methodist (Harry Blackmun) instead. Scholars have suggested that the Jewish seat ended on the court because Republican presidents did not find it advantageous, as the Jewish vote was typically Democratic,[79] and Jewish leaders did not significantly pursue this issue. Barbara Perry has suggested that it came to an end because Jews had been better assimilated into US society by that time, and gender now began to take precedence on the court.[80] Others have suggested that the Jewish seat had outlived its usefulness since the Jewish community had shed its insecurity, and the community was not 'overly disturbed' when the seat was done away with.[81]

Religion has generally been less relevant for appointments to the court in the latter half of the 20th century, perhaps since the time of President Nixon.[82] For example, the fact that Antonin Scalia and Anthony Kennedy were Catholic was entirely coincidental to their appointments.[83] As one commentator noted, '[r]eligious tensions have also cooled',[84] which is why religious 'seats' on the court have disappeared. Today, the court has six Roman Catholic justices (Chief Justice John Roberts, Antonin Scalia, Anthony Kennedy, Clarence Thomas, Samuel Alito, and Sonia Sotomayor) and three Jewish justices (Ruth Bader Ginsburg, Stephen Breyer, and Elena Kagan). With Elena Kagan's appointment to the court in 2010, for the first time since its establishment in 1789, the US Supreme Court does

---

[79] Strum, 'Book Review'.
[80] Perry, *"Representative" Supreme Court*, pp. 80–1.
[81] Karfunkel and Ryley, *Jewish Seat*, p. 146.
[82] Goldman, 'Politics of Appointing Catholics'.
[83] Perry, 'Life and Death'.
[84] Toobin, 'Diverse Opinions'.

not have a Protestant justice.[85] However, one scholar has argued that religion was still a 'plus' or 'minus' factor for recent appointments made or sought to be made to the US Supreme Court, as was the case with John Roberts, who was questioned whether his religious beliefs would conflict with his ability to decide abortion cases.[86] To some extent, the confirmation hearings for John Roberts' appointment to the court suggest that religion has ceased to become a form of descriptive or symbolic representation on the court, and some consider religious 'representation' on the court to be substantive or active representation—religion on the court is no longer a symbol of inclusiveness, but its presence on the court signals a fear that it may cloud legal interpretation.

Religious 'seats' on supreme courts are not limited to the United States alone. In the Netherlands,[87] a practice existed until 1968 that a vacancy on its supreme court arising out of the retirement or death of a Catholic judge would be followed by the appointment of a Catholic judge to the court. By 1913, the court had four Catholic judges. Seats were reserved on the court for Protestants, and a Jewish judge was appointed occasionally. Although this custom is no longer followed on the supreme court, it is still 'widely practiced' in other courts in the Netherlands.[88] On the Supreme Court of Israel,[89] a seat has typically been reserved for an Orthodox Jew, and since 1962, a seat has unofficially been reserved for a Spharadic judge. There have been calls to appoint judges from different religious and ethnic backgrounds to the Supreme Court of Israel, in order to make the court more 'reflective' (as opposed to 'representative') of different

[85] Cf. Adam Liptak. 2010. 'Stevens, the Only Protestant on the Supreme Court', *New York Times*, 10 April, available online at http://www.nytimes.com/2010/04/11/weekinreview/11liptak.html (last accessed on 23 January 2012).
[86] Horwitz, 'Religious Tests'.
[87] Peter J. van Koppen. 1990. 'The Dutch Supreme Court and Parliament: Political Decisionmaking Versus Nonpolitical Appointments', *Law and Society Review*, 24(3): 745–80, p. 770; Leeuwen, 'Merit Selection and Diversity'.
[88] Van Koppen, 'Dutch Supreme Court', p. 770.
[89] Eli M. Salzberger. 2006. 'Judicial Appointments and Promotions in Israel: Constitution, Law and Politics', in Kate Malleson and Peter H. Russell (eds), *Appointing Judges in an Age of Judicial Power: Critical Perspectives from around the World*, pp. 241–59. Toronto: University of Toronto Press, p. 250.

groups within society.[90] Even in Germany, one scholar has suggested that a religious equilibrium (that is, a balance between the Catholic and Protestant members of the court) is sought to be maintained on the Federal Constitutional Court, and there is some suggestion of an informal norm that judges with Jewish ancestry will be appointed to the court.[91] Informal barriers existed in the United Kingdom against the appointment of Catholic and Jewish justices to higher courts, although in more recent times, the proportion of Jewish justices serving on higher courts is believed to be more than the number of Jews in the population of the United Kingdom.

In the United States, gender and race have replaced geography and religion as informal diversity criteria in making judicial appointments—as one commentator has put it, 'the rules of diversity have changed'.[92] There is a large volume of scholarly literature on the question of whether any particular system of appointing judges to state courts makes it more or less likely that racial minorities and women will be appointed.[93] When Thurgood Marshall was appointed by President Lyndon B. Johnson to the US Supreme Court in 1967, the primary consideration was race[94] (Marshall was the court's first African American justice). Similarly, gender was the primary consideration when Sandra Day O'Connor was appointed the first female justice on the US Supreme Court by President Ronald Reagan in 1981.[95] Jimmy Carter is widely considered to be the first president to seriously appoint women and racial minorities to the lower federal courts.[96] However, ethnic and racial minorities are still considered

---

[90] Salzberger, 'Judicial Appointments and Promotions', p. 253.

[91] Kommers, 'Judicial Politics in West Germany', pp. 121, 148.

[92] Toobin, 'Diverse Opinions'.

[93] See Mark S. Hurwitz. 2010. 'Selection System, Diversity and the Michigan Supreme Court', *Wayne Law Review*, 56(2): 691–704; Adam Goldstein. 2007. 'Judicial Selection as It Relates to Gender Equality on the Bench', *Cardozo Journal of Law and Gender*, 13(2): 369–406; Graham, 'Toward an Understanding'; Malia Reddick. 2002. 'Merit Selection: A Review of the Social Scientific Literature', *Dickinson Law Review*, 106(4): 729–45.

[94] Perry, *"Representative" Supreme Court*, p. 100.

[95] Abraham, *Justices, Presidents, and Senators*, pp. 282–3.

[96] Goldman and Saronson, 'Clinton's Nontraditional Judges'; Perry, *"Representative" Supreme Court*.

under-represented on federal and state courts,[97] although great progress has been made in recent decades.[98] Today, the US Supreme Court has three female justices (Ruth Bader Ginsburg, Sonia Sotomayor, and Elena Kagan), one of whom also happens to be of Hispanic background (Sonia Sotomayor), and one African American justice (Clarence Thomas).

Again, this form of diversity is not limited to the United States alone. In the United Kingdom there has been 'official support' for increasing diversity in the judiciary since the 1990s.[99] In order to thwart some of the problems associated with 'tap on the shoulder'–type appointments—where candidates are approached and invited to become judges—judicial positions are now advertised and non-traditional candidates are encouraged to apply. The Judicial Appointments Commission under the Constitutional Reform Act, 2005, established in 2006, has a statutory duty to 'have regard to the need to encourage diversity in the range of persons available for selection for appointments'.[100] Yet, the judiciary is still criticized for being largely elite, male, white, old, upper class, and out of touch.[101] Baroness Hale of Richmond was the first female Law Lord appointed to the House of Lords, and even as of 2012, she is the only female judge on the Supreme Court of the United Kingdom. In her own words, she was not the first woman lawyer good enough to sit with the other male judges, only the first one who was 'visible to them'.[102] The Australian judicial system has been criticized for its absence of diversity—judges are typically male, and of Anglo-Saxon or Celtic background.[103] More recently, however, female justices have increasingly been appointed to the High Court of Australia. The first female

[97] Graham, 'Toward an Understanding'.

[98] Hurwitz and Lanier, 'Women and Minorities'.

[99] Kate Malleson, 'Diversity in the Judiciary'; Kate Malleson. 2006. 'The New Judicial Appointments Commission in England and Wales: New Wine in New Bottles?' in Kate Malleson and Peter H. Russell (eds), *Appointing Judges in an Age of Judicial Power: Critical Perspectives from around the World*, pp. 39–55. Toronto: University of Toronto Press.

[100] Section 64(1), Constitutional Reform Act, 2005.

[101] Malleson, 'New Judicial Appointments'.

[102] Hale, 'Making a Difference', p. 291.

[103] Davis and Williams, 'Reform of the Judicial Appointments Process', p. 827.

justice to be appointed to that court was Mary Gaudron in 1987—
who was only one amongst 44 justices appointed to the high court
in the last century.[104] However, the court now has three female justices serving on it (Susan Crennan, Susan Kiefel, and Virginia Bell,
appointed in 2005, 2007, and 2009 respectively). The Constitution
of South Africa contains an explicit requirement that the need to
broadly reflect the 'racial and gender composition of South Africa'
must be considered while appointing judicial officers.[105] There,
women and black judges have increasingly been appointed to the
courts.[106] However, gender diversity is considered subordinate to
racial diversity.[107] Consequently, Chief Justice Arthur Chaskalson
noted in his retirement speech in 2005 that although 50 per cent
of the judiciary was black, only 15 per cent consisted of women.[108]
Two original members of the Constitutional Court of South Africa
were women (Kate O'Regan and Yvonne Mokgoro), and the court
presently has two women serving on it (Bess Nkabinde-Mmono and
Sisi Khampepe). Canada has possibly made the most serious efforts
at attaining gender diversity.[109] Bertha Wilson was the first female
justice appointed to the court, in 1982. The court currently has
three female justices serving on it, a list that includes its chief justice
(Chief Justice Beverley McLachlin, Rosalie Silberman Abella, and
Andromache Karakatsanis). As of 2012, the ICC has more female
judges serving on it than male judges, a phenomenon seen on the
court since 2009.

[104] Davis and Williams, 'Reform of the Judicial Appointments Process',
p. 827.
[105] Section 174(2), Constitution of South Africa.
[106] Hugh Corder. 2001. 'Seeking Social Justice? Judicial Independence and
Responsiveness in a Changing South Africa', in Peter H. Russell and David
M. O'Brien (eds), *Judicial Independence in the Age of Democracy: Critical Perspectives from around the World*, pp. 194–206. Charlottesville: University Press of
Virginia.
[107] Ruth B. Cowan. 2006. 'Women's Representation on the Courts in the Republic of South Africa', *University of Maryland Law Journal of Race, Religion, Gender
and Class*, 6(2): 291–317, p. 309.
[108] Cowan, 'Women's Representation', p. 303.
[109] Hale, 'Making a Difference', p. 285. See Claire L'Heureux-Dubé. 2001. 'Out-
siders on the Bench: The Continuing Struggle for Equality', *Wisconsin Women's
Law Journal*, 16(1): 15–31.

GEOGRAPHIC DIVERSITY

Background

The geographic division of India before independence did not coincide with any ethnic, racial, or linguistic divisions.[110] Geographically, there were 'two Indias'[111]: one—British India—was governed by the British Crown according to the statutes of the British Parliament and enactments of the Indian legislature;[112] the other—the Indian states or princely States—were subject to the suzerainty of the Crown, but had not been annexed by the Crown, and were under the personal rule of the princes. When the new Indian Constitution came into being in 1950, it recognized three types of states, listed in the Constitution's First Schedule: Part A, Part B, and Part C states. Roughly translated, Part A states were the former Governor's Provinces of British India, Part B states were the former Indian states (though not all Indian states became Part B states), and Part C states were the former Chief Commissioners' Provinces of British India.

When the Indian Constitution came into effect, Article 1(1) proclaimed, 'India, that is Bharat, shall be a Union of States'. The term 'Union' was deliberately used by the framers of India's Constitution to signal that though India was a federation, the federation was indestructible.[113] The constituent states of India were not formerly sovereign entities that had decided to join the federation, and they did not have the right to secede. The Constitution expressly permitted

[110] See Indian States Committee. *Report of the Indian States Committee*, 1928–9, para. 10. See further, V.P. Menon. 1956. *Story of the Integration of the Indian States*. Bombay: Orient Longmans.

[111] *Report of the Indian States Committee*, para. 10. See further, Government of India. 1948. 'Foreword', *White Paper on Indian States*. Delhi: Ministry of States, Government of India.

[112] On the eve of the partition of India, British India consisted of 12 Governor's Provinces and 6 Chief Commissioners' Provinces. See Government of India. 1955. *Report of the States Reorganisation Commission*. New Delhi: Government of India. See further, S.R. Maheshwari. 2000. *State Governments in India*. New Delhi: Macmillan, p. 14, stating that there were 12 Governor's Provinces and 6 Chief Commissioners' Provinces.

[113] M.R. Palande. 1951. *Introduction to Indian Administration*. New York: Oxford University Press, p. 155.

Parliament, India's central legislative authority, to do as it pleased with the states—states could be merged or demerged, their area could be increased or diminished, their boundaries and names could be altered.[114] The Constitution only required that the legislatures of the state governments concerned first be consulted on these matters, in some cases,[115] but the consent of the concerned state's legislature was not required. Perhaps most significantly, an amendment to the Constitution effected for the purposes of altering state boundaries and so on was deemed not to be a constitutional amendment,[116] and consequently, it did not need to comply with any of the supermajority requirements for enacting constitutional amendments prescribed by the Constitution.[117] All this suggests that the federal system in India is characterized by a strong central government, and weak state governments. Over the years, state boundaries, even state identities, have not been immutable in India and were capable of being altered.[118] Often, this was done by means of an ordinary law, and though the law amended the Constitution, it was deemed not to be an amendment of the Constitution by virtue of the deeming fiction contained in the Constitution.[119]

[114] Article 3, Constitution of India.
[115] Proviso to Article 3, Constitution of India.
[116] Article 4, Constitution of India.
[117] Article 368, Constitution of India.
[118] It is also worth noting that the boundaries of states were often revised, and territories were often transferred from one state to another. See for example, Assam (Alteration of Boundaries) Act, 1951; Chandernagore (Merger) Act, 1954; Bihar and West Bengal (Transfer of Territories) Act, 1956; Rajasthan and Madhya Pradesh (Transfer of Territories) Act, 1959; Andhra Pradesh and Madras (Alteration of Boundaries) Act, 1959; Acquired Territories (Merger) Act, 1960; Bihar and Uttar Pradesh (Alteration of Boundaries) Act, 1968; Andhra Pradesh and Mysore (Transfer of Territory) Act, 1968; Haryana and Uttar Pradesh (Alteration of Boundaries) Act, 1979; Government Notification No. GSR-702E dated 14 September 1983 (transferring villages from Haryana to Uttar Pradesh).
[119] Article 4, Constitution of India. This is important to bear in mind because though it is commonly said that the Constitution has 'only' been amended 97 times so far (since there have been 97 'Constitution (Amendment) Acts' as of 2012), in reality it has been amended numerous more times—though such instances are not 'officially' counted as amendments because of the deeming fiction in the Constitution.

By the end of 1956, India had 14 states and 6 union territories.[120] As of 2013, India has 28[121] states and 7[122] union territories.[123] Each state has its own high court, except two states in the north (Punjab and Haryana), two states in the west (Maharashtra and Goa), and four states in the north-east (Assam, Nagaland, Mizoram, and Arunachal Pradesh), which share one high court each. The National

[120] In 1953, consequent to a popular movement for the reorganization of states on linguistic lines, the state of Andhra (later Andhra Pradesh) was created and made a Part A state, carved out of the state of Madras. In 1956, Parliament enacted the States Reorganisation Act. The Constitution (Seventh Amendment) Act, 1956, removed the distinction between Part A and Part B states altogether.
[121] Andhra Pradesh, Assam, Bihar, Gujarat, Kerala, Madhya Pradesh, Tamil Nadu, Maharashtra, Karnataka, Odisha, Punjab, Rajasthan, Uttar Pradesh, West Bengal, Jammu and Kashmir, Nagaland, Haryana, Himachal Pradesh, Manipur, Tripura, Meghalaya, Sikkim, Mizoram, Arunachal Pradesh, Goa, Chhattisgarh, Uttarakhand, and Jharkhand.
[122] Delhi, Andaman and Nicobar Islands, Lakshadweep, Dadra and Nagar Haveli, Daman and Diu, Puducherry (name changed from 'Pondicherry' in 2006 [Section 5, Pondicherry (Alteration of Name) Act, 2006]), and Chandigarh.
[123] In 1960, the bilingual state of Bombay was bifurcated into Maharashtra and Gujarat. In 1961, Dadra and Nagar Haveli, and in 1962, Goa, Daman and Diu, and Pondicherry, became the seventh, eighth and ninth union territories in India. In 1962, Nagaland became the 16th state in India, carved out of the state of Assam. In 1966, Haryana was carved out of the state of Punjab, and it became the 17th state in India. Consequently, Chandigarh became a union territory— the capital city of both states. (Meanwhile, in 1969, the name of the state of Madras was changed to 'Tamil Nadu'.) In 1971, the union territory of Himachal Pradesh became a full-fledged state—the 18th in India, dropping the number of union territories in the country down to nine. In 1972, the union territories of Manipur and Tripura became full-fledged states—the 19th and 20th states of India. Two new union territories (Mizoram and Arunachal Pradesh) were created as well, so the number of union territories in India remained the same, nine. Simultaneously, Meghalaya, which had previously become an 'autonomous state' carved out of the state of Assam, became a full-fledged state as well—the 21st state of India. (Meanwhile, in 1973, the state of Mysore was renamed the state of 'Karnataka', and the Union Territory of Laccadive, Minicoy, and Amindivi Islands was renamed 'Lakshadweep'.) In 1975, Sikkim became the 22nd state of India, with its own high court. In 1987, the union territories of Mizoram and Arunachal Pradesh became full-fledged states—the 23rd and 24th states in India respectively. In 1987, the Goa district of the Union Territory of Goa, Daman, and Diu became a separate state, the state of Goa—the 25th state in India. The remaining districts were rechristened the Union Territory of Daman and Diu. Finally, in the year 2000, three new states were carved out of the

Capital Territory[124] of Delhi has its own high court, and is the only non-state listed in the First Schedule to the Constitution to have its own high court. There are, thus, 24 high courts in the country.[125,*]

The Big States

More than 70 per cent of the population of India now resides in less than one-third of the states of India. Uttar Pradesh has historically always been the most populous state in India, accounting for over 16 per cent of the country's population, even after Uttaranchal (later Uttarakhand) was carved out of its territory, and even though it is not the largest state in terms of its area. Bihar (over 10 per cent until the year 2000, afterwards, over 8 per cent of the country's population) and Maharashtra (over 9 per cent of the country's population) follow as the next most populous states, although Maharashtra has overtaken Bihar as the second most populous state in the last two decades after Jharkhand was carved out of Bihar. West Bengal and Andhra Pradesh follow suit, typically at around 7–8 per cent of the population, while Tamil Nadu and Madhya Pradesh come next, typically at 5–7 per cent of the population in relatively recent times. Interestingly, Delhi, not a state, surpasses several states in terms of its population. Further, despite the enormous size of their population relative to the rest of India, the states of Bihar and West Bengal do not figure in a list of the 10 largest states by area. In the quantitative analysis of geographic diversity, an attempt will be made to determine whether the type of diversity seen in the Supreme Court corresponds with the size of the state in terms of its population.[126]

---

states of Madhya Pradesh, Uttar Pradesh, and Bihar—these were Chhattisgarh, Uttaranchal (later 'Uttarakhand'), and Jharkhand respectively. (In 2011, the name of the state of Orissa was changed to 'Odisha'.) In 2013, three north-eastern states, namely, Manipur, Tripura, and Meghalaya, got their own high courts.

[124] Though Delhi is still listed in the First Schedule to the Indian Constitution as a 'Union Territory', it is referred to as the 'National Capital Territory' of India. Constitution (Sixty-Ninth Amendment) Act, 1991.

[125] Typically, a high court is named after the state (or states) over which it exercises jurisdiction, except the letters patent high courts (High Courts of Calcutta, Bombay, Madras, Allahabad, and Patna) and the Gauhati High Court.

[126] Data has been obtained from the following sources: Census of India (1971) Series 1-India Part II-A(i) (General Population Tables); Census of India (1991)

India's Parliament consists of the president and two houses—the Council of States (Rajya Sabha) and the House of the People (Lok Sabha)—the upper and lower houses of Parliament respectively. The seat-sharing arrangement amongst states and union territories in the Council of States does not appear to perfectly correlate with the size of the population of a state or union territory, relative to the others.[127] However, generally speaking, there is naturally a very high statistically significant correlation between the population of states and the allocation of seats in the Council of States.[128] For example, consider that Uttar Pradesh has always had the strongest share of seats in the Council of States, corresponding with the size of its population. Similarly, seats allocated in the House of the People to the states do not perfectly correlate with the size of the population of that state.[129] Further, the share of seats allocated to states in the House of the People does not appear to perfectly correlate with the share of seats allocated to states in the Council of States either.[130] However, there is once again a high statistically significant correlation between the size of the population of a state and the number of seats that the state is allocated in the

<hr>

Series 1 Part II-A(i) (General Population Tables); Census of India (2001), website of the Census of India; Provisional Population Tables, Census of India (2011), website of the Census of India, available online at http://censusindia. gov.in/2011-prov-results/data_files/bihar/Provisional%20Population%20 Totals%202011-Bihar.pdf (last accessed on 2 February 2012).

[127] Thus, since 1956, Andhra Pradesh has had 18 seats in the Council of States, and West Bengal has had 16—in 1961 this would perhaps have accurately reflected the size of the population of the two states relative to one another, but it no longer does. In fact, from 1971 onwards, West Bengal has repeatedly had a larger population than Andhra Pradesh according to every census conducted since then—this change has not been reflected in the Fourth Schedule to the Constitution.

[128] See note 131.

[129] For example, Bihar became the third most populous state consequent to the creation of Jharkhand in the year 2000 but, as in the Council of States, it has fifth strongest share of seats in the House of the People.

[130] For example, Tamil Nadu has 18 seats in the Council of States, two more than the 16 seats belonging to West Bengal, although West Bengal has a larger population size and a larger share of seats in the House of the People than Tamil Nadu.

House of the People, typically even more so than in the Council of States.[131]

Gauging by the size of the population of the states, and their share of seats in the Council of States and the House of the People, over the last two decades, the states of India can be placed into two categories for the purposes of this chapter: 'Tier 1' states, which are the least number of states it takes (in descending order of size of population or share of seats) to get to 50 per cent of the population of India or 50 per cent of the total number of seats in the Council of States and House of the People—in other words, the fewest number of states (in descending order of size of population or share of seats) that can collude to 'veto' or block legislation in India's Parliament;[132] and 'Tier 2' states, which are the least number of states it takes (in descending order of size of population or share of seats), aggregating the figures of Tier 1 states, to get to 66.7 per cent of the population of India or to 66.7 per cent of the total number of seats in the Council of States and House of the People—in other words, the fewest number of states (in descending order of size of population or share of seats), who, along with the Tier 1 states can collude to 'veto' or block a constitutional amendment in India's Parliament.[133] Data available for the last 20 years tell us that the states of Uttar Pradesh, Maharashtra, Bihar, West Bengal, Andhra Pradesh,** and Tamil Nadu[134] are Tier 1 states. These six states out of 28 account for over half of the total population of India. In Parliament, these six states are the fewest number of states that can theoretically collectively block or 'veto' legislation since they have 50 per cent of the vote. In general elections for the central

[131] Correlation coefficients on file with me; the correlation coefficients range from 0.9535 to 0.9980. P values are all 0.0000 for every correlation coefficient.

[132] Legislation is passed by a majority of the members present and voting. See Article 100(1), Constitution of India.

[133] A constitutional amendment is passed by a vote of two-thirds the number of members present and voting, subject to a quorum requirement (that is, even a majority of the membership of the house must vote in favour of the amendment). See Article 368(2), Constitution of India.

[134] The population of Madhya Pradesh is larger than in Tamil Nadu according to the provisional figures available from the 2011 census. However, both in the House of the People and the Council of States, the seats allocated to Tamil Nadu exceed those allocated to Madhya Pradesh. For this reason, Tamil Nadu is counted here as a Tier 1 state.

government, these six states have the capacity to significantly impact outcomes. Data available for the last 20 years tell us that the states of Madhya Pradesh, Karnataka, Gujarat, Odisha, and Rajasthan[135] are Tier 2 states. Together with the Tier 1 states, these five states account for over 70 per cent of the voting power in Parliament, and for approximately 80 per cent of the population of India. Accordingly, the Tier 1 states and Tier 2 states are the fewest number of states (in descending order of size of population or share of seats) that can collude to 'veto' or block a constitutional amendment.

In this book, an arbitrary, artificial bright line has been used to draw a distinction between Tier 1, Tier 2, and other states, but the distinction is perhaps a useful estimate that gives us an idea of how politically significant the different states of India are. An attempt will be made in this chapter to determine whether the norm of geographic diversity on the Supreme Court of India correlates with this understanding of the relative political significance of states in India.

The Busy High Courts

Data[136] concerning the total sanctioned strength[137] of each high court, that is, the maximum number of judges that can serve on the high court simultaneously, may be an effective proxy that indicate the volume of work or the total arrears of cases in each high court. In other words, one could surmise that courts with a larger volume of work, or with a higher backlog of cases, are likely to have a sanctioned strength of more judges. The size of a high court in India does

---

[135] Together with the Tier 1 states, the states of Madhya Pradesh, Karnataka, and Gujarat exceed 66.7 per cent of the voting power in the House of the People. However, they do not get to that level of representation in the Council of States, where the states with the next highest share of seats, at 10 seats each, are Odisha and Rajasthan. The population of Rajasthan is also much higher than most of the Tier 2 states.

[136] Data have been compiled using the following sources: 'Judges of the Supreme Court of India and the High Courts' as on 1 April 2011, 'Court News'. April-June 2011. 6(2); press release by the Press Information Bureau dated 30 October 2003. Data was only available for the period 1992–2011.

[137] The sanctioned strength of a high court is the maximum number of both permanent and additional judges that can serve simultaneously on the court.

not perfectly correspond either with the size of the population or with the total share of seats in the Council of States or House of the People of the state over which its jurisdiction extends. For example, the sanctioned strength of the High Court of Delhi—the only high court which does not exercise jurisdiction over a state in India—is higher than the High Court of Bihar (categorized in this chapter as a Tier 1 state), and higher than the High Courts of Madhya Pradesh, Gujarat, Orissa (now Odisha), and Rajasthan (categorized in this chapter as Tier 2 states). The states of Punjab and Haryana share one high court between themselves—had Punjab and Haryana been considered one state for the purposes of this book, they would have qualified as a Tier 2 state based on their cumulative population and share of seats in Parliament. However, the High Court of Punjab and Haryana has a higher sanctioned strength today than all Tier 1 states except Uttar Pradesh and Maharashtra. This may indicate that the volume of litigation in the High Courts of Delhi and Punjab and Haryana is higher than in several Tier 1 and Tier 2 states. An attempt will be made in this chapter to determine whether there is any correlation between the size of a high court (in terms of its sanctioned strength) and the share of seats a state gets on the Supreme Court. After all, judges on busier courts, who have experience dealing with a greater volume of work, might be considered more attractive for a post on the Supreme Court, given the preference for prior judicial experience seen in Chapter 4.

That apart, there is generally a high statistically significant correlation between the sanctioned strength of a high court on the one hand, and the size of the population of, number of seats allocated in the House of the People to, and number of seats allocated in the Council of States to, the state over which the court exercises jurisdiction, on the other.[138] For example, consider that the high courts for the states of Uttar Pradesh and Maharashtra have a sanctioned strength commensurate with the size of their population and their share of seats in Parliament relative to the rest of the country.

[138] Correlation coefficients on file with me; the correlation coefficients range from 0.8252 to 0.9060. P values are all 0.0000 for every correlation coefficient.

Geographic Diversity in the Supreme Court of India

The discussion in Chapter 2 indicates that geographic diversity has always been considered a norm relevant for selecting and appointing judges to the Supreme Court of India. The picture that emerges from a quantitative analysis of the appointments made to the Supreme Court between 1950 and 2009 is that seats on the Court are sought to be distributed between states. Not more than two (or in rare cases, three) judges belonging to the same high court serve on the Supreme Court at the same time. If 'merit' were the sole criterion for appointment to the Court, then this would not be so—one would typically have seen a larger number judges from a smaller number of states serve on the Supreme Court simultaneously. However, no single state monopolizes seats on the Court. Further, it is often seen that when a judge from a state retires (or in rare cases, resigns or dies) from the Supreme Court, another judge from that state is appointed to compensate for the vacancy. The most striking illustration of this occurred during Chief Justice K.G. Balakrishnan's term, during which the retirement of a judge each from the states of Tamil Nadu, West Bengal, Uttar Pradesh, Punjab and Haryana, Madhya Pradesh, Odisha, and Assam (including Nagaland, Meghalaya, Manipur, Tripura, Mizoram, and Arunachal Pradesh), and from the National Capital Territory of Delhi, was compensated by appointing to the Supreme Court a judge from that state or territory respectively.[139]

---

[139] Similarly, Patanjali Sastri maintained Bombay at one seat; Mahajan maintained Madras at one seat; S.R. Das maintained Bombay, Madras, and Madhya Pradesh at one seat each; P.B. Gajendragadkar maintained West Bengal at two seats; Subba Rao maintained West Bengal at two seats; M. Hidayatullah maintained West Bengal at two seats; S.M. Sikri maintained Punjab and Haryana at three seats, West Bengal at two seats, and Kerala at one seat; A.N. Ray maintained Tamil Nadu and Kerala at one seat each, and West Bengal at two seats; Y.V. Chandrachud maintained Uttar Pradesh and Gujarat at two seats each, and Tamil Nadu at one seat; P.N. Bhagwati maintained Uttar Pradesh at two seats, and Tamil Nadu at one seat; R.S. Pathak maintained Madhya Pradesh at two seats; E.S. Venkataramiah maintained Tamil Nadu at two seats; K.N. Singh maintained Odisha at one seat; M.H. Kania maintained Karnataka at two seats; M.N. Venkatachaliah maintained Kerala at one seat; A.M. Ahmadi maintained Andhra Pradesh at two seats, and Tamil Nadu at one seat; J.S. Verma maintained Andhra Pradesh at two seats; A.S. Anand maintained Andhra Pradesh and Delhi

In the 1950s, seven states dominated the seats on the Supreme Court of India: Madras, West Bengal, Bombay, Bihar, Punjab, Uttar Pradesh, and Madhya Pradesh. It will be recalled that India had 14 states in 1956—only half of these consistently had a seat (sometimes two) on the Supreme Court in the 1950s. The remaining seven states (Andhra Pradesh, Assam, Mysore [later Karnataka], Odisha, Kerala, Rajasthan, and Jammu and Kashmir) which were all in existence by 1956, did poorly on the Court during this period despite the fact that the Court had eight seats (including the chief justice) until 1956, but 11 seats thereafter.[140] With one exception for the state of Odisha,[141] no appointments were made from the other states during this decade. However, the states of Andhra Pradesh and Rajasthan did not go entirely without representation on the Court during this time—one chief justice of the high courts of these states each was appointed to the Supreme Court in the 1950s, although these would strictly not be considered Andhra Pradesh or Rajasthan judges.

The Supreme Court has grown more geographically inclusive with every passing decade. In the 1960s, three more states began to see representation in the Supreme Court: Andhra Pradesh,[142] Kerala,[143] and Mysore[144] (later Karnataka). In 1962, there were 16 states in India, but appointments were made to the Supreme Court from only 10 states. The remaining six states (Gujarat, Jammu and

---

at two seats each, and Punjab and Haryana at one seat; S.P. Bharucha maintained Assam (including Nagaland, Meghalaya, Manipur, Tripura, Mizoram, and Arunachal Pradesh) at one seat; B.N. Kirpal maintained Maharashtra at two seats; R.C. Lahoti maintained Madhya Pradesh at two seats; and Y.K. Sabharwal maintained Delhi at three seats.

[140] Supreme Court (Number of Judges) Act, 1956.

[141] Justice B. Jagannadhadas. The state of Odisha would not see another appointment made to the Supreme Court of India until the 1980s.

[142] Chief Justice Gajendragadkar was the first to appoint a judge (P. Satyanarayana Raju) from Andhra Pradesh to the Court in 1965, and since then, a judge from that state periodically served on the Court, with a few interruptions.

[143] After Chief Justice Subba Rao appointed a judge from the state of Kerala to the Court in 1966 (C.A. Vaidialingam), the state consistently had a seat in the Court.

[144] Chief Justice K.N. Wanchoo appointed a judge (K.S. Hegde) from Mysore (Karnataka) to the Court in 1967, after which the state consistently had a judge in the Court.

Kashmir, Assam, Nagaland, Rajasthan, and Odisha) did not see any appointments being made to the Court on their account. However, the state of Gujarat and the National Capital Territory of Delhi were partially represented on the Court, as some judges who had served as chief justices of these high courts were appointed to the Supreme Court, although these judges would not be considered Gujarat or Delhi judges, strictly speaking. In the 1970s, during the tenure of Chief Justice A.N. Ray, appointments were made to the Court from eight more states: Gujarat,[145] Jammu and Kashmir,[146] Assam[147] (including Nagaland, Meghalaya, Manipur, and Tripura), and Rajasthan.[148] Of the 21 states of India that were in existence by 1971, only Odisha and Himachal Pradesh did not see appointments made to the Court during that decade. However, Odisha had seen one of its judges appointed to the Court in the 1950s, and two chief justices of the Himachal Pradesh High Court were appointed to the Supreme Court in the 1970s although they would not be considered Himachal Pradesh judges, strictly speaking. A judge each was appointed to the Supreme Court from Odisha[149] and the National Capital Territory of Delhi[150] in the 1980s. The trend towards inclusiveness was also perhaps facilitated by the fact that more seats were added to the Court— the Court's strength rose to 14 seats (including the chief justice's seat) in 1960,[151] 18 seats (including the chief justice's seat) in 1977,[152] and

---

[145] A.N. Ray appointed a judge (P.N. Bhagwati) from the state of Gujarat to the Court in 1973, after which the Court consistently saw a judge from that state serve on the bench.

[146] Chief Justice A.N. Ray appointed two judges (Murtaza Fazal Ali and Jaswant Singh) from the Jammu and Kashmir High Court in 1975–6.

[147] Chief Justice A.N. Ray appointed a judge (P.K. Goswami) from the Gauhati High Court in 1973.

[148] Chief Justice A.N. Ray appointed a judge (P.N. Shingal) from Rajasthan to the Court in 1975.

[149] Although Chief Justice Patanjali Sastri had appointed a judge (B. Jagannadhadas) from the state of Odisha to the Court back in 1953, it was not until Chief Justice Y.V. Chandrachud appointed a judge (Ranganath Misra) from that state to the Court in 1983 that Odisha quite consistently had a seat on the Court.

[150] Chief Justice R.S. Pathak appointed a judge (S. Ranganathan) from Delhi to the Court in 1987.

[151] Supreme Court (Number of Judges) Amendment Act, 1960.

[152] Supreme Court (Number of Judges) Amendment Act, 1977.

26 seats (including the chief justice's seat) in 1986.[153] By 1987, there were 25 states in India, and judges from all but three states (Jammu and Kashmir, Himachal Pradesh, and Sikkim) were appointed to the Court during that decade. A chief justice of the High Courts of Jammu and Kashmir and Himachal Pradesh were each appointed to the Court during this decade, although they would, strictly speaking, not be considered judges from those states.

The 1990s and 2000s coincided with the Supreme Court's decision in the second and third Judges cases discussed in Chapter 2. During this period of time, the Court's most senior judges usurped the power to appoint judges to the Supreme Court of India. It would therefore be interesting to ask whether the Supreme Court's institutional independence impacted the geographic diversity criterion for appointment to the Court. After all, entirely unbounded by political pressures, the Court's most senior judges were now free to appoint whomever they wished—even the most 'meritorious' judges, even if they all came from the same region, state, or city. However, the data tell us that this is not what happened. If anything, the Court grew even more inclusive during this period, as no single state received more than 10 per cent of the appointments made to the Court. No previously unrepresented states were represented on the Court in the 1990s, but in 2006, a judge (L.S. Panta) was appointed to the Court from the state of Himachal Pradesh for the first time. As of 2012, Sikkim, and the new states created in the year 2000 (Chhattisgarh, Jharkhand, and Uttaranchal [later Uttarakhand]) remain the only states from whose high courts judges have not yet been appointed to the Supreme Court, despite the fact that the strength of the Court presently stands at 31 (including the chief justice).[154, †]

However, there is one significant difference in the Supreme Court's geographic composition in the last two decades, when it is compared with its previous geographic composition. Between the 1990s and 2000s, the National Capital Territory of Delhi saw as many as eight of its judges get appointed to the Court—a disproportionately large share of appointments for a territory that is not a state. Chief Justice R.S. Pathak appointed a judge (S. Ranganathan) from Delhi

---

[153] Supreme Court (Number of Judges) Amendment Act, 1986.
[154] Supreme Court (Number of Judges) Amendment Act, 2008.

in 1987, and Chief Justice Ranganath Misra appointed a second judge (Yogeshwar Dayal) to the Court from Delhi in 1991. However, when these seats became vacant during the terms of Chief Justices M.H. Kania and M.N. Venkatachaliah in 1992 and 1994 respectively, they were not replaced by judges from Delhi. However, after Chief Justice Ahmadi appointed two judges (B.N. Kirpal and D.P. Wadhwa) from Delhi in 1995 and 1997 respectively, Delhi has consistently had two seats (sometimes three) on the Court. Delhi's rise in the Supreme Court consequently coincides with the Court's rising institutional independence following the second and third Judges cases.

In the 1990s, Delhi had as many judges appointed to the Supreme Court of India as the states of Maharashtra and Tamil Nadu, and more of its judges were appointed to the Court than the state of Bihar (each identified in this chapter as a Tier 1 state). In the 2000s, Delhi outstripped all Tier 1 states—more of its judges were appointed to the Supreme Court than the states of Tamil Nadu, Andhra Pradesh, Bihar, West Bengal, Maharashtra, and Uttar Pradesh. Delhi has consequently seen a share of seats in the Supreme Court disproportionate to the size of its population, to its representation in Parliament, and to the sanctioned strength of its court, relative to the other states in India.[155] Further, consider that amongst Supreme Court judges who served on multiple high courts as chief justices, the highest number of Delhi High Court transferee chief justices, that is, those who had already served as chief justices on other courts before being transferred as chief justices to Delhi, were appointed to the Supreme Court in the 2000s. In that decade, no state except Maharashtra had more of its high court chief justices appointed to the Supreme Court than Delhi.

The Delhi High Court came into existence in 1966, but how did its share of appointments rise from one in the 1980s to as many as three–five in the past two decades? One answer could be that the Delhi High Court has increasingly become known as one of the country's finest courts. Today, its opinions are often subjects of national news. In the not-so-distant past, the court issued a decision decriminalizing homosexuality.[156] In another decision,[157] the court

---

[155] See further, Abhinav Chandrachud. 2011. 'Regional Representation on the Supreme Court', *Economic and Political Weekly*, 46(20): 13.

[156] *Naz Foundation* v. *Delhi*, (2010) Cri LJ 94.

[157] *Maqbool Fida Husain* v. *Raj Kumar Pandey*, (2008) Cri LJ 4107.

quashed warrants of arrest and all summoning orders against M.F. Hussain—a renowned Indian painter who had received death threats for depicting Hindu goddesses in the nude in his art. The Delhi High Court's disproportionate share of seats in the Supreme Court of India may therefore be attributed to its status as a premier court in India. Another answer could be that Delhi has clearly become one of India's key financial and commercial centres—available data suggest that more companies were registered in Delhi than in any other state in India, including Maharashtra, almost without interruption since 2005.[158] The Delhi High Court may consequently be deciding high-quality cases that reflect the towering commercial stature of the capital. However, cynics could also argue that the Delhi High Court's geographic proximity to the Supreme Court (both courts are located in the city of New Delhi) makes its judges more 'visible' to the collegium, that the collegium is more 'accessible' to the Delhi High Court than to the other courts of India, and that the rise of the collegium system in the last two decades has consequently increased Delhi's representation in the Supreme Court. However, such arguments can only be speculative, at best.

A quantitative analysis of the seat-sharing arrangement on the Supreme Court of India reveals that four states have historically dominated seats on the Court: West Bengal in the east, Maharashtra in the west, Tamil Nadu in the south, and Uttar Pradesh in the north. Other states have seen highs and lows in their representation on the Court.[159] However, a theme of regional representation is discernible from the data. As Figure 5.1 demonstrates, appointments to the Supreme Court have roughly been distributed, between four[160] regions

---

[158] Data from 2001 is available on the website of the Ministry of Corporate Affairs, Government of India, available online at http://www.mca.gov.in/Ministry/annual_report.html and http://www.mca.gov.in/Ministry/corporate_growth.html (last accessed on 30 April 2012).

[159] For example, the state of Bihar had as many as four of its judges appointed to the Court in the 1950s, second only to Madras in that decade, but only one judge from Bihar was appointed to the Court in every decade thereafter, until suddenly in the 2000s, four of its judges were appointed to the Court.

[160] The four regions of India are: north (Uttar Pradesh, Punjab and Haryana, Rajasthan, Jammu and Kashmir, Himachal Pradesh, Uttarakhand, and Delhi), south (Andhra Pradesh, Tamil Nadu, Karnataka, and Kerala), east (West Bengal, Bihar, Odisha, Assam, Nagaland, Manipur, Tripura, Meghalaya, Mizoram,

in India. The regional distribution of seats on the Supreme Court has not always been symmetrical or equal. For example, the east in the 1950s, the north in the 1970s, the south in the 1980s, and the north in the 2000s, each received a share of a third or more of the appointments made to the Court during that decade respectively. Similarly, in the 1960s, the west received a comparatively smaller share of the appointments made to the Court during that decade. However, there does not appear to be a heavily disproportionate balance in favour of any one region or state. Although some regions have done better than others in different decades, no region had more than 40 per cent of the seats on the Court, and no state had more than two or three of its judges serving on the Court simultaneously. Gadbois has demonstrated that the regional representation on the Court roughly corresponds with the population of each region.[161] Further, each region does not have the same number of states in it, which may potentially justify unequal seat distributions amongst different regions.

Generally speaking, the number of judges appointed from each state to the Supreme Court of India bears a statistically significant positive correlation with that state's representation in Parliament, with the size of its respective population, and the size of its respective high court.[162] However, the correlation is not nearly as strong as the one between the population of a state and its representation in Parliament.[163] The correlation appears to be the strongest between the number of seats a state has on the Supreme Court and the size of that state's high court. Accordingly, the size of a state's high court may be a good indicator (though not a perfect indicator) of how well a state will do on the Supreme Court. This tends to confirm the hypothesis that judges of busier courts (where the number of judges on the court serves as a proxy to determine how busy the court is)

Arunachal Pradesh, Sikkim, Chhattisgarh, and Jharkhand), and west (Maharashtra, Goa, Gujarat, and Madhya Pradesh). See George H. Gadbois, Jr. 2011. *Judges of the Supreme Court of India: 1950–1989.* New Delhi: Oxford University Press, p. 354.

[161] Gadbois, *Judges of the Supreme Court.*

[162] Correlation coefficients on file with me; correlation coefficients range from 0.4638 to 0.6536. P values range from 0.0013 to 0.0608.

[163] See note 131 above.

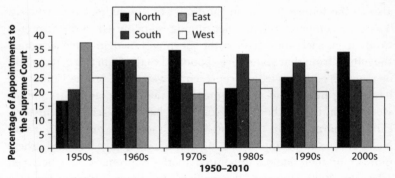

Figure 5.1 Regional Distribution of Appointments to the Supreme Court of India
Source: Author.

are likely to be considered more attractive candidates for appointment to the Supreme Court.

Unlike members of Parliament who typically serve fixed terms in office, Supreme Court judges in India serve in office for unequal lengths of time. It has been seen in Chapter 3 that the age at which a judge is appointed to the Supreme Court impacts the length of the judge's tenure on the Court, since the mandatory retirement age is 65. Consequently, when two judges from different states are appointed to the Court at the same time, it would not be accurate to say that both states have been given equal representation on the Court if one judge is significantly younger than the other. For example, Justices D.P. Madon (Maharashtra) and Sabyasachi Mukherjee (West Bengal) were appointed to the Court on the same day,[164] but Madon was nearly 62, while Mukherjee was only 55 and would go on to serve in office for nearly five years more than Madon. Under these circumstances, it would not be accurate to say that the appointment of these two judges to the Supreme Court accorded equal status to the states of Maharashtra and West Bengal.

Any study of state representation in the Supreme Court of India must account for this nuance—that in measuring how well states have done on the Supreme Court, regard must be had not merely of the number of appointments made from a state to the Court, but

[164] 15 March 1983.

also to the tenure served on the Court by the judges. Accordingly, Table 5.1 compares the number of judges appointed to the Supreme Court from each state against the mean and median age[165] at which the judges from that state were appointed to the Court. A state would be considered to have been represented very well on the Court if it has a high number of appointments to the Court, and if its judges were appointed to the Court young. It has been seen that historically, Maharashtra in the west, Uttar Pradesh in the north, Tamil Nadu in the south, and West Bengal in the east, have had the highest number of their judges appointed to the Supreme Court between 1950 and 2009. However, the median age of appointment of judges of only three of these states—Maharashtra, West Bengal, and Uttar Pradesh—is comparatively low, which perhaps explains why these states have had the highest number of their judges serve as chief justices of India (Maharashtra—seven,[166] West Bengal—five, and Uttar Pradesh—five).

Table 5.1 also illustrates the proposition that was put forth in Chapter 4, namely, that the eligibility criterion of seniority does not play out equally in different regions. For example, Bihar judges who came to the Supreme Court had a median age of appointment to the high court of 42.79 years, and were appointed at a median age of 59.30 years to the Supreme Court. By contrast, judges who came to the Supreme Court from Karnataka had a median age of appointment of 46.36 years to the high court, and were appointed at a median age of 58.3 years to the Supreme Court. Consequently, Bihar judges served close to 17 years in a high court before getting to the Supreme Court, while Karnataka judges spent 12 years in a high court before getting to the Supreme Court, and both spent comparable lengths of time in the Supreme Court. The criterion of geographic diversity therefore conflicts not merely with the principle of 'merit', but also with the criterion of seniority and prior judicial experience—junior judges might get selected over senior ones, or less experienced judges might get selected over more experienced

[165] The mean or median tenure served by judges is capable of being influenced by extraordinary factors such as premature resignation or death.
[166] Judges of the former state of Bombay are counted as judges of the Bombay High Court, which is the high court for the state of Maharashtra.

Table 5.1   Mean and Median Age of Judges Appointed to the High Courts and Supreme Court of India, and Number of Judges Appointed (1950–2009)

State	Age of Appointment to High Court Mean (Median)	Age of Appointment to Supreme Court Mean (Median)	Number of Judges Appointed to Supreme Court
Uttar Pradesh	45.50 (45.62)	59.32 (59.65)	18
Andhra Pradesh	46.59 (46.52)	59.23 (59.62)	10
Assam	50.02 (48.53)	61.49 (61.83)	7
Bihar	43.23 (42.79)	58.46 (59.30)	12
Maharashtra	44.86 (43.69)	58.11 (58.68)	18
West Bengal	46.00 (46.14)	58.84 (59.07)	22
Delhi	45.69 (44.84)	59.75 (59.93)	9
Gujarat	44.34 (44.42)	58.45 (59.36)	9
Himachal Pradesh	47.32 (47.32)	61.78 (61.78)	1
Jammu and Kashmir	44.15 (42.12)	58.14 (57.87)	5
Karnataka	46.78 (46.36)	58.66 (58.44)	10
Kerala	48.91 (49.74)	60.09 (60.51)	13
Tamil Nadu	49.34 (49.11)	60.32 (60.60)	18
Madhya Pradesh	45.29 (46.51)	58.86 (59.74)	11
Odisha	46.42 (45.45)	58.46 (57.73)	7
Punjab and Haryana	48.94 (49.84)	58.55 (58.78)	13
Rajasthan	44.76 (44.56)	59.48 (59.64)	6

Source: Author.

ones, because their region or state requires representation on the Supreme Court.

Seniority has, at times, been sacrificed in favour of geographic representation. In the 2000s, a judge was appointed to the Supreme Court from an under-represented state for the first time in the Court's history, despite the fact that the judge was not a chief justice of a high court. A member of the erstwhile collegium informed me that before that judge was appointed to the Court, his judgments had to be scrutinized by the collegium, because 'nobody knew who he was' (Interview 4). Strict adherence to the norm of seniority often appears to have been sacrificed in favour of what appears to be a concern to preserve the geographic 'balance' of the Court.

In the 1950s, although the highest number of judges were appointed to the Supreme Court of India from the state of Madras, these judges ended up spending less time on the Court than judges from Bombay, West Bengal, and Bihar. The lone judge appointed to the Court from the state of Maharashtra in the 1960s spent more time on the Court than the two judges appointed to the Supreme Court from the state of Andhra Pradesh during that decade. Similarly, in the 1970s, judges from Gujarat trumped those from West Bengal, Uttar Pradesh, and Punjab and Haryana; in the 1980s judges from Punjab and Haryana trumped those from Kerala, Maharashtra, and Uttar Pradesh; in the 1990s, judges from Jammu and Kashmir trumped those from the states of Tamil Nadu and Odisha; and in the 2000s, judges from Odisha trumped those from the state of Madhya Pradesh; even though in each instance more judges were appointed to the Supreme Court from the latter state or states during that respective decade. In this sense, the interaction between the geographic representation norm and the system of unequal tenures caused by mandatory retirement for Supreme Court judges, discussed in Chapter 3, adds wrinkles to state representation on the Supreme Court. However, the theme of regional representation described in Figure 5.1 does not collapse when Supreme Court appointments are viewed in the context of tenure, and the conclusions that were drawn from Figure 5.1 still hold true.

RELIGION, CASTE, AND GENDER

The quantitative data suggest that three religious minority communities have been represented on the Supreme Court of India: Muslims, Christians, and Sikhs, which are the three largest religious minority communities in India according to the census conducted in the years 1991 and 2001.

Muslim representation on the Court is the strongest amongst religious minority communities, although in the last decade it has diminished in strength. Approximately 16 per cent of the judges appointed to the Court in the 1950s were Muslim, but this figure has dipped ever since, and it fell to a staggering low of 4 per cent during the last decade (2000–9). Although the strength of the Supreme

Court rose over the years, no substantial attempts appear to have been made to effect a corresponding increase in the number of Muslim judges on the Court, which is why the proportion of Muslim judges has fallen. The number of Muslim judges appointed to the Court in each decade has hovered between zero and four. The Court of the first Chief Justice of India had a Muslim judge (S. Fazl Ali) serving on it. Chief Justice S.R. Das appointed a second Muslim judge (M. Hidayatullah) to the Court in 1958 when a Muslim judge (S.J. Imam) was already serving on the Court, but this was an aberration,[167] and it was not until Chief Justice A.N. Ray's tenure in 1975 that the Court would nearly consistently have a second Muslim judge on it.[168] Between 2000 and 2007, the Court had between zero and one Muslim judge serving on it, but the second Muslim seat was restored by Chief Justice K.G. Balakrishnan in 2007. Only two Muslim judges were appointed to the Court between 2000 and 2009 amongst approximately 50 judges appointed to the Court during that decade. Available census data indicate that Muslims accounted for 12–13 per cent of the population of India in 1991 and 2001. By contrast, Muslim representation on the Court between 1990 and 2009 was only between 8 per cent and 4 per cent.

Christian representation on the Supreme Court has not been as strong. Barring the 1960s when no Christian judge was appointed to the Court, at least one Christian judge was appointed to the Court in every decade. The first Chief Justice of India appointed a Christian judge (Vivian Bose) to the Court in 1951, and at least one Christian

---

[167] M. Hidayatullah. 1981. *My Own Boswell.* Gulab, pp. 181–2; Gadbois, *Judges of the Supreme Court*, pp. 60–1. After S.J. Imam resigned in 1964, the Court had only one Muslim judge for a considerable period of time.

[168] After the retirement of Chief Justice M.H. Beg, Chief Justice Y.V. Chandrachud appointed Baharul Islam, then V. Khalid, to preserve two seats for Muslim judges on the Court (Justice M. Fazal Ali, a Muslim judge, was also serving on the Court at the time). During 1985–9, the Court had between zero and one Muslim judge on it, but the second seat was restored by Chief Justice E.S. Venkataramiah in 1989, with the appointment of Justice M. Fathima Beevi (Justice A.M. Ahmadi was serving on the Court at the time). Barring a few exceptions, the Court consistently had two Muslim judges serving on it roughly until the end of the 1990s.

judge was appointed to the Court by a chief justice[169] in each decade. Available census data indicate that Christians accounted for approximately 2.3 per cent of the population of India between 1991 and 2001. Christian judges accounted for between 2.6 per cent and 4 per cent of the total number of judges appointed to the Court between 1990 and 2009.

Sikh representation on the Supreme Court has been more sporadic. One Sikh judge was appointed to the Court in each of only three decades—the 1970s, the 1980s, and the 2000s. The first Sikh judge (R.S. Sarkaria) was appointed to the Court by Chief Justice A.N. Ray. A Sikh judge each was appointed thereafter by Chief Justices R.S. Pathak and Y.K. Sabharwal. Available census data indicate that the Sikh community accounted for approximately 1.9 per cent of the population of India between 1991 and 2001. Sikh judges accounted for between 0 per cent and 2 per cent of the total number of judges appointed to the Supreme Court between 1990 and 2009.

The mean age of appointment of Supreme Court judges belonging to the Muslim (mean: 58.97 years) and Sikh (mean: 58.33 years) communities was lower than that of forward caste Hindu judges (mean: 59.12 years) on the Court, but only marginally so. It is plausible that, on average, judges belonging to these two religious minority communities might have been given longer tenures on the Supreme Court to compensate for their smaller numbers on the Court. However, the difference in means did not prove statistically significant in a two-sample mean comparison test, perhaps on account of the small number of the judges belonging to these two communities.

Figure 5.2 depicts the caste of judges appointed to the Supreme Court of India in each decade between 1950 and 2009. Here, the term 'Backward' Caste is used to denote Scheduled Caste, Scheduled Tribe, and Other Backward Class judges.[170] All other judges have been placed in the 'Forward' Caste category. No Backward Caste judges

---

[169] S.M. Sikri in the 1970s, R.S. Pathak in the 1980s, A.M. Ahmadi in the 1990s, and S.P. Bharucha and K.G. Balakrishnan in the 2000s.

[170] See Marc Galanter. 1978. 'Who Are the Other Backward Classes? An Introduction to a Constitutional Puzzle', *Economic and Political Weekly*, 13(43/44): 1812–28; A. Ramaiah. 1992. 'Identifying Other Backward Classes', *Economic and*

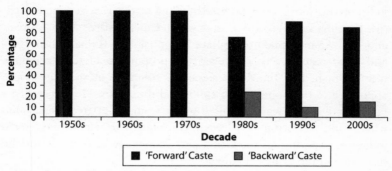

Figure 5.2 Caste of Judges Appointed in Each Decade to the Supreme Court of India
Source: Author.
Notes:
1. As far as possible, a judge has been placed in the 'Backward' Caste category only if his caste was recognized as such at the time of his appointment to the Supreme Court.
2. If a judge informed me that he belonged to a Backward Caste, I took that as sufficient evidence that he did, in fact, belong to a Backward Caste.

were appointed to the Court in the first two decades of its existence. Chief Justice Y.V. Chandrachud appointed the first Backward Caste judge to the Court in 1980. The number of Backward Caste judges serving simultaneously on the Court rose during the terms of Chief Justices R.S. Pathak and E.S. Venkataramiah. Roughly speaking, there have typically been between one and three Backward Caste judges serving simultaneously on the Court ever since. At times, some of these judges were not high court chief justices, and one gets the sense that seniority was at times sacrificed in order to appoint them to the Court, as appeared to be the case for geographic diversity as well.

No women were appointed to the Supreme Court of India during the first three decades of its existence. One female judge was appointed to the Court in every decade thereafter. The first female

Political Weekly, 27(23): 1203–7; Christophe Jaffrelot. 2000. 'The Rise of the Other Backward Classes in the Hindi Belt', *Journal of Asian Studies*, 59(1): 86–108.

judge on the Court was appointed by Chief Justice E.S. Venkataramiah (M. Fathima Beevi) in 1989, after which Chief Justices A.M. Ahmadi and A.S. Anand appointed Sujata Manohar and Ruma Pal in 1994 and 2000 respectively. However, the proportion of female judges has diminished on the Court since the 1980s, as more judges were appointed to the Court in the 1990s and the 2000s. More recently, a female judge each was appointed to the Court in 2010 (Gyan Sudha Misra) and 2011 (Ranjana Desai), consequent to which two female judges are serving on the Court simultaneously, as of 2012, for the first time in the Court's history.

* * *

This chapter demonstrates that there is some evidence to suggest that an informal quota system exists while making judicial appointments to the Supreme Court of India, a system that naturally lives on the fringes of the Indian Constitution, which is silent about whether such criteria ought to be taken into account while appointing judges to the Supreme Court. It is interesting that despite the change in the process of appointing judges examined in Chapter 2, consequent to the second and third Judges cases, the collegium—that is, the Chief Justice of India and four senior Supreme Court judges—has continued to appoint judges to the Supreme Court while adopting a system of geographic and demographic diversity. In the interest of preserving the Court's own legitimacy, the collegium has cooperated with political authorities in preserving the diversity criterion of appointment to the Supreme Court. However, it must be emphasized that not all diversity criteria have been given equal weight by the collegium, and geographic diversity puzzlingly ranks higher than other kinds of diversity based on gender, religion, and caste.

Is geographic diversity in the Supreme Court of India merely symbolic or is it also substantive? Do judges from different regions decide cases differently, do they actually bring a diversity of perspectives to the cases they decide, or do they merge into a unified decision-making culture in the Supreme Court? These are complex questions which perhaps cannot be answered without conducting sophisticated multivariate regression analyses. However, though the diversity in the Supreme Court might be symbolic, there are cracks in its symbolism.

A judge is considered to belong to a region or state where he was first appointed as a high court judge, irrespective of where he was born, where he lived for most of his life, or what his mother tongue is. It is difficult to imagine how a judge who was born in Delhi, and who practised there as a lawyer for most of his life, can be considered to represent the state of Maharashtra merely because he was first appointed there as a judge, and merely because he served as a judge there for 12–14 years—ignoring the 30–40 years that he spent in another region. Geographic diversity in the Supreme Court of India is linguistically blind. Thus, a judge whose mother tongue is Marathi is considered to represent the state of Madhya Pradesh if he was first appointed there as a high court judge, and not Maharashtra. Kannada-speaking judges in the Bombay High Court will be considered not to represent the state of Karnataka, perhaps justifiably so if their only bond with the state of Karnataka is a linguistic one. However, if a geographic 'balance' is sought to be maintained in the Supreme Court, the exclusion of factors like place of residence and language—though divisive—renders the norm of geographic diversity on the Court tenuous. Of course, it would be hard to devise an objective formula to account for such factors in making appointments to the Court. Should a judge who was born in Assam, who spent several years in south India, and who practised as a lawyer in West Bengal, be considered a judge from the south or from the east? Should a Gujarati-speaking judge, born and raised in the city of Mumbai, be considered to represent the state of Gujarat only because he speaks the Gujarati language? The norm of geographic diversity in the Supreme Court presently ensures that the Court's judges have some level of familiarity with local problems afflicting the different regions of India. High court judges are valued not for being symbols of the state to which they are initially appointed as high court judges, but for their judging experiences in that state. Of course, this policy may give rise to 'circuit effects',[171] that is, a phenomenon in which an appellate court judge more frequently affirms decisions of the subordinate court on which he served, than those of other courts.

[171] See Lee Epstein, Andrew D. Martin, Kevin M. Quinn, and Jeffrey A. Segal. 2009. 'Circuit Effects: How the Norm of Federal Judicial Experience Biases the Supreme Court', *University of Pennsylvania Law Review*, 157(3): 833–80. Also see, note 12, and accompanying text.

However, it cannot be gainsaid that India sustains several types of geographic diversity, and the norm of geographic diversity prevalent in the Supreme Court today does not embrace India's geographic diversity in its entirety.

Judges represent the state in which they were first appointed to the high court. However, consequent to the second and third Judges cases examined in Chapter 2, Supreme Court and high court judges in India are not appointed by elected representatives, but by judges themselves. Consequently, no matter how symbolic the presence of judges from different regions or states might appear on the Supreme Court, it cannot conceal the democratic illegitimacy of the judges themselves. Judges are picked in such a manner that they appear to 'represent' the states and regions of India, but in reality they arguably represent no one—having been appointed not by legitimate sources of democratic authority, but by an unelected pocket of counter-majoritarianism, the collegium of senior judges.

Further, because the geographic diversity norm is informal, the allocation of Supreme Court seats to states is not scientifically perfect, and consequently, the quest for geographic 'balance' is susceptible to arbitrariness—states that otherwise account for a relatively large proportion of India's population and which have a large proportion of seats allocated to them in Parliament, may not get commensurate representation in the Supreme Court. Thus, two Tier 1 states which account for a large proportion of India's population and for a large proportion of seats in Parliament—Bihar and Andhra Pradesh—have historically not done very well in terms of representation in the Supreme Court. Two Tier 2 states—Odisha and Rajasthan—have, likewise, not done too well on the Court historically. In more recent times, in the last 20 years, Andhra Pradesh and Odisha have gained some representation on the Court, although Tamil Nadu's representation on the Court has diminished. The figures do not appear to perfectly correspond with the size of the high courts either. For example, although the high court for the states of Punjab and Haryana is relatively large, its representation in the Supreme Court has not been very high in the last 20 years. In other words, the informal norm of geographic diversity may maintain a loose regional 'balance', on tenuous political foundations, but its definitions are not scientifically perfect, and it is consequently susceptible to arbitrariness. If 'merit' were the sole criterion for appointment to the Supreme Court then this discussion would have been irrelevant—however, in a system which seeks out a geographic 'balance', it is hard to justify deviations from constitutionally designed schemes for power sharing at the centre,[172] and it is difficult to argue that 'powerful' states in India's Parliament should not likewise be given a strong share of seats on the Supreme Court. Of course, no system of regional representation on a constitutional court can be perfect. However, in order to be legitimate, a system of regional representation on a court must take account of the relative standing of states vis-à-vis one another.

Representation given on the Supreme Court of India to some religious communities, and to women, leaves much to be desired. Although the number of judges on the Court has increased over the years, and although more judges have been appointed to the Court almost with each passing decade, no attempt seems to have been made to raise the number of Muslim judges on the Court. Consequently, Muslim representation in the Supreme Court falls short of a proportion that is commensurate with the Muslim population of India. Similarly, the fact that only three women were appointed to the Supreme Court in six decades says volumes about how inclusive the Court really is. Surely it cannot be argued that only three women amongst the 189 judges appointed to the Court between 1950 and 2009 had the 'merit' to be appointed Supreme Court judges? Perhaps only these three women satisfied the criteria of prior judicial experience and seniority examined in Chapter 4. The other informal criteria of appointing judges to the Supreme Court might consequently limit the number of non-traditional candidates that are appointed to the Court.

Finally, and perhaps most importantly, although there is an informal norm that diversity will be engendered on the Supreme Court of India, it is doubtful if that diversity finds its way into the opinions of the Court. The vast majority of cases are decided today by small panels of two judges of the Court. Although the 31 judges on the Court come from different regions, although some belong to minority communities, and some are women, since each individual

---

[172] See Chandrachud, 'Regional Representation'.

case is only decided by a small number of these judges sitting together, the diversity of the Court does not make its way into the Court's opinions. This is significant if one believes that diversity on a court is substantive, and not merely symbolic—that the diverse background of a judge is not merely a token which attempts to enhance the court's legitimacy, but a tool which gives the court access to different points of view, to diverse ways of thinking, and makes the opinions of the court themselves more reflective. Of course, Supreme Court judges may naturally meet one another outside the courtroom, and even though they may not decide cases sitting in a bench with each other, they may be exposed to one another's ways of thinking. However, since the vast majority of cases—often important ones—are decided only by two-judge benches, as opposed to being decided by a larger bench of the Court, it is arguable that diversity on the Supreme Court of India is more symbolic than substantive. Each case, after all, only reflects the diversity of the few judges who decide it, and no case embraces the diversity of the entire Court.

NOTES

* Readers should bear in mind that this book was written before the creation of the Telangana High Court and the union territories of Jammu and Kashmir and Ladakh.

** Readers should bear in mind that this book was written before the creation of the state of Telangana.

† The number of judges of the Supreme Court was increased to 34 (including the Chief Justice) in 2019.

CONCLUSION

IT HAS BEEN DEMONSTRATED IN the preceding chapters that informal norms govern appointments to the Supreme Court of India—norms that have not formally been prescribed or written down in any constitutional or legislative document. Although India's Constitution prescribes three formal criteria that make a person eligible for appointment to the Supreme Court, an entirely different set of eligibility criteria—informal, unwritten criteria—determine who will be considered fit and eligible for appointment to the Court. The formal law prescribes that a person must either be: (*a*) a high court judge for five years, (*b*) a high court lawyer for 10 years, or (*c*) a distinguished jurist, in order to be considered eligible for appointment to the Supreme Court. On the contrary, the informal norms examined in this book suggest that these formal rules convey little or no meaning, that in practice, in order to be considered eligible for appointment to the Supreme Court: (*a*) a person must now be a high court chief justice—and at that level of seniority, judges typically have double, often triple, the prescribed number of years of experience, (*b*) he must be quite senior—of the age of 55 or above—so as to ensure that his tenure on the Court will not be too long, and finally, (*c*) he must fit the diversity puzzle of the Supreme Court, that is, (i) his parent high court must need representation on the Court, or, in more rare circumstances, (ii) if he belongs to one of the three largest religious minority communities in India, then he will especially be considered eligible if his community needs representation on the Court, or (iii) if the candidate is a woman, then she will especially be considered eligible if her gender needs representation on the Court. Significantly, these norms exist despite India's written Constitution, and the lesson that must be derived from the preceding chapters is that even within written constitutional systems, unwritten, informal conventions do invariably surface.

It must be underscored that these norms are certainly not the only criteria employed in deciding whom to appoint to the Supreme Court of India. They are only eligibility criteria—necessary, but not sufficient, conditions precedent to earning an appointment to the Supreme Court. As between candidates who satisfy these criteria, a range of other informal criteria may be applied in deciding whom to appoint to the Court, and such criteria may at times be more intuitive than the ones examined in this book, for example, honesty, personal integrity, impartiality, case-disposal rate, or 'merit' generally. However, this book suggests that it is an informal norm that no matter how meritorious a person may be, no matter how honest or impartial a high court judge may be, and no matter how high a judge's disposal rate may be, he will not be considered eligible for appointment to the Supreme Court unless he satisfies the criteria examined in this book. Of course, there may be exceptions. For example, one lawyer was directly appointed to the Supreme Court in the 1990s, amongst 39 high court judges or chief justices appointed to the Court during that decade—a decade during which high court chief justices were increasingly being appointed to the Court. However, exceptions are rare, and do not materially diminish the strength of the informal criteria examined in this book.

The informality of these criteria is both advantageous and disadvantageous. The fact that none of these eligibility criteria have been prescribed by the Constitution or by a formal Act of Parliament, means that these norms can evolve organically. For example, since there is no formal rule that judges appointed to the Supreme Court of India must belong to diverse regional and religious communities, this informal norm can be abandoned according to the felt necessities of the time. Decades from now, geographic identity may become irrelevant in a more mature Indian republic. At that point in time, other diversity factors such as gender, sexual orientation, disability, or professional background may trump regional considerations in appointing judges to the Supreme Court. For example, the Supreme Court, 60 years from now, may be considered legitimate despite the fact that all its judges hail from one region in India, but special efforts may need to be made to ensure that persons from the lesbian, gay, bisexual, or transgendered (LGBT) community, disabled persons, transactional lawyers, or academics, get appointed to the Court, without which the Court may lose its credibility, or worse, its legitimacy. The benefit of informal criteria is that they can tie themselves more easily to the pulse of the times, and change more easily than formal rules.

However, the informality of these criteria is also deeply disadvantageous. Since the three informal eligibility criteria examined in this book have not been written down in any formal legal document, they have not been defined. Absent a precise, coherent set of rules governing who shall and who shall not be considered eligible for appointment to the Supreme Court, these informal eligibility criteria are susceptible to arbitrary application. They can be bent or broken, or subjected to unexplained exceptions. Further, the fact that these informal criteria have not been written down in any formal enactment means that there has been a democratic deficit in their adoption—they have not been extensively debated, or subjected to public comment or criticism, unlike when formal laws are enacted. Not having been subjected to rigorous democratic scrutiny, to the rough and tumble of an arduous adversarial debate, these informal criteria do not have the same level of political value, or the same sacrosanct status, as ordinary law. After all, the formal eligibility criteria now prescribed by Article 124 of the Constitution have been debated since at least 1933, first by the Joint Committee on Indian Constitutional Reform, then by the Constituent Assembly of India itself. Of course, the Law Commission of India, especially in its 14th and 80th reports published in 1958 and 1979 respectively, has examined these criteria in detail, but their informality has generally precluded substantial normative policy debates as to their existence.

This book used both quantitative and qualitative research techniques to determine whether these informal norms exist. Since there was no control group against which the quantitative data could be tested—that is, there was no readily available list of judges considered, but rejected, for appointment to the Supreme Court of India—the quantitative data could only reveal one piece of the puzzle. For example, the quantitative data tell us that between 1950 and 2009, only three amongst 189 judges appointed to the Court were female—however, this does not mean that there is an informal norm that only males will usually be appointed to the Supreme Court. Similarly, the quantitative data suggest that a large proportion of judges appointed to the Court during that time belonged to legal families, that is, a close family member, typically, the father, was a lawyer or judge. However, this does not mean that there is an informal norm that only persons whose fathers are lawyers will be appointed to the Supreme Court. Although judges on the Supreme Court are typically male, and although they often belong to legal families, their common gender and family background are characteristics, not eligibility criteria. Correlation is not causation, and merely because judges appointed to the Supreme Court have certain common characteristics amongst them does not necessarily mean that those characteristics have metamorphosed into eligibility criteria. For this reason, the quantitative data in this book were supplemented by semi-structured qualitative interviews with 29 former judges of the Supreme Court, and the interviews suggested that three characteristics of Supreme Court judges examined in this book—age, seniority, diversity—are considered eligibility criteria in making appointments to the Supreme Court.

Over a period of 60 years, these eligibility criteria have not remained the same—their content has changed, but their character has generally remained the same.

The data tell us that the judges being appointed to the Supreme Court of India are increasingly older—that no more than a handful of judges amongst over 120 appointed to the Court in the last three decades were of the age of 55, that none were appointed to the Court below the age of 55 during that time, and that it has now become an informal norm that judges will be considered eligible for appointment to the Supreme Court only after they turn 55. This may not have been an informal eligibility criterion for appointment to the Supreme Court in the 1950s, but it certainly appears to have been a criterion in the last two, perhaps three, decades. The age at which a judge is appointed to the Supreme Court is significant because it determines the length of time that the judge will serve in office—Supreme Court judges retire at the age of 65. The older the judge, the shorter the tenure that the judge will serve on the Court. The Indian Constitution does not prescribe any minimum age for appointment to the Supreme Court.[1] We saw that one of the comments received by the Constituent Assembly of India, from R.R. Diwakar and S.V. Krishnamoorthy Rao, was that there should be a minimum age for appointing judges to the Court, that is, that judges appointed to the court should not be below the age of 55. We saw that the Constitutional Adviser to the Constituent Assembly of India, B.N. Rau, was against this proposal, as it would prevent the President of India from appointing a person of 'outstanding merit' if he were less than 55 years of age. Though this proposal did not become a part of the formal law under India's Constitution, it now lives in the shadows of Article 124 of the Constitution, and has become an informal eligibility norm.

Why is it considered important to fix a minimum age for appointing judges to the Supreme Court of India? Chapter 3 examines this question in detail, but the short answer is that older judges are considered more mature than younger ones. We saw that the Law Commission of India, in its 80th report published in 1979, recommended that judges should not be appointed to the Court below the age of 54, despite the fact that judges appointed younger than that had 'distinguished themselves' on the Court—this was felt necessary in order to ensure that judges appointed to the Supreme Court had a certain level of maturity. We saw in the first Judges case that Justice Desai hoped that judges would be appointed to the Court at a 'sufficiently mature age'—a 'good guide for a sombre approach in a law court'. Several former Supreme Court judges interviewed for this book emphasized maturity as being tied to age—that the minimum age of 55 perhaps ensures that judges appointed to the Court have attained a certain level of maturity. However, maturity may also be a

---

[1] It could be argued that a minimum age is implied by the formal eligibility criteria prescribed by the Constitution, but we saw in Chapter 3 that the minimum age implied by the Constitution was far below the age of 55.

code word for path dependency, and older judges may perhaps lack the enthusiasm necessary to make radical or substantial changes to the system. Some of the Court's most activist judges were appointed to the Court young, and to set limits on the age of appointment to the Court may be equivalent to setting limits on the Court's activism itself. Chapter 3 suggested that this could very well be a compromise offered by the judiciary to the executive, in order to make the second and third Judges cases seem less unacceptable to the executive. Consequent to these decisions, the collegium of judges appoints judges to the Supreme Court—this power may seem less unbearable to the executive if the collegium only appoints non-threatening, older judges to the Court, judges less willing or able to become activist or menacing to the executive's personal or policy objectives.

This is also a function of the shorter tenures that older judges appointed to the Court can serve. Supreme Court judges retire at age 65—a limit set by the Joint Committee on Indian Constitutional Reform in 1933, when life expectancy in India was 26 years. In the Constituent Assembly of India, it was asked why judges should retire at the age of 65—that the Court was losing its talented members to an arbitrary retirement age. Citing Albert Einstein and Oliver Wendell Holmes, Pandit Jawaharlal Nehru agreed that 'first-rate' judges could be older than 65, but that this retirement age was 'by no means unfair'. B.R. Ambedkar too agreed that the age of 65 did not represent the 'zero hour in a man's intellectual ability', but he argued that even retired judges could be called back to work in the Supreme Court of India—citing this as a justification for the retirement age. It is now perhaps necessary to seriously rethink the age of retirement from the Supreme Court. Life expectancy today is not what it was in 1933. The number of judges who died in harness has also steadily declined, and retired Supreme Court judges typically continue to work either as arbitrators or on tribunals. Today, retired judges are seldom, if ever, called back to serve as temporary judges on the Court as they were before, contrary to what Ambedkar had expected—and an argument is capable of being made that the Court is losing its talented and experienced judges to an arbitrary retirement age. We saw in Chapter 3 that the retirement age of 65 is also typically lower than the retirement age on constitutional courts in other countries. The Law Commission of India, in its 14th report published in 1958, recommended that the minimum term that Supreme Court judges should serve on the Court is 10 years, thereby implying, given the retirement age, that Supreme Court judges should not be appointed to the court older than 55. The Law Commission of India in 1979, in its 80th report, suggested a different ceiling for appointing judges to the Supreme Court—that judges should not be appointed to the court above the age of 60. As of now in 2012, a large proportion of the judges appointed to the Court since 2009 were above the age of 60 when appointed. Even the Supreme Court's majority opinion in the second Judges case had emphasized that judges appointed to the Court should be young enough to ensure that their tenures are not 'unduly short'. Not unlike the Japanese Supreme Court, older judges appointed to the Supreme Court have a shorter period of time within which they can make a difference, and a short tenure imposes an inherent limit on judicial activism. It may take a year or so for a Supreme Court judge to settle in, and several more years to rise to a position of seniority in order to become the presiding judge in a bench on the Court. By this time, if the judge has only a few months left before he is to retire, there are limits to how activist he can be. The Chief Justice of India is the single most powerful actor in India's judiciary—not only does he drive the process of judicial appointments, but he also composes benches and assigns cases. We saw in Chapter 3 that the tenure of judges in the post of Chief Justice of India is also incredibly short. In 1958, the Law Commission of India suggested that chief justices of India should serve in office for at least five or seven years, but in practice the term served by successive chief justices of India in office has been overwhelmingly shorter—an inherent limit on the potential of Chief Justices of India to be activist, or to substantially lead the Court in any direction.

The second eligibility criterion examined in this book, namely, seniority, has not remained stagnant over the decades. It began as a norm which dictated that a judge appointed to the Supreme Court of India should have prior judicial experience. We saw in Chapter 1 that prior to Indian independence, discussions in the Central Legislative Assembly and Council of State concerning the setting up of a proposed supreme court presupposed that the court's judges would be retired high court judges. It was of some concern, even then, that 'eminent and successful' lawyers would be unlikely to take up positions on the court because of poor compensation. For example, in 1927, the Law Member of the Viceroy's Executive Council, S.R. Das, pointed out that 'great lawyers' were refusing to accept judgeships on high courts because the salary of a high court judge did not compensate them well enough to encourage them to give up their 'lucrative practice'. It was therefore envisioned, even prior to the setting up of the Federal Court of India, that the supreme court's judgeships would be staffed from amongst high court judges. Even B.R. Puri—who successfully moved a resolution in the Central Legislative Assembly in 1932 recommending to the Governor General that a supreme court be set up in India—said that judges of the Supreme Court, 'perhaps for all time to come', would be appointed from amongst the existing personnel of high courts. Only half the judges who served on the Federal Court of India between 1937 and 1947 were former high court judges, but the character of the bench changed rapidly after independence—between 1947 and 1950, every single judge who served on the Federal Court of India was a former high court judge. The composition of the Federal Court of India therefore offers early insights into the norm of seniority—even at that point in time, high court judges dominated the bench. Similarly, in his memorandum to the Provincial Constitution Committee, B.N. Rau noted that high court judges in India were 'potential judges of the Supreme Court'.

In the early years of the Court's existence, typically, only senior high court judges, or high court chief justices, were appointed to the Supreme Court of India. For the Law Commission of India in 1958, this was a cause for concern. '[T]oo great an emphasis', it said, was being placed 'on the need for judicial experience'. It was suggested that eminent lawyers would be willing to give up their lucrative practice in exchange for a 'fairly long tenure on the Bench'. The Law Commission also observed that because of the norm of prior judicial experience, older judges were being appointed to the Court, who were serving shorter tenures on the Court, that short tenures went against the 'interests of the stability of the judicial administration of the country'. Only four lawyers* were ever appointed directly to the Court after then—only one in each decade from amongst scores of judges appointed to the Court during that time. To be fair though, attempts were perhaps made during this time to appoint eminent lawyers directly to the Supreme Court, but these lawyers probably refused either because the money was too little, or the tenure too short. Each of the four lawyers directly appointed to the Supreme Court had served as a high-ranking government lawyer—and as government lawyers their practice was presumably not as 'lucrative' as some of their contemporaries' in private practice. This suggests that private lawyers may be unwilling to accept judgeships on the Supreme Court because the salary of a Supreme Court judge, and even the prestige of the office (being one amongst as many as 31 Supreme Court judges), is insufficient to compensate a lawyer for the sacrifice of a 'lucrative practice'. Further, despite these hurdles, private lawyers may be willing to accept judgeships on the Supreme Court if they were to be offered long tenures on the Court—but it is not clear that this is on offer. S.M. Sikri in the 1960s and S.C. Roy in the 1970s were lawyers appointed directly to the Supreme Court— and each was appointed young enough that he could go on to become Chief Justice of India.[2] However, appointed to the Court in the 1980s, Justice Kuldip Singh did not become Chief Justice of India despite the fact that by the conventional norm of calculating seniority, he could have risen to the office. It was seen in Chapter 2 that he made references to his fate in his opinion in the second Judges case. Today, it is therefore highly unlikely that a lawyer directly appointed to the Court will become Chief Justice of India,** and therefore equally unlikely that a lawyer will accept a judgeship on the Supreme Court in exchange for his 'lucrative practice'. In fact, in the second Judges case, the majority opinion observed that senior judges had a 'legitimate expectation' of being appointed to the Supreme Court, that this was a part of the constitutional principle of non-arbitrariness. Of course, there were contrary viewpoints—Justice Pandian perhaps worried that non-traditional candidates—'meritorious and suitable candidates practicing in forums other than the High Courts'—may not get to the Supreme Court, on account of the eligibility norm of seniority. In the third Judges case, the Court re-characterized the 'legitimate expectation' as only a 'hope'—it was held that senior high court judges only had a 'hope' that they would be appointed to the

[2] S.C. Roy passed away early, and did not rise to the position of Chief Justice of India.

Supreme Court, and that the collegium should 'bear this in mind'. Seniority, the Court seemed to emphasize in the third Judges case, was not an entitlement—it was only an eligibility criterion.

The norm that a person must be a senior high court judge in order to be considered eligible for appointment to the Supreme Court of India has metamorphosed into something different. Now, in order to be considered eligible for appointment to the Court, a person must, in most cases, be a high court chief justice. This change coincides with the second and third Judges cases, and though correlation does not amount to causation, it is safe to hypothesize that the emphasis on high court chief justices is a direct product of the collegium system consequent to the second and third Judges cases. For reasons discussed in Chapter 4, the collegium, consisting of the Chief Justice of India and the four most senior Supreme Court judges, increasingly seems to be insisting that only high court chief justices are eligible candidates for appointment to the Supreme Court. Of course, there have been exceptions to this norm—but the exceptions are typically driven by other eligibility criteria, for example, if the candidate is a woman or belongs to a backward caste.

Diversity is a more controversial eligibility criterion for appointment to the Supreme Court. The seniority of a judge is a badge of honour, but the diversity of a judge is only spoken of in hushed whispers. Early debates even prior to independence reveal that legislators in India were always aware of the 'merit–diversity paradox'. In a speech made in the Council of State in 1927, Law Member S.R. Das worried that if a supreme court were established, 'communal questions will arise'—that judges would be appointed to the court on account of their religion, and not their merit. At the third session of the Round Table Conference held in 1932, former Law Member of the Viceroy's Executive Council, Sir Tej Sapru, argued that no 'religious or racial considerations' should be taken into account while appointing judges to the proposed Federal Court— that judges should be appointed from 'any community, European or Indian', provided that they were independent, competent, and impartial. However, communal considerations prevailed on the Federal Court of India—of the three judges who sat on the court at any given point in time between 1937 and 1947, the Chief Justice was always British, and one judge each was either Hindu or Muslim.

Sir John Beaumont—former Chief Justice of the Bombay High Court—
seemed to have been one of the few proponents of regional representation at the time, which, he believed, the Privy Council lacked. The
Constituent Assembly did not seem to apply itself to the question
of whether judges on the Supreme Court of India would come
from different regions, but in 1958, the Law Commission of India
'regretted' that judges were being appointed to the Supreme Court
on regional and communal grounds, hinting that this was perhaps on
account of executive influence in the judicial appointments process.
By 1979, however, the Law Commission of India tacitly accepted the
principle that judges were appointed on considerations of diversity,
and argued that merit should still be taken into account in considering whom to appoint to the Court, consistently with diversity.
In 1987 too, the Law Commission of India noted that diversity, in
terms of region and minority representation, was a criterion taken
into account in making appointments to the Supreme Court. In the
second Judges case, Justice Ahmadi found that the eligibility norm
of seniority could be sacrificed in favour of preserving the representative character of the Court. '[P]eople of all hues', he held,
should 'have confidence in the institution', and for this reason non-
traditional candidates could be appointed to the Court despite their
lack of rank in terms of seniority. In the same case, Justice Pandian
added that 'outstanding and meritorious candidates belonging to all
sections of the society' must be appointed to the Supreme Court, and
not merely those of 'any selective or insular group'.

Diversity on the Court today is not what it was in the 1950s or
even in the 1980s. The proportion of judges from the High Court of
Delhi in the Supreme Court of India has gone up—perhaps a tacit
acknowledgement of its status as a premier court in India, and of the
towering commercial status of Delhi. Further, although the number
of judges appointed to the Supreme Court has increased with each
passing decade, the total number of judges from religious minority
communities appointed to the Supreme Court has not commen-
surately increased. However, perhaps one of the most interesting
revelations of this book is that the diversity criterion has continued
to be prevalent even after the second and third Judges cases. One
would intuitively have hypothesized that only popularly elected
officials are keen on appointing 'diverse' candidates to the Supreme

Court, on compulsions of vote-bank politics. However, even after seizing control of the power to appoint judges to the Supreme Court, the collegium of judges continues to appoint judges based on considerations of diversity. In the last two decades, an attempt still appears to have been made to ensure that the regions of India, India's minority religious communities, and women, are each represented on the Court. This suggests that the 'diversity' of judges on the Supreme Court enhances the Court's legitimacy, and that as a rational actor, the collegium is interested in preserving the Court's legitimacy. It is also arguable that in preserving the norm of diversity on the Court, the collegium seems to be cooperating with the executive, in order to make the Court's power to appoint judges consequent to the second and third Judges cases seem less unbearable to the executive. However, the collegium's attentiveness to diversity leaves much to be desired as region puzzlingly ranks higher than gender, religion, and caste on the collegium's list of priorities. Consequently, not enough women judges, and not enough judges from backward castes or religious minorities have made it to the Court.

In measuring appointments made to the Supreme Court in the last two decades, this book has also examined the Judges cases. Interestingly, the outcome arrived at in the second and third Judges cases was directly contrary to the express value choices of the framers of India's Constitution. The Constituent Assembly of India had expressly rejected the proposal that the opinion of the Chief Justice of India must bind the President of India in matters of judicial appointments. The suggestion, namely, that no appointment should be made without the 'concurrence' of the Chief Justice of India, was made to the Constituent Assembly by the conference of Federal Court judges and high court chief justices in 1948. This was felt necessary in order to prevent judicial appointments from being made on political, communal, or party grounds. In its 80th report in 1979, the Law Commission of India recommended that the Chief Justice of India consult three senior judges before making recommendations to the President—perhaps an early forerunner to the collegium system. It was seen that Chief Justice P.N. Bhagwati was the first to use the word 'collegium' in the Judges cases, but he used it in the first Judges case in an entirely different context from the one in which it is used today. In the second and third Judges cases, the Supreme Court of India broke away from the intentions of the framers of the Indian Constitution, but this may not be too worrisome given B.N. Rau's comments about the legitimacy of the Assembly, examined in Chapter 1.

So has the collegium system made a significant difference to the type of candidate selected for the Supreme Court of India? There are two answers to this question, one affirmative, the other negative, and both are equally interesting. Older judges are being appointed to the Supreme Court under the watch of the collegium. In the 1950s, the prototypic judge was 57.67 years old. In the 2000s, he was two years older—59.7. A mean difference of a couple of years may not seem significant at first, but it clearly is if one considers the age of a Supreme Court judge in context. Supreme Court judges retire at the age of 65, and a 57-year-old judge serves a 33 per cent longer term than a 59-year-old judge. Older judges serve shorter terms on the Court, and are less threatening to the executive—perhaps the collegium's insistence on older judges makes the collegium system itself non-threatening, even acceptable, to the executive. The collegium has also intensified its insistence on seniority—high court chief justices are now making it to the Supreme Court in overwhelming numbers, where, at one point, the Court was composed of roughly even numbers of former senior puisne high court judges and chief justices. Thus, the collegium system has affirmatively had an impact on the type of candidate selected for the Court in two ways—the collegium's candidate is older, and he is almost always a high court chief justice. At the same time, the collegium still insists on diversity, especially geographic diversity, in selecting judges for the Court. To this extent, the collegium has continued to apply a norm that predates the collegium system itself. In order to preserve its legitimacy, the collegium has cooperated with the executive in perpetuating a system of diversity in the Court.

Despite not being in the Constitution then, age, seniority, and diversity have become informal eligibility criteria for selecting and appointing judges to the Supreme Court of India. Each of these is tied to a policy objective: age ensures maturity, seniority ensures experience, and diversity ensures legitimacy. Each of these objectives lives within the shadows of the written text of India's Constitution.

The policy assumes that older judges appointed to the Court are more mature than younger ones. It assumes that senior high court judges and chief justices have a better, more legitimate, claim to the Court on account of the relative length of their judicial experience— their seniority makes them the least controversial choice. The informal policy also assumes that the Court needs diversity in order to preserve its legitimacy—that in order to be accepted as the Supreme Court of all of India, it must reflect the geographic and demographic character of most of India. Each of these assumptions is plausible, though refutable. A 50-year-old judge can hardly be termed 'immature' on account of his age, yet the policy seems to insist upon the arbitrary threshold age of 55. Seniority and experience do not necessarily go hand in hand either—the most senior judge on the high court of one state might have less experience than judges lower down on the list of seniority on other, bigger high courts, and despite seniority, controversies still surface when regional definitions of seniority trump all-India definitions of seniority. In turn, the age and seniority criteria threaten to produce an elderly, tired judiciary—or judges with barely enough time left on the Court to make any difference to the system, to provide leadership to the Court or coherence and consistency to its opinions. Ironically, although the Court is geographically and demographically diverse, its members still come from an overwhelmingly homogeneous professional background— all of them have spent a vast portion of their careers as high court judges. The Court has seen no career law professors, arbitration counsel, or transactional lawyers directly appointed to its bench. It is diverse only in one sense—the politically correct sense. Then, the diversity of the Court's composition does not necessarily find its way into its opinions either. The Court convenes most frequently in fractured two-judge panels, not in plenary sessions, and the differences of opinion that could arise as a consequence of the Court's diversity, instead do not, because strenuous compromise amongst a large group of judges is not essential to its daily functioning. If more judges were to hear each case, more disagreements would be likely to arise, and more compromises would have to be made—in judgments that would truly reflect the diversity of opinions on the Court. Instead, at present, benches are small, and disagreements on the bench seem discouraged, perhaps even unproductive. On the Court, to dissent is to delay, and expediency trumps diversity. Benches with five or more judges on them (that is, 'constitution benches') are uncommon because it is feared that if too many judges hear a case, then too few cases will be heard (cf. Interview 15), and since the Supreme Court does not confine its attention only to rare cases on appeal, India's sluggish judicial system will crumble beneath the weight of its own backlog. The Court's appearance of diversity, then, is an empty promise—its present system of decision-making renders its own diversity symbolic, but not substantive.

NOTES

* Between 2014 and 2018, four more lawyers were directly appointed to the Supreme Court.

** Appointed to the Supreme Court directly from the bar in 2014, Justice U.U. Lalit is likely to become the Chief Justice of India for a few months in 2022.

APPENDIX

JUDGES OF THE SUPREME COURT OF INDIA (1950–2011)

	Judge	Date of Birth	High Court Appointment Date	Parent High Court	High Court Chief Justice	Supreme Court Appointment Date	Date of Retirement/ Resignation/ Death	Comments
1.	Harilal J. Kania (CJI)	3 November 1890	June 1933	Bombay	N/A	20 June 1946 (Federal Court)	6 November 1951	***
2.	Syed Fazl Ali	19 September 1886	April 1928	Patna	Patna	9 June 1947 (Federal Court)	18 September 1951	
3.	M. Patanjali Sastri (CJI)	4 January 1889	15 March 1939	Madras	N/A	6 December 1947 (Federal Court)	3 January 1954	
4.	Mehr Chand Mahajan (CJI)	23 December 1889	27 September 1943	Lahore, East Punjab	N/A	4 October 1948 (Federal Court)	22 December 1954	
5.	B.K. Mukherjea (CJI)	15 August 1891	9 November 1936	Calcutta	N/A	14 October 1948 (Federal Court)	31 January 1956	**

(continued)

(*continued*)

	Judge	Date of Birth	High Court Appointment Date	Parent High Court	High Court Chief Justice	Supreme Court Appointment Date	Date of Retirement/ Resignation/ Death	Comments
6.	S.R. Das (CJI)	1 October 1894	1 December 1942	Calcutta	East Punjab	20 January 1950 (Federal Court)	30 September 1959	
7.	N. Chandrasekhara Aiyar	25 January 1888	July 1941	Madras	N/A	23 September 1950	24 January 1953	
8.	Vivian Bose	9 June 1891	9 January 1936	Nagpur	Nagpur	5 March 1951	8 June 1956	
9.	Ghulam Hasan	3 July 1891	August 1940	Oudh	Oudh	8 September 1952	5 November 1954	***
10.	N.H. Bhagwati	7 August 1894	27 August 1944	Bombay	N/A	8 September 1952	6 August 1959	
11.	B. Jagannadhadas	27 July 1893	26 July 1948	Orissa	Orissa	9 March 1953	8 September 1957	**
12.	T.L. Venkatarama Ayyar	25 November 1893	7 January 1951	Madras	N/A	4 January 1954	24 November 1958	
13.	B.P. Sinha (CJI)	1 February 1899	6 January 1943	Patna	Nagpur	3 December 1954	31 January 1964	
14.	Syed Jaffer Imam	18 April 1900	October 1943	Patna	Patna	10 January 1955	31 January 1964	**

15.	S.K. Das	3 September 1898	1945	Patna	Patna	30 April 1956	2 September 1963	
16.	P. Govinda Menon	10 September 1896	28 July 1947	Madras	N/A	1 September 1956	16 October 1957	***
17.	J.L. Kapur	13 December 1897	6 June 1949	Punjab	N/A	14 January 1957	12 December 1962	
18.	P.B. Gajendragadkar (CJI)	16 March 1901	6 March 1945	Bombay	N/A	17 January 1957	15 March 1966	
19.	A.K. Sarkar (CJI)	29 June 1901	25 January 1949	Calcutta	N/A	4 March 1957	28 June 1966	
20.	K. Subba Rao (CJI)	15 July 1902	22 March 1948	Madras	Andhra Pradesh	31 January 1958	11 April 1967	**
21.	K.N. Wanchoo (CJI)	25 February 1903	17 February 1947	Allahabad	Rajasthan	11 August 1958	24 February 1968	
22.	M. Hidayatullah (CJI)	17 December 1905	24 June 1946	Nagpur	Nagpur/Madhya Pradesh	1 December 1958	16 December 1970	
23.	K.C. Das Gupta	3 January 1900	June 1948	Calcutta	Calcutta	24 August 1959	2 January 1965	
24.	J.C. Shah (CJI)	22 January 1906	1 March 1949	Bombay	N/A	12 October 1959	21 January 1971	
25.	Raghubar Dayal	26 October 1900	22 July 1946	Allahabad	N/A	27 July 1960	25 October 1965	

(continued)

(continued)

	Judge	Date of Birth	High Court Appointment Date	Parent High Court	High Court Chief Justice	Supreme Court Appointment Date	Date of Retirement/ Resignation/ Death	Comments
26.	N. Rajagopala Ayyangar	15 December 1899	23 November 1953	Madras	N/A	27 July 1960	14 December 1964	
27.	J.R. Mudholkar	9 May 1902	11 November 1948	Nagpur	N/A	3 October 1960	3 July 1966	**
28.	S.M. Sikri (CJI)	26 April 1908	N/A	N/A	N/A	3 February 1964	25 April 1973	
29.	R.S. Bachawat	1 August 1904	23 January 1950	Calcutta	N/A	7 September 1964	31 July 1969	
30.	V. Ramaswami	30 October 1904	1 November 1947	Patna	Patna	4 January 1965	29 October 1969	
31.	P. Satyanarayana Raju	17 August 1908	1 November 1954	Andhra	Andhra Pradesh	20 October 1965	20 April 1966	***
32.	J.M. Shelat	16 July 1908	6 January 1957	Bombay	Gujarat	24 February 1966	30 April 1973	**
33.	Vashishtha Bhargava	5 February 1906	1 August 1949	Allahabad	Allahabad	8 August 1966	4 February 1971	
34.	G.K. Mitter	24 September 1906	24 November 1952	Calcutta	N/A	29 August 1966	23 September 1971	
35.	C.A. Vaidialingam	30 June 1907	26 March 1957	Kerala	N/A	10 October 1966	29 June 1972	

No.	Name							
36.	K.S. Hegde	11 June 1909	26 August 1957	Mysore	Delhi	17 July 1967	30 April 1973	**
37.	A.N. Grover	15 February 1912	10 October 1957	Punjab	N/A	11 February 1968	31 May 1973	**
38.	A.N. Ray (CJI)	29 January 1912	23 December 1957	Calcutta	N/A	1 August 1969	28 January 1977	
39.	P. Jaganmohan Reddy	23 January 1910	18 February 1952	Hyderabad	Andhra Pradesh	1 August 1969	22 January 1975	
40.	I.D. Dua	4 October 1907	11 August 1958	Punjab	Delhi	1 August 1969	3 October 1972	
41.	S. Chandra Roy	29 May 1912	N/A	N/A	N/A	19 July 1971	12 November 1971	***
42.	D.G. Palekar	4 September 1909	14 October 1961	Bombay	N/A	19 July 1971	3 September 1974	
43.	H.R. Khanna	3 July 1912	7 May 1962	Punjab	Delhi	22 September 1971	11 March 1977	**
44.	K.K. Mathew	3 January 1911	5 June 1962	Kerala	N/A	4 October 1971	2 January 1976	
45.	M.H. Beg (CJI)	22 February 1913	11 June 1963	Allahabad	Himachal Pradesh	10 December 1971	21 February 1978	
46.	S.N. Dwivedi	1 October 1913	12 May 1959	Allahabad	N/A	14 August 1972	8 December 1974	***

(continued)

(continued)

	Judge	Date of Birth	High Court Appointment Date	Parent High Court	High Court Chief Justice	Supreme Court Appointment Date	Date of Retirement/ Resignation/ Death	Comments
47.	A.K. Mukherjea	20 January 1915	27 February 1962	Calcutta	N/A	14 August 1972	23 October 1973	***
48.	Y.V. Chandrachud (CJI)	12 July 1920	19 March 1961	Bombay	N/A	28 August 1972	11 July 1985	
49.	A. Alagiriswami	17 October 1910	11 August 1966	Madras	N/A	17 October 1972	16 October 1975	
50.	P.N. Bhagwati (CJI)	21 December 1921	21 July 1960	Gujarat	Gujarat	17 July 1973	20 December 1986	
51.	V.R. Krishna Iyer	15 November 1915	12 July 1968	Kerala	N/A	17 July 1973	14 November 1980	
52.	P.K. Goswami	1 January 1913	12 May 1967	Gauhati	Gauhati	10 September 1973	31 December 1978	
53.	R.S. Sarkaria	16 January 1916	13 June 1967	Punjab and Haryana	N/A	17 September 1973	15 January 1981	
54.	A.C. Gupta	1 January 1917	24 February 1964	Calcutta	N/A	2 September 1974	31 December 1982	

55.	N.L. Untwalia	1 August 1915	2 January 1958	Patna	Patna	3 October 1974	31 July 1980
56.	S. Murtaza Fazal Ali	20 December 1920	9 April 1958	Jammu and Kashmir	Jammu and Kashmir	2 April 1975	20 August 1985	***
57.	P.N. Shingal	15 October 1915	21 June 1961	Rajasthan	Rajasthan	6 November 1975	14 October 1980
58.	Jaswant Singh	25 January 1914	3 December 1967	Jammu and Kashmir	Jammu and Kashmir	23 January 1976	24 January 1979
59.	P.S. Kailasam	12 September 1915	20 October 1960	Madras	Madras	3 January 1977	11 September 1980
60.	V.D. Tulzapurkar	9 March 1921	21 December 1963	Bombay	N/A	30 September 1977	8 March 1986
61.	D.A. Desai	9 May 1920	19 February 1968	Gujarat	N/A	30 September 1977	8 May 1985
62.	R.S. Pathak (CJI)	25 November 1924	1 October 1962	Allahabad	Himachal Pradesh	20 February 1978	18 June 1989	**
63.	A.D. Koshal	7 March 1917	28 May 1968	Punjab and Haryana	Punjab and Haryana	17 July 1978	6 March 1982
64.	O. Chinnappa Reddy	25 September 1922	21 August 1967	Andhra Pradesh	N/A	17 July 1978	24 September 1987

(continued)

(*continued*)

	Judge	Date of Birth	High Court Appointment Date	Parent High Court	High Court Chief Justice	Supreme Court Appointment Date	Date of Retirement/ Resignation/ Death	Comments
65.	A.P. Sen	20 September 1923	7 November 1967	Madhya Pradesh	Madhya Pradesh	17 July 1978	19 September 1988	
66.	E.S. Venkataramiah (CJI)	18 December 1924	25 June 1970	Karnataka	N/A	8 March 1979	17 December 1989	
67.	Baharul Islam	1 March 1918	20 January 1972	Gauhati	Gauhati	4 December 1980	12 January 1983	**
68.	A. Vardarajan	17 August 1920	15 February 1973	Madras	N/A	10 December 1980	16 August 1985	
69.	A.N. Sen	1 October 1920	15 November 1965	Calcutta	Calcutta	28 January 1981	30 September 1985	
70.	V. Balakrishna Eradi	19 June 1922	5 April 1967	Kerala	Kerala	30 January 1981	18 June 1987	
71.	R.B. Misra	15 June 1921	3 January 1968	Allahabad	N/A	30 January 1981	14 June 1986	
72.	D.P. Madon	7 April 1921	25 September 1967	Bombay	Bombay	15 March 1983	6 April 1986	
73.	Sabyasachi Mukharji (CJI)	1 June 1927	31 July 1968	Calcutta	N/A	15 March 1983	25 September 1990	***
74.	M.P. Thakkar	4 November 1923	2 July 1969	Gujarat	Gujarat	15 March 1983	3 November 1988	

75.	Ranganath Misra (CJI)	25 November 1926	4 July 1969	Orissa	Orissa	15 March 1983	24 November 1991
76.	V. Khalid	1 July 1922	7 March 1974	Kerala	Jammu and Kashmir	25 June 1984	30 June 1987
77.	G.L. Oza	12 December 1924	29 July 1968	Madhya Pradesh	Madhya Pradesh	29 October 1985	11 December 1989
78.	B.C. Ray	1 November 1926	10 June 1974	Calcutta	N/A	29 October 1985	31 October 1991
79.	M.M. Dutt	30 October 1924	18 September 1969	Calcutta	N/A	10 March 1986	29 October 1989
80.	K.N. Singh (CJI)	13 December 1926	25 August 1970	Allahabad	N/A	10 March 1986	12 December 1991
81.	S. Natarajan	29 October 1924	15 February 1973	Madras	N/A	10 March 1986	28 October 1989
82.	M.H. Kania (CJI)	18 November 1927	4 November 1969	Bombay	Bombay	1 May 1987	17 November 1992
83.	K. Jagannatha Shetty	15 December 1926	25 June 1970	Karnataka	Allahabad	1 May 1987	14 December 1991
84.	L.M. Sharma (CJI)	12 February 1928	12 April 1973	Patna	N/A	5 October 1987	11 February 1993
85.	M.N. Venkatachaliah (CJI)	25 October 1929	6 November 1975	Karnataka	N/A	5 October 1987	24 October 1994

(continued)

(continued)

	Judge	Date of Birth	High Court Appointment Date	Parent High Court	High Court Chief Justice	Supreme Court Appointment Date	Date of Retirement/ Resignation/ Death	Comments
86.	S. Ranganathan	31 October 1927	14 November 1977	Delhi	N/A	5 October 1987	30 October 1992	
87.	N.D. Ojha	19 January 1926	3 September 1971	Allahabad	Madhya Pradesh	18 January 1988	18 January 1991	
88.	S. Ratnavel Pandian	13 February 1929	27 February 1974	Madras	N/A	14 December 1988	12 February 1994	
89.	T.K. Thommen	26 September 1928	9 May 1975	Kerala	N/A	14 December 1988	25 September 1993	
90.	A.M. Ahmadi (CJI)	25 March 1932	2 September 1976	Gujarat		14 December 1988	24 March 1997	
91.	K.N. Saikia	1 March 1926	12 February 1979	Gauhati	Gauhati	14 December 1988	28 February 1991	
92.	Kuldip Singh	1 January 1932	N/A	N/A	N/A	14 December 1988	31 December 1996	
93.	J.S. Verma (CJI)	18 January 1933	12 September 1972	Madhya Pradesh	Madhya Pradesh, Rajasthan	3 June 1989	17 January 1998	
94.	V. Ramaswami	15 February 1929	31 January 1971	Madras	Punjab and Haryana	6 October 1989	14 February 1994	

95.	P.B. Sawant	30 June 1930	29 March 1973	Bombay	N/A	6 October 1989	29 June 1995
96.	N.M. Kasliwal	4 April 1928	15 June 1978	Rajasthan	Himachal Pradesh	6 October 1989	3 April 1993
97.	M.M. Punchhi (CJI)	10 October 1933	24 October 1979	Punjab and Haryana	N/A	6 October 1989	9 October 1998
98.	K. Ramaswamy	13 July 1932	29 September 1982	Andhra Pradesh	N/A	6 October 1989	12 July 1997
99.	M. Fathima Beevi	30 April 1927	4 August 1983	Kerala	N/A	6 October 1989	29 April 1992
100.	K. Jayachandra Reddy	15 July 1929	7 March 1975	Andhra Pradesh	N/A	11 January 1990	14 July 1994
101.	S.C. Agrawal	5 September 1933	15 June 1978	Rajasthan	N/A	11 January 1990	4 September 1998
102.	R.M. Sahai	25 June 1930	27 January 1976	Allahabad	N/A	11 January 1990	24 June 1995
103.	Yogeshwar Dayal	18 November 1930	28 February 1974	Delhi	Delhi, Andhra Pradesh	22 March 1991	2 August 1994 ***
104.	S. Mohan	11 February 1930	27 February 1974	Madras	Madras, Karnataka	7 October 1991	10 February 1995

(continued)

(*continued*)

Judge	Date of Birth	High Court Appointment Date	Parent High Court	High Court Chief Justice	Supreme Court Appointment Date	Date of Retirement/ Resignation/ Death	Comments
105. B.P. Jeevan Reddy	14 March 1932	17 July 1975	Andhra Pradesh	Allahabad	7 October 1991	13 March 1997	
106. G.N. Ray	1 May 1933	23 December 1976	Calcutta	Gujarat	7 October 1991	30 April 1998	
107. A.S. Anand (CJI)	1 November 1936	26 May 1975	Jammu and Kashmir	Jammu and Kashmir, Madras	18 November 1991	31 October 2001	
108. R.C. Patnaik	28 July 1935	18 September 1981	Orissa	N/A	3 December 1991	30 May 1992	***
109. N.P. Singh	25 December 1931	12 April 1973	Patna	Calcutta	15 June 1992	24 December 1996	
110. S.P. Bharucha (CJI)	6 May 1937	19 September 1977	Bombay	Karnataka	1 July 1992	5 May 2002	
111. N.G. Venkatachala	3 July 1930	28 November 1977	Karnataka	N/A	1 July 1992	2 July 1995	
112. M.K. Mukherjee	1 December 1933	17 June 1977	Calcutta	Allahabad, Bombay	14 December 1993	30 November 1998	
113. Faizan Uddin	5 February 1932	27 November 1978	Madhya Pradesh	N/A	14 December 1993	4 February 1997	

114. B.L. Hansaria	25 December 1931	12 February 1979	Gauhati	Orissa	14 December 1993	24 December 1996
115. S.C. Sen	21 December 1932	23 November 1981	Calcutta	N/A	11 June 1994	20 December 1997
116. K.S. Paripoornan	12 June 1932	23 December 1982	Kerala	Patna	11 June 1994	11 June 1997
117. S.B. Majmudar	20 August 1935	3 October 1978	Gujarat	Andhra Pradesh, Karnataka	19 September 1994	19 August 2000
118. Sujata V. Manohar	28 August 1934	23 January 1978	Bombay	Bombay, Kerala	8 November 1994	27 August 1999
119. G.T. Nanavati	17 February 1935	19 July 1979	Gujarat	Orissa, Karnataka	6 March 1995	16 February 2000
120. S. Saghir Ahmad	1 July 1935	2 November 1981	Allahabad	Jammu and Kashmir, Andhra Pradesh	6 March 1995	30 June 2000
121. K. Venkataswami	19 September 1934	24 July 1983	Madras	Patna	6 March 1995	18 September 1999
122. B.N. Kirpal (CJI)	8 November 1937	20 November 1979	Delhi	Gujarat	11 September 1995	7 November 2002
123. G.B. Pattanaik (CJI)	19 December 1937	1 June 1983	Orissa	Patna	11 September 1995	18 December 2002

(continued)

(continued)

Judge	Date of Birth	High Court Appointment Date	Parent High Court	High Court Chief Justice	Supreme Court Appointment Date	Date of Retirement/ Resignation/ Death	Comments
124. S.P. Kurdukar	16 January 1935	25 April 1978	Bombay	Punjab and Haryana	29 March 1996	15 January 2000	
125. K.T. Thomas	30 January 1937	12 August 1985	Kerala	N/A	29 March 1996	29 January 2002	
126. M. Jagannadha Rao	2 December 1935	29 September 1982	Andhra Pradesh	Kerala, Delhi	21 March 1997	1 December 2000	
127. V.N. Khare (CJI)	2 May 1939	25 June 1983	Allahabad	Calcutta	21 March 1997	1 May 2004	
128. D.P. Wadhwa	5 May 1935	12 August 1983	Delhi	Patna	21 March 1997	4 May 2000	
129. M. Srinivasan	12 January 1937	2 June 1986	Madras	Himachal Pradesh	25 September 1997	25 February 2000	***
130. S. Rajendra Babu (CJI)	1 June 1939	19 February 1988	Karnataka	N/A	25 September 1997	31 May 2004	
131. A.P. Misra	1 September 1936	24 May 1984	Allahabad	Delhi	4 December 1997	31 August 2001	
132. S.S.M. Quadri	5 April 1938	11 July 1986	Andhra Pradesh	N/A	4 December 1997	4 April 2003	

	Name						
133.	M.B. Shah	25 September 1938	28 January 1983	Gujarat	Bombay	9 December 1998	24 September 2003
134.	D.P. Mohapatra	3 August 1937	18 November 1983	Orissa	Allahabad	9 December 1998	2 August 2002
135.	U.C. Banerjee	18 November 1937	9 January 1984	Calcutta	Andhra Pradesh	9 December 1998	17 November 2002
136.	R.C. Lahoti (CJI)	1 November 1940	3 May 1988	Madhya Pradesh	N/A	9 December 1998	31 October 2005
137.	N. Santosh Hegde	16 June 1940	N/A	Karnataka	N/A	8 January 1999	15 June 2005
138.	R.P. Sethi	7 July 1937	30 May 1986	Jammu and Kashmir	Karnataka	8 January 1999	6 July 2002
139.	S.N. Phukan	1 April 1937	11 October 1985	Gauhati	Himachal Pradesh, Orissa	28 January 1999	30 March 2002
140.	Y.K. Sabharwal (CJI)	14 January 1942	17 November 1986	Delhi	Bombay	28 January 2000	13 January 2007
141.	Doraiswamy Raju	2 July 1939	14 June 1990	Madras	Himachal Pradesh	28 January 2000	1 July 2004
142.	Ruma Pal	3 June 1941	6 August 1990	Calcutta	N/A	28 January 2000	2 June 2006
143.	S.N. Variava	8 November 1940	21 November 1986	Bombay	Delhi	15 March 2000	7 November 2005

(continued)

(*continued*)

Judge	Date of Birth	High Court Appointment Date	Parent High Court	High Court Chief Justice	Supreme Court Appointment Date	Date of Retirement/ Resignation/ Death	Comments
144. Shivaraj V. Patil	12 January 1940	29 March 1990	Karnataka	Rajasthan	15 March 2000	11 January 2005	
145. K.G. Balakrishnan (CJI)	12 May 1945	26 September 1985	Kerala	Gujarat, Madras	8 June 2000	11 May 2010	
146. Brijesh Kumar	10 June 1939	24 May 1984	Allahabad	Gauhati	19 October 2000	9 June 2004	
147. B.N. Agrawal	15 October 1944	17 November 1986	Patna	Orissa	19 October 2000	14 October 2009	
148. Ashok Bhan	2 October 1943	15 June 1990	Punjab and Haryana	N/A	17 June 2001	1 October 2008	
149. Venkatarama Reddi	10 August 1940	16 March 1990	Andhra Pradesh	Karnataka	17 August 2001	9 August 2005	
150. Arijit Pasayat	10 May 1944	20 March 1989	Orissa	Kerala, Delhi	19 October 2001	9 May 2009	
151. B.P. Singh	9 July 1942	9 March 1987	Patna	Bombay	14 December 2001	8 July 2007	
152. D.M. Dharmadhikari	14 August 1940	24 March 1989	Madhya Pradesh	Gujarat	5 March 2002	13 August 2005	

153. H.K. Sema	1 June 1943	24 May 1989	Gauhati	Jammu and Kashmir	9 April 2002	31 May 2008
154. S.B. Sinha	8 August 1944	9 March 1987	Patna	Andhra Pradesh, Delhi	3 October 2002	7 August 2009
155. Arun Kumar	12 April 1941	13 July 1990	Delhi	Rajasthan	3 October 2002	11 April 2006
156. B.N. Srikrishna	21 May 1941	30 July 1990	Bombay	Kerala	3 October 2002	20 May 2006
157. A.R. Lakshmanan	22 March 1942	14 June 1990	Madras	Rajasthan, Andhra Pradesh	20 December 2002	21 May 2007
158. G.P. Mathur	19 January 1943	6 July 1990	Allahabad	N/A	20 December 2002	18 January 2008
159. S.H. Kapadia (CJI)	29 September 1947	8 October 1991	Bombay	Uttaranchal	18 December 2003	28 September 2012
160. A.K. Mathur	7 August 1943	13 July 1985	Rajasthan	Madhya Pradesh, Calcutta	7 June 2004	6 August 2008
161. C.K. Thakker	10 November 1943	21 June 1990	Gujarat	Himachal Pradesh, Bombay	7 June 2004	9 November 2008
162. P.P. Naolekar	29 June 1943	15 June 1992	Madhya Pradesh	Gauhati	28 July 2004	28 June 2008

(continued)

(continued)

Judge	Date of Birth	High Court Appointment Date	Parent High Court	High Court Chief Justice	Supreme Court Appointment Date	Date of Retirement/ Resignation/ Death	Comments
163. Tarun Chatterjee	14 January 1945	6 August 1990	Calcutta	Allahabad	27 August 2004	13 January 2010	
164. P.K. Balasubramanyan	28 August 1942	4 June 1992	Kerala	Orissa, Jharkhand	27 August 2004	27 August 2007	
165. Altamas Kabir	19 July 1948	6 August 1990	Calcutta	Jharkhand	9 September 2005	18 July 2013	
166. R.V. Raveendran	15 October 1946	22 February 1993	Karnataka	Madhya Pradesh	9 September 2005	14 October 2011	
167. Dalveer Bhandari	1 October 1947	19 March 1991	Delhi	Bombay	28 October 2005	27 April 2012	**
168. L.S. Panta	23 April 1944	20 August 1991	Himachal Pradesh	N/A	3 February 2006	22 April 2009	
169. D.K. Jain	25 January 1948	19 March 1991	Delhi	Punjab and Haryana	10 April 2006	24 January 2013	
170. Markandey Katju	20 September 1946	30 November 1991	Allahabad	Madras, Delhi	10 April 2006	19 September 2011	
171. H.S. Bedi	5 September 1946	15 March 1991	Punjab and Haryana	Bombay	12 January 2007	4 September 2011	

172.	V.S. Sirpurkar	22 August 1946	9 November 1992	Bombay	Uttaranchal, Calcutta	12 January 2007	21 August 2011
173.	B Sudershan Reddy	8 July 1946	2 May 1995	Andhra Pradesh	Gauhati	12 January 2007	7 July 2011
174.	P. Sathasivam	27 April 1949	8 January 1996	Madras	N/A	21 August 2007	
175.	G.S. Singhvi	12 December 1948	20 July 1990	Rajasthan	Andhra Pradesh	12 November 2007	18 April 2013
176.	Aftab Alam	19 April 1948	27 July 1990	Patna	N/A	12 November 2007	
177.	J.M. Panchal	6 October 1946	22 November 1990	Gujarat	Rajasthan	12 November 2007	5 October 2011
178.	Mukundakam Sharma	18 September 1946	10 January 1994	Gauhati	Delhi	9 April 2008	17 September 2011
179.	Cyriac Joseph	28 January 1947	6 July 1994	Kerala	Uttaranchal, Karnataka	7 July 2008	27 January 2012
180.	Asok Kumar Ganguly	3 February 1947	10 January 1994	Calcutta	Orissa, Madras	17 December 2008	2 February 2012
181.	R.M. Lodha	28 September 1949	31 January 1994	Rajasthan	Patna	17 December 2008	
182.	H.L. Dattu	3 December 1950	18 December 1995	Karnataka	Chhattisgarh, Kerala	17 December 2008	

(continued)

(*continued*)

Judge	Date of Birth	High Court Appointment Date	Parent High Court	High Court Chief Justice	Supreme Court Appointment Date	Date of Retirement/ Resignation/ Death	Comments
183. Deepak Verma	28 August 1947	15 December 1994	Madhya Pradesh	Rajasthan	11 May 2009		
184. B.S. Chauhan	2 July 1949	5 April 1995	Allahabad	Orissa	11 May 2009		
185. A.K. Patnaik	3 June 1949	13 January 1994	Orissa	Chhattisgarh, Madhya Pradesh	17 November 2009		
186. T.S. Thakur	4 January 1952	16 February 1994	Jammu and Kashmir	Punjab and Haryana	17 November 2009		
187. K.S. Panicker Radhakrishnan	15 May 1949	17 May 1995	Kerela	Jammu and Kashmir, Gujarat	17 November 2009		
188. S.S. Nijjar	7 June 1949	8 April 1996	Punjab and Haryana	Calcutta	17 November 2009		
189. Swatanter Kumar	31 December 1947	10 November 1994	Delhi	Bombay	18 December 2009		
190. C.K. Prasad	15 July 1949	8 November 1994	Patna	Allahabad	8 February 2010		

191.	H.L. Gokhale	10 March 1949	Bombay	20 January 1994	Allahabad, Madras	30 April 2010
192.	Gyan Sudha Misra	28 April 1949	Rajasthan	16 March 1994	Jharkhand	30 April 2010
193.	A.R. Dave	19 November 1951	Gujarat	18 September 1995	Andhra Pradesh, Bombay	30 April 2010
194.	S.J. Mukhopadhaya	15 March 1950	Patna	8 November 1994	Gujarat	13 September 2011
195.	Ranjana P. Desai	30 October 1949	Bombay	15 April 1996	N/A	13 September 2011
196.	J.S. Khehar	28 August 1952	Punjab and Haryana	8 February 1999	Uttarakhand, Karnataka	13 September 2011
197.	Dipak Misra	3 October 1953	Orissa	17 January 1996	Patna, Delhi	10 October 2011
198.	Jasti Chelameswar	23 June 1953	Andhra Pradesh	23 June 1997	Gauhati, Kerala	10 October 2011

Sources:

1. Website of the Supreme Court of India (http://supremecourtofindia.nic.in).
2. Websites of high courts (where such data are available).
3. Government of India. 1983, 1990, 2001. *Judges of the Supreme Court and the High Courts.* New Delhi: Department of Justice, Ministry of Law and Justice, Government of India.

(*continued*)

4. George H. Gadbois, Jr. 2011. *Judges of the Supreme Court of India: 1950–1989.* New Delhi: Oxford University Press.
5. Personal conversations with judges in some instances.

Notes:

1. In the 'Chief Justice' column, an acting Chief Justice is not counted as a Chief Justice of a high court.
2. As a rule, for the sake of consistency, the date of retirement in this table is the day before the judge's 65th birthday.
3. As a rule, column 4 ('High Court Appointment Date') sets out the date on which a judge was appointed as an additional judge, unless the judge was directly appointed a permanent judge, or unless, in rare cases, a temporary judgeship was continuous.
4. It has been assumed that where a judge is appointed to a high court ('High Court 1') as an additional judge, transferred to another high court ('High Court 2') where he later becomes a permanent judge, his parent high court is still the first mentioned high court, that is, High Court 1.
5. Justice Ghulam Hasan's parent high court is listed in this table as being Oudh, even though the Oudh Chief Court was not a high court, because it had the status of a high court.[1]
6. N/A indicates 'not applicable'/'not available'.
7. ** indicates 'resigned'.
8. *** indicates 'died'.
9. (CJI) indicates 'later became Chief Justice of India'.

[1] See George H. Gadbois, Jr. 2011. *Judges of the Supreme Court of India: 1950–1989.* New Delhi: Oxford University Press, p. 42.

INDEX

ABOUT THE AUTHOR

Abhinav Chandrachud is an advocate at the Bombay High Court. He graduated from the LL.M. Program at Harvard Law School where he was a Dana Scholar, and from the JSM and JSD programs at Stanford Law School where he was a Franklin Family Scholar. In 2008, he graduated from the Government Law College, Mumbai, where he was a university rank-holder, winning academic awards like the Hon'ble Justice D.P. Madon prize in Constitutional Law, the Ranganath Rao prize for best student, and the Yashwant Dalal Prize for best student. He worked as an associate attorney at Gibson, Dunn & Crutcher, LLP in Los Angeles and Singapore from 2009 to 2011. He also worked as a paralegal (student associate) at AZB & Partners between 2005 and 2008, and as a trainee law clerk in the office of the Chief Justice of the Supreme Court of India in 2006. In his free time, he enjoys playing the guitar. He can be reached at abhinav.chandrachud@gmail.com.